TOPOGRAPHICAL BIBLIOGRAPHY OF ANCIENT EGYPTIAN HIEROGLYPHIC TEXTS, RELIEFS, AND PAINTINGS

III.² MEMPHIS

Part 2. Ṣaqqâra to Dahshûr

Fascicle 3 (III.² 777—1014)

BY

THE LATE BERTHA PORTER

AND

ROSALIND L. B. MOSS

B.Sc. and Hon. D.Litt. (Oxon.), F.S.A.

Assisted by

ETHEL W. BURNEY

SECOND EDITION

REVISED AND AUGMENTED

BY

PHDR. JAROMÍR MÁLEK

GRIFFITH INSTITUTE

ASHMOLEAN MUSEUM, OXFORD

Part II ISBN 0 9000416 238

Fasc. 3 ISBN 0 9000416 246

Printed in Great Britain
at the University Press, Oxford
by Eric Buckley
Printer to the University

TOPOGRAPHICAL BIBLIOGRAPHY OF ANCIENT EGYPTIAN HIEROGLYPHIC TEXTS, RELIEFS, AND PAINTINGS

MEMPHIS

Ṣaqqâra to Dahshûr

TOPOGRAPHICAL BIBLIOGRAPHY OF ANCIENT EGYPTIAN HIEROGLYPHIC TEXTS, RELIEFS, AND PAINTINGS

III.[2] MEMPHIS

Part 2. Ṣaqqâra to Dahshûr

BY

THE LATE BERTHA PORTER

AND

ROSALIND L. B. MOSS

B.Sc. and Hon. D.Litt. (Oxon.), F.S.A.

Assisted by

ETHEL W. BURNEY

SECOND EDITION

REVISED AND AUGMENTED

BY

PHDR. JAROMÍR MÁLEK

GRIFFITH INSTITUTE

ASHMOLEAN MUSEUM, OXFORD

1981

Part II ISBN 0 9000416 238

Printed in Great Britain
at the University Press, Oxford
by Eric Buckley
Printer to the University

CONTENTS

INTRODUCTION

The first part of the revised edition of Volume III of this work, published in 1974, recorded a more than fourfold increase in the number of pages required for the same section of the Memphite necropolis in the first edition, and soon it became clear that a similar ratio was to be expected for the second part of the volume. This was one of the reasons why we decided to depart from tradition and publish the remaining text in the form of three fascicles, thus spreading over a longer period the considerable printing costs, as well as the time needed for seeing the book through the press. Perhaps even more importantly, the new method of publication enabled us to give Egyptologists at least parts of the work several years earlier than would otherwise have been possible, even though the unavoidable lack of indexes in the first two fascicles made their use somewhat more difficult.

This part of Volume III of the *Topographical Bibliography* deals with the southern half of the Memphite necropolis and the structures at Mît Rahîna. The dividing line between Abûṣîr and Ṣaqqâra is, admittedly, rather tenuous and may become even more so when the area has been more thoroughly excavated. Ṣaqqâra is by far the most important necropolis here, merging almost imperceptibly into Dahshûr in the south, while Mît Rahîna, in the cultivation zone to the east, nearer the river, is a temple and town site.

The pyramid-field of Ṣaqqâra has been dealt with using the pattern established in the first edition. Although numerous pyramids of the Old Kingdom and Dynasty XIII at Ṣaqqâra have never ceased to attract the attention of scholars, much work still remains to be done. The publication of the mortuary temple of Unis was in the press while this book was being prepared, and we are grateful to Professor Leclant for allowing us to see it in proof and so at least partly to complete our documentation. The important reliefs which once adorned the causeway leading to the pyramid have not yet been systematically published, but we have been very fortunate to have at our disposal copies of texts of inscribed blocks made by Professor Černý. In a similar way, we have been able to use Professor Gunn's unpublished descriptions and copies of texts in the mortuary temple of Khuit, one of the Queens of Teti.

For the northern part of the extensive necropolis of Ṣaqqâra we have used the Step Pyramid enclosure of Neterikhet (Zoser) as our area of reference and divided the private tombs into those situated north, east, and west of it (this is somewhat different from the system employed in the first edition). The width of the Step Pyramid enclosure has also provided the convenient dimension on which to base our grid on maps XLV, XLVI, LI, LVIII, LXIX, and LXX, which is also used in Appendix D and occasionally in the text to indicate the position of tombs. Concentrations of tombs near pyramid-complexes suggested further divisions, with the large area, as yet little explored, between the Monastery of Apa Jeremias and the enclosure of Sekhemkhet in the west being treated as on a par with them. In the case of the tombs near the pyramid of Teti, we have been able to quote extensively from Professor Gunn's copies of monuments excavated by Cecil M. Firth almost sixty years ago. These, as well as the other manuscript sources mentioned above, are kept in the archives of the Griffith Institute.

There is no agreed system of numbering Ṣaqqâra tombs. The position of many of them can only be derived from old maps, without the possibility of verifying their accuracy and, in view of the lack of a modern survey of the area, it seemed unwise to try to introduce a uniform numbering system, ill-equipped as we are for such a step at present. Each section of the necropolis has, therefore, been treated on its own, usually by dealing with tombs belonging to different numbering schemes in turn or by dividing them according to their relative position and date. The list of contents, Appendix D, and the appropriate maps at the end are designed to help in case of difficulty.

The very substantial sections entitled Tombs of Position Unknown and Objects from Tombs conclude the Ṣaqqâra necropolis. The number of monuments where a Ṣaqqâra origin might be suggested could, no doubt, be increased even further, but it has been our policy to err on the side of caution. Our next project, Volume VIII (Objects of Unknown Provenance), will give us an opportunity to include all such pieces and, if desirable, mention a suggested provenance.

It now seems clear that the Serapeum with the tombs of Apis-bulls is only part of a large complex of galleries with burials of sacred animals which, together with temples and shrines, grew up in the northern part of Ṣaqqâra from the XVIIIth Dynasty and were particularly prominent during the Late and Ptolemaic Periods. Our section called Sacred Animal Complexes has been divided into the Eastern Group, where so far only a few monuments covered by this work have been found, the Western Group, containing the Serapeum with a large number of votive Apis-stelae, and the interesting Northern Group, with the temple of Nektanebos II, the burial place of the Isis Mother-of-Apis cows, and the galleries of mummified ibises, hawks, and baboons. The amount of quoted material, mostly stelae, found by A. Mariette at the site of the Serapeum in the middle of the last century has been greatly increased, and here we owe a great debt of gratitute to Professor Posener who allowed us to consult and use some of the unpublished transcriptions of the texts of Apis-stelae in the Louvre prepared by him, J. Vercoutter and the late M. Malinine.

Although the importance of Mît Rahîna as part of ancient Memphis is not in doubt, only small sections of the site have been systematically explored. We have followed the natural disposition of the remaining structures, as it appears on available maps, thus dividing the area into the Northern Enclosure with the palace of Apries, the large Ptaḥ Enclosure with subsidiary buildings and monuments inside or outside its walls, and the series of *kôms* encircling the enclosures. Compared with the first edition, the most obvious new features are some of the smaller structures near the Enclosure of Ptaḥ, such as the embalming house of Apis-bulls of Sesonchis I, the chapel of Sethos I, the two small temples of Ramesses II, and the tombs of High Priests of Memphis of Dynasty XXII. The last is, with the exception of some First Intermediate Period or Middle Kingdom tombs at Kôm el-Fakhry, the only evidence for burials at Mît Rahîna and corresponds to similar cases of Third Intermediate Period tombs inside or near temple enclosures elsewhere. A temple of Ḥatḥor built by Ramesses II has been partly excavated at Kôm el-Rabîʿa. A temple of Merneptaḥ, explored by C. S. Fisher at Kôm el-Qalʿa between 1915 and 1920, has not yet been published, but we are able to quote the most important objects thanks to the help of various Egyptologists, in particular the late Professor J. Černý and the staff of the University Museum in Philadelphia, who have provided us with copies of the texts and answered our queries over many years.

The excavation of the lower temple of the southern pyramid-complex of Snefru by A. Fakhry and the work currently carried out on the Middle Kingdom pyramids by German Egyptologists have been the main new developments at Dahshûr. The material has been re-arranged to conform to the other sites in the volume.

The work on the *Topographical Bibliography* would not be possible without the active participation and interest of many other scholars. This not only applies to the period during which the manuscript of a particular volume is being prepared, but is true all the time. To acknowledge this help fully would be an impossible task and the list would have to contain the names of most of those who actively contribute to the progress of the discipline. However, in addition to those already mentioned above, we have to thank specifically at least D. Abou-Ghazi, H. Altenmüller, Dieter Arnold, H. G. Fischer, T. G. H. James, G. T. Martin, H. De Meulenaere, A. M. Moussa, and W. K. Simpson.

Much of the material used in this volume was collected by the previous Editors, Dr. R. L. B. Moss and Mrs. E. W. Burney. Few of us can ever aspire to contributing to Egyptology to the extent they have done by their foresight, sheer hard work and, above all, unfailing optimism.

Although their names do not appear on the title-page of this publication, it owes much to the work done by the other members of the *Topographical Bibliography* team at the Griffith Institute. Miss Helen Murray and Miss Kathleen Lorimer have been involved in the preparation of the whole volume, while Mrs. V. Raisman, Mrs. A. G. Hobby, Miss S. McLachlan and Mrs. J. Wiggin have helped with parts of it. I am also grateful to Mrs. C. Dupuis for her work on our main royal index, to Mrs. E. Hine for typing the manuscript, and to Mrs. M. E. Cox for drawing the maps and plans. The combination of the Ashmolean Library and the Griffith Institute archives has provided an ideal setting for this type of work. My thanks are also due to the Oxford University Press for their competent handling of the complicated printing.

The British Academy has very generously contributed towards the printing costs for each fascicle.

The completion of the Memphite volume marks a point of departure for the whole project. Our next volume, VIII (Objects of Unknown Provenance), will appear in a new form, and the presentation of material will be very different. The main reasons for this are the need for more frequent revisions of the existing volumes, the ever increasing amount of material for inclusion, and the constantly rising printing costs. The new scheme will be computer-based and should enable us to catch up with the technological advances we are witnessing elsewhere.

J. MÁLEK

Oxford, January 1981

LIST OF PLANS

LIST OF MAIN SOURCES OF MAPS AND PLANS

All adapted. Full references and sources of plans of individual tombs in the letterpress

Source	Plates
de Morgan, *Carte de la Nécropole Memphite*	XLI, XLII, XLV, XLVI, LI, LVIII, LXI, LXII, LXIX, LXX, LXXIII, LXXIV
Maragioglio and Rinaldi, *Notizie*	XLIII [1, 2]
Lauer, *Pyr. à deg.* ii	XLIII [3]
Jéquier, *Le Monument funéraire de Pepi II*, iii	XLIV
Smith (W. S.) in Reisner, *Tomb Development*	XLV, XLVI
Quibell, *Saqqara (1905–1906)*	LI
id. *(1906–1907)*	LI
id. *(1912–1914)*	XLV
Emery, *Great Tombs*, i	XLV
id. in *J.E.A.* 52 (1966)	XLV
Firth and Gunn, *Teti Pyr. Cem.* ii	LII
Hassan, *Mastabas of Princess Ḥemet-Rʿ and Others*	LX
id. *The Mastaba of Neb-Kaw-Ḥer*	LXI, LXII
Barsanti in *Ann. Serv.* ii (1901)	LXI
Zayed in ib. lv (1958)	LXII
Moussa and Altenmüller, *Das Grab des Nianchchnum und Chnumhotep*	LXII
Maspero, *Trois années de fouilles* [etc.] in *Mém. Miss.* i	LXVII [1]
Jéquier, *Tombeaux de particuliers*	LXVII [2]
Mariette, *Sérapéum, Texte*	LXVIII [1]
Lauer and Picard, *Les Statues ptolémaïques du Sarapieion de Memphis*	LXVIII [2]
Malinine [etc.], *Cat.* i	LXVIII [3]
Martin, *Ḥetepka*	LXIX
Rhoné, *L'Égypte à petites journées* (1877)	LXIX
Smith (H. S.) and Jeffreys in *J.E.A.* 64 (1978)	LXX
Dimick (J.) in Anthes, *Mit Rahineh 1955*	LXXI
El-Sayed Mahmud, *A New Temple for Hathor at Memphis*	LXXI
Anthes, *Mit Rahineh 1956*	LXXII [1]
C. S. F[isher] in *Penn. Mus. Journ.* viii (1917)	LXXII [2]
Fakhry, *Sneferu*, i	LXXIII, LXXIV
Arnold and Stadelmann in *Mit. Kairo*, 31 (1975)	LXXIII
de Morgan, *Dahchour*, i	LXXV
id. ib. ii	LXXIV, LXXV

NOTE TO READERS

Registers are counted from the top and numbered in Roman figures, heavy type; scenes in registers are described starting with the one nearest to the large figure of deceased unless otherwise stated.

Destroyed scenes or details are indicated by square brackets.

Numbers in round brackets at the begining of a paragraph refer to position on plans.

When authors are quoted without the title of the book, the full reference will be found at the beginning of the section.

Original copies and publications only are usually included, though secondary ones are given in special cases. For some very extensively published objects, scenes, or views, only selected references are given (indicated by footnotes); however, all important publications have been included.

Tombs shown in heavier outline on the plans of cemeteries are those mentioned in the letterpress.

III. *Sacred Animal Complexes*

Maps LXIX, LXX

Plan of Eastern and Western Groups, RHONÉ, *L'Égypte à petites journées* (1877), plan on p. 216; MARIETTE, *Sérapéum, Texte*, 1st plan at end; id. in *Bibl. Ég.* xviii, pl. ii; see WILCKEN, *Urkunden der Ptolemäerzeit*, i, pp. 9–12 with Abb. 2 (from MARIETTE).

A. EASTERN GROUP

('Greek Serapeum')

Map LXX

SMITH (H. S.) in *Glimpses of Ancient Egypt. Studies in Honour of H. W. Fairman*, pp. 164–5; MARIETTE, *Sérapéum, Texte*, pp. 72–5; RHONÉ, op. cit. pp. 255–8. Description of building containing colossal statue of Imḥōtep, in Arabic MS. of 10th century, see STRICKER in *Acta Orientalia*, xix (1943), pp. 101–18.

NORTHERN ENCLOSURE. 'Es-Sign Yusuf.'

SMITH (H. S.) and JEFFREYS in *J.E.A.* 64 (1978), pp. 12–20, with plan, fig. 1.

Blocks. Ptolemy II Philadelphus; see SMITH (H. S.) in *Glimpses of Ancient Egypt. Studies in Honour of H. W. Fairman*, p. 164. Ptolemy V Epiphanes; (a) cornice, QUIBELL, *Saqqara (1905–1906)*, pl. xxxi [5], p. 29; (b) heads of the King and Anubis, SMITH (H. S.) and JEFFREYS, op. cit. pl. v [3], p. 19.

Chapel of Bes. Ptolemaic.

QUIBELL, *Saqqara (1905–1906)*, pp. 12–14; plan, on pl. iii.

Clay statue-groups of Bes with nude goddesses, and one with ape, and painted decoration on walls above and at sides, including bees on vine, Apis-bull, remains of soldier and a king slaying foe. One group, in Cairo Mus., id. ib. frontispiece, pl. xxvii, pp. 17, 28; MILNE Photo. Album, 2.9 [lower right]; others and paintings, QUIBELL, op. cit. pls. i, xxvi, xxviii, xxix, pp. 17, 28–9; Apis-bull, see KATER-SIBBES and VERMASEREN, *Apis, I*, p. 12 [32], cf. pl. xxiv (from QUIBELL).

Found in Northern Enclosure

Stela, Bes holding sword and snake, with small female figure, no text, Ptolemaic, formerly in von Bissing Colln. and The Hague, Scheurleer Mus., now in Amsterdam, Allard Pierson Mus. 7762. VON BISSING in *Mitteilungen des Deutschen archäologischen Instituts, Athenische Abteilung*, l (1925), Taf. v [2], p. 124 note 2; see *Allard Pierson Museum. Algemeene Gids* (1937), p. 10 [48].

JACKAL GALLERIES.

Position, DE MORGAN, *Carte de la Nécropole Memphite*, on pl. 10.

Coffins of jackals, wood, Ptolemaic or Roman, probably from here, in Cairo Mus. (a) Decorated and inscribed, CG 29765; MASPERO in *Ann. Serv.* iii (1902), pp. 283–5 with plate; GAILLARD and DARESSY, *La Faune momifiée de l'antique Égypte* (*Cat. Caire*), pl. lv, pp. 129–30. (b) With decoration of barks and jackals, CG 29760; id. ib. pl. liv, pp. 127–8.

Fragments of false-doors of Sit-wernu [hieroglyphs] (presumably woman) and Sebkemkhent [hieroglyphs], 1st Int. Period, intrusive. CAIRO, CENTRE OF DOCUMENTATION photo. S.A., 2088. Names, GUNN Notebook, 21, p. 1.

B. WESTERN GROUP WITH THE SERAPEUM

Maps LXVIII, LXIX

AVENUE OF HUMAN-HEADED SPHINXES. Probably Nektanebos I.

MARIETTE, *Sérapéum, Texte*, pp. 7–10, 13–15, 75–6; id. *Choix de Monuments*, pp. 6–7; RHONÉ, *L'Égypte à petites journées* (1877), pp. 213–15, 218–19; WILCKEN, *Urkunden der Ptolemäerzeit*, i, pp. 7–8, 10. Notes of HARRIS (A. C.) mentioning Avenue of Sphinxes and identifying the Serapeum in 1847–8, SAYCE MSS. 18.

Sphinxes.

Two, in Berlin Mus. 7777–8 (latter in East). No. 7778 (probably), *Aeg. und Vorderasiat. Alterthümer*, Taf. 132; sketches, BORCHARDT in *Amtliche Berichte*, xxxix (1917–18), Abb. 35, col. 107. See *Ausf. Verz.* pp. 312–13.

Five, in Cairo Mus. CG 685, 1193–6; BORCHARDT, *Statuen*, iii, Bl. 126 (CG 685), p. 29; iv, Bl. 168 (CG 1193), pp. 95–6; CG 1193, HASSAN, *The Sphinx*, fig. 23 facing p. 110; id. *The Great Sphinx and its Secrets*, fig. 137, p. 197. Two heads, CG 1024–5; BORCHARDT, op. cit. iv, Bl. 160 (CG 1025), p. 30.

Six, in Louvre, N.391. One, DE MONTGON, *L'Égypte*, fig. on p. 115. See BOREUX, *Guide*, i, p. 168; VANDIER, *Guide* (1948 and 1952), p. 25; (1973), p. 57.

Twelve, in Vienna Mus. Inv.5756–67. See REINISCH, *Miramar* (1865), p. 230 [7–19]; *Uebersicht* (1895), p. 45 [II, IV, VI]; (1923), p. 18 [II, IV, VI].

Others, QUIBELL, *Saqqara (1905–1906)*, pl. xxiv [1], p. 27; LAUER in *Bull. Inst. Ég.* xxxiv (1951–2), fig. 2 on p. 210, cf. p. 207; id. *Saqqara*, pl. 1; id. and PICARD, *Les Statues ptolémaïques du Sarapieion de Memphis*, figs. 2, 13, cf. on pl. 1, p. 3; BINDER-HAGELSTANGE, *Ägypten. Ein Reiseführer* (1966), fig. on p. 346 [right].

EAST TEMPLE. Nektanebos II.

Plan LXVIII [2]

MARIETTE, *Sérapéum. Texte*, pp. 16–19, 23, 76–7, cf. pl. D on p. 26; LAUER and PICARD, op. cit. pp. 7–10, 25, with plan on pl. 26 (from drawing by Mariette).

(1) and (2) Two sphinxes of Nektanebos II, present location unknown.

See MARIETTE, op. cit. pp. 16–17 (as Nektanebos I); LAUER and PICARD, op. cit. pp. 7–8 note 1, 15 [3], 25. Base of one, in Louvre, N.424; BOREUX, *Guide*, i, pl. xxi [lower]; SCHARFF in *Miscellanea Gregoriana*, Abb. 2 [lower], p. 196.

(3) Statue of Onuris, sandstone, present location unknown.

See LAUER and PICARD, op. cit. p. 15 [1].

Found in Temple.

Jamb-fragment, heads of the King and Isis, in Louvre, N.402 [S.993]. VANDIER, *Guide* (1948), pl. vii [2], p. 25; (1952), pl. vii [2], p. 26; (1973), pl. vi [2], p. 57; DEVÉRIA squeezes, 6170C, 1, 1a–c. King, WOLF, *Kunst*, Abb. 689. See DE ROUGÉ, *Notice sommaire* (1876), p. 59; BOREUX, *Guide*, i, p. 175.

Block, upper part of the King before bull-headed Apis, in Louvre, N.423 [S.119]. See id. ib. i, pp. 174–5.

Statue of Bes, Dyn. XXX, in Louvre, N.437. Id. ib. i, pl. xix, p. 168; GALVANO, *L'Arte egiziana antica*, fig. 60; RANKE, *The Art of Ancient Egypt*, and BREASTED, *Geschichte Aegyptens* (1936), 177; DESROCHES, *L'Art égyptien au Musée du Louvre* (1941), fig. on 29th p. [lower]; LAUER, *Saqqara*, pl. 6; id. and PICARD, op. cit. fig. 5, p. 9; *Egyptian Mythology*, fig. on p. 113; MICHALOWSKI, *Art*, fig. 620; ARCHIVES phot. E.63; MARBURG INST. photo. 48797. See MARIETTE, op. cit. p. 17; VANDIER, *Guide* (1948), p. 25; (1952), p. 26; (1973), p. 57.

Perhaps from here.

Stela, Nektanebos II kneeling before Apis-bull, year 2, quartzite, found reused in Monastery of Apa Jeremias, in Cairo Mus. Temp. No. 2.12.24.3. SPIEGELBERG in QUIBELL, *Saqqara (1907–1908)*, pl. lii, pp. 10, 89–93, 112; text, DARESSY in *Ann. Serv.* ix (1908), pp. 154–6; see KATER-SIBBES and VERMASEREN, *Apis, I*, p. 24 [85] (as Nektanebos I).

Block with cartouches of Nektanebos I, in Louvre, B 33. See DE ROUGÉ, *Notice des monuments* (1883), p. 62.

Found near Hemicycle with Hellenistic Statues, etc.

Blocks from pillars or jambs of Ramesses II. See LAUER and PICARD, op. cit. p. 23.

Statuette of Apis-bull, schist, Late Period or Ptolemaic, in Cairo Mus. JE 89607. LAUER in *Ann. Serv.* liv (1957), pl. iv, pp. 111–12; see KATER-SIBBES and VERMASEREN, *Apis, I*, p. 11 [28], cf. pl. xxii (from LAUER).

Upper part of statuette of a Queen or Isis, schist, Ptolemaic. EL-KHOULY in *J.E.A.* 59 (1973), pl. xli [2], p. 155.

APPROACH TO SERAPEUM ENCLOSURE. 'Dromos' of Mariette.

Plan LXVIII [2]

Plan, LAUER and PICARD, *Les Statues ptolémaïques du Sarapieion de Memphis*, on pl. 26 (from drawing by Mariette); view, on pls. 2 [a], 18; LAUER, *Saqqara*, pl. 2. See MARIETTE, *Sérapéum, Texte*, pp. 77–8.

(4) Lion-statue, Dyn. XXX, in Louvre, N.432a [A.F.2962; S.1091].

MARIETTE, *Sérapéum, Atlas*, pl. 4 [d], *Texte*, p. 29; LAUER, *Saqqara*, pl. 7; id. and PICARD, op. cit. fig. 6, pp. 11, 16 [6], 18–19; DE MONTGON, *L'Égypte*, fig. on p. 94; DESROCHES, *L'Art égyptien au Musée du Louvre* (1941), fig. on 30th p. [lower]; ARCHIVES phot. E.992. See ROEDER in *Miscellanea Gregoriana*, pp. 185–6, 188–9; BOREUX, *Guide*, i, p. 174; VANDIER, *Guide* (1948 and 1952), p. 15.

(5) Statue of Horus as hawk, probably Late Period or Ptolemaic, now destroyed except for base.

See MARIETTE, *Sérapéum, Texte*, p. 29; LAUER and PICARD, op. cit. pp. 16 [11], 17.

(6) Two sphinxes of Merneptaḥ, sandstone, one (headless) in Louvre, IM.223 [N.393], the other destroyed.

Louvre sphinx, ARCHIVES phot. E.623. See MARIETTE, *Sérapéum, Texte*, p. 29; LAUER and PICARD, op. cit. pp. 16 [15], 18, 23–4; BOREUX, *Guide*, i, p. 170.

(7) Lion-statue, Late Period or Ptolemaic, now displaced.

MARIETTE, *Sérapéum, Atlas*, pl. 5 [a]. Two similar lion-statues, see LAUER and PICARD, op. cit. pp. 16 [17], 18, with figs. 11 (from MARIETTE), 12 (one).

Chapel of Apis.

Statue of Apis-bull, Dyn. XXX, in Louvre, N.390 [S.98]. MARIETTE, *Sérapéum*, *Atlas*, pl. 3 [a]; *Texte*, p. 29; BOREUX, *Guide*, i, pl. xx, pp. 168–9; GALVANO, *L'Arte egiziana antica*, fig. 59; DESROCHES, op. cit. fig. on 30th p. [upper]; DE MONTGON, *L'Égypte*, fig. on p. 112; VANDIER and SOUGEZ, *La Sculpture égyptienne au Musée du Louvre*, 27th pl. [lower]; LAUER, *Saqqara*, pl. 10; id. and PICARD, op. cit. figs. 8, 9, pp. 14, 16 [14], 19; MONTET, *Eternal Egypt*, pl. 69; KATER-SIBBES and VERMASEREN, *Apis*, *I*, p. 5 [1] with pls. i, ii; ARCHIVES phot. E.73. See DE ROUGÉ, *Notice sommaire* (1876), pp. 57–8; VANDIER, *Guide* (1948 and 1952), p. 14; (1973), p. 57.

SERAPEUM ENCLOSURE WITH TOMBS OF APIS-BULLS

Plans LXVIII [2] and [3]

PYLON. Nektanebos I.

Cornice-blocks with name of the King. See MARIETTE, *Sérapéum*, *Texte*, p. 27 (as Nektanebos II).

(8) Two lion-statues, in Louvre, N.432b, c [A.F.2963–4; S.971–2].

N.432b [A.F.2963; S.971], BOREUX, *Guide*, i, pl. xxi [upper], p. 169; SCHARFF in *Miscellanea Gregoriana*, Abb. 2 [upper], p. 196; *L'Égypte des Pharaons* (Marcq-en-Baroeul, Oct. 1977–Jan. 1978), No. 1 with fig. (as N.432c); ARCHIVES phot. E.606. See ROEDER in *Miscellanea Gregoriana*, pp. 185–6, 188–9; DE ROUGÉ, *Notice sommaire* (1876), p. 58; VANDIER, *Guide* (1948 and 1952), p. 23; (1973), p. 46.

Donation-stela of Nektanebos I to Khons, originally set in pedestal of one of lion-statues, in Louvre, C 318 [IM.131]. See MARIETTE, *Sérapéum*, *Texte*, p. 27; VANDIER, *Guide* (1948 and 1952), p. 17; (1973), p. 27.

ISOLATED TOMBS

Plan LXVIII [3]

Plan showing position, RHONÉ, *L'Égypte à petites journées* (1877), on pl. facing p. 228; MALININE [etc.], *Cat.* i, on pl. facing p. xvi. Section of a tomb, MARIETTE, *Sérapéum*, *Texte*, fig. 1 on p. 117 = id. *Renseignements* (1855), fig. 1 on p. 47 (repr. in *Bibl. Ég.* xviii, fig. 1 on p. 138); MASPERO, *L'Arch. ég.* (1887), fig. 145; (1907), fig. 151.

APIS I [I OF DYN. XVIII] of Mariette. Temp. Amenophis III.

Tomb C1 of Rhoné, A of Mariette.

Chapel. Above burial chamber.

Amenophis III and son Ḏḥutmosi before Apis-bull. Texts, MARIETTE, *Sérapéum*, *Texte*, pp. 124–5 = id. *Renseignements* (1855), p. 53 (repr. in *Bibl. Ég.* xviii, p. 149).

Burial chamber.

Four canopic-jars and inscribed block. Id. *Sérapéum*, pl. 1.

Four magical bricks, found in niches, in Louvre, IM.5336–9 [N.842]. MONNET in *Rev. d'Ég.* 8 (1951), pls. 8, 9, 10 [B, C], pp. 153 with note 3, 155–60 [2].

Monuments of Ḏḥutmosi. In Louvre.

Vase of [Ḏḥutmosi], alabaster, N.482. Name and title, GAUTHIER, *Livre des Rois*, ii, p. 336 [ciii, B.3]. See PIERRET, *Cat.* No. 364.

Four vases, pottery, N.455, 484. See id. ib. No. 365.

APIS II [V OF DYN. XVIII] of Mariette. Probably Dyn. XVIII.

Tomb C2 of Rhoné, B of Mariette.

Four canopic-jars, in Louvre, S.1164–7. MARIETTE, *Sérapéum*, pl. 5; one, WILKINSON MSS. xxiv. 5 [middle].

Stelae. In Louvre.

May , Servant of Amūn and Apis, two registers, **I,** hawk-headed Horus and deified King Teti(?) before Osiris, with Isis and Nephthys beyond, **II,** May adoring Apis-bull, IM.5305 [E.3012; A.F.125; S.1168]. MALININE [etc.], *Cat.* i, pl. i [1], pp. 1–2; MARIETTE, *Sérapéum*, pls. 6, 7 [1, 2]. Cartouche, id. *Sérapéum, Texte*, fig. 7, pp. 131–5 = id. *Renseignements* (1855), fig. 7, pp. 56–7 (repr. in *Bibl. Ég.* xviii, fig. 7, pp. 158–64); GAUTHIER, *Livre des Rois*, iii, p. 148 [ii]; DEVÉRIA squeezes, 6166, i. 82. See PIERRET, *Cat.* No. 274.

Two registers, **I,** Apis-bull and Osiris, **II,** two men (no names) kneeling adoring before offerings, IM.5306 [S.1170; No. 2]. MALININE [etc.], *Cat.* i, pl. i [2], pp. 2–3. Texts, CHASSINAT in *Rec. Trav.* xxi (1899), p. 70 [xxxiii]. See REVILLOUT, *Cat.* No. 386.

Two registers, **I,** Apis-bull and Osiris seated, **II,** two men (no names) kneeling adoring, IM.5307 [S.1169; No. 1]. MALININE [etc.], *Cat.* i, pl. i [3], p. 3. See REVILLOUT, *Cat.* No. 385.

APIS III [II OF DYN. XVIII] of Mariette. Temp. Tutʿankhamūn.

Tomb C3 of Rhoné, C of Mariette.

Four canopic-jars, in Louvre, S.1151–4. MARIETTE, *Sérapéum*, on pl. 2; three, GOODWIN MSS. 31279, 25–7; one, DESROCHES, *L'Art égyptien au Musée du Louvre* (1941), fig. on 24th p. [middle]; text of another, WILKINSON MSS. xxiv. 5 [right]. Lid of one, BÉNÉDITE in *Mon. Piot*, xxiv (1921), fig. 10, p. 65. See DE ROUGÉ, *Notice sommaire* (1876), p. 59; BOREUX, *Guide*, i, p. 170.

Three glass pendants with name of Tutʿankhamūn, in Louvre, No. 456. One, MARIETTE, *Sérapéum*, on pl. 2; PETRIE, *History*, ii (1924), fig. 150, pp. 235, 237; MICHAÏLIDIS in *Ann. Serv.* xlv (1947), fig. 16, p. 125. Text, MARIETTE, *Sérapéum*, *Texte*, fig. 4, pp. 125–6 = id. *Renseignements* (1855), fig. 4, p. 53 (repr. in *Bibl. Ég.* xviii, fig. 4, p. 150); HELCK, *Urk.* iv. 2062 [785], cf. *Übersetz.* (1961), p. 382. See BOREUX, *Guide*, ii, p. 546 [bottom].

APIS IV AND V [III AND IV OF DYN. XVIII] of Mariette. Temp. Ḥaremḥab.

Tombs C4 and C5 of Rhoné, D and E of Mariette.

See MARIETTE, *Sérapéum*, *Texte*, pp. 66–7.

Block with name of the King, from débris of chapel. See id. ib. p. 126 = id. *Renseignements* (1855), p. 53 (repr. in *Bibl. Ég.* xviii, p. 151).

First Room. Apis IV. Painted decoration.

Apis-bull, four Sons of Horus, Anubis, Isis, and Nephthys; MARIETTE, *Sérapéum*, pl. 3.

Second Room. Apis V.

Canopic-jars, in Louvre, S.1160–3. Id. ib. pl. 4 [2–6]. See BOREUX, *Guide*, i, p. 170; VANDIER, *Guide* (1948 and 1952), p. 6; (1973), p. 56.

Text of coffin, MARIETTE, *Sérapéum*, *Texte*, p. 129 = id. *Renseignements*, p. 55 (repr. in *Bibl. Ég.* xviii, p. 156).

APIS VI [I OF DYN. XIX] of Mariette. Temp. Sethos I.

Tomb C6 of Rhoné, F of Mariette.

Block with name of the King, from débris of chapel. See MARIETTE, *Sérapéum*, *Texte*, p. 137 = id. *Renseignements* (1855), p. 66.

APIS VII AND IX [II AND IV OF DYN. XIX] of Mariette. Years 16 and 30 of Ramesses II.[1]

Tomb C8 of Rhoné, G of Mariette.

MARIETTE, *Sérapéum*, *Texte*, pp. 62–4, 137–42; id. *Renseignements* (1855), pp. 66–8.

South wall with painted decoration. Double-scene, Ramesses II with son Khaᶜemwēset censing and libating before bull-headed Apis, with four Sons of Horus behind; id. *Sérapéum*, pl. 8; left half, BRUGSCH, *Recueil*, pl. viii [1]; texts, KITCHEN, *Ram. Inscr.* ii. 367 [131, A].

Finds.

Canopic-jar dedicated by Khaᶜemwēset, in Louvre (unnumbered). MARIETTE, *Sérapéum*, pl. 10 [upper middle]; text, KITCHEN, op. cit. 368 [131, D]; see MARIETTE, *Sérapéum*, *Texte*, pp. 61–2, 138; id. *Renseignements* (1855), p. 66; GOMAÀ, *Chaemwese* [etc.], pp. 78–9 [22], cf. Abb. 8.

Two magical bricks, in Louvre, IM.3597–8 [N.842]. MONNET in *Rev. d'Ég.* 8 (1951), pls. 10 [A], 11, pp. 154, 156–8 [6]; texts, KITCHEN, op. cit. 368 [131, C].

Pectoral[2] with name of Ramesses II, gold inlaid with glass, in Louvre, IM.2886 [N.767; E.79]. MARIETTE, *Sérapéum*, pl. 9; SCHUMANN-ANTELME in *Göttinger Miszellen*, No. 21 (1976), pp. 77–82 with figs.; *recto*, RHONÉ, *L'Égypte à petites journées* (1877), pl. facing p. 229 [middle]; PERROT and CHIPIEZ, *Hist. de l'Art*, i, fig. 566; DEVILLE, *Histoire de l'art de la verrerie dans l'antiquité* (1873), pl. cx [A]; MASPERO, *Hist. anc.* ii, fig. on p. 492; id. *Eg. Art*, pl. facing p. 148 [upper], cf. pp. 148–50; id. *Essais*, fig. 56, pp. 183–5; id. *Égypte*, fig. 408; WHYTE in *P.S.B.A.* xv (1893), pl. i facing p. 408, cf. p. 411; VERNIER, *La Bijouterie et la joaillerie égyptiennes*, pl. vii [1]; BÉNÉDITE, *L'Art égyptien dans ses lignes générales*, pl. xxxiv, p. 72; CAPART, *L'Art ég.* iv, pl. 750 [lower]; PETRIE, *Arts and Crafts*, fig. 105 facing p. 94; BOREUX, *L'Art ég.* pl. lxiii [D, middle]; id. *Guide*, ii, pl. xlvii [lower], p. 350; DESROCHES, *L'Art égyptien au Musée du Louvre* (1941), fig. on 25th p. [bottom]; DESROCHES-NOBLECOURT, *Le Style égyptien*, pl. liii [upper], p. 160; id. *L'Art ég.* fig. 73 [top]; id. and DU BOURGUET, *L'Art égyptien*, pl. xxxi; DAUMAS, *Civ. de l'Ég.* pl. 219; CHARBONNEAUX, *Les Merveilles du Louvre*, i, pl. on p. 79 [upper]; WOLDERING, *Ägypten. Die Kunst der Pharaonen*, pl. on p. 185 (reversed); id. *Götter*, fig. on p. 248 [Kat. 102]; KAYSER, *Ägyptisches Kunsthandwerk*, Abb. 202; MICHALOWSKI, *Art*, fig. 796; WILKINSON (A.), *Ancient Egyptian Jewellery*, pl. lxi [A]; FEUCHT-PUTZ, *Die königlichen Pektorale*, Taf. x [24], p. 172; ALDRED, *Jewels of the Pharaohs*, pl. 145; LAUER, *Saqqara*, pl. 14; VANDIER, *Guide* (1973), pl. xii [1], p. 92; ARCHIVES phot.

[1] From stela of Piay, in Louvre, IM.4963, see *infra*. Year 25 refers to the death of a Mnevis-bull.
[2] Selected references.

E.337. Name, KITCHEN, *Ram. Inscr.* ii. 366 [130, A (ii)]. See DE ROUGÉ, *Notice sommaire* (1876), p. 73; PIERRET, *Cat.* No. 521; VANDIER, *Guide* (1948), p. 48 [middle], cf. pl. xi [upper]; (1952), p. 49 [middle], cf. pl. xi [upper].

Jewellery dedicated by Paser, Vizier (Theb. tb. 106), in Louvre. (a) Pectoral, IM.2894 [N.762; E.68]; MARIETTE, *Sérapéum*, pl. 12 [middle]; BOREUX, *Guide*, ii, pl. xlvii [upper left], p. 350; id. *L'Art ég.* pl. lxiii [D, right]; DAUMAS, *Civ. de l'Ég.* pl. 226; ARCHIVES phot. E.337; texts, KITCHEN, op. cit. 366–7 [130, B (ii)]; see PIERRET, *Cat.* No. 524; FEUCHT, *Pektorale nichtköniglicher Personen*, pp. 65–6 [11 B], 70 [29]. (b) Colonnette, N.760 [E.69]; BOREUX, *Guide*, ii, pl. xlvi [middle], p. 342; ARCHIVES phot. E.722; see PIERRET, *Cat.* No. 522. Both, see DE ROUGÉ, *Notice sommaire* (1876), p. 74; VANDIER, *Guide* (1948), p. 48; (1952), p. 49.

Stelae. Temp. Ramesses II. In Louvre.

Amenemḥab [hieroglyphs], Head of outline-draughtsmen of the ḥarîm at Memphis, before bull-headed Apis, probably from here, IM.5954 [No. 11]. MALININE [etc.], *Cat.* i, pl. vi [17], p. 16; see REVILLOUT, *Cat.* No. 395.

Amenmosi, Overseer of the royal apartments of the ḥarîm at Memphis, two registers, **I,** before Osiris and Isis, **II,** before Apis-bull, IM.5268 [S.1466; No. 6]. MALININE [etc.], *Cat.* i, pl. iv [10], pp. 10–11; text, CHASSINAT in *Rec. Trav.* xxi (1899), p. 73 [xxxvi]; KITCHEN, *Ram. Inscr.* ii. 374 [132, H]; see REVILLOUT, *Cat.* No. 390.

Ḏḥutemḥab [hieroglyphs], Royal scribe, Overseer of the royal apartments of the ḥarîm at Memphis, two registers, **I,** kneeling adoring bull-headed Apis, **II,** Ḥori [hieroglyphs], Deputy in Memphis, kneeling adoring bull-headed Apis, probably from here, IM.5952 [No. 10]. MALININE [etc.], *Cat.* i, pl. vi [15], p. 15; MARIETTE, *Sérapéum*, pl. 17 [right]; see REVILLOUT, *Cat.* No. 394.

Ipy [hieroglyphs], Scribe of the Temple of Ptaḥ, IM.5271 [S.1465; No. 12]. MALININE [etc.], *Cat.* i, pl. iv [13], p. 13; text, KITCHEN, op. cit. 375 [132, K]; see REVILLOUT, *Cat.* No. 396.

Khons [hieroglyphs], Head of the *shaytiu*, two registers, **I,** Khons, wife Nezet [hieroglyphs] and daughter before Apis-bull in shrine, **II,** family before Osiris seated, IM.4964 [No. 13]. MALININE [etc.], *Cat.* i, pl. iii [7], pp. 7–8; MARIETTE, *Sérapéum*, pl. 17 [left]; text, KITCHEN, op. cit. 373 [132, F]; names and titles, LIEBLEIN, *Dict.* No. 965; see REVILLOUT, *Cat.* No. 397.

Meriḥu [hieroglyphs], Retainer of His Majesty, two registers, **I,** before Apis-bull and Osiris, **II,** family, fragmentary, S.N.81 [No. 16]. MARIETTE, *Sérapéum*, pl. 17 [middle]; omitting top, MALININE [etc.], *Cat.* i, pl. iv [11], pp. 11–12; text, KITCHEN, op. cit. 374 [132, I]; see REVILLOUT, *Cat.* No. 400.

Neḥeḥ-endisu [hieroglyphs], Head of the store-room of Ptaḥ, two registers, **I,** Neḥeḥ-endisu and wife before bull-headed Apis, **II,** Neḥeḥ-endisu and Neferronpet [hieroglyphs] with oryx before Osiris, fragmentary, IM.5270 [No. 14]. MALININE [etc.], *Cat.* i, pl. v [12], pp. 12–13; MARIETTE, *Sérapéum*, pl. 18 [middle]; text, KITCHEN, op. cit. 374–5 [132, J]; see REVILLOUT, *Cat.* No. 398.

Piay [hieroglyphs], Royal scribe, Overseer of embalmers in the two embalming houses, etc. (a) Apis-bull (died in year 16) and Mnevis-bull (died in year 25), and two registers below, **I,** Piay and Ḏḥutmosi Raʿmosi, Chief lector-priest in the embalming house, etc., before Apis-bull with statue in shrine, **II,** text and two men, year 30, IM.4963 [N.411; S.1457; No. 3]. MALININE [etc.], *Cat.* i, pl. ii [4], pp. 3–5; MARIETTE, *Sérapéum*, pl. 15; upper part, VAN DER LEEUW, *De Godsdienst van het oude Aegypte*, pl. 63 facing p. 112; text, BRUGSCH, *Thes.* 964–6 (as IM.4969); CHASSINAT in *Rec. Trav.* xxi (1899), pp. 70–2 [xxxiv]; KITCHEN, *Ram.*

Inscr. ii. 369–70 [132, A]; date and some names and titles, LIEBLEIN, *Dict.* No. 899 (as No. 2); see MARIETTE, *Sérapéum, Texte*, p. 142 (part of text) = id. *Renseignements* (1855), p. 68; DE ROUGÉ, *Notice sommaire* (1876), p. 59 (as S.1553); REVILLOUT, *Cat.* No. 387. (b) Two registers, **I,** Piay and Riya [hieroglyphs], Embalmer in the embalming house, etc., before Apis-bull in shrine, **II,** text and Riya and another man, year 30, IM.5936 [No. 5 (as No. 4 in 1st ed. in error)]; MALININE [etc.], *Cat.* i, pl. ii [5], pp. 5–6; MARIETTE, *Sérapéum*, pl. 16; **I,** PRISSE, *L'Art ég. Texte*, fig. on p. 25; text, CHASSINAT, op. cit. xxi (1899), pp. 72–3 [xxxv]; KITCHEN, op. cit. 370–1 [132, B]; names, titles, and date, LIEBLEIN, *Dict.* No. 898 (as No. 1); see REVILLOUT, *Cat.* No. 389. (c) Piay and Yy [hieroglyphs], Embalmer in the embalming house, etc., before Apis-bull in shrine, fragments, S.N.84 [No. 4]; MALININE [etc.], *Cat.* i, pl. i [6], pp. 6–7; text, KITCHEN, op. cit. 371–2 [132, C]; see REVILLOUT, *Cat.* No. 388.

Ptaḥmosi, Royal scribe, Steward, three registers, **I,** Ptaḥmosi and wife Yuhebet [hieroglyphs] before Ptaḥ seated, **II,** man and wife before Apis-bull, **III,** people, IM.5269 [No. 9]. MALININE [etc.], *Cat.* i, pl. iii [9], pp. 9–10; MARIETTE, *Sérapéum*, pl. 18 [left]; text, KITCHEN, op. cit. 372–3 [132, E, II]; names and titles of Ptaḥmosi and wife, LIEBLEIN, *Dict.* No. 964; see REVILLOUT, *Cat.* No. 393.

Sekhmetnefert [hieroglyphs], Mourner of Apis (woman), two registers, **I,** before Apis-bull, **II,** people before Osiris seated, IM.6153 [No. 8]. MALININE [etc.], *Cat.* i, pl. iv [8], pp. 8–9; MARIETTE, *Sérapéum*, pl. 18 [right]; text, KITCHEN, op. cit. 373 [132, G]; see REVILLOUT, *Cat.* No. 392.

Thaia [hieroglyphs], Head of workmen of the Necropolis of the ḥarîm at Memphis, before bull-headed Apis, probably from here, IM.5953 [No. 7]. MALININE [etc.], *Cat.* i, pl. vi [16], pp. 15–16; text, CHASSINAT in *Rec. Trav.* xxi (1899), p. 73 [xxxvii]; see REVILLOUT, *Cat.* No. 391.

GALLERIES

Plan, RHONÉ, *L'Égypte à petites journées* (1877), on pl. facing p. 228; MALININE [etc.], *Cat.* i, on pl. facing p. xvi; part, MARIETTE, *Sérapéum, Texte*, pl. F on p. 43.

'LESSER VAULTS'.

Plan LXVIII [3]

See MARIETTE, *Sérapéum, Texte*, pp. 56–60, 80. Plan of north part, VERCOUTTER in *Kush*, viii (1960), fig. 1, p. 66 note 30.

APIS X–XIV [V–IX OF DYN. XIX] of Mariette. Temp. Ramesses II.

Chambers I, J, K of Mariette, D, D′ of Rhoné.

MARIETTE, *Sérapéum, Texte*, pp. 142–3, 145–6, mentioning date 'year 55' on wall of one chamber (presumably K of Mariette); id. *Renseignements* (1855), pp. 85, 86 (repr. in *Bibl. Ég.* xviii, pp. 167, 171–2).

Stela, Merneptaḥ (son of Ramesses II, later King), two registers, **I,** before Apis-bull, **II,** Thay [hieroglyphs] To [hieroglyphs], Scribe of the Hereditary prince, and father Smentaui [hieroglyphs], Retainer of the Hereditary prince, in Louvre, IM.3747 [N.412; S.1555; No. 15]. MALININE [etc.], *Cat.* i, pl. v [14], p. 14; MARIETTE, *Sérapéum*, pl. 21 (as Apis X); DEVÉRIA squeezes, 6166, ii. 132. Text, KITCHEN, *Ram. Inscr.* ii. 377 [B (ii)]. See DE ROUGÉ, *Notice sommaire* (1876), p. 60; REVILLOUT, *Cat.* No. 399; CHRISTOPHE in *Ann. Serv.* li (1951), p. 343 note 1.

APIS XVI [II OF DYN. XX] of Mariette. Temp. Ramesses VI.

MARIETTE, *Sérapéum, Texte*, p. 147 = id. *Renseignements* (1855), p. 87 (repr. in *Bibl. Ég.* xviii, pp. 173–4).

Jar dedicated by Ramesses VI, in Louvre, N.5415. Id. *Sérapéum*, pl. 22 [3]; see PIERRET, *Cat.* No. 379; VANDIER, *Guide* (1973), p. 99.

APIS XVII [III OF DYN. XX] of Mariette. Temp. Ramesses IX.

Chamber M of Mariette, E′ of Rhoné.

Cylindrical jars, (a) small, Ramesses IX, (b) large, Ramesses-Siptaḥ, both in Louvre, N.442. MARIETTE, *Sérapéum*, pl. 22 [5, 7] (latter as Apis IV); cartouches, id. *Sérapéum, Texte*, p. 148 = id. *Renseignements* (1855), p. 87 (repr. in *Bibl. Ég.* xviii, p. 174); see PIERRET, *Cat.* Nos. 375–6; BOREUX, *Guide*, ii, p. 528; VANDIER, *Guide* (1973), p. 99. (b) Id. in *Rev. d'Ég.* 23 (1971), fig. 4, p. 189.

Vase of Ramesses-Siptaḥ, in Louvre, N.5418. Id. ib. fig. 5, pp. 189–91; MARIETTE, *Sérapéum*, pl. 22 [6] (as Apis IV); see PIERRET, *Cat.* No. 374; VANDIER, *Guide* (1973), p. 99.

Faience *zad*-amulet of Ramesses IX, in Louvre, N.5416. MARIETTE, *Sérapéum*, pl. 22 [4]; ARCHIVES phot. E.1064; see BOREUX, *Guide*, ii, p. 526; VANDIER, *Guide* (1973), p. 99.

APIS XXVII [I OF DYN. XXII] of Mariette. Year 23 of Osorkon II.

MARIETTE, *Sérapéum, Texte*, pp. 158–9 = id. *Renseignements* (1855), pp. 93–4 (repr. in *Bibl. Ég.* xviii, pp. 188–91).

Stela with date, two men (one of them Amenemōpet, Royal scribe, etc.) before bull-headed Apis seated, painted, much effaced, in Louvre, IM.3090 [N.5419; S.1883]. MALININE [etc.], *Cat.* i, pl. vi [18], p. 17; see PIERRET, *Cat.* No. 275.

Statues.

Block-statue of Ḥuy [hieroglyphs], Chief Governor of Memphis, temp. Ramesses II, in Louvre, N.519. MARIETTE, *Sérapéum*, pl. 23; ARCHIVES phot. E.899; see PIERRET, *Cat.* No. 27; VANDIER, *Guide* (1973), p. 125.

Sheshonḳ [hieroglyphs], son of Osorkon II and Keramama, kneeling with naos of Ptaḥ-Sokari-Osiris, in Budapest, Szépművészeti Múzeum, 51.2050. OROSZLÁN and DOBROVITS, *Az Egyiptomi Gyűjtemény* (1939), pl. 1, pp. 21–2 [32] (text); VARGA and WESSETZKY, *Egyiptomi kiállítás. Vezető* (1955), pl. vii, p. 17; (1961), pl. xix, p. 26; (1964), pl. xiii, p. 25; id. *Az ókori Egyiptom* (1970), pl. 22; VARGA in *Bull. Soc. fr. d'Ég.* 36 (June 1963), fig. on p. 27 [right], cf. p. 29; id. *Egyiptomi kiállítás. Vezető* (1976), pl. 26. Titles, BUDGE, *The Kings of Egypt*, ii, p. 48 [bottom]; DARESSY in *Rec. Trav.* xxxv (1913), p. 142 [bottom]; BRUGSCH, *Thes.* 1450 [79].

APIS XXVIII [II OF DYN. XXII] of Mariette. Year 14 of Takelothis II.

MARIETTE, *Sérapéum, Texte*, p. 159 = id. *Renseignements* (1855), p. 94 (repr. in *Bibl. Ég.* xviii, p. 191).

Block of Merneptaḥ, Greatest of the Directors of craftsmen of Ptaḥ, with cartouches of Takelothis II, in Louvre, S.N.82 [No. 119]. MALININE [etc.], *Cat.* i, pl. vii [19], p. 18; cartouches, GAUTHIER, *Livre des Rois*, iii, p. 354 [xii].

Lower part of stela, name lost, year 14, perhaps from here, in Alexandria, Graeco-Roman Mus. Text, DARESSY in *Ann. Serv.* v (1904), p. 121 [xxiv]; see BOTTI, *Catalogue des monuments* [etc.], p. 353 [22].

Stela of Zeptaḥef'ankh, Servant of Ḥatḥor Mistress of the Southern Sycamore, inscribed in ink, much effaced, probably temp. Takelothis II and from here, in Louvre, IM.2810 [S.1890; No. 21]. MALININE [etc.], *Cat.* i, pl. vii [20], pp. 18–19.

APIS XXIX [III OF DYN. XXII] of Mariette. Year 28 of Sesonchis III.

Chamber P of Mariette, F of Rhoné.

Stela, Pedēsi, son of Thekerti, both Great chiefs of the Ma, and Thesubastepert, with two other men before bull-headed Apis, year 28 of Sesonchis III, in Louvre, IM.3749 [N.413; S.1898; No. 18]. MARIETTE, *Sérapéum*, pl. 24; MALININE [etc.], *Cat.* i, pl. vii [21], pp. 19–20; SCHMIDT, *Levende og Døde*, fig. 887; DEVÉRIA squeezes, 6169, i. 39; WILKINSON MSS. xxiv. 19 [1]. Text, CHASSINAT in *Rec. Trav.* xxii (1900), pp. 9–10 [xxxviii]. Names and titles, LIEBLEIN, *Dict.* No. 1011; id. in *Rev. Arch.* N.S. xviii (1868), p. 283; LEGRAIN in *Rec. Trav.* xxix (1907), pp. 178–9. See MARIETTE, *Sérapéum, Texte*, pp. 159–60; YOYOTTE in *Mélanges Maspero*, i [4], p. 124 [3]; DE ROUGÉ, *Notice sommaire* (1876), p. 60; REVILLOUT, *Cat.* No. 401.

Statue-group, two men (unfinished) kneeling supporting stela of Esptaḥ, God's father of Ptaḥ, Prophet of the Temple of Mut foremost of 'Abuy-neteru, son (more likely descendant) of Shedsunefertem, Greatest of the Directors of craftsmen, etc., in Louvre, N.436. VANDIER in *J.E.A.* 35 (1949), pl. xiv, pp. 135–8; stela, MARIETTE, *Sérapéum*, pl. 25 [1].

APIS XXX [IV OF DYN. XXII] of Mariette. Year 2 of Pemu.

Dated stelae. In Louvre. See DE ROUGÉ, *Notice sommaire* (1876), p. 60.

Pedēsi (same as dedicator of stela IM.3749, see *supra*) and son Ḥarsiēsi before bull-headed Apis and Western goddess, giving the date of birth of the Apis-bull as year 28 of Sesonchis III, two stelae, IM.3697, 3736 [S.1904–5; Nos. 34, 36]. MARIETTE, *Sérapéum*, pls. 26–7; MALININE [etc.], *Cat.* i, pl. viii [22–3], pp. 21–3; DEVÉRIA squeezes, 6165, i. 39, 38; WILKINSON MSS. xxiv. 15, 16; names and titles, LEGRAIN in *Rec. Trav.* xxix (1907), pp. 179–80; LIEBLEIN, *Dict.* Nos. 1012–13; see YOYOTTE in *Mélanges Maspero*, i [4], p. 124 [4, 5]. IM.3697, ARCHIVES phot. E.654; text, CHASSINAT in *Rec. Trav.* xxii (1900), pp. 10–11 [xxxix]; incomplete, MARIETTE, *Sérapéum*, *Texte*, pp. 161–3 = id. *Renseignements* (1855), pp. 95–6 (repr. in *Bibl. Ég.* xviii, pp. 194–7); BRUGSCH, *Thes.* 967 [bottom]–968.

Pezai, God's father of Ptaḥ, Prophet of Ḥatḥor Mistress of Ḥetept in Khanūfer, etc., son of Pemu, with King Pemu offering bread to bull-headed Apis and [Ḥatḥor], and Pezai behind, painted, IM.3441 [N.414; A.F.122; S.1907]. MALININE [etc.], *Cat.* i, pl. ix [25], pp. 24–5; WILKINSON MSS. xxiv. 24 [right upper], 34 [left lower]; text, CHASSINAT in *Rec. Trav.* xxi (1899), pp. 58–9 [i]; ČERNÝ Notebook, 117, p. 23 [upper]; titles, see VANDIER in *Rev. d'Ég.* 17 (1965), p. 97 [E.lxxiii]; see PIERRET, *Cat.* No. 276.

Senbef, Prophet of the phyle of the 3rd month, etc., IM.4205 [S.1906; No. 35]. MARIETTE, *Sérapéum*, pl. 28 [right]; MALININE [etc.], *Cat.* i, pl. ix [24], p. 24; WILKINSON MSS. xxiv. 14 [right].

Perhaps this Apis.

Stela, Ḥarwen [hieroglyphs], God's father of Amūn, son of Iufꜥankh [hieroglyphs], and another man before bull-headed Apis, now lost. MARIETTE, *Sérapéum*, pl. 25 [3]; MALININE [etc.], *Cat.* i, pl. xiv [45] (from MARIETTE), p. 43.

APIS XXXI [V OF DYN. XXII] of Mariette.

Year 4 of Sesonchis V according to Mariette, but this is unlikely since none of the known stelae of year 4 (see *infra*) bears this name. Chamber Q of Mariette, F′ of Rhoné.

Stelae. Ascribed to this Apis-bull by Mariette. In Louvre.

Rekhsuptaḥ [hieroglyphs] and brother Zeptaḥefꜥankh, both Singers of the Temple of Ptaḥ, IM.3432 [S.1977; No. 38]. MARIETTE, *Sérapéum*, pl. 29 [lower left]; MALININE [etc.], *Cat.* i, pl. xiv [46], p. 44. Text, CHASSINAT in *Rec. Trav.* xxii (1900), pp. 11–12 [xl]. Three names, LIEBLEIN, *Dict.* No. 1023. See REVILLOUT, *Cat.* No. 412.

Wenamūn [hieroglyphs], IM.3034 [N.419; No. 58]. MALININE [etc.], *Cat.* i, pl. xx [68], p. 60; text, CHASSINAT, op. cit. xxii (1900), p. 14 [xlv]; see REVILLOUT, *Cat.* No. 419.

APIS XXXII [VI OF DYN. XXII] of Mariette. Year 11 of Sesonchis V.

Stelae. In Louvre.

Year 11.

ꜥAnkhefenubaste [hieroglyphs], son of Pashenēsi [hieroglyphs], both God's fathers, etc., IM.3719 [No. 37]. MALININE [etc.], *Cat.* i, pl. ix [27], pp. 26–7.

Ḥor, Inspector of *sem*-priests, etc., kneeling before Apis-bull at top, with three people prostrate behind, IM.3049 [N.469; A.F.124; S.1933]. MARIETTE, *Sérapéum*, pl. 30 [upper]; MALININE [etc.], *Cat.* i, pl. ix [26], pp. 25–6; see PIERRET, *Cat.* No. 277.

Zeptaḥefꜥankh, Door-opener of the Temple (of Ptaḥ), son of Ḥetep-ptaḥ [hieroglyphs], and Taruy [hieroglyphs], IM.3061 [N.421/36; No. 388]. MARIETTE, *Sérapéum*, pl. 30 [lower left]; MALININE [etc.], *Cat.* i, pl. x [28], pp. 27–8; text, CHASSINAT in *Rec. Trav.* xxiii (1901), pp. 82–3 [cxxxix]; ČERNÝ Notebook, 117, p. 11 [upper]; see PIERRET, *Cat.* No. 280.

Probably temp. Sesonchis V.

Irꜥaḥap [hieroglyphs], Door-opener of the Temple of Ptaḥ, son of Ḥetep-ptaḥ (same as above), IM.2702 [No. 62]. MARIETTE, *Sérapéum*, pl. 30 [lower right]; MALININE [etc.], *Cat.* i, pl. x [29], pp. 28–9; text, CHASSINAT in *Rec. Trav.* xxii (1900), p. 15 [xlix]; see REVILLOUT, *Cat.* No. 423.

Thonūfer [hieroglyphs], IM.3110 [No. 124]. MALININE [etc.], *Cat.* i, pl. x [30], p. 29; see REVILLOUT, *Cat.* No. 456.

Pedeamūn-paiat [hieroglyphs], IM.3427 [N.421/35; S.1929; No. 59]. MALININE [etc.], *Cat.* i, pl. xxiii [77], p. 66; text, CHASSINAT in *Rec. Trav.* xxii (1900), p. 14 [xlvi]; see REVILLOUT, *Cat.* No. 420.

APIS XXXIII [VII OF DYN. XXII] of Mariette. Year 37 of Sesonchis V.

Chamber R of Mariette, F″ of Rhoné.

Stelae.

In Cairo Museum

ʿAnkhefenkhons, son of Pasenḥor, both Secretaries of the Place of Truth, two registers, **I,** Sesonchis V offering bread to Apis-bull, with ʿAnkhefenkhons kneeling behind, **II,** 8 lines of cursive text, year 37. MARIETTE, *Voyage*, i, on pl. 13, p. 44; id. *Album du Musée de Boulaq* (1872), on pl. 37; text, BRUGSCH, *Thes.* 998–1000; names, LIEBLEIN, *Dict.* No. 2291; see MASPERO, *Guide* (1914), p. 458 [4497].

In Louvre

Year 37.

Gemnefḥarbak(?), son of ʿAnkh-khons, both God's fathers, IM.2690 [No. 40]. MALININE [etc.], *Cat.* i, pl. xiii [40], pp. 39–40; text, ČERNÝ Notebook, 117, p. 5 [lower]; names, LIEBLEIN, *Dict.* No. 1199.

Ḥarwoz, Inspector of *sem*-priests in the Temple of Sokari, etc., son of Tadeneb(t)hen (woman), sides in form of obelisks, year [3]7, IM.3595 [No. 83]. MARIETTE, *Sérapéum*, pl. 32 [lower right]; MALININE [etc.], *Cat.* i, pl. xi [34], pp. 33–4; see REVILLOUT, *Cat.* No. 431.

Ḥepiu, God's father, etc., son of Irefʿa(en)ptaḥ, with double-scene at top, Sesonchis V followed by Ḥepiu and son Ptaḥḥotp respectively offering to bull-headed Apis, IM.3085 [No. 80]. MALININE [etc.], *Cat.* i, pl. xii [36], pp. 35–6; text, ČERNÝ Notebook, 117, p. 17; see REVILLOUT, *Cat.* No. 428.

Heribek, son of Khuwennefer, Ptaḥḥotp, son of Estaneb . . ., and others, IM.3079 [No. 75]. MALININE [etc.], *Cat.* i, pl. xi [32], pp. 31–2; WILKINSON MSS. xxiv. 13 [left lower].

Ḳereferptaḥ, God's father, etc., son of Tentnefertem (woman), IM.3084 [No. 77]. MALININE [etc.], *Cat.* i, pl. xi [33], pp. 32–3.

Khaʿsu(en)amūn, Inspector of *sem*-priests, *wnrw*-priest in Letopolis, etc., son of Nemareth, IM.3143 [No. 85]. Id. ib. i, pl. xiii [39], pp. 38–9; CHASSINAT in *Rec. Trav.* xxii (1900), p. 16 [lii].

Pasenḥor, Prophet of Neith, son of Ḥemptaḥ, Overseer of the prophets in Heracleopolis Magna, Commander of the army, etc., and Irterau, Prophetess of Ḥatḥor in Heracleopolis Magna, with genealogy including Nemareth, son of Osorkon II and Wezmutʿankhes, giving the date of birth of the Apis-bull as year 11, IM.2846 [N.481; A.F.123; S.1959]. MARIETTE, *Sérapéum*, pl. 31; MALININE [etc.], *Cat.* i, pl. x [31], pp. 30–1; WILKINSON MSS. xxiv. 24 [left]. Text in lower register, LEPSIUS, *Über die XXII. ägyptische Königsdynastie* [etc.] in *Abhandlungen der Königl. Preuss. Akademie der Wissenschaften zu Berlin, Philos.-hist. Kl.* (1856), pp. 267–8. Genealogies (some incomplete), LIEBLEIN, *Dict.* No. 1008; id. in *Rev. Arch.* N.S. xviii (1868), pp. 282–3 [i]; LEGRAIN in *Rec. Trav.* xxxi (1909), pp. 1–2. See MARIETTE, *Sérapéum, Texte*, pp. 169–70 = id. *Renseignements* (1855), pp. 98–9 (repr. in *Bibl. Ég.* xviii, pp. 206–7); DE ROUGÉ, *Notice sommaire* (1876), p. 66; PIERRET, *Cat.* No. 278.

Pashenptaḥ, Prophet of Ptaḥ, Prophet in Smen-maʿet (), son of ʿAnkhsemtu, same titles, at top, Sesonchis V libating to Apis-bull, with Pashenptaḥ kneeling behind, IM.3078 [N.488]. MALININE [etc.], *Cat.* i, pl. xii [37], p. 37; text (incomplete), DARESSY in *Rec. Trav.* xxxv (1913), p. 136 [vii]; part, xi (1889), p. 80 [middle]; see PIERRET, *Cat.* No. 279.

Pemu [ ] [ ], Prophet of Khonspekhrod and of (Ḥatḥor) Mistress of Ḥetept in Khanūfer, etc., son of Pezai , Prophet of Khons, IM.3092 [No. 78]. MALININE [etc.], *Cat.* i, pl. xiii [41], pp. 40–1.

Pezai, son of Pemu (probably same as owner of preceding stela), IM.3091 [No. 79]. Id. ib. i, pl. xiii [42], p. 41.

Zeptaḥefʿankh , IM.3054 [No. 91]. Id. ib. i, pl. xii [38], p. 38; see REVILLOUT, *Cat.* No. 436.

Name lost, year 37, IM.3721 [No. 76]. MALININE, *Cat.* i, pl. xii [35], pp. 34–5.

Probably year 37.

ʿAnkh-sheshonḳ , much defaced, IM.3012 [N.421/77; No. 87]. MALININE [etc.], *Cat.* i, pl. xiv [43], p. 42.

Diptaḥiau , Craftsman of the Temple of Ptaḥ, son of Pedeamūn, IM.3728 [N.421/309; No. 328]. Id. ib. i, pl. xiv [44], pp. 42–3.

APIS XXXIV = XXXV [I OF DYN. XXIV = I OF DYN. XXV] of Mariette. Year 6 of Bocchoris = year 2 of Sabacon.

Chamber S of Mariette, G of Rhoné.

Graffito with names of Bocchoris and date on wall, MARIETTE, *Sérapéum*, pl. 34 [top], *Texte*, p. 175.

Stela of Sabacon, see id. *Sérapéum*, *Texte*, p. 184 (repr. in *Bibl. Ég.* xviii, p. 228).

Stelae. In Louvre.

Year 6 of Bocchoris.

ʿAnkh-unnūfer , IM.2704 [No. 110]. MALININE [etc.], *Cat.* i, pl. xxvi [92], p. 76.

[Be]kenptaḥ , IM.3068 [No. 120]. Id. ib. i, pl. xxvii [96], pp. 78–9; see REVILLOUT, *Cat.* No. 453.

Ḥarsiēsi, Head of servants of the Temple of Ptaḥ, son of Ḥarbes , IM.3050 [No. 114]. MALININE [etc.], *Cat.* i, pl. xxvii [95], pp. 77–8; see REVILLOUT, *Cat.* No. 449.

Painmu , God's father, *sem*-priest, son of Thonūfer , IM.3424 [No. 112]. MALININE [etc.], *Cat.* i, pl. xxvii [93], pp. 76–7.

Pashenēsi, son of Pashenptaḥ, before bull-headed Apis on *recto*, probably temp. Bocchoris, S.N.22. Id. ib. i, pl. xxix [102], pp. 83–4.

Pawen , Head of the door-openers of Bubastis Mistress of the Two Lands, IM.3592 [N.476]. Id. ib. i, pl. xxix [101], pp. 82–3; MARIETTE, *Sérapéum*, pl. 34 [middle]; see PIERRET, *Cat.* No. 298.

Pe(n)ēsi , *waʿb*-priest of the Great Place, son of Zeptaḥefʿankh, IM.2718 [No. 115]. MALININE [etc.], *Cat.* i, pl. xxvii [94], p. 77; see REVILLOUT, *Cat.* No. 450.

Pentazer , Craftsman, Servant of the House of Eternity, IM.2680 [No. 100]. MALININE [etc.], *Cat.* i, pl. xxviii [97], pp. 79–80; text, ČERNÝ Notebook, 117, p. 7 [upper]; see REVILLOUT, *Cat.* No. 443.

Name uncertain, lower part, N.471. MALININE [etc.], *Cat.* i, pl. xxvi [91], p. 75; text, WILKINSON MSS. xxiv. 25 [right lower]; see PIERRET, *Cat.* No. 299.

Probably year 6 of Bocchoris.

ʿAnkh-ḥor, Craftsman, son of Paneḥesi , same title, IM.2682 [S.1995]. MALININE [etc.], *Cat.* i, pl. xxxiv [121], pp. 96–7; see DE ROUGÉ, *Notice sommaire* (1876), p. 60.

Paiuenḥor [hieroglyphs] (also [hieroglyphs]), Craftsman, son of ʿAnkhpekhrod [hieroglyphs], IM.2692 [No. 98]. MALININE [etc.], *Cat.* i, pl. xxviii [98], p. 80; see REVILLOUT, *Cat.* No. 441.

Senbef [hieroglyphs], *wnrw*-priest in Letopolis, etc., son of ʿAnkh-sheshonḳ [hieroglyphs], IM.5947 [No. 106]. MALININE [etc.], *Cat.* i, pl. xxviii [100], pp. 81–2; see REVILLOUT, *Cat.* No. 446.

Name uncertain, Door-opener of Ptaḥ, son of Ḏhout [hieroglyphs], same title, IM.3035 [N.421/284; S.2198; No. 299]. MALININE [etc.], *Cat.* i, pl. xxviii [99], p. 81.

Probably Dyn. XXIV and from here.

Afti [hieroglyphs] (perhaps also [hieroglyphs]), daughter(?) of ʿAnkh-ḥor, IM.2679 [No. 430]. MALININE [etc.], *Cat.* i, pl. xxx [105], pp. 85–6.

ʿAkheperrēʿ(?) [hieroglyphs](?)[hieroglyphs], Door-opener of Ptaḥ, son of Pash(en)meḥyt [hieroglyphs] and Ḥathoremḥēt [hieroglyphs], with bull-headed Apis, IM.3580 [N.677]. Id. ib. i, pl. xxxiv [120], pp. 95–6; see PIERRET, *Cat.* No. 285.

Amen(em)ḥēt-pameshaʿ [hieroglyphs], God's father, son of Paneḥesi [hieroglyphs], Inspector of *sem*-priests, etc., IM.3118 [No. 108]. MALININE [etc.], *Cat.* i, pl. xxxii [115], p. 92; MARIETTE, *Sérapéum*, pl. 34 [bottom right]; text, CHASSINAT in *Rec. Trav.* xxii (1900), p. 17 [lvi]; see REVILLOUT, *Cat.* No. 447.

ʿAnkhpekhrod(?) [hieroglyphs](?), IM.5948 [N.421/107; No. 118]. MALININE [etc.], *Cat.* i, pl. xxxi [109], p. 88; see REVILLOUT, *Cat.* No. 451.

Bekenrenef [hieroglyphs], God's father, son of Ḥarwoz, same title, IM.3106 [N.677]. MALININE [etc.], *Cat.* i, pl. xxxii [113], pp. 90–1; text, CHASSINAT in *Rec. Trav.* xxi (1899), p. 61 [xii]; see PIERRET, *Cat.* No. 302.

Ḥepuser [hieroglyphs], son of Pakharkhons [hieroglyphs], IM.2653 [N.679]. MALININE [etc.], *Cat.* i, pl. xxxi [108], p. 87; text, CHASSINAT in *Rec. Trav.* xxi (1899), p. 64 [xviii]; see PIERRET, *Cat.* No. 312.

Hererem [hieroglyphs], God's father, son of Pedes [hieroglyphs], same title, IM.3113 [N.677]. MALININE [etc.], *Cat.* i, pl. xxxii [114], p. 91; text, CHASSINAT in *Rec. Trav.* xxi (1899), p. 61 [x]; names and titles, LIEBLEIN, *Dict.* No. 1174; see PIERRET, *Cat.* No. 300.

Heribes [hieroglyphs], IM.2847 [N.679; No. 323]. MALININE [etc.], *Cat.* i, pl. xxx [104], p. 85; text, CHASSINAT in *Rec. Trav.* xxii (1900), p. 177 [cxxi]; see PIERRET, *Cat.* No. 292.

Ḥetep-ptaḥ, Door-opener of Nefertem Protector of the Two Lands, son of Men [hieroglyphs], IM.2757 [N.421; No. 116]. MALININE [etc.], *Cat.* i, pl. xxxi [110], pp. 88–9.

Irʿaḥap [hieroglyphs], IM.3756 [N. 421/38; No. 104]. MALININE [etc.], *Cat.* i, pl. xxxi [111], p. 89; see REVILLOUT, *Cat.* No. 445.

Khaʿsuenamūn [hieroglyphs], God's father, son of Pasenenkhons [hieroglyphs]. (a) IM.2863 [N.677]; MALININE [etc.], *Cat.* i, pl. xxxii [112], p. 90; text, CHASSINAT in *Rec. Trav.* xxi (1899), p. 59 [iv]; see PIERRET, *Cat.* No. 286. (b) Perhaps same man, IM.3037 [No. 107]; MALININE [etc.], *Cat.* i, pl. xxxiv [122], pp. 97–8; names and titles, LIEBLEIN, *Dict.* No. 1198.

Paneḥesi [hieroglyphs], IM.5939 [No. 201]. MALININE [etc.], *Cat.* i, pl. xxx [106], p. 86; text, CHASSINAT in *Rec. Trav.* xxii (1900), p. 22 [lxvi]; see REVILLOUT, *Cat.* No. 467.

Pedubaste, son of Pen-ḥarwoz [hieroglyphs], with names of Neterikhet (Zoser) at top, IM.3036 [N.5442]. MALININE [etc.], *Cat.* i, pl. xxxiii [117], pp. 93–4; MARIETTE, *Sérapéum*, pl. 28 [left] (as Apis IV of Dyn. XXII); WILKINSON MSS. xxiv. 37; see PIERRET, *Cat.* No. 281.

Pefʿa-ḥor(?) [hieroglyphs](?)[hieroglyphs], with men kneeling before Apis-bull on sledge at top, IM.4208 [No. 117]. MALININE [etc.], *Cat.* i, pl. xxxiii [116], pp. 92–3.

Pentaōnet [hieroglyphs](?)[hieroglyphs], *waʿb*-priest, Craftsman, IM.2735 [S.2009; No. 113]. Id. ib. i, pl. xxix [103], p. 84; see REVILLOUT, *Cat.* No. 448.

Ptaḥḥotp, Scribe of the divine offerings, son of Paiuenḥor, IM.2673 [No. 90]. Malinine [etc.], *Cat.* i, pl. xxx [107], pp. 86–7; see Revillout, *Cat.* No. 435.

Zeptaḥefʿankh, son of Pedes, IM.4162 [N. 421/39; No. 61]. Malinine [etc.], *Cat.* i, pl. xxxiii [118], p. 94; text, Chassinat in *Rec. Trav.* xxii (1900), pp. 14–15 [xlviii]; see Revillout, *Cat.* No. 422.

. . . nakht, IM.2659 [No. 188]. Malinine [etc.], *Cat.* i, pl. xxxiii [119], p. 95.

Apis XXXVI [II of Dyn. XXV] of Mariette. Year 24 of Taharqa.

Chamber (T′) of Mariette, (H*) of Rhoné.

Stelae. In Louvre.

Year 24.

ʿAnkh-khons, son of Irʿa[ḥap] (?), with two goddesses, IM.2675. Malinine [etc.], *Cat.* i, pl. xxxv [126], pp. 100–1; Vercoutter in *Kush*, viii (1960), pl. xxi [a], p. 68 note 35 (as IM.3146).

[Ḥar]siēsi, son of Ḏḥutardais, IM.2705. Malinine [etc.], *Cat.* i, pl. xxxv [127], pp. 101–2.

Irʿaḥap, son of Ḏḥutardais, demotic, IM.2746 [N.454]. Id. ib. i, pl. xxxvi [128], pp. 102–3; Vercoutter, op. cit. pl. xxi [b], pp. 68–9 with note 39 (as IM.2705 in error); see Pierret, *Cat.* No. 303.

Pashensekhmet, IM.2707 [N.421/112; No. 123]. Malinine [etc.], *Cat.* i, pl. xliii [158], pp. 122–3.

Senbef, Hereditary prince, Prophet of Ptaḥ, etc., son of ʿAnkh-unnūfer and Naʿa-tesnakht, before bull-headed Apis, IM.2640 [N.417; S.2018; No. 121]. Id. ib. i, pl. xxxv [125], pp. 99–100; Mariette, *Sérapéum*, pl. 35 [left]; Wilkinson MSS. xxiv. 6 [right bottom]. Text, Chassinat in *Rec. Trav.* xxii (1900), p. 18 [lvii]; incomplete, Revillout in *Revue Égyptologique*, vii (1896), p. 136 note 1; Vercoutter in *Kush*, viii (1960), p. 71. Date, names, and titles, Lieblein, *Dict.* No. 1046. See de Rougé, *Notice sommaire* (1876), p. 60; Revillout, *Cat.* No. 454.

Probably year 24.

Paraʿarʿa, son of Pederēʿ, probably IM.2732. Malinine [etc.], *Cat.* i, pl. xliv [159], p. 123.

Pashenēsi, son of Pedenefertem, IM.2763 [N. 421/118]. Id. ib. i, pl. xliv [160], p. 124; text, Černý Notebook, 117, p. 22 [bottom].

Thonūfer, son of Painmu (owner of stela IM.3424, see *supra*), remains of date, IM.3306 [No. 213]. Malinine [etc.], *Cat.* pl. xlviii [178], p. 136; text, Chassinat in *Rec. Trav.* xxii (1900), p. 24 [lxxiv] (as Apis I of Dyn. XXVI).

Apis XXXVII [I of Dyn. XXVI] of Mariette. Years 20/21 of Psammetikhos I.

Chamber T of Mariette, H of Rhoné.

Mariette, *Sérapéum, Texte*, pp. 190–2 (repr. in *Bibl. Ég.* xviii, pp. 236–9).

Stelae. In Louvre.

Official stela, with King libating and censing to Apis at top, year 21, giving the date of birth of the Apis-bull as year 26 of Taharqa, IM.3733 [N.403; S.2035; No. 190]. Malinine [etc.], *Cat.* i, pl. lii [192], p. 146; Mariette, *Sérapéum*, pl. 36; Petrie, *History*, iii, fig. 137; Breasted, *History*, fig. 182; Parker in *Kush*, viii (1960), pl. xxxviii, pp. 267–9; Devéria squeezes, 6165, i. 44; Wilkinson MSS. xxiv. 2 [left]; Archives phot. E.635. Texts, Chassinat in *Rec. Trav.* xxii (1900), p. 19 [lxi]; Černý Notebook, 117, p. 14 [middle]. Main text, Piehl, *Inscr. hiéro.* 1 Sér. xxii [C]; Mariette, *Sérapéum, Texte*, p. 191 = id. *Renseignements* (1856), p. 75 (repr. in *Bibl. Ég.* xviii, p. 238); Revillout in *Revue Égyptologique*, vii (1896), p. 138 note 1. See id. *Cat.* No. 460; de Rougé, *Notice sommaire* (1876), p. 61.

Year 20 (death of the Apis-bull) or 21 (burial).

ʿAnkh-khons, son of Ḥarsiēsi, IM.2620 [N.485]. Malinine [etc.], *Cat.* i, pl. lv [205], p. 157; text, Chassinat in *Rec. Trav.* xxi (1899), p. 68 [xxviii]; Černý Notebook, 117, p. 19 [upper]; see Pierret, *Cat.* No. 330.

ʿAnkh-unnūfer, Judge, son of Esptaḥ, God's father, and Takhar. (a) IM.2856 [No. 249]; Malinine [etc.], *Cat.* i, pl. lix [217], p. 166; text, Chassinat in *Rec. Trav.* xxii (1900), p. 169 [xcv]; names and titles, Lieblein, *Dict.* No. 1139; see Revillout, *Cat.* No. 482. (b) N.421/221 [S.N.54; No. 232], undated; Malinine [etc.], *Cat.* i, pl. lix [220], pp. 168–9; text, Chassinat, op. cit. xxii (1900), pp. 164–5 [lxxxv]; names and titles, Lieblein, *Dict.* No. 1222; see Revillout, *Cat.* No. 475.

Atemḥotp, son of Ḥeka, God's father, IM.2867 [No. 273]. Malinine [etc.], *Cat.* i, pl. lix [219], pp. 167–8; text, Chassinat, op. cit. xxii (1900), p. 172 [cvi]; see Revillout, *Cat.* No. 492.

Diptaḥiau, God's father, *sem*-priest, etc., son of Penamūn, IM.3043 [No. 208]. Malinine [etc.], *Cat.* i, pl. lviii [216], p. 165; text, Chassinat, op. cit. xxii (1900), p. 23 [lxxi].

Esamūn, IM.2676 [No. 294]. Malinine [etc.], *Cat.* i, pl. lxiv [239], pp. 183–4.

Ḥarenḥap, son of Paʿankhi, IM.3087 [N.421/297; S.2082; No. 285].

Ḥarkhebi, son of Esamūn, IM.3089 [N.421/111; S.2027; No. 166]. Id. ib. i, pl. lxiii [235], pp. 180–1.

Ḥarmosi, Door-opener of *waʿb*-priests of the Temple of Ptaḥ, son of Ptaḥardais and Thes-ḥap-pert, libating to Apis-bull, IM.3072 [S.2178; No. 221]. Id. ib. i, pl. lii [193], p. 147; text, Chassinat, op. cit. xxii (1900), p. 26 [lxxx]; names and titles, Lieblein, *Dict.* No. 1219.

Ḥarwoz, Door-opener of the Temple of Ptaḥ, son of Pennebt-nehet and Penʿaḳer, with Isis behind Apis-bull, IM.3009 [N.5417]. Malinine [etc.], *Cat.* i, pl. liv [202], p. 154; names, Lieblein, *Dict.* No. 1138; see Pierret, *Cat.* No. 304.

Ḥepardais, IM.2819 [S.2056].

Ḥor, son of ʿAnkh-thekerti, both Singers of the Temple of Ptaḥ, IM.3076 [N.485]. Malinine [etc.], *Cat.* i, pl. lvi [209], p. 160; see Pierret, *Cat.* No. 310 bis.

It, God's father, *sem*-priest, etc., son of Nefertemḥotp and Heribesnes, IM.3082 [N.3417; S.2106]. Malinine [etc.], *Cat.* i, pl. liii [195], p. 149; see Pierret, *Cat.* No. 303 bis.

Ḳerfamūn, son of Esptaḥ, God's father, etc., and Kapes (?), with Isis behind Apis-bull, IM.3129 [No. 250]. Malinine [etc.], *Cat.* i, pl. liv [199], p. 152; text, Chassinat in *Rec. Trav.* xxii (1900), p. 169 [xcvi]; names and titles, Lieblein, *Dict.* No. 1225; see Revillout, *Cat.* No. 483.

Khensardais, Door-opener of the Temple of Ptaḥ, son of Tadeparēʿ (mother), with Nephthys behind Apis-bull, IM.2623 [N.476; S.2038; No. 234]. MALININE [etc.], *Cat.* i, pl. lv [203], p. 155; text, CHASSINAT, op. cit. xxii (1900), p. 165 [lxxxvi]; ČERNÝ Notebook, 117, p. 19 [lower]; see REVILLOUT, *Cat.* No. 476.

Nana, IM.4058 [S.2159; No. 316]. MALININE [etc.], *Cat.* i, pl. lviii [214], p. 164; see REVILLOUT, *Cat.* No. 500.

Nefertemḥotp, God's father, *sem*-priest, etc., son of It and Imut, IM.3130 [S.2109; No. 247]. MALININE [etc.], *Cat.* i, pl. liii [196], pp. 149–50; text, CHASSINAT, op. cit. xxii (1900), p. 168 [xciii]; see REVILLOUT, *Cat.* No. 480.

Paneferiu, son of Zeptaḥefʿankh, IM.2619 [N.421/287; S.2166; No. 309].

Pashenḥor(?) (?), with bark on recto, IM.3046 [No. 150]. MALININE [etc.], *Cat.* i, pl. lviii [215], pp. 164–5; see REVILLOUT, *Cat.* No. 457.

Pashenmut, son of Zeptaḥefʿankh, IM.2681 [N.421/292; S.2048]. Text, ČERNÝ Notebook, 117, p. 21 [lower].

Pashenmut, Door-opener of the Temple of Ptaḥ, son of Pefteu, IM.3027 [S.2041; No. 176]. MALININE [etc.], *Cat.* i, pl. lv [206], pp. 157–8.

Pashentiḥet, Door-opener of the Temple of Ptaḥ, son of Pashenptaḥ, IM.3062 [S.2046; No. 216]. Id. ib. i, pl. lv [204], p. 156.

Pedeḥarenpe, son of Ḥor, S.N.24 [No. 288].

Pedeḥarmeden, son of Uzaḥor, both God's fathers, IM.3045 [S.2131]. Text, ČERNÝ Notebook, 117, p. 5 [upper].

Pedes, son of Ḥeka, IM.2685 [N.421/289]. Text, id. ib. p. 22 [top].

Pedēsi, son of ʿAnkh-thekerti, both Singers of the Temple of Ptaḥ, Clappers of Sokari, IM.2656 [N.485]. MALININE [etc.], *Cat.* i, pl. lvi [208], p. 159; text, CHASSINAT in *Rec. Trav.* xxi (1899), pp. 60–1 [ix]; see PIERRET, *Cat.* No. 297.

Pedēsi, S.N.59 [N.421/127; S.2055; No. 139].

Pedubaste, IM.2703.

Pedusiri, son of Amenardais, IM.2621 [S.2172; No. 202]. MALININE [etc.], *Cat.* i, pl. lx [223], p. 171; text, CHASSINAT in *Rec. Trav.* xxii (1900), p. 22 [lxvii]; see REVILLOUT, *Cat.* No. 468.

Pedusiri-pewaḥ, son of Bekenrenef, IM.3023 [S.2089; No. 161]. MALININE [etc.], *Cat.* i, pl. lxv [243], p. 186; text, ČERNÝ Notebook, 117, p. 21 [upper].

Pefḥerinūter, son of Pedeptaḥ, IM.2734 [S.2104]. MALININE [etc.], *Cat.* i, pl. lxvi [246], p. 188.

Pefḥerinūter, IM.2768 [S.2057; No. 149].

Pefḥerinūter, IM.3067 [S.2072; No. 128].

Pefteuʿaubaste, God's father, Inspector of *sem*-priests, son of Ḥory, IM.3039 [S.2648; No. 258]. Id. ib. i, pl. lvii [213], p. 163.

Penamenōpet, son of Pefḥerinūter, IM.2740 [N.421/156; S.2065; No. 162].

Penamūn, son of Iru, IM.2689 [S.2100; No. 238]. Id. ib. i, pl. lxii [229], pp. 175–6; text, ČERNÝ Notebook, 117, p. 15 [top].

Ptaḥḥotp, Judge, son of Iʿa and Ḳebḥatenēsi, IM.2624 [No. 241]. MALININE [etc.], *Cat.* i, pl. lx [222], p. 170; text, GOODWIN MSS. 31279, 30 [left]; names and titles, LIEBLEIN, *Dict.* No. 1203; see REVILLOUT, *Cat.* No. 479.

Ptaḥnūfer, son of It and Imut, IM.3077 [S.2105; No. 191]. MALININE [etc.], *Cat.*

i, pl. liii [197], pp. 150–1; WILKINSON MSS. xxiv. 2 [right]; text, CHASSINAT in *Rec. Trav.* xxii (1900), p. 19 [lxii]; see REVILLOUT, *Cat.* No. 461.

Senbef, son of ʿAnkh-sheshonḳ and Mer(yt)ptaḥ, IM.5342 [No. 353]. Text, CHASSINAT in *Rec. Trav.* xxiii (1901), p. 76 [cxxix].

Userken, IM.3053 [N.421/272; No. 422].

Uzaḥorresnet and Weḥebrēʿ, both sons of It and Imut, IM.3075 [No. 317]. MALININE [etc.], *Cat.* i, pl. liii [198], pp. 151–2; text, CHASSINAT in *Rec. Trav.* xxii (1900), p. 174 [cxiii]; names and titles, cf. LIEBLEIN, *Dict.* No. 1140; see REVILLOUT, *Cat.* No. 501.

Zeamūnefʿankh, IM.3591 [No. 194]. MALININE [etc.], *Cat.* i, pl. lxi [225], pp. 172–3; see REVILLOUT, *Cat.* No. 464.

Names lost or uncertain. E.5639 [S.N.63] (formerly in Rousset Bey Colln.). IM.2662 [No. 160]. IM.2706 [N.421/299; S.2168; No. 303]. IM.3063 [No. 225], MALININE [etc.], *Cat.* i, pl. lvi [207], pp. 158–9. IM.3105 [S.2079; No. 186]. S.2073 [No. 156]. S.2127. S.2128 [No. 301] (name of the King only).

Undated.

Amennezem, son of Zeamūnefʿankh, Door-opener, IM.2642 [S.2077].

ʿAnkhpefḥeri, with Isis behind Apis-bull, IM.3579 [N.421/244; S.2151; No. 270]. MALININE [etc.], *Cat.* i, pl. liv [200], p. 153; see REVILLOUT, *Cat.* No. 490.

ʿArptaḥ-ḥap, IM.3574 [S.2067; No. 185]. MALININE [etc.], *Cat.* i, pl. lxv [242], p. 185.

Esḥu, son of Paʿaenruz, IM.3134 [No. 218]. Text, CHASSINAT in *Rec. Trav.* xxii (1900), p. 25 [lxxvii].

Ḥarenḥap, son of (Pa)she(n)mut, IM.3057 [S.2101; No. 165]. MALININE [etc.], *Cat.* i, pl. lxiv [237], pp. 182–3.

Ḥarḥap, son of Shesepamūn-tefḥert, IM.3029 [N.421/256; No. 275].

Ḥarsiēsi, with Isis behind Apis-bull, IM.3318 [N.421/263; S.2152; No. 278]. Id. ib. i, pl. liv [201], pp. 153–4; see REVILLOUT, *Cat.* No. 494.

Ḥarsiēsi, son of Meḥamenwia, IM.3757 [No. 168]. MALININE [etc.], *Cat.* i, pl. lxvi [248], p. 189.

Ḥepardais, son of Amenardais, IM.2699 [S.2050; No. 155].

Ḥor, God's father, son of Pashenēsi, God's father in the Temple of Ptaḥ, IM.3132 [No. 259]. See REVILLOUT, *Cat.* No. 485.

Ḥui, *waʿb*-priest, son of Pashenēsi, IM.2764 [S.2197; No. 230]. Text, CHASSINAT, op. cit. xxii (1900), p. 164 [lxxxiii].

Ip, son of Ḥetep-ptaḥ. (a) IM.2665 [S.2092; No. 158], MALININE [etc.], *Cat.* i, pl. lxii [230], pp. 176–7; text, ČERNÝ Notebook, 117, p. 8; some names and titles, LIEBLEIN, *Dict.* No. 1200. (b) IM.2787 [S.2069; No. 169], MALININE [etc.], *Cat.* i, pl. lxiv [240], p. 184; text, CHASSINAT, op. cit. xxii (1900), p. 18 [lix].

Iputi, son of Tade (mother), IM.3031 [S.2213; No. 281].

Irʿaḥor(?) (?), IM.3104 [S.1892; No. 227]. MALININE [etc.], *Cat.* i, pl. lxi [226], p. 173; text, CHASSINAT, op. cit. xxii (1900), p. 26 [lxxxi]; see REVILLOUT, *Cat.* No. 472.

Irḥap, IM.2853 [N.421/293; S.2093; No. 284]. MALININE [etc.], *Cat.* i, pl. lxiii [236], pp. 181–2.

Iufʿa, God's father, *sem*-priest, IM.2866 [N.677]. See PIERRET, *Cat.* No. 316.

Memi(?) [hieroglyphs], God's father, son of Panehesi [hieroglyphs], Scribe of [hieroglyphs] of the Temple of Ptah, etc., IM.3428 [S.2196; No. 179].

Nefertemhotp [hieroglyphs], God's father, *sem*-priest, etc., son of Buiruteha [hieroglyphs] and Tata [hieroglyphs], libating to Apis-bull, IM.3142 [No. 248]. MALININE [etc.], *Cat.* i, pl. lii [194], p. 148; text, CHASSINAT in *Rec. Trav.* xxii (1900), pp. 168–9 [xciv]; names and titles, LIEBLEIN, *Dict.* No. 1224; see REVILLOUT, *Cat.* No. 481.

Nekht-haremhab [hieroglyphs], son of Hetep-ptah, IM.2854 [N.421/296; S.2090; No. 293]. MALININE [etc.], *Cat.* i, pl. lxiii [234], pp. 179–80.

Paba . . . [hieroglyphs], son of Pashenptah, IM.3112.

Pade [hieroglyphs], God's father, son of Harsiēsi, IM.2789 [N.421/254; S.1885; No. 274]. Id. ib. i, pl. lx [221], p. 169; text, CHASSINAT, op. cit. xxii (1900), p. 172 [cvii]; see REVILLOUT, *Cat.* No. 493.

Pairkap [hieroglyphs] (?) and Imhōtep, sons of Hepmen [hieroglyphs] and Ēsireshti [hieroglyphs], IM.2861 [No. 318]. Text, CHASSINAT, op. cit. xxii (1900), pp. 174–5 [cxiv]; see REVILLOUT, *Cat.* No. 502.

Paiuenhor [hieroglyphs], son of Keref [hieroglyphs], IM.3727 [S.2064; No. 184]. MALININE [etc.], *Cat.* i, pl. lxv [244], pp. 186–7.

Pakap [hieroglyphs], son of Senbef [hieroglyphs], IM.2815 [S.2173; No. 237]. Id. ib. i, pl. lx [224], pp. 171–2; text, CHASSINAT, op. cit. xxii (1900), pp. 165–6 [lxxxviii]; see REVILLOUT, *Cat.* No. 477.

Pakap, IM.2726 [S.2063; No. 137]. MALININE [etc.], *Cat.* i, pl. lxvii [250], pp. 190–1.

Pakebesh [hieroglyphs], Singer of Ptah. (a) IM.2858 [No. 271]; names and titles, LIEBLEIN, *Dict.* No. 1223. (b) IM.3108 [S.2186; No. 224].

[Pa]khar [hieroglyphs], son of Espaper-webekhet [hieroglyphs], IM.2709 [No. 308].

Pashentanaʿ [hieroglyphs], IM.3307 [N.421/279; S.2179; No. 307]. MALININE [etc.], *Cat.* i, pl. lxi [227], p. 174.

Pedeharde [hieroglyphs], son of Pashenmut [hieroglyphs], IM.3582 [S.2068; No. 142]. Id. ib. i, pl. lxvi [247], pp. 188–9.

Pedeneit, son of ʿAnkhemthenent [hieroglyphs], both Singers of the Temple of Ptah, Clappers of Sokari, inscribed on both sides, IM.2658 [No. 211]. Id. ib. i, pl. lvii [211], p. 161; text, CHASSINAT, op. cit. xxii (1900), p. 24 [lxxiii].

Pedeneit, son of ʿAnkh-hor, IM.2634 [N.421/258; S.2134; No. 276]. Text, id. ib. pp. 172–3 [cviii].

Pedeptah, son of Irʿahap [hieroglyphs], IM.2796 [No. 178]. MALININE [etc.], *Cat.* i, pl. lxiii [233], p. 179.

Pedesiptah [hieroglyphs], son of Hepiuiu [hieroglyphs], IM.2788 [N.421/137; No. 133].

Pede . . . [hieroglyphs], IM.2663 [S.2093; No. 164]. Id. ib. i, pl. lxii [231], pp. 177–8.

Pedusiri, son of Amenardais, IM.2650 [No. 148]. Id. ib. i, pl. lxvi [245], p. 187.

Pedusiri and Amenkhaʿ [hieroglyphs], sons of Iʿa [hieroglyphs], IM.2728 [N.421/260; S.2200; No. 277]. Text, CHASSINAT in *Rec. Trav.* xxii (1900), p. 173 [cix].

Pefherinūter [hieroglyphs], IM.5944 [S.2059; No. 129]. MALININE [etc.], *Cat.* i, pl. lxvii [251], p. 191.

Pefteuʿauēsi [hieroglyphs], son of Usirinakht [hieroglyphs] and Mehytardais [hieroglyphs], IM.3048 [S.2214; No. 245]. Text, CHASSINAT, op. cit. xxii (1900), p. 168 [xcii].

Psammethek, Treasurer of the King of Lower Egypt, etc., son of Zeptaḥefʿankh, Singer of the Temple of Ptaḥ, and Ēsi(em)khebi [hieroglyphs], IM.1805 [N.679]. Text, id. ib. xxi (1899), pp. 64–5 [xx]; see PIERRET, *Cat.* No. 315.

Ptaḥardais(?) [hieroglyphs], son of Pashenptaḥ, N.421/132 [S.N.75; No. 136]. MALININE [etc.], *Cat.* i, pl. lxi [228], pp. 174–5.

Ptaḥḥotp, son of Ptaḥwēr and Ia [hieroglyphs], IM.2859 [N.421/264; No. 264]. Text, CHASSINAT in *Rec. Trav.* xxii (1900), p. 171 [ciii].

Ptaḥḥotp, God's father, son of Gem(n)efḥarbak [hieroglyphs], IM.3038 [N.421/115; No. 126]. Some names, LIEBLEIN, *Dict.* No. 1218 (as temp. Darius I).

Ptaḥ-khaʿ [hieroglyphs], son of Pashentanaʿ [hieroglyphs], IM.2797 [No. 265]. MALININE [etc.], *Cat.* i, pl. lix [218], p. 167; text, ČERNÝ Notebook, 117, p. 15 [middle]; see REVILLOUT, *Cat.* No. 487.

Ptaḥwēr, son of Zeamūnefʿankh, IM.3041 [N.421/338; No. 42]. Text, CHASSINAT, op. cit. xxii (1900), p. 170 [c] (as No. 258).

Shedsunefertem [hieroglyphs], God's father, *sem*-priest, son of Gem(n)efḥarbak and Sekhmetnefer(t) [hieroglyphs], IM.3442 [N.421/120; No. 127].

Shedsunefertem, son of Nefertemḥotp(?), God's father, *sem*-priest, unnumbered.

Uzaḥor, *waʿb*-priest of the Temple of Ptaḥ, son of Ze[ḥo], IM.3071 [No. 231]. Text, id. ib. p. 164 [lxxxiv]; see REVILLOUT, *Cat.* No. 474.

Zeamūnefʿankh, son of Ptaḥwēr and Ia, IM.3017 [No. 257]. Text, CHASSINAT, op. cit. xxii (1900), p. 170 [xcix].

Zeḥo [hieroglyphs], son of Amenardais, IM.2666 [S.2091; No. 163]. MALININE [etc.], *Cat.* i, pl. lxii [232], p. 178.

Zekhensefʿankh, IM.5428 [S.2142; No. 199]. See REVILLOUT, *Cat.* No. 466.

Zeptaḥefʿankh [hieroglyphs], Door-opener of the Temple of Ptaḥ, son of Pefti [hieroglyphs], E.10529. Text, ČERNÝ Notebook, 117, p. 13 [middle].

Zeptaḥefʿankh, God's father, IM.3304 [S.2139; No. 233].

. . . denebwen [hieroglyphs], Singer of the Temple of Ptaḥ, etc., son of Uzaḥor, IM.3042 [No. 252]. MALININE, *Cat.* i, pl. lvii [212], p. 162.

Names uncertain. IM.2693 [No. 220]; text, CHASSINAT, op. cit. xxii (1900), p. 26 [lxxix]. IM.2802 [S.2054]. IM.5945 [S.2097; No. 167]; MALININE [etc.], *Cat.* i, pl. lxiv [238], p. 183. S.2146 [No. 255]; text, CHASSINAT, op. cit. xxii (1900), p. 170 [xcviii].

'GREATER VAULTS'.

Plan LXVIII [3]

See MARIETTE, *Sérapéum*, *Texte*, pp. 46–8, 52–6, 80 [lower]–83. Plan, GUNN in *Ann. Serv.* xxvi (1926), fig. 1 on p. 82; of east part, VERCOUTTER in *Mitt. Kairo*, 16 (1958), fig. 2 (from Mariette papers), pp. 336–7 with note 10.

Doorway with demotic graffiti of year 30 of Ptolemy II Philadelphus, in Louvre, N.420. Texts on jambs, DEVÉRIA squeezes, 6170D, B, C; see BRUGSCH, *Thes.* 993–4 [B]; on south thickness, id. ib. 993 [A]. See DE ROUGÉ, *Notice sommaire* (1876), p. 62; MARIETTE, *Sérapéum*, *Texte*, p. 57, cf. pl. F [f] on p. 43; BOREUX, *Guide*, i, pp. 169–70; VANDIER, *Guide* (1948), p. 25; (1952), p. 26; (1973), pp. 55–6.

Hieroglyphic graffiti of Imḥōtep son of Ḥor, Ḥetepniḥap [hieroglyphs] son of Imḥōtep, Ḥarneziotef [hieroglyphs] son of Imḥōtep, and others. WILKINSON MSS. xviii. 36 [lower]–37.

Apis XXXVIII [II of Dyn. XXVI] of Mariette. Year 52 of Psammetikhos I.

Chamber U of Mariette, I of Rhoné.

Official stela, in Louvre, E.3335 [No. 239]. Devéria squeezes, 6168, 5. Text, Mariette, *Sérapéum, Texte*, pp. 198–9 = id. *Renseignements* (1856), pp. 78–80 (repr. in *Bibl. Ég.* xviii, pp. 248–9); Chassinat in *Rec. Trav.* xxii (1900), p. 166 [lxxxix]. See de Rougé, *Notice sommaire* (1876), p. 61; Boreux, *Guide*, i, p. 171; Vandier, *Guide* (1948), p. 25; (1952), p. 26; (1973), p. 57.

Apis XXXIX [III of Dyn. XXVI] of Mariette. Year 16 of Necho II.

Chamber V of Mariette, J of Rhoné.

Official stela, with bull-headed Apis at top, giving the date of birth of the Apis-bull as year 53 of Psammetikhos I, in Louvre, IM.133 [N.404; S.2243; No. 193]. Petrie, *History*, iii, fig. 143; Wilkinson MSS. xxiv. 1 [lower]; Archives phot. E.653. Text, Chassinat in *Rec. Trav.* xxii (1900), pp. 20–1 [lxiv]; main text, Piehl, *Inscr. hiéro.* 1 Sér. xxi [A]. See de Rougé, *Notice sommaire* (1876), p. 61; Revillout, *Cat.* No. 463; Boreux, *Guide*, i, p. 172; Vandier, *Guide* (1948), p. 25; (1952), p. 26; (1973), p. 56.

Apis XL [IV of Dyn. XXVI] of Mariette. Year 12 of Apries.

Chamber X of Mariette, K of Rhoné.

Official stela, with bull-headed Apis at top, giving the date of birth of the Apis-bull as year 16 of Necho II, in Louvre, IM.132 [N.405; S.2244; No. 240]. Mariette, *Choix de monuments*, pl. vii, pp. 10–11 (repr. in *Bibl. Ég.* xviii, pl. vii, pp. 316–18); Wilkinson MSS. xxiv. 4 [left]; Devéria squeezes, 6165, i. 46; 6169, 42; Archives phot. E.638. Text, Chassinat in *Rec. Trav.* xxii (1900), p. 167 [xc]; main text, Piehl, *Inscr. hiéro.* 1 Sér. xxi–xxii [B]. See de Rougé, *Notice sommaire* (1876), p. 61; Revillout, *Cat.* No. 478; Boreux, *Guide*, i, p. 172; Vandier, *Guide* (1948), p. 25; (1952), p. 26; (1973), p. 57.

Apis XLI [V of Dyn. XXVI] of Mariette. Year 23 of Amasis.

Chamber Y of Mariette, L of Rhoné.

Granite sarcophagus, with lid lying near entrance. Text, Brugsch, *Thes.* 966–7 [2]; Gunn in *Ann. Serv.* xxvi (1926), pp. 83–4; of lid, Devéria squeezes, 6170B, 1.

Stelae. In Louvre.

Official stela, with King kneeling before Apis-bull at top, giving the date of birth of the Apis-bull as year 5, IM.4131 [N.406; S.2259; No. 192]. Vercoutter in *Mitt. Kairo*, 16 (1958), Taf. xxxii, p. 334; *Encycl. phot. Louvre*, pls. 156–7; Wilkinson MSS. xxiv. 3; Devéria squeezes, 6169, i. 43; 6170D, 5; Archives phot. E.636; upper part, Maspero, *Hist. anc.* iii, fig. on p. 642. Text, Chassinat in *Rec. Trav.* xxii (1900), p. 20 [lxiii]; main text, Piehl, *Inscr. hiéro.* 1 Sér. xx [H]; beginning, Revillout in *Revue Égyptologique*, i (1880), p. 62 note 1. See Gunn in *Ann. Serv.* xxvi (1926), pp. 92–4; de Rougé, *Notice sommaire* (1876), p. 61; Revillout, *Cat.* No. 462; Boreux, *Guide*, i, p. 172; Vandier, *Guide* (1948), p. 25; (1952), p. 26; (1973), p. 57.

Year 23.

Penptaḥ, Director of the estates of Neith, etc., son of Uzaḥor-meḥent and Sitpep. (a) IM.3011 [N.421/346; No. 337]; text, Chassinat in *Rec. Trav.* xxii

(1900), p. 177 [cxx]; GOODWIN MSS. 31279, 32 [lower]; see VERCOUTTER, *Textes*, p. 24 [b] (as IM.3001); REVILLOUT, *Cat.* No. 511. (b) IM.4192 [N.421/331; No. 350], undated; text, CHASSINAT, op. cit. xxii (1900), p. 180 [cxxvii].

Ptaḥemmaʿet(?) (?) (?), *waʿb*-priest, son of Zeiuenptaḥ, God's father, and Mertiotes, IM.4002 [No. 503]. See PIERRET, *Cat.* No. 307.

Temp. Amasis, undated.

Upper part, [King] adoring Apis-bull and seated Osiris, IM.4074 [No. 325]. Text, CHASSINAT in *Rec. Trav.* xxii (1900), pp. 175–6 [cxvii]; see REVILLOUT, *Cat.* No. 505.

Pasenenkhons, son of King Amasis and Nekhtubasterau, IM.4053 [No. 266]. Text, CHASSINAT, op. cit. xxii (1900), p. 171 [civ]; see REVILLOUT, *Cat.* No. 488.

Psammethek (later King Psammetikhos III), son of King Amasis and Tent-kheta IM.4034 [N.486; S.2252]. VERCOUTTER, *Textes*, pl. v, pp. 37–43; WILKINSON MSS. xxiv. 24 [right lower]. Text, CHASSINAT in *Rec. Trav.* xxi (1899), p. 63 [xvi]; ČERNÝ Notebook, 117, p. 18 [upper]. See DE ROUGÉ, *Notice sommaire* (1876), p. 66; PIERRET, *Cat.* No. 309.

Probably temp. Amasis. Not necessarily Apis V of Dyn. XXVI.

ʿAḥmosi, son of Heribamūn, both Commanders of the army, and [Sety]erboni, IM.4175. Text, CHASSINAT in *Rec. Trav.* xxi (1899), pp. 68–9 [xxx] (as Apis V of Dyn. XXVI); see PIERRET, *Cat.* No. 333.

ʿAnkh-unnūfer, God's father, Prophet of Isis, son of Ptaḥḥotp and Thekhet, IM.4009 [N.421/350; No. 365]. VERCOUTTER, *Textes*, pl. iv, pp. 34–6; text, CHASSINAT, op. cit. xxiii (1901), pp. 79–80 [cxxxiv]; names and titles, LIEBLEIN, *Dict.* No. 1045; see REVILLOUT, *Cat.* No. 529.

Ḥarkhebi (perhaps not dedicator of the stela, but one of relatives), son of Tasenḥor (mother), IM.64.

Ḥarshefnakht(?), son of Weḥebrēʿ-mer(y)ptaḥ, both God's fathers and Prophets of Amen-rēʿ foremost of the Temples, Prophets of Pepy, etc., IM.4040 [No. 424]. Text, CHASSINAT, op. cit. xxv (1903), p. 51 [clx]; ČERNÝ Notebook, 117, p. 16 [upper]; see REVILLOUT, *Cat.* No. 539.

Khensardais, son of Atemardais and Mutar[dais], IM.4170.

Neferebrēʿ, Inspector of *sem*-priests, Secretary of the King, etc., son of Psammethek and Esnebttaui. (a) IM.3148 [N.479]; text, CHASSINAT, op. cit. xxi (1899), p. 62 [xiii] (as Apis IV of Dyn. XXVI); see PIERRET, *Cat.* No. 305 (as N.671/3148); VERCOUTTER, *Textes*, pp. 24–6 [c]. (b) IM.4110 [N.421/342; No. 336]; id. ib. pl. vii, pp. 48–58; text, CHASSINAT, op. cit. xxii (1900), pp. 176–7 [cxix]; see REVILLOUT, *Cat.* No. 510.

Paneḥesi Neferebrēʿ-sonb, *ḥwn*-priest of Bubastis, son of Pathenfi and Iʿoḥ-neferu, temp. Amasis, IM.4051 [No. 322]. VERCOUTTER, *Textes*, pl. vi, pp. 44–7; text, CHASSINAT, op. cit. xxii (1900), p. 175 [cxvi].

Psammethek-emakhet, son of ʿAnkh-weḥebrēʿ and Wendes-ḥes, IM.4174. Names and titles, LIEBLEIN, *Dict.* No. 1157.

Psammethek-meryptaḥ, Overseer of the royal freight boats, etc., son of Ḥarkhons and Pepy-meriotes, IM.4019 [No. 333]. Text, CHASSINAT, op. cit. xxii (1900), p. 176 [cxviii]; GOODWIN MSS. 31279, 33 [lower]; names and titles, LIEBLEIN, *Dict.* No. 1144.

Psammethek-sonb, Mayor in Sais, etc., son of Ḥory, God's father, and Sopdetiyti, IM.4128.

Thaiḥarimu, God's father, Secretary of Ra-setau, etc., son of Sekhemʿankh-ptaḥ and Ḥepet, IM.3114 [N.421/327; No. 349]. Text, CHASSINAT, op. cit. xxii (1900), p. 179 [cxxvi] (as IM.3714 in error); see REVILLOUT, *Cat.* No. 519.

Weḥebrēʿ-unnūfer, Overseer of the seal, Prophet of Isis and Nephthys, etc., son of Ḥarsiēsi and Estanefert, quartzite, IM.4100. VERCOUTTER, *Textes*, pl. iii, pp. 27–33.

APIS XLII of Mariette. Year 6 of Cambyses.

Chamber Z of Mariette, M of Rhoné.

Text on lid of sarcophagus, GUNN in *Ann. Serv.* xxvi (1926), p. 85.

Official stela, giving the date probably of birth of the Apis-bull as year 27 (of Amasis), in Louvre, IM.4133 [N.407; S.N.83; S.2287; No. 354]. POSENER, *La Première domination perse en Égypte*, pl. ii, pp. 30–5; ARCHIVES phot. E.896. Lines 1 and 2 of text, REVILLOUT in *Revue Égyptologique*, i (1880), pp. 71–2 note 1. See DE ROUGÉ, *Notice sommaire* (1876), p. 61.

APIS XLIII. See *infra*.

APIS XLIV of Mariette. Year 4 of Darius I.

Chamber B′ of Mariette, N′ of Rhoné.

Stelae. In Louvre.

Year 4.

Official stela, giving the date of birth of the Apis-bull as year 5 of Cambyses, fragmentary, IM.4187 [N.408; S.2274; No. 357]. POSENER, op. cit. pl. iii, pp. 36–41; ARCHIVES phot. E.655; DEVÉRIA squeezes, 6165, i. 53. Text, CHASSINAT in *Rec. Trav.* xxiii (1901), pp. 77–8 [cxxxi]. See DE ROUGÉ, *Notice sommaire* (1876), p. 61.

Ḥekaemsaf, son of Irefʿa(en)ptaḥ, both God's fathers, Heads of door-openers, etc., IM.4013. ARCHIVES phot. E.637; text, CHASSINAT, op. cit. xxiii (1901), pp. 76–7 [cxxx] (as IM.4012 and No. 355); names and titles, LIEBLEIN, *Dict.* No. 1051.

Pefneit, son of Ḥarkhebi, both *sem*-priests, *wp-nṯrwy*, etc., IM.4086. See PIERRET, *Cat.* No. 320.

Pensekhmet sic, son of Ptaḥshepses, both God's fathers, *wnrw*-priests in Letopolis, etc., and Irti, IM.4188. Text, ČERNÝ Notebook, 117, p. 7 [lower].

Psammethek-meryneit, son of Pashenptaḥ, God's father, *kʿḥ*-priest, IM.3131 [N.421/355].

Ptaḥḥotp, God's father in the 1st phyle, *sem*-priest, son of Esunnūfer, IM.4054 [No. 366]. Text, CHASSINAT, op. cit. xxiii (1901), pp. 80–1 [cxxxv].

Probably year 4.

ʿAḥmosi, son of Paiuenḥor, both Commanders of the army, and Taḳapenkhebi. (a) IM.4017 [No. 359]; VERCOUTTER, *Textes*, pl. viii, pp. 59–64; DEVÉRIA squeezes, 6165, i. 47; ARCHIVES phot. E.1175; text, PIERRET, *Rec. inscr.* i, pp. 67–9; CHASSINAT in *Rec. Trav.* xxiii (1901), p. 78 [cxxxii]; POSENER, *La Première domination perse en Égypte*, pp. 42–3, cf. 41, 44–6; names and titles, LIEBLEIN, *Dict.* No. 1214; see REVILLOUT, *Cat.* No. 527. (b) N.421/317 [S.N.88; No. 330]; text, POSENER, op. cit. pp. 47, cf. 46.

ʿAḥmosi, Director of the estates, *wnrw*-priest, etc., son of Psammethek-sineit [hieroglyphs], Chief lector-priest, and Tashentiḥet [hieroglyphs], IM.4129 [N.421/402; No. 417]. VERCOUTTER, op. cit. pl. xvi, pp. 105–8; text, CHASSINAT, op. cit. xxv (1903), p. 50 [clvi].

Ḥarwoz, Hereditary prince, etc., son of Tesnakht [hieroglyphs] (mother), IM.4057. See BOTHMER, *Eg. Sculp.* pp. 72, 73.

Pashenptaḥ, God's father and Prophet of Ptaḥ, son of Pedeptaḥ, God's father and Prophet of Bubastis Mistress of ʿAnkhtaui, IM.4118.

Pedeḥaremḥab [hieroglyphs], Royal scribe under Amasis, etc., son of Uzaḥorresnet [hieroglyphs], Prophet of Ḥa, etc., and Shep(en)sopdet [hieroglyphs], IM.4018 [No. 339]. VERCOUTTER, op. cit. pl. ix, pp. 65–9; text, CHASSINAT, op. cit. xxii (1900), p. 178 [cxxiii] (as Apis V of Dynasty XXVI); see REVILLOUT, *Cat.* No. 513.

Lower part of a stela, IM.4116.

APIS XLV of Mariette. Temp. Darius I.

Chamber C′ of Mariette, N″ of Rhoné.

Stelae dated between years 4 and 34 of Darius I.

Esbanebded [hieroglyphs], *sem*-priest, *wp-ntrwy*, son of Shedsunefertem [hieroglyphs] and Irterau, year 31, in Louvre. (a) IM.4016 [No. 362]; part of text, BRUGSCH, *Thes.* 969 [4]; id. in *Ä.Z.* xxii (1884), pp. 115–16; date and cartouche, WILKINSON MSS. xxiv. 19 [4]. (b) Probably same man, IM.4068.

Ptaḥḥotp, year 31 (or 34), in Louvre, S.N.74.

APIS XLIII of Mariette. Year 34 of Darius I.

Chamber A′ of Mariette, N of Rhoné. Identification doubtful.

Stelae.

Year 34.

In Louvre.

Official stela, inscribed in ink, IM.4039. VERCOUTTER, *Textes*, pl. x, pp. 70–7.

Ḥarkhebi [hieroglyphs], son of Tabes [hieroglyphs] (mother), IM.4045 [N.441a]. Text, WILKINSON MSS. xxiv. 26 [1]; ČERNÝ Notebook, 117, p. 20 [lower]; see PIERRET, *Cat.* No. 322.

Ḥarsiēsi, son of Zeḥarefʿankh [hieroglyphs], both God's fathers, *wnrw*-priests, IM.4104 [N.421/476]. Part of text, ČERNÝ Notebook, 117, p. 24 [upper].

Irʿaḥor [hieroglyphs] . . . ḥap [hieroglyphs], Secretary of Ra-setau, *khet*-priest of Ḥa, etc., IM.4063 [N.475]. Text, CHASSINAT in *Rec. Trav.* xxi (1899), p. 67 [xxvi]; see PIERRET, *Cat.* No. 326.

Irʿaḥor, *sem*-priest, *wnrw*-priest, etc., son of ʿAnkh-psammethek and Werek [hieroglyphs], IM.4046 [No. 394]. Text, CHASSINAT, op. cit. xxiii (1901), pp. 84–5 [cxlii] (as IM.4045).

Iufʿa [hieroglyphs] (same man as Berlin 3423, see *infra*) and Ḥor, *sem*-priests, *kʿḥ*-priests, etc., sons of Pashenptaḥ [hieroglyphs] and Neitikert [hieroglyphs], IM.4076 [N.441]. Text, id. ib. xxi (1899), pp. 66–7 [xxv]; see PIERRET, *Cat.* No. 325.

Children of Neferebrēʿ-mer(y)ptaḥ [hieroglyphs], God's father, Prophet of Sobk, and Tashenpashai [hieroglyphs], IM.4037 [N.421/652; No. 443]. Text, CHASSINAT, op. cit. xxv (1903), p. 55 [clxvii].

(Pa)shenptaḥ, God's father, *sem*-priest, etc., son of Ḥaremakhet and Tasokari, IM.4008 [N.441]. Text, id. ib. xxi (1899), pp. 65–6 [xxiii]; WILKINSON MSS. xxiv. 25 [left lower]; see PIERRET, *Cat.* No. 323.

Pedubaste, son of Pefteuᶜaubaste, IM.4072 [N.485]. Text, CHASSINAT, op. cit. xxi (1899), p. 65 [xxii]; see PIERRET, *Cat.* No. 321.

Psammethek-emakhet, Prophet of Ptaḥ, *wnrw*-priest, etc., son of Ḥarsiēsi and Takap, IM.4097 [S.2303; No. 364]. Text, CHASSINAT, op. cit. xxiii (1901), pp. 78–9 [cxxxiii] (as IM.4067); names and titles, LIEBLEIN, *Dict.* No. 1230; see DE ROUGÉ, *Notice sommaire* (1876), p. 62.

Ptaḥḥotp, son of Shesepamūn-tefḥert, probably year 34 (or 31), IM.4207.

Semtu-tefnakht, God's father, son of Irᶜaḥeka, Inspector of *sem*-priests, etc., and Renpetnefert, S.N.72.

Weḥebrēᶜ-emkhebi, son of ᶜAḥmosi-mer(y)ptaḥ, both *khet*-priests of Ḥa, Prophets of Ptaḥ and Isis foremost of Thenent, etc., and Neitiyti, IM.4033 [No. 398]. Text, CHASSINAT, op. cit. xxiii (1901), pp. 85–6 [cxliii].

Zeptaḥefᶜankh, *sem*-priest, Secretary of Ra-setau, etc., son of Ḥekaemsaf and Neferḥeres, IM.3999 [N.421/701; No. 446]. Text, id. ib. xxv (1903), p. 56 [clxx].

Zeptaḥefᶜankh(?), God's father and Prophet of Ptaḥ, son of Amenemsaf, IM.4125 [No. 471]. Text, id. ib. xxv (1903), p. 59 [clxxvii].

. . . ḥotp, son of Ḥaremmaᶜkheru, probably year 34 of Darius I, IM.4087 [No. 390]. Text, id. ib. xxiii (1901), p. 83 [cxl].

. . . wepᶜau (?) Pefteuᶜaubaste, Treasurer of the King of Lower Egypt, etc., son of Mutardais, Sistrum-player of Ḥatḥor Mistress of the Southern Sycamore (mother), IM.4109. VERCOUTTER, *Textes*, pl. xi, pp. 78–81.

Name lost, son of Psammethek-snefertaui and Setyerboni, IM.4214. Names, LIEBLEIN, *Dict.* No. 1208.

Name lost, N.421/347 [S.N.31; No. 374]. Text, CHASSINAT, op. cit. xxiii (1901), p. 81 [cxxxvi].

In Cairo Museum.

Lower part of stela, CG 50042. SPIEGELBERG, *Die demotischen Denkmäler*, iii, *Demotische Inschriften und Papyri*, Taf. x, p. 13.

Temp. Darius I, probably year 34. In Louvre.

ᶜAḥmosi, God's father, Scribe, N.421/382 [S.N.64; No. 404]. Text, CHASSINAT in *Rec. Trav.* xxiii (1901), pp. 87–8 [cxlviii] (as year 34); see REVILLOUT, *Cat.* No. 533.

Ḥory, God's father and Prophet of Harsaphes in the domain of the Temple of Sekhmet, son of ᶜAḥmosi-men Irᶜaḥeka, Greatest of the Directors of craftsmen, and Sekhmet-nefert, IM.4038 [N.421/614].

Ptaḥḥotp, Overseer of the House of Silver and of the House of Gold, *khet*-priest of Ḥa, etc., IM.1244 [N.677]. Text, CHASSINAT, op. cit. xxi (1899), pp. 67–8 [xxvii]; see COONEY in *Brooklyn Mus. Bull.* xv [2] (Winter 1953), p. 14; BOTHMER, *Eg. Sculp.* p. 77; PIERRET, *Cat.* No. 327.

Probably temp. Darius I, year 34. In Louvre.

ᶜAḥmosi-men, Greatest of the Directors of craftsmen, etc., son of Nekau-mer(y)ptaḥ [hieroglyphs] and grandson of Neferebrēʿ-men [hieroglyphs], IM.4213 [No. 485]. Genealogy, BRUGSCH, *Thes.* 947 [13], cf. 1256; LIEBLEIN, *Dict.* No. 2515.

Amenḥotp, son of Psammethek and Setyerboni [hieroglyphs], IM.4011 [N.677]. Text, CHASSINAT in *Rec. Trav.* xxi (1899), p. 64 [xix]; see PIERRET, *Cat.* No. 313 (as N.674/7011).

ʿAnkhefensekhmet [hieroglyphs], son of Psammethek, both Secretaries of the Great Place, Prophets of Sekhmet Mistress of Shendi, etc., and Setyerboni, IM.4080 [No. 219]. Text, CHASSINAT, op. cit. xxii (1900), pp. 25–6 [lxxviii] (as S.4080); names and titles, LIEBLEIN, *Dict.* No. 1205.

ʿAnkhefensekhmet, *waʿb*-priest of the Temples of Memphis, etc., son of Neferseshem-psammethek [hieroglyphs], Overseer of *waʿb*-priests of Sekhmet of the Temple of Ptaḥ, Prophet of the Temple of Merneptaḥ, etc., and Te(nt)nefertem [hieroglyphs], IM.4111.

ʿAnkh-unnūfer [hieroglyphs], IM.4060 [N.421/383; No. 399]. Text, CHASSINAT, op. cit. xxiii (1901), p. 86 [cxliv].

Diptaḥiau [hieroglyphs], son of Pedēsi, both God's fathers, and ʿAnkhes [hieroglyphs], IM.4029 [N.421/397; No. 421]. Text, id. ib. xxv (1903), pp. 50–1 [clviii] (as Apis of year 34 of Darius I); names and titles, LIEBLEIN, *Dict.* No. 1033.

Diptaḥiau, son of ʿAnkh-unnūfer, God's father, and Takap [hieroglyphs], IM.4056 [N.421/366; No. 405]. Text, CHASSINAT, op. cit. xxiii (1901), p. 88 [cxlix].

Diptaḥiau, son of Ptaḥḥotp and Takap, IM.4077.

Esbanebded, son of Shedsunefertem and Irterau, probably from here or year 31, although said to have been found in burial chamber of Apis XLI, IM.5341.

Espakhutaui [hieroglyphs], son of Esunnūfer [hieroglyphs], both Prophets of Ptaḥ, etc., IM.4099 [N.679]. Text, CHASSINAT, op. cit. xxi (1899), p. 60 [vii]; see PIERRET, *Cat.* No. 294.

Ḥardedef [hieroglyphs], son of Pefteuʿaubaste, God's father, IM.4050.

Ḥarem . . . ḥotp [hieroglyphs], son of Thesēsi-erboni(?) [hieroglyphs] (mother), IM.4149 [N.421/390; No. 406]. Text, CHASSINAT, op. cit. xxiii (1901), pp. 88 [cl].

Ḥepmen [hieroglyphs], son of Esbanebded, both *wnrw*-priests, and Khreduʿankh [hieroglyphs], IM.4121 [N.677]. Text, id. ib. xxi (1899), p. 69 [xxxi]; ČERNÝ Notebook, 117, p. 10 [lower]; see PIERRET, *Cat.* No. 686.

Ḥor, Overseer of the fields, Prophet of many gods, etc., son of Uzaḥorresnet [hieroglyphs], Royal scribe, etc., and Shepensopdet [hieroglyphs], C 317 [No. 428]. Text, CHASSINAT, op. cit. xxv (1903), pp. 52–3 [clxiii]; see BOREUX, *Guide*, i, p. 174.

Imḥōtep, son of Setyerboni (mother), IM.4025 [N.421/366; No. 383]. Text, CHASSINAT, op. cit. xxiii (1901), p. 82 [cxxxviii]; ČERNÝ Notebook, 117, p. 4 [lower]; see REVILLOUT, *Cat.* No. 532.

Imḥōtep, son of Ptaḥardais and Tadēsi, IM.4120 [N.421/697; No. 470]. Text, CHASSINAT, op. cit. xxv (1903), p. 58 [clxxvi].

Imḥōtep, son of Ḥeperiu [hieroglyphs], IM.4134 [N.421/598; No. 472]. Text, id. ib. xxv (1903), p. 59 [clxxviii]; ČERNÝ Notebook, 117, p. 20 [upper] (as IM.4130).

Inamūn-nefnebu [hieroglyphs] Neferebrēʿ-sineit [hieroglyphs], son of Ḥekaiotef [hieroglyphs], IM.4003 [N.421/393; No. 407]. Text, CHASSINAT, op. cit. xxiii (1901), p. 88 [cli].

Iʿoḥardai[s] [hieroglyphs], son of Pair[kap](?) [hieroglyphs], N.421/593 [S.N.55; No. 444]. Text, id. ib. xxv (1903), p. 55 [clxviii]; see REVILLOUT, *Cat.* No. 547.

Khnemebrēʿ [hieroglyphs], Director of the estates, *wnrw*-priest, etc., son of Psammethek-sineit [hieroglyphs], Chief lector-priest, and Setyerboni, IM.4032 [No. 410]. VERCOUTTER,

Textes, pl. xiii, pp. 88–92; WILKINSON MSS. xxiv. 17 [right]. Text, CHASSINAT, op. cit. xxiii (1901), pp. 89–90 [cliv]; main text, BRUGSCH, *Thes.* 989 [8, a]. Names and titles, LIEBLEIN, *Dict.* No. 1216. See REVILLOUT, *Cat.* No. 535.

Mem, son of Pawen, both God's fathers, *sem*-priests, etc., and Tayirterau, IM.4027 [N.421/403; No. 409]. Text, CHASSINAT, op. cit. xxiii (1901), p. 89 [cliii]; ČERNÝ Notebook, 117, p. 14 [bottom]; part, GOODWIN MSS. 31279, 34. Names and titles, LIEBLEIN, *Dict.* No. 1048. See REVILLOUT, *Cat.* No. 534.

Pashenptaḥ(?), son of Ḥor, IM.4052 [N.481]. Text, CHASSINAT, op. cit. xxv (1903), p. 62 [clxxxi].

Pashenptaḥ, son of Painmu, God's father, *sem*-priest, and Sopdetiyt, IM.4069.

Pedeḥor, son of Pedeḥarpekhrod, IM.4004.

Pedes, son of Senbef, both *sem*-priests, *wp-nṯrwy*, etc., IM.4001 [N.421/704; No. 474]. Text, CHASSINAT, op. cit. xxv (1903), p. 61 [clxxx].

Pedēsi, son of Ḥarwoz, IM.4169 [N.421/398; No. 463]. Text, id. ib. xxiii (1901), p. 87 [cxlvii].

Pedusiriwēr-nūfer, Door-opener of the Temple of Serapis, son of Pakap and Ḥetepubaste, IM.4150 [N.421/394; No. 402]. Text, id. ib. xxiii (1901), p. 87 [cxlvi].

Pefteuʿaukhons, Prophet of Amen-rēʿ Lord of Khentnūfer, etc., son of Semtu-tefnakht and Takapu, mentioning family with titles of Prophets of (a) a temple () of Ramesses II, (b) Sekhmet of Saḥurēʿ, IM.4107 [N.421/399; No. 413]. Text, id. ib. xxiii (1901), pp. 90–1 [clv]; WILKINSON MSS. xxiv. 17 [left upper]; names and titles, LIEBLEIN, *Dict.* No. 1217.

Psammethek, son of Khnemebrēʿ-siptaḥ Nekau, Greatest of the Directors of craftsmen of Ptaḥ, etc., and Ēsireshti, IM.4098 [No. 391]. Text, CHASSINAT, op. cit. xxiii (1901), pp. 83–4 [cxli].

Psammethek-ib(?), Door-opener of Serapis, etc., IM.3047.

Psammethek-menempe, Prophet of Isis Mistress of the Pyramid, Khufu, Raʿzedef, Khephren, and Ḥaremakhet, son of Ḥarwoz and Taremtenubaste, IM.2857 [N.444; No. 291]. Text, CHASSINAT, op. cit. xvii (1895), pp. 53–4 [iv]; xxii (1900), pp. 173–4 [cxi]; WILKINSON MSS. xxiv. 25 [right upper]; see PIERRET, *Cat.* No. 314.

Ptaḥemmaʿkheru Esptaḥ, son of Ḥor, both *sem*-priests, Secretaries of Ra-setau, etc., IM.137 [No. 401]. Text, CHASSINAT, op. cit. xxiii (1901), pp. 86–7 [cxlv]; name and titles, LIEBLEIN, *Dict.* 1231.

Semtu-tefnakht, *sem*-priest, etc., son of Irenḥor, IM.138 [N.421/647; No. 448]. Text, CHASSINAT, op. cit. xxv (1903), p. 57 [clxxii] (as IM.198).

Semtu-tefnakht, Director of the estates, Prophet of Harsaphes, etc., son of ʿAḥmosi-men, Greatest of the Directors of craftsmen, etc., and Sekhmetnefert, IM.4044 [N.677]. Text, id. ib. xxi (1899), p. 66 [xxiv]; see PIERRET, *Cat.* No. 324.

Semtu-tefnakht, son of Zeḥo, both God's fathers, *wnrw*-priests, and ʿAnkh-irterau, IM.4095 [N.421/660; No. 445]. Text, CHASSINAT, op. cit. xxv (1903), pp. 55–6 [clxix].

Senbef, son of Pedes, both God's fathers, and Ēsireshti, IM.42 [N.421/626; No. 441]. Text, id. ib. xxv (1903), p. 54 [clxv] (as N.421/624).

Sinebʿankh, son of Zeptaḥefʿankh, IM.4190.

Weḥebrēʿ-mer(y)neit, IM.4055.

Zeḥo Shednefertem, *sem*-priest, *wnrw*-priest in Letopolis, etc., son of Nubiyti (mother), IM.4021.

Zeubastefʿankh, son of Pedēsi and Irterau, IM.4000 [N.421/676; No. 447]. Text, id. ib. xxv (1903), p. 56 [clxxi].

UNNUMBERED APIS. Year 2 of Nepheritis I.

Stelae. In Louvre.

Dated.

IM.4092 [No. 451]; see REVILLOUT, *Notice des papyrus démotiques archaïques* [etc.], pp. 470–1 [123].

IM.4101 [No. 458]; text, DEVÉRIA squeezes, 6165, i. 60–1; see REVILLOUT, op. cit. pp. 469–70 [122].

Ḥor, God's father, *sem*-priest, son of Pawen, IM.4103 [N.421/564]; text of probably this, DEVÉRIA squeezes, 6170D, 18; date and cartouches, VERCOUTTER, *Textes*, p. 100.

Probably year 2 of Nepheritis I.

Name lost, son of Paḥeter, Overseer of prophets, and Tairterau, IM. 4114. Id. ib. pl. xv, pp. 100–4.

APIS XLVI of Mariette. Year 2 of Khebebesh.

Chamber D′ of Mariette, O of Rhoné.

Text on lid of black granite sarcophagus, with date, BRUGSCH, *Thes.* 968 [3]; id. in *Ä.Z.* ix (1871), p. 13; GUNN in *Ann. Serv.* xxvi (1926), p. 87; DEVÉRIA squeezes, 6165, i. 55; WILKINSON MSS. xviii. 42 [upper left]; xxiv. 6 [right top].

APIS LV of Mariette. Year 17 of Ptolemy VI Philometor.

Chamber P (2nd on right) of Rhoné.

Official stela, year 6 of the three Philometors (*i.e.* Ptolemies VI and VIII and Cleopatra II), giving the date of birth of the Apis-bull as year 19 of Ptolemy V Epiphanes, granite, in Louvre, N.409 (upper part) and E.3866 (lower part). ARCHIVES phot. E.982; DEVÉRIA squeezes, 6165, i. 68, and 6168, 29; text, BRUGSCH in *Ä.Z.* xxii (1884), p. 125; names, id. *Thes.* 865 [middle].

APIS LVII of Mariette. Year 52 of Ptolemy VIII Euergetes II.

Official stela, giving the date of birth of the Apis-bull as year 28 and death as year 51, black granite, in Louvre, IM.4246 [N.410]. ARCHIVES phot. E.983; DEVÉRIA squeezes, 6165, i. 69 and 6196, 17; text, DE ROUGÉ in *Revue Égyptologique*, iv (1887), pp. 110–18, and v (1888), pp. 8–9 (repr. in *Bibl. Ég.* xxii, pp. 424–38, 454–6); WILKINSON MSS. xxiv. 4 [right], 18; lines 2–3, BRUGSCH, *Thes.* p. 867 [upper]. See DE ROUGÉ, *Notice sommaire* (1876), p. 62.

APIS OF AN UNKNOWN PTOLEMY (?).

Chamber R of Rhoné.

Sarcophagus with lid, inscribed, black granite. Dümichen, *Photo. Result.* xiv; Petrie in Wright, *Twentieth Century Impressions of Egypt*, fig. on p. 132 [upper]; Capart, *Propos*, fig. 141; Desroches-Noblecourt, *Les Religions égyptiennes* in *L'Histoire générale des religions*, fig. on p. 224 [lower]; Wood and Drower, *Egypt in Colour*, pl. 11; Lauer, *Saqqara*, pl. 12; Ruffle, *Heritage of the Pharaohs*, fig. 135. Texts, Gunn in *Ann. Serv.* xxvi (1926), pp. 88–90; Wilkinson MSS. xviii. 38–40.

Apis-Stelae not assigned to a particular Apis-bull

In Louvre

Probably Dyn. XXII.

ʿAnkh-ḥor, adoring, IM.2865 [N.679]. Malinine [etc.], *Cat.* i, pl. xxiii [80], p. 68; text, Chassinat in *Rec. Trav.* xxi (1899), p. 60 [vi]; see Pierret, *Cat.* No. 291.

ʿAnkh-khons, *ỉmy-ḫnt*, IM.2849 [No. 94]. Malinine [etc.], *Cat.* i, pl. xx [66], p. 59.

ʿAnkh-unnūfer, IM.3107 [S.1093; No. 33]. Id. ib. i, pl. xvii [55], p. 51; see Revillout, *Cat.* No. 409.

ʿAshōkhi, God's father, *sem*-priest in the Temple of Sokari Lord of Ra-setau, son of Pakhar, same titles, with long genealogy, IM.3429 [No. 96]. Malinine [etc.], *Cat.* i, pl. xvi [52], pp. 48–9; Mariette, *Sérapéum*, pl. 34 [bottom left] (as Dyn. XXIV); text, Chassinat in *Rec. Trav.* xxii (1900), pp. 16–17 [liv]; genealogy, Lieblein, *Dict.* No. 1027; end of text, Brugsch, *Thes.* 1012 [bottom]; Sottas, *La Préservation de la propriété funéraire* [etc.], p. 167 [top]; see Revillout, *Cat.* No. 440.

Ḥarsiēsi, son of Ḥarwoz(?), IM.3032 [S.2914; No. 32]. Malinine [etc.], *Cat.* i, pl. xxi [71], pp. 62–3; see Revillout, *Cat.* No. 408.

Ḥarwoz, *waʿb*-priest of the Great Place, etc., son of Ten-tho (woman), IM.5937 [No. 19]. Malinine [etc.], *Cat.* i, pl. xviii [59], pp. 53–4; some names and titles, Lieblein, *Dict.* No. 1197; see Revillout, *Cat.* No. 402.

Ḥarwoz-paḥeka, IM.3059 [N.421/38; No. 44]. Malinine [etc.], *Cat.* i, pl. xix [64], pp. 57–8; text, Černý Notebook, 117, p. 12 [upper].

Ḥepiu, IM.19 [No. 93]. Malinine [etc.], *Cat.* i, pl. xxv [87], p. 72; see Revillout, *Cat.* No. 438.

Ḥerenḥepu, son of Pashenmut, IM.4215 [S.1951; No. 89]. Malinine [etc.], *Cat.* i, pl. xix [62], p. 56; see Revillout, *Cat.* No. 434.

Ḥor, Head of door-openers of the Temple of Ptaḥ, S.N.58 [No. 53]. Malinine [etc.], *Cat.* i, pl. xxvi [90], pp. 74–5.

Irneferenptaḥ, Craftsman, IM.3093 [S.1890; No. 27]. Id. ib. i, pl. xv [47], pp. 44–5.

Merneptaḥ, Prophet of the Temples of Bubastis and Shesmetet (both called Mistress of ʿAnkhtaui), etc., son of Esunnūfer, *sem*-priest, and his son Ptaḥḥotp, God's father, *sem*-priest, etc. (owner of stela IM.3024, see *infra*), IM.3745 [N.421/63; No. 41]. Id. ib. i, pl. xvi [50], pp. 46–7; Mariette, *Sérapéum*, pl. 33 (as Apis VII of Dyn. XXII); Vercoutter, *Textes*, pl. i, pp. 1–15 [A]; text, Chassinat in *Rec. Trav.* xxii (1900), pp. 12–13 [xli].

Mes-unnūfer [hieroglyphs], IM.3311 [No. 69]. MALININE [etc.], *Cat.* i, pl. xxiv [83], p. 70; see REVILLOUT, *Cat.* No. 426.

Naʿsu [hieroglyphs], Head of the servants of Apis, son of Ḥatneferu [hieroglyphs], same title, IM.3081 [N.421/94; No. 99]. MALININE [etc.], *Cat.* i, pl. xvii [53], p. 49; see REVILLOUT, *Cat.* No. 442.

Paʿazab [hieroglyphs], *waʿb*-priest of the Great Place, son of Ḥarwoz, same title (owner of stela IM.5937, see *supra*), IM.3141 [No. 95]. MALININE [etc.], *Cat.* i, pl. xx [67], pp. 59–60; see REVILLOUT, *Cat.* No. 439.

Paḥethi(?) [hieroglyphs], Workman of the Necropolis, IM.3033 [N.421/37; No. 60]. MALININE [etc.], *Cat.* i, pl. xxi [72], p. 63; text, CHASSINAT in *Rec. Trav.* xxii (1900), p. 14 [xlvii]; see REVILLOUT, *Cat.* No. 421.

Paḳerer [hieroglyphs], son of Pashenptaḥ, IM.3065 [No. 25]. MALININE [etc.], *Cat.* i, pl. xxi [69], p. 61.

Pashensekhmet [hieroglyphs], son of Ptaḥḥotp, God's father, *sem*-priest, IM.5432 [S.1895; No. 23]. Id. ib. i, pl. xxiv [84], pp. 70–1.

Pawenḥētef [hieroglyphs], Workman of the Necropolis, son of Paweredu [hieroglyphs], and others, IM.3083 [N.421/48; No. 47]. Id. ib. i, pl. xviii [60], pp. 54–5; text, CHASSINAT in *Rec. Trav.* xxii (1900), pp. 13–14 [xliii]; some names and titles, LIEBLEIN, *Dict.* No. 1017.

Pedekherbeḳ . . . [hieroglyphs], son of Pedēsi, IM.3103 [N.679]. MALININE [etc.], *Cat.* i, pl. xxv [85], p. 71; text, CHASSINAT in *Rec. Trav.* xxi (1899), p. 68 [xxix]; see PIERRET, *Cat.* No. 332.

Pedēsi, God's father, Inspector of *sem*-priests, before Amen-rēʿ, bull-headed Apis, Ptaḥ and Sokari-Osiris at top, much effaced, S.N.2 [No. 17]. MALININE [etc.], *Cat.* i, pl. xvii [54], pp. 50–1.

Pedesopdu [hieroglyphs] sic [hieroglyphs], son of Pe(n)tent-khebi [hieroglyphs], IM.3128 [N.421/46; No. 65]. Id. ib. i, pl. xix [63], pp. 56–7; see REVILLOUT, *Cat.* No. 425.

Pefteuʿaukhons [hieroglyphs], son of Ḥarmaʿkheru [hieroglyphs], God's father, with sides in form of obelisks and pyramidion in centre, IM.3008 [N.421/74; No. 81].[1] MALININE [etc.], *Cat.* i, pl. xxi [70], pp. 61–2; MARIETTE, *Sérapéum*, pl. 32 [lower left] (as Apis VII of Dyn. XXII); see REVILLOUT, *Cat.* No. 429.

Penptaḥ [hieroglyphs], son of Esunnūfer [hieroglyphs], IM.3305 [N.421/64; No. 73]. MALININE [etc.], *Cat.* i, pl. xix [61], p. 55; see REVILLOUT, *Cat.* No. 427.

Ptaḥḥotp, Singer of the Temple of Ptaḥ, IM.3051 [N.421/65; No. 74]. MALININE [etc.], *Cat.* i, pl. xv [48], p. 45.

Ptaḥḥotp (stela of father Merneptaḥ, IM.3745, see *supra*), IM.3024 [No. 295]. Id. ib. i, pl. xv [51], pp. 47–8; MARIETTE, *Sérapéum*, pl. 35 [middle] (as Apis II of Dyn. XXV).

Ptaḥḥotp, inscribed on both sides, IM.2660. MALININE [etc.], *Cat.* i, pl. xxv [88], p. 73.

Ptaḥ-khaʿ [hieroglyphs], son of Wenemdi-amūn [hieroglyphs], IM.2637 [S.1903; No. 26]. Id. ib. i, pl. xviii [58], p. 53; see REVILLOUT, *Cat.* No. 404.

Sheshonḳ [hieroglyphs] and father Pedeamūn, IM.3016 [N.421/16; No. 52]. MALININE [etc.], *Cat.* i, pl. xv [49], pp. 45–6; MARIETTE, *Sérapéum*, pl. 25 [2] (as Apis III of Dyn. XXII); see REVILLOUT, *Cat.* No. 417.

Taped [hieroglyphs], Head of *ʿḳr* of Upper and Lower Egypt, daughter of Puerem [hieroglyphs], Commander of the army, libating before Apis-bull, IM.3088 [No. 82]. MALININE [etc.], *Cat.* i, pl. xxiii [79], pp. 67–8; MARIETTE, *Sérapéum*, pl. 32 [upper right]; text,

[1] Modern copy formerly in Paris, Mus. Guimet, Inv.2494, now in Louvre, E.19993; MORET, *Catalogue du Musée Guimet. Galerie égyptienne* in *Annales du Musée Guimet*, xxxii (1909), pl. xlix, pp. 111–12.

CHASSINAT in *Rec. Trav.* xxii (1900), p. 15 [l]; some names and titles, LIEBLEIN in *Rev. Arch.* N.S. xviii (1868), p. 290 [bottom]; id. *Dict.* No. 1018; see REVILLOUT, *Cat.* No. 430.

Uzaḥor, Door-opener of Ptaḥ, IM.3426 [N.421/57; No. 70]. MALININE [etc.], *Cat.* i, pl. xxii [76], pp. 65–6.

Uzaḥor, IM.3101 [N.677]. Id. ib. i, pl. xxv [86], p. 72; see PIERRET, *Cat.* No. 329.

Uzarenu(?), IM.3302 [No. 268]. MALININE [etc.], *Cat.* i, pl. xvii [56], p. 52; see CHASSINAT in *Rec. Trav.* xxii (1900), pp. 171–2 [cv].

Zeptaḥefʿankh, Head of craftsmen, son of Nana, IM.3123 [N.421/1; No. 88]. MALININE [etc.], *Cat.* i, pl. xxvi [89], pp. 73–4; text, CHASSINAT in *Rec. Trav.* xxii (1900), p. 16 [liii]; see REVILLOUT, *Cat.* No. 433.

. . . iau, IM.3060 [No. 66]. MALININE [etc.], *Cat.* i, pl. xxii [75], p. 65.

Several names, top missing, IM.2821 [S.2928; No. 49]. Id. ib. i, pl. xx [65], p. 58; see REVILLOUT, *Cat.* No. 415.

Man (name uncertain), IM.3022 [N.421/59]. MALININE [etc.], *Cat.* i, pl. xxiv [81], p. 69.

Man (no name), IM.38 [N.421/606]. Id. ib. i, pl. xviii [57], p. 52; see CHASSINAT in *Rec. Trav.* xxv (1903), p. 62 [clxxxii]; REVILLOUT, *Cat.* No. 566.

Dyn. XXII–XXV.

Year 4 of an unidentified King.

Ḥarwoz, son of Usirinakht, IM.3440 [No. 43]. MALININE [etc.], *Cat.* i, pl. xxxvi [129], p. 103; MARIETTE, *Sérapéum*, pl. 29 [lower right] (as Apis V of Dyn. XXII). Text, CHASSINAT in *Rec. Trav.* xxii (1900), p. 13 [xlii]. Date, see VERCOUTTER in *Kush*, viii (1960), p. 68 with note 36.

Pedusiri, with bull-headed Apis, IM.3019 [S.2661; No. 111]. MALININE [etc.], *Cat.* i, pl. xxxvi [130], p. 104.

Tha-amenemwēset, probably year 4, IM.3146 [N.421/31; No. 56]. Id. ib. i, pl. xxxvi [131], pp. 104–5.

Year 14 of an unidentified King.

Pef . . . (?) . . ., Door-opener of the Temple of Ptaḥ, IM.2686 [No. 28]. MALININE [etc.], *Cat.* i, pl. xxxiv [123], p. 98; VERCOUTTER in *Kush*, viii (1960), pl. xxii [a], p. 69 note 41; text, ČERNÝ Notebook, 117, p. 15 [bottom]; see REVILLOUT, *Cat.* No. 405.

Thaenkhonsenimu, Door-opener of the Temple of Ptaḥ, no date but almost certainly contemporary with preceding stela, IM.3117 [S.1889; No. 22]. MALININE [etc.], *Cat.* i, pl. xxxv [124], p. 99; VERCOUTTER, op. cit. pl. xxii [b], p. 69 note 43.

Others.

ʿAnkh-ḥor, IM.3100 [N.679]. MALININE [etc.], *Cat.* i, pl. xxxviii [136], p. 108; see CHASSINAT in *Rec. Trav.* xxi (1899), p. 59 [ii]; PIERRET, *Cat.* No. 283.

ʿAnkh-ḥor, with two men with hoes at bottom, IM.3056 [N.421/51; No. 48]. MALININE [etc.], *Cat.* i, pl. xxxviii [139], p. 110; see REVILLOUT, *Cat.* No. 414.

ʿAnkh-sheshonḳ, God's father, son of Ḥarsiēsi, IM.3127 [No. 86]. MALININE [etc.], *Cat.* i, pl. xlii [151], p. 118; names, LIEBLEIN, *Dict.* No. 1024.

Ḥekaen . . ., son of Pueher, with man with basket before shrine with Apis-bull, IM.3025 [No. 51]. MALININE [etc.], *Cat.* i, pl. xxxviii [137], pp. 108–9; see REVILLOUT, *Cat.* No. 416.

Ḥepaʿa, Judge, son of Ipu, IM.2631 [No. 195]. MALININE [etc.],

Cat. i, pl. xl [146], pp. 114–15; names, LIEBLEIN, *Dict.* No. 1053; see REVILLOUT, *Cat.* No. 465.

Ihy, son of Bekenrenef, God's father, etc., prostrate before Apis-bull, IM.2775 [No. 46]. MALININE [etc.], *Cat.* i, pl. xxxvii [132], p. 105; MARIETTE, *Sérapéum*, pl. 29 [upper right] (as Apis V of Dyn. XXII); names and titles, LIEBLEIN, *Dict.* No. 1047.

Iref‘a(en)ptaḥ, *wa‘b*-priest, Craftsman, unfinished, IM.3308 [N.421/97; No. 103]. MALININE [etc.], *Cat.* i, pl. xxxvii [135], p. 107; text, ČERNÝ Notebook, 117, p. 16 [lower]; see REVILLOUT, *Cat.* No. 444.

Irḥepiaut, IM.2799 [No. 105]. MALININE [etc.], *Cat.* i, pl. xxxviii [138], p. 109.

Iry, son of Ptaḥemakhet(?) (?), S.N.52 [probably IM.3760; No. 173]. Id. ib. i, pl. xliii [157], p. 122; text, CHASSINAT in *Rec. Trav.* xxii [1900], p. 19 [lx]; see REVILLOUT, *Cat.* No. 458.

Iuiu, son of Iuf‘ankh, N.421/52 [S.N.70; No. 68]. MALININE [etc.], *Cat.* i, pl. xliii [156], p. 121.

Ḳeref-ptaḥ, son of Ḥarḥap, S.N.16. Id. ib. i, pl. xli [148], p. 116.

Paḥesa(?), IM.3144 [N.677]. Id. ib. i, pl. xlii [153], pp. 119–20; see PIERRET, *Cat.* No. 296.

Pairsespet-khema‘-amūn(?), IM.3133 [No. 84]. MALININE [etc.], *Cat.* i, pl. xlii [152], pp. 118–19; MARIETTE, *Sérapéum*, pl. 32 [upper left] (as Apis VII of Dyn. XXII). Text, CHASSINAT in *Rec. Trav.* xxii (1900), p. 15 [li]. See REVILLOUT, *Cat.* No. 432.

Paiu(en)ḥor, Door-opener of the Temple of Ptaḥ, son of Pashenēsi, with Isis and deceased before Apis-bull in shrine, IM.3439 [N.677]. MALININE [etc.], *Cat.* i, pl. xxxix [142], p. 112; see PIERRET, *Cat.* No. 282.

Pay, IM.3064 [N.421/44; No. 64]. MALININE [etc.], *Cat.* i, pl. xxxix [141], p. 111; see REVILLOUT, *Cat.* No. 424.

Pawenḥētef, God's father, IM.2717 [N.421/50; No. 67]. MALININE [etc.], *Cat.* i, pl. xli [150], p. 117.

Pedes, Judge, IM.4168 [No. 205]. Id. ib. i, pl. xl [144], p. 113. Text, CHASSINAT in *Rec. Trav.* xxii (1900), p. 23 [lxix] (as Apis I of Dyn. XXIV); ČERNÝ Notebook, 117, p. 1 [upper]. Names, LIEBLEIN, *Dict.* No. 1220. See REVILLOUT, *Cat.* No. 469.

Pedēsi, prostrate before Apis-bull, with text of Pedeḥor(?), son of Pefneferiu, below, IM.2784 [No. 45]. MALININE [etc.], *Cat.* i, pl. xxxvii [133], p. 106.

Pedēsi, son of Ra‘mosi, Goldsmith, IM.3316 [N.421/321; S.2226]. Id. ib. i, pl. xl [145], p. 114; see REVILLOUT, *Cat.* No. 506.

Pefteu‘aubaste, kneeling before Apis-bull and Nephthys, No. 200. MALININE [etc.], *Cat.* i, pl. xli [147], p. 115; text, CHASSINAT in *Rec. Trav.* xxii (1900), p. 21 [lxv].

Pemu, prostrate before Apis-bull, IM.2809 [N.421/32; No. 57]. MALININE [etc.], *Cat.* i, pl. xxxvii [134], pp. 106–7; text, CHASSINAT, op. cit. xxii (1900), p. 14 [xliv].

Penameny(?) (?), S.N.60 [No. 55]. MALININE [etc.], *Cat.* i, pl. xxxix [140], p. 110; see REVILLOUT, *Cat.* No. 418.

Ptaḥḥotp, son of Ḥor, *khet*-priest of Ḥa, etc., S.N.56 [No. 172]. MALININE [etc.], *Cat.* i, pl. xl [143], pp. 112–13.

Ptaḥḥotp, son of Nefertemḥotp, God's father, etc., IM.2782 [N.421/285; S.2222; No. 290]. Id. ib. i, pl. xlv [163], p. 126; see REVILLOUT, *Cat.* No. 498.

Ptaḥnakht, son of ʿAnkhefensekhmet(?) (?), S.N.43 [No. 54]. MALININE [etc.], *Cat.* i, pl. xliii [155], pp. 120–1.

Ptaḥnūfer, son of ʿAnkhpekhrod, IM.3587 [No. 24]. Id. ib. i, pl. xlii [154], p. 120; see REVILLOUT, *Cat.* No. 403.

Ptaḥwēr, Priest of the Temple of Ptaḥ, IM.3097 [N.677; S.1933]. MALININE [etc.], *Cat.* i, pl. xli [149], pp. 116–17; see PIERRET, *Cat.* No. 287.

Probably Dyn. XXV.

Amenardais, IM.3109 [No. 72]. MALININE [etc.], *Cat.* i, pl. xlv [166], p. 128.

Ameniʿaseb(?), IM.3028 [S.2218; No. 310]. Id. ib. i, pl. xlvi [167], p. 129.

Bekenrenef, IM.3102 [N.677; S.2025]. Id. ib. i, pl. xlv [165], pp. 127–8; incomplete text, CHASSINAT in *Rec. Trav.* xxi (1899), p. 61 [xi] (as Dyn. XXIV); see PIERRET, *Cat.* No. 301.

Espekafaiʿa, son of Ḥepardais and Irterau. (a) IM. 3080 [S.2198; No. 242], MALININE [etc.], *Cat.* i, pl. xlvi [170], p. 131; text, CHASSINAT in *Rec. Trav.* xxii (1900), pp. 167–8 [xci]. (b) IM.2661 [S.2199; No. 292], MALININE [etc.], *Cat.* i, pl. xlvii [171], p. 132; text, CHASSINAT, op. cit. xxii (1900), p. 174 [cxii].

Esptaḥ, son of Sekhmetka, both Overseers of the Necropolis, S.N.78 [No. 39]. MALININE [etc.], *Cat.* i, pl. xlvi [169], pp. 130–1; MARIETTE, *Sérapéum*, pl. 29 [upper left] (as Apis V of Dyn. XXII); names and titles, LIEBLEIN, *Dict.* No. 1201; see REVILLOUT, *Cat.* No. 413.

Ḥekaemḥēt, son of Pedes, Prophet of Ptaḥ, IM.3030 [No. 215]. MALININE [etc.], *Cat.* i, pl. xlix [179], pp. 136–7; text, CHASSINAT in *Rec. Trav.* xxii (1900), pp. 24–5 [lxxvi] (as Apis V of Dyn. XXII); ČERNÝ Notebook, 117, p. 3 [lower].

Kemkap, son of Pedekherbek, IM.2762 [No. 187]. MALININE [etc.], *Cat.* i, pl. xlv [164], p. 127.

Pashensekhmet, IM.3058 [No. 246]. Id. ib. i, pl. xlix [180], pp. 137–8.

Pedes, IM.2672 [No. 102]. Id. ib. i, pl. xlvii [174], p. 134; texts, CHASSINAT in *Rec. Trav.* xxii (1900), p. 17 [lv] (as Apis VI of Dyn. XXII).

Pedubaste, son of Ḥarsiēsi, IM.3010 [No. 378]. MALININE [etc.], *Cat.* i, pl. xlviii [176], p. 135; MARIETTE, *Sérapéum*, pl. 35 [right] (as Apis II of Dyn. XXV). Text, CHASSINAT in *Rec. Trav.* xxiii (1901), pp. 81–2 [cxxxvii]. See REVILLOUT, *Cat.* No. 531.

Shedsunefertem, son of Siptaḥ (owner of stela IM.2785, see below), IM.2807 [S.2190; No. 214]. MALININE [etc.], *Cat.* i, pl. xlvii [173], p. 133; text, CHASSINAT in *Rec. Trav.* xxii (1900), p. 24 [lxxv] (as Apis I of Dyn. XXVI).

Siptaḥ, Count, Prophet of Wert-ḥekau Mistress of the Palace, etc., IM.2785 [N.5442; S.2189; No. 439]. MALININE [etc.], *Cat.* i, pl. xlvii [172], pp. 132–3.

. . . amūn, son of ʿAnkhpefḥeri, with Isis and Nephthys, IM.2795 [S.1888; No. 229]. Id. ib. i, pl. xlix [181], p. 138; text, CHASSINAT in *Rec. Trav.* xxii (1900), pp. 163–4 [lxxxii].

Dyn. XXV to early Dyn. XXVI.

Ḥarnakht and Ḥarwoz, sons of Ptaḥḥotp, God's father, and Khnemnūfer, IM.2724 [No. 223]. MALININE [etc.], *Cat.* i, pl. xliv [161], pp. 124–5; text, ČERNÝ Notebook, 117, p. 3 [upper]; names, LIEBLEIN, *Dict.* No. 1221; see REVILLOUT, *Cat.* No. 470.

Ḥarwoz, Door-opener of Ptaḥ, IM.3116 [No. 20]. MALININE [etc.], *Cat.* i, pl. li [187], pp. 142–3.

Irterau, Door-opener of Ptaḥ, son of ʿAnkh-kh[ons], IM.3020 [No. 287]. Id. ib. i, pl. l [184], pp. 140–1; see REVILLOUT, *Cat.* No. 497.

Khaʿsuenēsi, son of Uzaḥor, IM.3139 [S.2083; No. 144]. MALININE [etc.], *Cat.* i, pl. lii [191], p. 145.

Nefer . . . ptaḥ, IM.3070 [No. 269]. Id. ib. i, pl. li [188], p. 143.

Paneḥesi, IM.2710 [N.421/150; S.2125; No. 154]. Id. ib. i, pl. xliv [162], p. 125.

Pede . . .(?), S.N.48. Id. ib. i, pl. l [186], p. 142; text, ČERNÝ Notebook, 117, p. 1 [lower].

Ptaḥardais(?), IM.4218 [S.1982; No. 92]. MALININE [etc.], *Cat.* i, pl. l [185], p. 141; see REVILLOUT, *Cat.* No. 437.

Ptaḥḥotp, God's father, IM.3588 [No. 138]. MALININE [etc.], *Cat.* i, pl. li [190], pp. 144–5.

Shedsunefertem, IM.3586 [N.421/271; No. 280]. Id. ib. i, pl. li [189], p. 144; text, CHASSINAT in *Rec. Trav.* xxii (1900), p. 173 [cx] (as Apis IV of Dyn. XXII); see REVILLOUT, *Cat.* No. 495.

Siptaḥ, IM.3312 [S.2209; No. 329]. MALININE [etc.], *Cat.* i, pl. xlix [182], p. 139.

Wenptaḥ, IM.5949 [N.421/303; S.2216; No. 304]. Id. ib. i, pl. l [183], p. 140.

Dyn. XXVI.

ʿAḥmosi . . ., son of Psammethek-sirēʿ, both Charioteers, N.5442/4130 [S.2278]. Text, CHASSINAT in *Rec. Trav.* xxi (1899), p. 63 [xvii]; names and titles, LIEBLEIN, *Dict.* No. 1260; see PIERRET, *Cat.* No. 311.

Amenḥotp, IM.3577 [S.2016].

ʿAnkh-ḥap, son of Ēsiemḥēt (mother), N.677 [S.2211]. Text, CHASSINAT, op. cit. xxi (1899), p. 60 [viii]; see PIERRET, *Cat.* No. 295.

ʿAshʿash, son of Paensupesez, IM.2860 [N.677]. Text, CHASSINAT, op. cit. xxi (1899), p. 62 [xiv] (as Apis V of Dyn. XXVI); see PIERRET, Cat. No. 306.

Dwensupanūfer, son of Ḥarwoz and Khaʿsumin, IM.2864 [N.677]. Text, CHASSINAT, op. cit. xxi (1899), pp. 62–3 [xv] (as Apis V of Dyn. XXVI); ČERNÝ Notebook, 117, p. 10 [upper]; see PIERRET, *Cat.* No. 308.

Ḥaremmaʿkheru, son of Ḥarnakht, IM.3135.

Ḥarwoz, Prophet of Horus, Noble (*sʿḥ*) of Ḥebnu, with Ptaḥ-Sokari and bull-headed Apis at top, IM.4065. VERCOUTTER, *Textes*, pl. xvii, pp. 109–12; text, ČERNÝ Notebook, 117, p. 6 [lower].

Imut, son of Zeamūnefʿankh, IM.2862 [S.2227, No. 226]. See REVILLOUT, *Cat.* No. 471.

Iʿoḥweben(?), God's father, IM.5941 [S.2085; No. 228]. See id. ib. No. 473.

Khnemebrēʿ, Director of the estates, *wnrw*-priest in Letopolis, etc., son of Uzaḥor-resnet and Pespermeḥ, IM.4193.

Neferebrēʿ-meryptaḥ, Prophet of the Ram of Mendes, dedicated by son Weḥebrēʿ-mererptaḥ, same title, IM.4042. Text, WILKINSON MSS. xxiv. 7 [right lower]; names and titles, LIEBLEIN, *Dict.* No. 1213.

Neferseshem-psammethek, *waʿb*-priest of the Temples of Memphis, son of Weḥebrēʿ-mer(y)ptaḥ [hieroglyphs], *sem*-priest, Secretary of the Temple of Ptaḥ, etc., and Ēsiwert [hieroglyphs], IM.4067 [N. 418; S.2254]. RICHER, *Le Nu*, fig. 155 [upper]; DEVÉRIA squeezes, 6165, ii. 107; ARCHIVES phot. E.570; deceased kneeling, GROUSSET, *The Civilizations of the East*, i, fig. 44. Names and titles, LIEBLEIN in *Rev. Arch.* N.S. xviii (1868), pp. 274–5; id. *Dict.* No. 1207. See DE ROUGÉ, *Notice sommaire* (1876), p. 61.

Pedepep [hieroglyphs], son of Pedeptaḥ, Prophet of Ptaḥ and Bubastis Mistress of ʿAnkhtaui, and Neferḥeres [hieroglyphs], IM.3098 [No. 209]. Text, CHASSINAT in *Rec. Trav.* xxii (1900), pp. 23–4 [lxxii].

Pedes [hieroglyphs], Craftsman, IM.3111 [N.421/522; No. 321]. Text, id. ib. xxii (1900), p. 175 [cxv].

Pefteuʿaukhons [hieroglyphs], IM.3096 [N.679]. Text, id. ib. xxi (1899), p. 65 [xxi]; see PIERRET, *Cat.* No. 317.

Psammethek, Greatest of the physicians of Upper and Lower Egypt, etc. (tomb, see *supra*, p. 649), perhaps temp. Amasis, IM.4084 [No. 338]. Text, CHASSINAT, op. cit. xxii (1900), pp. 177–8 [cxxii] (as Apis V of Dyn. XXVI); MASPERO in *Ann. Serv.* i (1900), p. 185 (by Chassinat); see REVILLOUT, *Cat.* No. 512.

Psammethek, God's father, Prophet, N.421/12 [No. 260]. Text, CHASSINAT, op. cit. xxii (1900), pp. 170–1 [ci]; see REVILLOUT, *Cat.* No. 486.

Ptaḥḥotp, Secretary of Ra-setau, Prophet of Amūn, etc., son of Pedēsi and Sit-ḥap [hieroglyphs], IM.4062 [N.421/328; No. 344]. Text, CHASSINAT, op. cit. xxii (1900), pp. 178–9 [cxxiv]; see REVILLOUT, *Cat.* No. 515.

Ptaḥnūfer, son of Diptaḥiau [hieroglyphs], IM.3136 [N.421; No. 306]. Text, ČERNÝ Notebook, 117, p. 13 [top]; see REVILLOUT, *Cat.* No. 499.

Uzaḥor, son of Ḏḥutardais, IM.2645 [S.2144; No. 189].

Weḥebrēʿ-unnūfer and Weḥebrēʿ-mer(y)ptaḥ [hieroglyphs], sons of Menkhib-weḥebrēʿ, and others, IM.4217 [N.421/339; No. 352]. Text, CHASSINAT, op. cit. xxiii (1901), p. 76 [cxxviii] (as Apis IV of Dyn. XXVI); see REVILLOUT, *Cat.* No. 522.

Weḥebrēʿ . . ., Inspector of *sem*-priests, etc., son of Sit-ḥap [hieroglyphs] (mother), IM.3095.

Zeptaḥefʿankh, *wnrw*-priest in Letopolis, etc., son of Sinūhet [hieroglyphs], IM.4189.

Zeptaḥefʿankh, Door-opener of the Temple of Ptaḥ, son of Taḥert [hieroglyphs] (mother), probably temp. Psammetikhos I. Names and titles, LIEBLEIN, *Dict.* No. 1143.

Zeubastefʿankh, Royal scribe, son of Pedēsi and Irterau, No. 435 (probably).

Name uncertain, IM.2651 [N.421/307; No. 296].

Name lost, fragment, temp. Amasis (probably year 4 or 5), IM.4113. VERCOUTTER, *Textes*, pl. ii, pp. 16–26.

Dyn. XXVI–XXVII.

ʿAḥmosi, Overseer of *waʿb*-priests of Sekhmet, etc., son of Weḥebrēʿ-[mery]ptaḥ [hieroglyphs], IM.4108.

ʿAḥmosi, son of Weḥebrēʿ-ḥarenpe [hieroglyphs], both Charioteers, and Setyerboni, IM.4126 [N.421/570; No. 449]. Text, CHASSINAT in *Rec. Trav.* xxv (1903), p. 57 [clxxiii]; see REVILLOUT, *Cat.* No. 549.

ʿAnkhef(en)mut [hieroglyphs], God's father, Secretary of Ra-setau, son of Senbef(?), Prophet of Amūn, and Tashensekhmet [hieroglyphs], IM.4089.

Diptaḥiau [hieroglyphs], God's father, son of Pedēsi and ʿAnkh-tes-ḥert [hieroglyphs](?), IM. 5343 [N.421/344; No. 348]. Text, CHASSINAT, op. cit. xxii (1900), p. 179 [cxxv] (as Apis V of Dyn. XXVI); names and titles, LIEBLEIN, *Dict.* No. 1229.

Ḥaremmaᶜet, God's father, *wnrw*-priest in Letopolis, IM.4079.

Imḥōtep, Prophet of Serapis, etc., IM.4106.

Mer(y)ptaḥ, *wnrw*-priest in Letopolis, Prophet of all the gods in Khanūfer, etc., son of Pashenptaḥ, *wnrw*-priest, etc., and Mernubtiotes, IM.4030. VERCOUTTER, *Textes*, pl. xii, pp. 82–7 (as temp. Amasis, or more likely year 34 of Darius I); text, ČERNÝ Notebook, 117, p. 24 [lower].

Neferebrēᶜ, son of Shedsunefertem, both *wp-nṯrwy*, etc., IM.4119. One name and titles, JELÍNKOVÁ in *Ann. Serv.* lv (1958), p. 124 [96].

Pashenptaḥ ᶜAnkh-ḥap, son of Esptaḥ and Irterau, IM.4043 [N.421/605].

Shep(en)-iusᶜas, God's father, Prophet, son of Painmu and Sit-ḥap, IM.4020. Text, ČERNÝ Notebook, 117, p. 13 [bottom].

Weḥebrēᶜ-mer(y)neit, Prophet of Ḥeḳet Mistress of Ḥerwēr and Nekhbet Mistress of Nekheb, Deputy of the Temple of Ptaḥ, etc., son of Uzaḥorresnet, Chief lector-priest, and Hert, Sistrum-player of Sekhmet, top part lost, IM.4112 [N.421/620; No. 473]. VERCOUTTER, op. cit. pl. xiv, pp. 93–9; text, CHASSINAT, op. cit. xxv (1903), pp. 59–61 [clxxix] (as Apis of year 34 of Darius I).

Weḥebrēᶜ-meryptaḥ, Overseer of the Two Granaries, Overseer of scribes of the Great Prison, son of Irterau (mother), IM.4073 [N.421/324].

Weḥebrēᶜ-nebpeḥti, son of Semtu-tefnakht, IM.4066.

Dyn. XXVII.

Fragment of official stela, IM.4198 [N.421/644]. VERCOUTTER in *Mitt. Kairo*, 16 (1958), Taf. xxxi, pp. 333–45 with fig. 1.

Ptolemaic.

ᶜAḥmosi, Prophet of the Sanctuary () of Ramesses of the Temple () of Memphis, Prophet of Sekhmet of the *mert* of Saḥurēᶜ, etc., son of Herib and Tiamūn, temp. Ptolemy V Epiphanes, C 316 [No. 427]. Text, CHASSINAT in *Rec. Trav.* xxv (1903), pp. 51–2 [clxii]; OTTO in *Ä.Z.* 81 (1956), pp. 119–20 [1], cf. 109; see BOREUX, *Guide*, i, p. 174.

Ḏḥuti-herib, *waᶜb*-priest of the Temples of Memphis, etc., IM.6.

Esnuwēr, *waᶜb*-priest of the Temples of Memphis, Prophet of the statues of Nektanebos II in the Temple of the domain of Great Sekhmet 'at the head of the valley', etc., son of Unnūfer, Prophet of the statues of Nektanebos II in various temples, Prophet of Menes and Teti, etc., and Semsem, Sistrum-player of Anubis upon his mountain, temp. Ptolemy IV Philopator and V Epiphanes, IM.3689. DEVÉRIA squeezes, 6169, i. 46; text, CHASSINAT, op. cit. xxi (1899), pp. 69–70 [xxxii]; OTTO, op. cit. pp. 127–8 [10], cf. 110; some titles, see DE MEULENAERE in *Chron. d'Ég.* xxxv (1960), pp. 94–5 [6]; see PIERRET, *Cat.* No. 328.

Ḥepmeneḥ, son of Ḥarwoz and Renpet, hieroglyphic and demotic texts, IM.3345 [N.421/526]. Text, REVILLOUT in *Revue Égyptologique*, vi (1891), pl. 1 facing p. 104, cf. pp. 95–6 (as No. 59).

Iᶜoḥ, IM.3717.

Irtḥarerau, S.N.1. WILKINSON MSS. xxiv. 36, with squeeze.

Thaiḥepimu, Door-opener of Apis, son of Irᶜaḥap, IM.4167.

Unnūfer, son of Pashentiḥet, hieroglyphic and demotic texts, IM.16. Text, REVILLOUT, op. cit. pl. 2 after p. 104, cf. pp. 97–8 (as No. 117).

Weḥebrēʿ(em)khebi, Chief lector-priest, etc., son of Ḥarwoz and Ēsiwert, and others, S.N.79.

Name illegible, Prophet of the statues of Nektanebos II of the temple in the domain of Osiris Lord of Ra-setau, IM.176 [N.421/601]. Title, DE MEULENAERE, op. cit. p. 95 [7].

Procession of different aspects of Horus, and effaced text below, IM.3 [S.1006]. Short texts, ČERNÝ Notebook, 117, p. 6 [upper].

Date uncertain. Mostly Dyn. XXVI–XXX.

ʿAḥmosi, son of Uzaḥorresnet, both *wnrw*-priests in Letopolis, Prophets of Buto Mistress of Pe and Dep, Overseers of the town, etc., and Her(?), Sistrum-player of Neith Mistress of Sais, IM.4012. Text, ČERNÝ Notebook, 117, p. 9.

ʿAnkh-ḥap, Prophet of Harpocrates, etc., son of Unnūfer, E.6246.

ʿAnkhpefḥeri, IM.3758 [N.677].

ʿAth, *wnrw*-priest, son of Pakha and Renpetnefert. Text, GOODWIN MSS. 31279, 30 [right]; names, LIEBLEIN, *Dict.* No. 1204.

Ḏḥutiptaḥ, God's father, son of ʿAnkh-unnūfer, S.1889 [No. 235]. Text, CHASSINAT in *Rec. Trav.* xxii (1900), p. 165 [lxxxvii].

Diptaḥiau and Imḥōtep, IM.3729.

Duarēʿ ʿAnkh-ḥor, son of Pefteuʿaubaste and Meḥytwērt-nebtʿankh, IM.4135 [No. 143]. Text, id. ib. xxii (1900), p. 18 [lviii] (as S.4135).

Gemniḥarbak, *sem*-priest, Prophet of Ptaḥ, son of Neferebrēʿ and Shepenubaste, IM.4041 [No. 420]. Text, id. ib. xxv (1903), p. 50 [clvii]; see REVILLOUT, *Cat.* No. 537.

Ḥarbes, son of Pashenḥatḥor and Irterau, IM.4083 [N.421/579].

Ḥaremḥab, Treasurer of the King of Lower Egypt, etc., son of ʿAnkh-ḥap, on *recto*, and Psammethek-sonb, Prophet of the statue of Amasis, etc., on *verso*, IM.4115. Name and title, JELÍNKOVÁ in *Ann. Serv.* lv (1958), p. 124 [98] (as Pasetemsonb).

Ḥarkhebi, son of Te(n)tḥap (mother), IM.4071. See PIERRET, *Cat.* No. 293.

Ḥarmaʿkheru, [*wnrw*-priest] in Letopolis, etc., son of Weḥebrēʿ . . ., N.421/698 [S.N.50].

Ḥarsiēsi, son of Sekhmetnefert (mother), IM.4082.

Ḥarsiēsi, son of Ḥekaemsaf, both God's fathers, IM.4085 [N.421/613; No. 464]. Text, CHASSINAT, op. cit. xxv (1903), pp. 57–8 [clxxiv]; see REVILLOUT, *Cat.* No. 555.

Ḥarsiēsi, *wnrw*-priest in Letopolis, etc., son of Psammethek. Names and titles, LIEBLEIN, *Dict.* No. 1209.

Ḥor, son of Thesubastepert, IM.3145 [No. 327].

Ḥor, God's father, *wnrw*-priest in Letopolis, IM.4015. One name, JELÍNKOVÁ, op. cit. p. 124 [91].

Irʿaḥor, son of Pairkap Psammethek-[meryneit], both God's fathers, Directors of the estates, etc., S.N.47. Text, ČERNÝ Notebook, 117, p. 23 [lower]; name and two titles, JELÍNKOVÁ, op. cit. p. 124 [97] (as Irʿa).

Kanūfer, son of Tutu-imḥōtep, IM.4075 [N.421/662; No. 442]. Text, CHASSINAT, op. cit. xxv (1903), p. 54 [clxvi].

Khaʿemwēset, son of Pemu and Sit-ḥapʿankh, IM.129 [N.421/658]. See PIERRET, *Cat.* No. 311 bis.

Nefʿarud, son of Perka, IM.5427 [S.4045; No. 251]. Text, CHASSINAT, op. cit. xxii (1900), pp. 169–70 [xcvii]; names, LIEBLEIN, *Dict.* No. 1226; see REVILLOUT, *Cat.* No. 484.

Nekhten . . ., IM.4122 [N.421/404; No. 423]. Text, CHASSINAT, op. cit. xxv (1903), p. 51 [clix]; see REVILLOUT, *Cat.* No. 538.

Painmu, God's father, Prophet, IM.4216 [N.677; No. 204]. Text, CHASSINAT, op. cit. xxii (1900), p. 22 [lxviii] (as N.677/4210); see PIERRET, *Cat.* No. 288.

Pakap, son of Ptaḥḥotp, IM.4191.

Pashenptaḥ, God's father, *sem*-priest, etc., son of Ḥaremakhet, IM.4026. Names and titles, LIEBLEIN, *Dict.* No. 1234.

Pashenptaḥ, son of Mer(y)ptaḥ, both God's fathers, *wnrw*-priests in Letopolis, and Khedeb-yerboni, IM.4117. Text, WILKINSON MSS. xxiv. 17 [lower].

Pashe(n)sekhmet-ʿankh-ḥeka(?) (?), IM.4210 [N.421/648]. See PIERRET, *Cat.* No. 318.

Pashentiḥet, *wp-nṯrwy*, Prophet of Buto Opener of the Ways, etc., son of ʿAnkh-ḥap, IM.3732.

Pashentiḥet, son of Pemu and Ēsireshti, IM.4005 [No. 425]. Text, CHASSINAT, op. cit. xxv (1903), p. 51 [clxi]; names and titles, LIEBLEIN, *Dict.* No. 1032.

Pedubaste, son of Pedenefertem, both God's fathers, *sem*-priests, etc., No. 78. Text, ČERNÝ Notebook, 117, p. 11 [lower].

Pefteuʿauēsi, God's father, Secretary of Ra-setau, son of Painmu, IM.4123.

Pefteuʿaukhons, son of Shepenubaste, IM.47 [N.421/473; S.993].

Psammethek, son of ʿAnkh-(the)kerti and Tathenef, IM.4010.

Psammethek-sonb, son of Pedenebwen and Irterau, IM.4047.

Psammethek-sonb, *fkt*-priest of the Temple of Ptaḥ, son of Neferebrēʿ-[mery]ptaḥ, with Zeḥo, *fkt*-priest of the Temple of Ptaḥ, IM.4105. Some names and titles, JELÍNKOVÁ in *Ann. Serv.* lv (1958), p. 124 [92–5].

Ptaḥḥotp, IM.36.

Ptaḥḥotp, son of Ptaḥwēr and Mery(t)ptaḥ, IM.43.

Ptaḥḥotp, God's father, *sem*-priest, son of Esunnūfer, IM.3431.

Ptaḥḥotp and brothers, sons of Sekhmetardais (mother), S.N.62. Text, ČERNÝ Notebook, 117, p. 2 [lower].

Ptaḥḥotp, son of Neferḥōtep, God's father, etc. Names and titles, LIEBLEIN, *Dict.* No. 1206.

Ptaḥwēr, son of Esbanebded, both God's fathers, *wp-nṯrwy*, etc., IM.4127 [No. 408]. Text, CHASSINAT, op. cit. xxiii (1901), p. 89 [clii].

Senbef, IM.37.

Senbef, son of Ptaḥḥotp, IM.3040. Names, LIEBLEIN, *Dict.* No. 1227.

Shedsunefertem, God's father, *wp-nṯrwy*, etc., son of Ptaḥḥotp, God's father, IM.4091. Names and titles, id. ib. No. 1228.

Thaiḥepimu sic, Door-opener of Serapis, etc., son of Psammethek, IM.139.

Thaiḥepimu, Head of door-openers of Serapis, etc., son of ʿAnkh-ḥap and Ēsireshti, IM.4209.

Unnūfer and ʿAnemḥo, both God's fathers and Prophets, sons of Pedenefertem, IM.78.

Unnūfer Psammethek-ibsonb [hieroglyphs], son of Basa [hieroglyphs], IM.4006.

Unnūfer, Prophet, son of Psammethek-sonb and Irterau. Names and titles, id. ib. No. 1152.

Weḥebrēʿ Amentefnakht [hieroglyphs], son of Psammethek and Tanefertem, IM.4022.

Zeamūnefʿankh [hieroglyphs], IM.5943 [N.421/411; No. 261]. Text, CHASSINAT, op. cit. xxii (1900), p. 171 [cii] (as Apis I of Dyn. XXVI).

Ze-ēsefʿankh, son of Pentahayet [hieroglyphs], IM.3099 [N.677]. Text, id. ib. xxi (1899), p. 59 [iii]; see PIERRET, *Cat.* No. 284.

Zeḥo, son of Ḥepmen [hieroglyphs] and Khedeb-yerboni, IM.136.

Zeḥo, son of Uzaḥor, IM.4163 [N.421/408]. Text, ČERNÝ Notebook, 117, p. 4 [upper].

Names uncertain or lost. IM.4061, originally with cartouches of Saḥurēʿ, now completely effaced. IM.4244, son of Ḥarbes [hieroglyphs]. N.679/3094 [S.1890]; text, CHASSINAT, op. cit. xxi (1899), pp. 59–60 [v]; see PIERRET, *Cat.* No. 290.

ʿAḥmosi [hieroglyphs] (good name), son of Mutardais [hieroglyphs], S.N.10 [No. 440]. Text, CHASSINAT, op. cit. xxv (1903), pp. 53–4 [clxiv].

In other museums

Late Period unless otherwise dated

Antwerp, Museum Vleeshuis.

Man kneeling before Apis-bull, No. 79.1.457. *Oudheidkundige Musea. Vleeshuis. Cat. viii, Egypte* (1959), pl. ix [11], p. 26.

Berlin Museum.

Iufʿa (same man as Louvre, IM.4076, see *supra*), son of Pashenptaḥ, *kʿḥ*-priest, etc., and Neitiḳert, fragment, temp. Darius I, No. 3423. Text, BURCHARDT in *Ä.Z.* 49 (1911), p. 72 [3]. See *Ausf. Verz.* p. 312.

Stela inscribed on both sides, of a son of Paneferrekh(?), No. 2144 (East). See id. ib. p. 312.

Bologna, Museo Civico.

Apis-bull and 4 lines of demotic, No. 1946. See KMINEK-SZEDLO, *Catalogo di Antichità Egizie* (1895), p. 215; CURTO, *L'Egitto antico* (1961), p. 151 [394].

Brussels, Musées Royaux d'Art et d'Histoire.

Ḥarsiēsi, son of [Pa]iuenḥor [hieroglyphs] and Ḳewenēsi [hieroglyphs], Dyn. XXVI, E.3468 (formerly in Prince Napoleon and Ravestein Collns.). DE MEULENAERE, *Het leven na de dood in het Oude Egypte* (Tentoonstelling van 21 juni tot 28 september 1969. Provinciaal Gallo-Romeins Museum—Tongeren), No. 71 with pl. 14; LIMME in *Chron. d'Ég.* xlvii (1972), fig. 3, pp. 103–9; id. *Stèles égyptiennes*, No. 16 with fig. See DE MEESTER DE RAVESTEIN, *Musée de Ravestein*, i (1871), p. 28 [25].

Cairo Museum.

ʿAnkh-ḥor [hieroglyphs] Weḥebrēʿ, Overseer of infantry, etc., son of Peḳen [hieroglyphs] and Tadeusiri, Dyn. XXVI–XXVII, re-used in Monastery of Apa Jeremias, JE 43204. VERCOUTTER, *Textes*, pl. xix, pp. 117–21; QUIBELL, *Saqqara (1908–10)*, pl. lxxxiii, p. 146.

Ḥepmen [hieroglyphs], son of Ḥepardais [hieroglyphs] and Takhyay [hieroglyphs], Dyn. XXVI–XXVII, CG 31086. SPIEGELBERG, *Die demotischen Inschriften*, Taf. i, pp. 12–13.

Ka, Scribe of divine books, Secretary, son of Pedeneit, re-used in Monastery of Apa Jeremias, JE 40043. Text, QUIBELL, *Saqqara (1907–8)*, p. 16.

Pedepenpen, son of Es-zad and Irterau. LANZONE, *Diz.* pl. cci [2], p. 530.

Pedēsi, God's father, Secretary of Ra-setau, son of Pashenptaḥ, God's father, and Tahaib(?), with hieroglyphic and demotic texts, CG 31157. SPIEGELBERG, op. cit. Taf. xx, pp. 63–4.

Psammethek, son of Pedeḥarkhebi [ ] and Irterau, JE 15037. LANZONE, *Diz.* pl. cciii [1], pp. 531–2. Names, LIEBLEIN, *Dict.* No. 1159.

Ptaḥḥotp, God's father, *wp-ntrwy*, etc., son of Nekau-mer(y)neteru and Renpetnefert, probably Dyn. XXVII, JE 20014. VERCOUTTER, *Textes*, pl. xviii, pp. 113–16. Text, PIEHL in *Ä.Z.* xxv (1887), pp. 122–3 [xlvii] (as No. 2316). See MASPERO, *Guide*, p. 472 [4496].

Siēsi (?), Inspector of *sem*-priests, Secretary of Ra-setau, etc., son of ʿAnkh-unnūfer, Secretary of the Great Place, etc. Text, PIEHL, *Inscr. hiéro.* 3 Sér. lxxxiii [S].

Unnūfer, JE 4889.

Chicago, Oriental Institute.

Mersurēʿ, Scribe of the Lord of the Two Lands, New Kingdom, No. 9375.

Grenoble, Musée de Peinture et de Sculpture.

Pedēsi, son of Irḥepiaut and Tent, No. 14 [Inv. 1950]. KUÉNY, *L'Égypte ancienne au Musée de Grenoble*, fig. on 15th p. [3]; DEVÉRIA squeezes, 6167, ii. 151. Text, MORET in *Revue Égyptologique*, N.S. i (1919), p. 172 [x]. See TRESSON, *Catalogue descriptif des antiquités égyptiennes de la Salle Saint-Ferriol* (repr. from *Bulletin de l'Académie delphinale*, 6 Sér. iv [1933]), pp. 21–2 [3].

Hildesheim, Roemer-Pelizaeus-Museum.

Zeptaḥefʿankh and Ḥarsiēsi, sons of Thonūfer, all God's fathers, *sem*-priests, etc., No. 2372. LIMME in *Chron. d'Ég.* xlvii (1972), fig. 1, pp. 83–92. See IPPEL and ROEDER, *Die Denkmäler des Pelizaeus-Museums zu Hildesheim*, p. 90; KAYSER, *Die ägyptischen Altertümer im Roemer-Pelizaeus-Museum in Hildesheim* (1973), p. 120.

Leningrad, State Hermitage Museum.

Irefʿaenubaste, No. 1095. Text, STRUVE, *Etyudy po istorii severnogo Prichernomor'ya, Kavkaza i Sredney Azii*, pp. 305 [55], cf. 290 (as Ptolemaic). See GOLÉNISCHEFF, *Inventaire de la collection égyptienne* (1891), p. 167.

Mesḥotp, son of Ptaḥardais, No. 1096. Text, STRUVE, op. cit. pp. 305 [53], cf. 290 (as Ptolemaic). Names, LIEBLEIN, *Dict.* No. 2549. See GOLÉNISCHEFF, op. cit. p. 167 (as Dyn. XXVI).

London, University College Museum.

Kha . . . . . ., Mourner of Apis, No. 14610.

Pedubaste, son of Psammethek, formerly in Amherst and Harding Smith Collns., No. 15807. Two names, LIEBLEIN, *Dict.* No. 2382. See *Sotheby Sale Cat.* (AMHERST), June 13–17, 1921, No. 238 [3]; id. November 1–2, 1922, No. 220.

Pefteuʿauneit [hieroglyphs], son of Pakap [hieroglyphs] and Ēsiardais [hieroglyphs], No. 15993.

Marseilles, Musée d'archéologie.

Peḳʿa [hieroglyphs], son of Ḥarkhebi [hieroglyphs] and Tiamūn [hieroglyphs], before bull-headed Apis, Imḥōtep and Ptaḥ, Dyn. XXX, No. 246. *Le Nil et la société égyptienne* (Musée Borély, Marseille, 6 décembre–1er mars 1973), No. 173 with fig.; WILDUNG, *Imhotep und Amenhotep*, pp. 40–2 [19] with Taf. v and fig.; id. *Egyptian Saints. Deification in Pharaonic Egypt*, fig. 30; CAIRO, CENTRE OF DOCUMENTATION photo. S.R., Box 173, P. 5019. Text, MASPERO in *Rec. Trav.* xiii (1890), pp. 123–4 [46]. See id. *Catalogue du Musée Égyptien de Marseille* (1889), p. 28 [46].

Vienna, Kunsthistorisches Museum.

Diptaḥiau, *wnrw*-priest, etc., Inv.5833. REINISCH, *Miramar*, Taf. xxxviii, pp. 254–5 [16].

Pedeḥarpekhrod, son of Pede . . . [hieroglyphs] and Zeubastesʿankh, Inv.5852. Id. ib. Taf. xxxvi, pp. 253–4 [14].

Zeḥo [hieroglyphs] Nebʿankh [hieroglyphs], son of Ḥarmosi [hieroglyphs], both Door-openers of Ptaḥ, and Tashentiḥet [hieroglyphs], Inv.6126.

Mentioning Hager(?) [hieroglyphs], son of Pemu [hieroglyphs], Inv.5853. Text, id. ib. Taf. xl [5], pp. 257–8 [32].

. . . beḥēsi . . . [hieroglyphs], son of Ptaḥnaḳay(?) [hieroglyphs], Inv.5824. Id. ib. Taf. xxxvii, p. 254 [15].

Others, Inv.5827, 5831, 5841. Inv.5831, id. ib. Taf. xxxv, p. 253 [3].

Present location unknown

Psammethek (good name), son or husband of Te(nt)ubaste [hieroglyphs], fragment, Late Period, at one time in Verlaque Colln. Texts, MASPERO in *Mélanges d'archéologie égyptienne et assyrienne*, ii (1875), pp. 212–13 [18].

Panūfer [hieroglyphs]. MARIETTE, *Fouilles*, pl. li [top left].

Apis-bull in shrine being conveyed in bark on wheels, Ptolemaic or Roman. FARAG in *J.E.A.* 61 (1975), pl. xxiii [1], pp. 165–6. (Others, see *supra*, p. 573, where the date is to be corrected, and Mît Rahîna, Embalming House of Apis-bulls.)

OBJECTS CONNECTED WITH THE SERAPEUM

Statues.

Base with cartouches of Ramesses II, granite. Cartouches, MARIETTE, *Mastabas*, p. 445 [lower middle].

Khaʿemwēset (son of Ramesses II). (a) Holding naos with statue of bull-headed Apis, with a princess (text lost) in relief by left leg, lower part, in court of the house of the Service des Antiquités at Ṣaqqâra; DRIOTON in *Ann. Serv.* xli (1942), pl. i, pp. 21–7; princess, see DESROCHES-NOBLECOURT in SCHAEFFER, *Ugaritica III*, p. 202 with note 2; see GOMAÀ, *Chaemwese* [etc.], p. 80 [33], cf. Abb. 12 [a]; KATER-SIBBES and VERMASEREN, *Apis, I*, p. 10 [26], cf. pl. xxi (from DRIOTON). (b) Statue-base, re-used in Monastery of Apa Jeremias; text, QUIBELL, *Saqqara (1908–10)*, pp. 45–6, cf. *(1907–8)*, p. 2; see GOMAÀ, op. cit. p. 81 [37]. (c) Statue-base, granite; id. ib. p. 81 [39] with Taf. iii, Abb. 14 [a].

Raʿmeses-emperamūn [hieroglyphs], Steward and Overseer of the Treasury of his lord

Khaʿemwēset (son of Ramesses II), holding naos, headless, temp. Ramesses II, in court of the house of the Service des Antiquités at Ṣaqqâra. DRIOTON, op. cit. pl. ii, pp. 27–35. See GOMAÀ, op. cit. p. 80 [34], cf. Abb. 12 [b]; KATER-SIBBES and VERMASEREN, op. cit. pp. 10–11 [27], cf. pl. xxi (from DRIOTON).

Man kneeling with naos of Ptaḥ-Sokari-Osiris, with remains of text, late Ramesside, in Vienna Mus. Inv.5773. HALL in *Apollo*, lxxxv (1967), fig. 12, p. 95; *Meisterwerke. Führer durch das Kunsthistorische Museum*, 1 (1958 and 1968), fig. 3 [middle]; KOMORZYNSKI, *Das Erbe des alten Ägypten*, Abb. 13 [middle]; see REINISCH, *Miramar*, pp. 241–2 [28], 257 [31], cf. Taf. xl [4] (naos); *Uebersicht* (1895), p. 34 [XIII]; (1923), p. 9 [XIII].

Block-statue, text effaced, granite, late New Kingdom, in Brussels, Mus. Roy. E.2147. CAPART in *Bull. Mus. Roy.* 2 Sér. iii (1910), p. 15 with fig.

Triple block-statue of Amenḥotp, Penamūn, and Tairi-sherit (woman), granite, Ramesside, probably from here, in Louvre, N.435. VANDIER, *Manuel*, iii, pl. clii [5], p. 672.

Ptaḥʿaba, Guardian of the house, double block-statue with remains of text, fragmentary, Dyn. XXVI, probably from here, in Louvre, E.17449. See BOTHMER, *Eg. Sculp.* p. 36.

Statue-base of Psammethek, son of Pefḥerinūter and ʿArptaḥ-ḥap, Late Period. Text, MARIETTE, *Mastabas*, p. 457 [H 15].

Apis-bull protecting man kneeling with offering-table, heads lost, Late Period, in Cairo Mus. CG 683. BORCHARDT, *Statuen*, iii, Bl. 125, p. 28; MASPERO, *Eg. Art*, pl. facing p. 112, cf. pp. 115 and 116 with note; id. *Essais*, fig. 37, p. 134 with note 2 (description in both confused with Cairo CG 676).

Ḥeresʿankh, Prophetess of Philotera (daughter of Ptolemy I Soter), etc., daughter of Neferebrēʿ, Prophet, and Ḥeresʿankh, headless, Ptolemaic, in Louvre, N.2456. RICHER, *Le Nu*, fig. 173; text, PIERRET, *Rec. inscr.* ii, p. 83 [top] (with sketch); BRUGSCH, *Thes.* 946; names and some titles, LIEBLEIN, *Dict.* No. 2520; see PIERRET, *Cat.* No. 33; BOREUX, *Guide*, ii, p. 491; VANDIER, *Guide* (1948), p. 80; (1952), p. 82; (1973), pp. 154–5.

Man or god, head, arms, and lower parts of legs lost, with text on back pillar, Ptolemaic, probably from here, in Stafford Colln. BOTHMER, *Eg. Sculp.* pl. 120, pp. 168–9 [129].

Head ('Boston Green Head'), with remains of text on back pillar, green schist, Ptolemaic, formerly in Prince Napoleon Colln., now in Boston Mus. 04.1749. FERRI PISANI in *Gazette des Beaux-Arts*, i (1859), fig. on p. 281 [upper] (reversed), cf. p. 275; LENORMANT in ib. xxiii (1867), fig. on p. 31 (reversed); DELBRÜCK, *Antike Porträts*, Taf. 12, p. xxviii; *Handbook* (1910), fig. on p. 34 [upper]; (1920), fig. on p. 53; (1925), fig. on p. 26; (1930 and 1935), fig. on p. 25; (1947 and 1956), fig. on p. 26; (1964), fig. on p. 201 [top]; (1976), fig. on p. 177 [bottom]; DUNHAM in *Boston Mus. Bull.* xxxv (1937), figs. on p. 71, cf. p. 70; id. *The Egyptian Department and its Excavations*, fig. 12; SMITH, *Anc. Eg.* (1942), fig. 101; (1952), fig. 100; (1960), fig. 113; id. in *Boston Mus. Bull.* xlvii (1949), fig. 6, p. 26; id. *Art . . . Anc. Eg.* pl. 185, p. 252; HALL in HAMMERTON, *Universal History of the World*, ii, fig. on p. 1020 [upper right]; PIJOÁN, *Summa Artis*, iii (1945), fig. 637; WOLF, *Kunst*, Abb. 662, p. 628; id. *Die Kultur Ägyptens*, Abb. 85; ATARASHI, *Egypt*, pl. 69; WOLDERING, *Götter und Pharaonen*, Abb. 114; BOTHMER, *Eg. Sculp.* pls. 100, 101 [272], pp. 138–40; id. in *The Brooklyn Museum Annual*, iv (1962–3), fig. 8, p. 46; TERRACE in *The Connoisseur*, clxix (1968), col. pl. 3 on p. 120, cf. p. 118; McKEON and CARR, *Portraiture in Ancient Egypt* (Gallery Guide, Mus. of Fine Arts, Boston, Nov. 28, 1972–Jan. 7, 1973), fig. 16; BRECKENRIDGE, *Likeness. A Conceptual History of Ancient Portraiture*, fig. 88.

Divinities.

Osiris, basalt, Dyn. XXVI, in Cairo Mus. CG 38368. Text, DARESSY, *Statues*, p. 100; MARIETTE, *Mon. div.* pl. 77 [e] (as bronze); DE ROUGÉ, *Inscr. hiéro.* pl. ccc [top].

Osiris, with figures of ʿAḥmosi, Greatest of the five of Thoth, Overseer of the Treasury, etc., and wife Mutnezemt on base, Dyn. XIX, in Cairo Mus. CG 38411. DARESSY, *Statues*, pl. xxi, pp. 108–9.

Tuēris, inscribed, black schist, Dyn. XXVI, in Cairo Mus. CG 39147. Id. ib. pl. lv, pp. 285–6; MARIETTE, *Album du Musée de Boulaq* (1872), pl. 5 [right].

Stelae (other than Apis-stelae).

Apries offering to Ptaḥ, with hieroglyphic and Carian texts, probably from here, in Cairo Mus. JE 49060. MASSON and YOYOTTE, *Objets pharaoniques à inscription carienne*, pl. i, figs. 11, 12, pp. 17–20; Carian text, SAYCE in *Transactions of the Society of Biblical Archaeology*, ix (1893), pl. i [ii, 2], pp. 125–6, 146 [ii, 2]; see MASPERO, *Guide* (1902), p. 260 [701 bis].

Blocks of Khaʿemwēset (son of Ramesses II).

Remains of 8 lines of text. Text, BRUGSCH, *Thes.* 957 [lower]–958; DEVÉRIA squeezes, 6170C, 5; GOMAÀ, *Chaemwese* [etc.], Abb. 10, 11 (from BRUGSCH), p. 80 [31].

Upper part of Khaʿemwēset, in Louvre, N.518. WENIG in *Forschungen und Berichte*, 14 (1972), Taf. 1 [1], pp. 41–2 [1]; REVILLOUT, *Le Roman de Setna* (1877), frontispiece; id. in *Rev. Arch.* N.S. xxxvii (1879), pl. xiv facing p. 335; GOMAÀ, op. cit. Taf. viii [a], p. 80 [32]; DEVÉRIA squeezes, 6170C, 6; head, MYŚLIWIEC, *Le Portrait royal dans le bas-relief du Nouvel Empire*, pl. cix [242]. See PIERRET, *Cat.* No. 3; BOREUX, *Guide*, ii, p. 481.

Two registers, **I** (incomplete), Khaʿemwēset kneeling offering to Ptaḥ, **II,** [Khaʿemwēset] with Opening-the-Mouth instruments before Apis-bull in shrine on sledge (**II** now in Louvre, E.25497). GOMAÀ, op. cit. pp. 81–2 [40] with Taf. v [b]; WENIG, op. cit. Taf. 2 [1, 2], pp. 42–3 [3]; **II,** VANDIER in *La Revue du Louvre*, xv (1965), fig. 8, p. 42; *Vingt ans*, p. 20 [Cat. 77] with plate.

Six fragments of jambs, with personifications led by Khaʿemwēset, in Vienna Mus. Inv. 5081–3, 5095–7. KOMORZYNSKI in *Archiv für Orientforschung*, xix (1959–60), pp. 67–73 with Abb. 1–4; see GOMAÀ, *Chaemwese* [etc.], p. 81 [35] with Abb. 13 (Inv. 5095–7). Inv. 5081–2, *200 Meisterwerke. Führer durch die Kunsthistorischen Sammlungen in Wien*, 13 (1931), fig. 15; *Meisterwerke. Führer durch das Kunsthistorische Museum*, 1 (1958 and 1968), fig. 5; DEMEL, *Ägyptische Kunst*, Abb. 26; LEIBOVITCH in *J.N.E.S.* xii (1953), fig. 18, p. 107 (as Ptolemaic); see *Uebersicht* (1895), p. 38 [143]; (1923), p. 13 [143]. Inv.5083, see Vienna. *5000 Jahre*, p. 79 [118].

Various

Offering-table of Pedusiri, son of Ḥaremḥab and Neḥemesēsi, dedicated to Apis, Late Period, in Louvre, D 79. ARCHIVES phot. E.684; text, GOODWIN MSS. 31279, 29 [top]; names, LIEBLEIN, *Dict.* No. 1202.

Hawk-coffin dedicated by Ḳenamūn, Craftsman of Pharbaethos, son of Weramūn, limestone, late New Kingdom, in Louvre, A.F.448. Text, WIEDEMANN in *P.S.B.A.* xiii (1891), p. 273 [3]. See VANDIER, *Guide* (1973), p. 123.

Apis canopic-jars. (a) Ramesses II, alabaster, in Louvre, N.5438; see PIERRET, *Cat.* No.

367. (b)–(d) Three (two inscribed), Dyn. XXVI, brought from Egypt by Borély in 18th century, in Marseilles, Mus. d'archéologie, 300–2; texts, Wilbour MSS. iii.D.11 [near top]; see Maspero, *Catalogue du Musée Égyptien de Marseille*, pp. 65–6 [100–2]. (e)–(i) Five, Late Period, three of them at one time in the possession of Le Maire, two in the possession of Sicard; Lucas, *Voyage . . . dans la Turquie, l'Asie, Sourie, Palestine, Haute & Basse Egypte*, &c., ii (1724), pl. facing p. 100.

Vase-fragment of Ramesses IX, faience, in Louvre, N.2255. See Pierret, *Cat.* No. 380 (as Ramesses VIII).

Cylindrical vase of Necho II, alabaster, in Louvre, N.462. See Boreux, *Guide*, ii, p. 572; Pierret, *Cat.* No. 383.

Jar with cartouche of Apries, dedicated to Apis, alabaster, in Cairo Mus. CG 18489. Von Bissing, *Steingefässe* (*Cat. Caire*), Taf. v, pp. 96–7 with text (as from Abûṣîr).

Flat-bottomed jar dedicated to Apis by Unnūfer, son of Psammethek, faience, Dyn. XXVI, in Cairo Mus. CG 18037. Id. *Fayencegefässe* (*Cat. Caire*), pp. 107–8 with fig. and text (as from Abûṣîr).

Bronze aegis with cartouches of Amasis, in Cairo Mus. Temp. No. 30.5.26.1. Mariette, *Album du Musée de Boulaq* (1872), pl. 37 [558]; de Rougé, *Album photo.* pl. 133.

Intrusive or re-used reliefs.

From New Kingdom tombs.

King Menkauḥor, with texts of Amenemōnet, Head of craftsmen of the Lord of the Two Lands (tomb, p. 552), end of Dyn. XVIII, in Louvre, B 48 [IM.2614; N.151; E.3028]. Berlandini-Grenier in *B.I.F.A.O.* 76 (1976), pls. liii–lv, pp. 303–15; Berlandini in *Bull. Soc. fr. d'Ég.* No. 83 (Oct. 1978), fig. 1, p. 25; de Rougé, *Recherches sur les monuments* [etc.] (1866), pl. vi, p. 99 (repr. in *Bibl. Ég.* xxvi, pl. vi, p. 95); id. *Album photo.* pl. 102; Meyer, *Geschichte des alten Aegyptens*, ii, fig. on p. 45; Maspero, *Hist. anc.* i, fig. on p. 415; id. *Égypte*, fig. 97; Boreux, *Guide*, ii, pl. lxiii [left], pp. 451–2; Petrie, *History*, i, fig. 59; Galvano, *L'Arte egiziana antica*, fig. 10; Richer, *Le Nu*, fig. 77; Michalowski, *Art*, fig. 234; Devéria squeezes, 6166, i. 3; Wilkinson MSS. xxiv. 12 [lower left]; Archives phot. E.1020. Head, L. *D.* iii. 291 [19]. See de Rougé, *Notice des monuments* (1883), p. 66; Vandier, *Guide* (1948), pp. 23–4; (1952), p. 24.

Two remaining registers, **I,** Thuthu, Scribe, Physician, and probably wife Nemau(?) before Duamutf and Nephthys, **II,** Thuthu and sister Naia before Ḳebḥsenuf and King Menkauḥor, end of Dyn. XVIII, in Louvre, B 50 [N.152]. Jonckheere, *Les Médecins de l'Égypte pharaonique*, fig. 24, p. 72; Ḳebḥsenuf and Menkauḥor, Berlandini in *Bull. Soc. fr. d'Ég.* No. 83 (Oct. 1978), fig. 2, p. 25; Devéria squeezes, 6166, ii. 161. Names and titles, Pierret, *Rec. inscr.* ii, p. 28; Lieblein, *Dict.* No. 432, *Suppl.* p. 953. See de Rougé, *Notice des monuments* (1883), pp. 67–8; Berlandini-Grenier in *B.I.F.A.O.* 76 (1976), pp. 315–16.

C. NORTHERN GROUP

Map LXIX

Emery and Smith (H. S.), *The Sacred Animal Necropolis at North Saqqâra. The Main Temple Complex and the Northern Dependencies*, in preparation; Martin, *The Sacred Animal Necropolis at North Saqqâra. The Southern Dependencies of the Main Temple Complex*, in press (1979). Plans, EMERY in *J.E.A.* 52 (1966), fig. 1 on p. 4; 53 (1967), fig. 1 on p. 142; 55 (1969), fig. 1 on p. 32; 56 (1970), pl. xviii after p. 10; 57 (1971), pl. xiv facing p. 12; SMITH (H. S.), *A Visit to Ancient Egypt*, fig. 2; MARTIN in *J.E.A.* 60 (1974), figs. 1, 2, 5, 10, 11, cf. 3 (sections) facing pp. 15, 16, 26, 27 and on pp. 17, 20; id. *Ḥetepka*, pl. 2. Ibis Galleries, POCOCKE, *A Description of the East* (1743), i, p. 54, with plan on pl. xxi [B]; L. *D. Text*, i, pp. 141–2 [LS 4] with plan.

TEMPLE. Nektanebos II.

EMERY in *J.E.A.* 53 (1967), pp. 142–3 (= id. in *Antiquity*, xlii (1968), pp. 99–100), with plan and section, pls. xix, xx, cf. fig. 2; 55 (1969), pp. 31–5, with plan and views, pls. x, xi; 56 (1970), pp. 5–7, with plans, pls. ii, iii; 57 (1971), p. 4, with plan, pl. i; SMITH (H. S.) in ib. 62 (1976), pp. 14–17, with plan, fig. 1; id. *A Visit to Ancient Egypt*, pp. 29–37, with plans, figs. 5, 6, 8.

Blocks with remains of scenes with the King, texts, and royal titles, etc., MARTIN, *Ḥetepka*, Nos. 340–411B. Upper part of the King before bull-headed Apis, and before [Mother-of-Apis] (= No. 363 of MARTIN), EMERY in *J.E.A.* 55 (1969), pl. ix [2]; SMITH (H. S.), *A Visit to Ancient Egypt*, pl. i [B], p. 34. Cornice-blocks with cartouches (= Nos. 352–3 of MARTIN), EMERY in *J.E.A.* 55 (1969), pl. ix [3, 4], p. 34.

Finds from Temple Terrace and neighbourhood of Animal Galleries

Texts, MARTIN, *Ḥetepka* (numbers in square brackets are those of the publication).

Statues and statuettes.

Lower part of seated statue, granite, Dyn. III, in Brit. Mus. 67154. [9]; see EMERY in *J.E.A.* 53 (1967), p. 143; *Brit. Mus. Quarterly*, xxxiv (1969–70), p. 186.

Fragment of statue-base of Khuit[rē]ʿ (woman), Dyn. V–VI, in Edinburgh, Roy. Scot. Mus. 1969.81. [86].

Statuette-fragment(?), Ptaḥshepses, Dyn. V–VI. [105].

Front part of prostrate King, probably Ramesses II, schist, in Edinburgh, Roy. Scot. Mus. 1971.130. *On View* (*A Guide to Museum and Gallery Acquisitions in Great Britain*), 6 (1971–2), 12th pl. [middle left] after p. 10, cf. p. 27. See ALDRED in *Triennial Report 1971–3*, p. 27.

Miniature block-statuette of Paser, Vizier (Theb. tb.106), temp. Sethos I to Ramesses II, faience, in Hildesheim Mus. 4886. [140]; *Meisterwerke altägyptischer Keramik*. Höhr-Grenzhausen, 16. Sept. bis 30. Nov. 1978, No. 293 with fig.

Double-statuette, Ma[ḥu](?), . . . of the fields of Amūn, and wife Tia, both seated, schist, Dyn. XIX, in Cairo Mus. JE 91915. [144].

Kanūfer, God's father and Prophet of the Ram 'Lord of Per-ka', squatting with figure of Ptaḥ, wood, New Kingdom, in Cairo Mus. JE 91118. [203]; EMERY in *J.E.A.* 53 (1967), pls. xxiv [2], xxi [4, middle], p. 143; id. in *Antiquity*, xlii (1968), pls. xiv [d], xv [b, middle], p. 99; *I.L.N.* March 25, 1967, fig. 6 on p. 30; BACON in ib. July 29, 1967, on fig. 4 on p. 25; Aug. 5, 1967, fig. 2 on p. 25.

Lower part of statue of Sety, Custodian of the Treasury, son of Ptaḥ-khaʿ, kneeling with figure of Ptaḥ, schist, New Kingdom, in Brit. Mus. 67156. [201].

Torso and legs of statue of Sesonchis V, glass frit, in Cambridge, Fitzwilliam Mus. E.6. 1969. [155]; see EMERY in *J.E.A.* 53 (1967), p. 143 [near bottom] (as Tuthmosis II).

A kneeling King, unfinished, wood, 3rd Int. Period, in Brit. Mus. 67143. See *Brit. Mus. Quarterly*, xxxiv (1969–70), p. 186.

Man holding figure of Ptaḥ, wood, 3rd Int. Period, in Brit. Mus. 67138. EMERY in *J.E.A.* 53 (1967), pls. xxiii [3], xxi [4, left], p. 143; id. in *Antiquity*, xlii (1968), pls. xiv [b], xv [b, left], p. 99; BACON in *I.L.N.* July 29, 1967, figs. 6 on p. 24, on 4 on p. 25; *Exhibition of Recent Discoveries in Egypt and the Sudan by the Egypt Exploration Society*. Brit. Mus. 16th Oct.–30th Nov. 1968, frontispiece; SMITH (H. S.), *A Visit to Ancient Egypt*, pl. vi [A]; *On View (A Guide to Museum and Gallery Acquisitions in Great Britain)*, 4 (1969–70), 9th pl. after p. 32 [right bottom], cf. p. 50. See *Brit. Mus. Quarterly*, xxxiv (1969–70), p. 186.

Bekennanefu [hieroglyphs] Psammethek-menkhib [hieroglyphs], Royal scribe, etc., son of ʿAnkh-sinebʿankh [hieroglyphs], kneeling with naos of Ptaḥ, re-dedicated in demotic by Ḥarpaēsi, son of Ḥaremḥab, schist, late Dyn. XXVI or Dyn. XXVII, in Toronto Mus. 969. 137.1. [199]; EMERY in *J.E.A.* 53 (1967), pls. xxiii [1, 2], cf. xxi [1], p. 143; id. in *Antiquity*, xlii (1968), pl. xiv [a], p. 99; *I.L.N.* March 25, 1967, fig. 3 on p. 30; BACON in ib. Aug. 5, 1967, figs. 4–6 on p. 26; NEEDLER in *Rotunda. The Bulletin of the Royal Ontario Museum*, 2 [4] (1969), fig. on p. 31; *Gazette des Beaux-Arts*, lxxvii (1971), Supp. Feb. 1971, fig. 203; SMITH (H. S.), *A Visit to Ancient Egypt*, pl. vi [D].

Man with figure of Ptaḥ, wood, Dyn. XXVI, in Cairo Mus. JE 91115. EMERY in *J.E.A.* 53 (1967), pl. xxiii [5]; id. in *Antiquity*, xlii (1968), pl. xiv [c], p. 99; BACON in *I.L.N.* July 29, 1967, fig. 2 on p. 23; SMITH (H. S.), op. cit. pl. vi [B]; id. in *Bull. Soc. fr. d'Ég.* Nos. 70–1 (June–Oct. 1974), fig. on p. 19.

Pentashendyt [hieroglyphs], son of ʿAnkhpefḥeri [hieroglyphs], Prophet of Amūn, and Theskhenspert [hieroglyphs], kneeling with figure of Osiris, schist, Dyn. XXVI–XXVII, in Cairo Mus. JE 91113. [202]; EMERY in *J.E.A.* 53 (1967), pl. xxiv [1], p. 143; BACON in *I.L.N.* Aug. 5, 1967, fig. 11 on p. 27 (as diorite).

[Pede]atum(?), Regulator of the Temple of Ptaḥ, with figure of Ptaḥ, wood, Late Period, in Cambridge, Fitzwilliam Mus. E.8.1969. [204]; EMERY in *J.E.A.* 53 (1967), pl. xxi [4, right]; id. in *Antiquity*, xlii (1968), pl. xv [b, right], p. 99; *On View (A Guide to Museum and Gallery Acquisitions in Great Britain)*, 4 (1969–70), 7th pl. after p. 16 [top left], cf. p. 21.

Bekenkhons [hieroglyphs], *sem*-priest, etc., kneeling with figure of Osiris(?), lower part, damaged, schist, Late Period, in Brit. Mus. 67155. [205].

Bekenptaḥ [hieroglyphs], *waʿb*-priest of Ptaḥ, Scribe of the army in Memphis, etc., seated clad in long robe, headless, probably granite, Late Period. [200].

Double-statuette, man and wife, wood, Late Period, in Cambridge, Fitzwilliam Mus. E.12.1969. BACON in *I.L.N.* July 29, 1967, fig. 11 on p. 24; *On View (A Guide to Museum and Gallery Acquisitions in Great Britain)*, 4 (1969–70), 7th pl. after p. 16 [top middle], cf. p. 21.

Divinities. Late Period.

Osiris. (a) Seated, dedicated by Deubasteiau [hieroglyphs], son of Pefteuʿaubaste [hieroglyphs], schist, in Cairo Mus. JE 91116; [207]; EMERY in *J.E.A.* 53 (1967), pl. xxiv [3], p. 143. (b) Seated, dedicated by Mosi, son of Zeamūnefʿankh(?) [hieroglyphs], diorite with traces of gilt, in Toronto Mus. 972.51.16; [206]. (c) Dedicated by Pedēsi, son of ʿAnkh-khons [hieroglyphs], basalt, originally gilded, in Bolton Mus. A-76. 1969; [208]; see *On View (A Guide to Museum and Gallery Acquisitions in Great Britain)*, 5 (1970–1), p. 13. (d) Perhaps Osiris, fragment, dedicated by a son of Tademeḥyt [hieroglyphs] (mother), granite, in Edinburgh, Roy. Scot. Mus. 1969.80; [210]. (e) Dedicated by a *waʿb*-priest of Ptaḥ, Sistrum-player of Ḥatḥor Mistress of the Sycamore, wood, in Cairo Mus. JE 91114; [209].

Ptaḥ. (a) Throne and legs, dedicated by Shedsunefertem [hieroglyphs], Greatest of the Directors of craftsmen, etc., faience, temp. Sesonchis I, in Edinburgh, Roy. Scot. Mus. 1971.165; [214]. (b) Base, dedicated by Iufʿankh-nūfer [hieroglyphs], wood, in Birmingham, City Mus. 460.69; [213].

A goddess, bust, schist; EMERY in *J.E.A.* 53 (1967), pl. xxvi [3] facing p. 145; BACON in *I.L.N.* July 29, 1967, fig. 14 on p. 25.

Animals and sphinxes.

Uraeus-serpent and Sokari as hawk on sledge, statue-group with cartouche of Ramesses II, incomplete, glass, in Cairo Mus. JE 91117. [123]; EMERY in *J.E.A.* 53 (1967), pl. xxv [5], p. 143; id. in *Antiquity*, xlii (1968), pl. xv [a], p. 100; BACON in *I.L.N.* Aug. 5, 1967, fig. 7 on p. 26.

Baboon, faience, Late Period, in Cairo Mus. JE 91112. SMITH (H. S.), *A Visit to Ancient Egypt*, pl. vii [D]; EMERY in *J.E.A.* 55 (1969), pl. vi [4].

Head of lioness, wood, Late Period. Id. ib. 53 (1967), pl. xxvi [5], p. 143; SMITH (H. S.), op. cit. pl. vi [C].

Jackal, three statues, Late Period. (a) In London, Univ. Coll. 30565; EMERY in *J.E.A.* 53 (1967), pl. xxii [6], p. 143. (b) In New York, M.M.A. 69. 105; id. ib. pls. xxi [2], xxii [5], p. 143; BACON in *I.L.N.* July 29, 1967, fig. 8 on p. 24; LILYQUIST in *The Metropolitan Museum of Art. Notable Acquisitions 1965–1975*, fig. on p. 73 [middle]; *Report on Projects funded by the Adelaide Milton de Groot Fund* (New York, M.M.A., 1977), fig. on p. 9 [top]; see FISCHER in *M.M.A. Bull.* N.S. xxviii (Oct. 1969), p. 70.

Sphinx, Ptolemaic, in Birmingham, City Mus. 65.71.

False-doors and stelae.

Ḳednas [hieroglyphs], Supervisor of the Treasury, upper part, Dyn. V–VI. [26].

Senezem . . . [hieroglyphs], Overseer of scribes of the Two Granaries, etc., fragment, Dyn. V–VI. [33].

Zadptaḥ [hieroglyphs], Craftsman, upper part, Dyn. III or late Old Kingdom. [13].

Stela-fragment with Nefer(t), Songstress of Bubastis, in lower register, Dyn. XIX. [130].

Mutnefert (woman), Dyn. XIX. [137].

Stela-fragment mentioning King Teti, Ramesside. [151].

Pente[nt]-khebi [hieroglyphs], Chiseller (*by*), son of Pedesopdu [hieroglyphs], probably Dyn. XXII. [168].

Ḥeribni [hieroglyphs], son of Unnūfer, before cow Setyerboni [hieroglyphs] on sledge, probably Dyn. XXVII. [165]; SMITH (H. S.), *A Visit to Ancient Egypt*, pl. ii [D].

Ptaḥardais [hieroglyphs], son of Thaiḥepimu [hieroglyphs], Late Period. [164].

Takhet [hieroglyphs], daughter of Taḳernefer(t) [hieroglyphs] (mother), Late Period. [163].

Upper part of donation-stela(?), with Apries offering field to Bubastis and Neḥi. [159].

Lintels, blocks, etc.

Two blocks of Inti [hieroglyphs], Judge and Keeper of Nekhen, late Old Kingdom. [100–1].

Drum-fragment of Perneb [hieroglyphs], Royal acquaintance, Dyn. V–VI. [31].

Offerings, and [wife Ḥemtrēʿ [hieroglyphs], Royal acquaintance], Dyn. V–VI. [44].

Block of Shesethef [hieroglyphs], Inspector of oils of King's adorners, Dyn. V–VI. [99].

Ducks in pool, Dyn. V–VI, in Cairo Mus. JE 91104. [53]; *The Egyptian Museum, Cairo in ten years 1965–1975*, pl. i, p. 42.

Lintel-fragment of a Director of bowmen, Assistant royal scribe, etc., Dyn. V. [98].

Blocks with names of Ramesses II. [121–2].

Relief-fragments from shrine of ʿAnta, probably temp. Ramesses II. [147].

Blocks mentioning brother Paraʿemḥab [hieroglyphs], Overseer of the cabinet, Dyn. XIX. [131–2].

Column-base of Raʿmosi, Chief steward of Khons, etc., alabaster, Ramesside. [143].

Block with remains of text of Ptolemy II Philadelphus. [338].

Offering-tables and basins. Some fragmentary. Late Period unless otherwise stated.

ʿAnkhpekhrod, in Cairo Mus. JE 91518, [268]. Ḥarardais [hieroglyphs], son of Pedēsi, [267]. Ḥarnakht and Ḥarsiēsi, sons of Esby [hieroglyphs], [270]. Ḥarsiēsi, son of Imḥōtep, in Brit. Mus. 67243, [266]. Half-brothers Ḥarwoz [hieroglyphs], son of Weḥebrēʿ-ḥarenpe [hieroglyphs], and Pedepamenkh [hieroglyphs], son of Esbi [hieroglyphs], both sons of Tashentnehy [hieroglyphs] (mother), in Cairo Mus. JE 91143, [263]. Mesthu [hieroglyphs], Royal acquaintance, late Old Kingdom, [79]. Pedeḥor, [272]. Pedeneit, son of ʿAnkhpekhrod, [269]. Pedēsi, [235]. Pefḥerinūter [hieroglyphs] and Esḥor [hieroglyphs], mentioning cow Setyerboni [hieroglyphs], probably Dyn. XXVII, in Cairo Mus. JE 91519, [260]. W[ash]ptaḥ [hieroglyphs], Dyn. V–VI, [113]. Zeḥo [hieroglyphs], son of Pawenḥētef, [265]. A Prophet of Khufu, etc., Dyn. V–VI, in Cairo Mus. JE 91916, [80].

Other objects.

Vase of Nezem-seshet [hieroglyphs], Scribe of divine books, alabaster, Dyn. I–III. [3].

Furniture-fragment of Ramesses XI, wood, in London, Univ. Coll. 30629. [154]; see EMERY in *J.E.A.* 53 (1967), p. 143 (as Ramesses IX).

Standing sphinx, presumably part of furniture, wood, Late Period, in Cairo Mus. JE 91111. Id. ib. pl. xxiii [4], p. 143; *I.L.N.* March 25, 1967, fig. 4 on p. 30.

Wooden shrines or similar. (a) Fragment with Horus-name of Sethos II or Ramesses VI, in Brit. Mus. 68173; [125]. (b) Fragment of Amasis, with glass inlay and gold leaf, in Toronto Mus. 969.137.2; [160]; NEEDLER in *Rotunda. The Bulletin of the Royal Ontario Museum*, 2 [4] (1969), fig. on p. 30 [lower]; see EMERY in *J.E.A.* 53 (1967), p. 143. (c) Door fragment of Amasis, in Brit. Mus. 68169; [161]. (d) Door, man offering vase, with demotic text in ink on back, gilded, Late or Ptolemaic Periods, in Cambridge, Fitzwilliam Mus. E.5. 1969; [286]; *On View* (*A Guide to Museum and Gallery Acquisitions in Great Britain*), 4 (1969–70), 7th pl. after p. 16 [top right], cf. p. 21. (e) Panel, a King offering to Isis and Harpocrates, inscribed, inlaid with glass, Late or Ptolemaic Periods, in Cairo Mus. JE 91103; [337]; EMERY in *J.E.A.* 53 (1967), pl. xxv [3]. (f) Panel, man and two gods in relief, Late Period, in Birmingham, City Mus. 442.69; id. ib. pl. xxii [3]. (g) Panels, with dedications in ink to Isis by Pedeneshmet, son of Pedepaneshmet [hieroglyphs], Late Period, in London, Univ. Coll. 8576–7; [288, 287]. (h) Panel, head of a king, probably Dyn. XXVI; SMITH (H. S.) and JEFFREYS (D. G.) in ib. 63 (1977), pl. iv [3], p. 25.

White Crown flanked by arms, wood, probably Late Period, in Cairo Mus. JE 91110. EMERY in ib. 53 (1967), pl. xxvi [1, 2], p. 143; BACON in *I.L.N.* Aug. 5, 1967, fig. 8 on p. 26.

Fragment of sarcophagus-lid of Ḥuy [hieroglyphs], First prophet of Sekhmet, etc., New Kingdom, re-used. [238].

Wooden plank from coffin with remains of texts and scenes, Late Period, re-used. MARTIN in *J.E.A.* 60 (1974), fig. 6, p. 21.

Dummy mummy of Apis-bull, skull attached to wooden body, Late Period, in Cairo Mus. JE 91318. EMERY in ib. 55 (1969), pl. viii [1–4], p. 33; id. in *Antiquity*, xliii (1969), pl. xiv [a, b], p. 108; SMITH (H. S.), *A Visit to Ancient Egypt*, pl. ii [E] and front cover; *The Egyptian Museum, Cairo in ten years 1965–1975*, pl. xii, p. 40 [54]; *A Brief Description of the Principal Monuments* (*Cairo Museum, 1976*), No. 6368 with fig.; KATER-SIBBES and VERMASEREN, *Apis*, *I*, p. 24 [86] with pls. lviii, lix.

Probably from here.

Shrine of Nektanebos II, parts of back and sides, wood with glass inlay, formerly in Abbott and N.Y. Hist. Soc. Collns., now in Brooklyn Mus. 37.258–60E. RIEFSTAHL, *Ancient Egyptian Glass and Glazes in the Brooklyn Museum* (1968), figs. 69–71, p. 109. Nos. 37.258E and 37.260E, id. *Glass and Glazes from Ancient Egypt*, figs. 16a, b. See *N.Y.H.S. Cat.* p. 48 [759–61].

SOUTH IBIS GALLERIES.

EMERY in *J.E.A.* 51 (1965), pp. 4, 6–7; 52 (1966), pp. 3–6. Plan, id. ib. 51 (1965), fig. 2 on p. 7, cf. fig. 1 on p. 5 (section); 52 (1966), fig. 2 on p. 6; id. in *I.L.N.* March 6, 1965, fig. 4 on p. 21; SMITH (H. S.), *A Visit to Ancient Egypt*, figs. 4, cf. 3, pp. 22–9. View of fore-court, LECLANT in *Orientalia*, N.S. 42 (1973), pl. viii [9], pp. 400–1; of entrance, EMERY in *J.E.A.* 52 (1966), pl. i [3], p. 5; of galleries, some showing pots with mummies, 51 (1965), pl. iv [1, 2] facing p. 6; 52 (1966), pls. ii, iii [1, 2], p. 5; id. in *I.L.N.* March 6, 1965, figs. 2 on p. 21, 7 on p. 23; LAUER, *Saqqara*, pl. 166. View of rock-cut statues, Old Kingdom, restored in Late Period, EMERY in *I.L.N.* March 6, 1965, fig. 9 on pp. 22–3; id. in *J.E.A.* 51 (1965), pl. ii [2], p. 6; 52 (1966), pl. i [4], p. 5. Decorated wrappings of mummies, id. ib. 51 (1965), pl. v, p. 4; 52 (1966), fig. 4, pp. 6, 8; id. in *I.L.N.* March 6, 1965, fig. 10 on p. 23; one, with Nefertem, in Brit. Mus. 67149, MACQUITTY, *Island of Isis*, figs. on p. 52, cf. on p. 53; LAUER, *Saqqara*, pl. 168.

Probably from here.

Ibis mummy, in Vienna Mus. Inv.8639. Text, BRUGSCH, *Thes.* 970 [left], cf. 969–70.

Sarcophagus of Thaenmu, Scribe of all accounts of the Treasury, son of Tadeimḥōtep (mother), Dyn. XXVI. Texts, DEVÉRIA squeezes, 5372A.

Head of block-statue, Late Period, in Cairo Mus. CG 871. See BORCHARDT, *Statuen*, iii, p. 131.

HAWK GALLERIES.

EMERY in *J.E.A.* 57 (1971), pp. 4–8, with plan, pl. iii, and views, pls. iv, v [2]; SMITH (H. S.), *A Visit to Ancient Egypt*, pp. 45–9, with plan, fig. 10. Decorated wrappings of mummies, EMERY, op. cit. pl. vi [1], p. 5. Texts of objects, MARTIN, *Ḥetepka* (numbers in square brackets are those of the publication).

Base for statuette of Ptaḥ, with Souls of Nekhen and Pe and name of Neterikhet (Zoser), bronze. EMERY, op. cit. pl. ix [1].

Statuette of Mut, dedicated by Pedubaste, son of Paḥor, schist, Late Period, in Cairo Mus. JE 91459. [227].

Canopic-jar of Psammetikhos I, re-used, in Cairo Mus. JE 91520. [157]; EMERY, op. cit. pl. vi [2], p. 5.

Hand censer with figure of a kneeling king, inscribed, bronze, Late Period, from deposit of temple equipment. EMERY, op. cit. pl. x [4], p. 6.

Sistrum-handle of Nektanebos II, fragment, faience. [300].

Inscribed wooden hawk-coffin, Ptolemaic. [289].

Fragment of text, gold leaf on plaster, from hawk-mummy wrapping, Late or Ptolemaic Periods. [304].

BABOON GALLERIES.

EMERY in *J.E.A.* 56 (1970), pp. 7–9, with plan, fig. 1 on p. 9, and views, pls. xi [1, 2], xii, xiii; SMITH (H. S.), *A Visit to Ancient Egypt*, pp. 41–4, with plan, fig. 9, and views, pls. i [C], iii [A]. View, LAUER, *Saqqara*, pl. 167; of chapel and entrance, SMITH (H. S.) in *Bull. Soc. fr. d'Ég.* Nos. 70–1 (June–Oct. 1974), figs. on pp. 13, 14. Plan, EMERY in *J.E.A.* 57 (1971), pl. ii, p. 4. Texts of objects, MARTIN, *Ḥetepka* (numbers in square brackets are those of the publication).

Statues.

Fragment with speech of Ptaḥ to Amenophis III, over life-size, faience, in Cairo Mus. JE 91304. [118].

Isis suckling Horus, inscribed, Late Period(?), in Cairo Mus. JE 91301. [211]; EMERY in *J.E.A.* 56 (1970), pl. xiv [1], p. 8; head of Horus, 55 (1969), pl. vii [5, 6].

Two baboons, Ptolemaic, one in Cairo Mus., other in New York, M.M.A. 1971.51. Id. ib. 56 (1970), pl. xiv [2, 3], p. 8. Cairo Mus., SMITH (H. S.), *A Visit to Ancient Egypt*, pl. iii [B]. M.M.A. 1971.51, LILYQUIST in *The Metropolitan Museum of Art. Notable Acquisitions 1965–1975*, fig. on p. 73 [bottom]; *Report on Projects funded by the Adelaide Milton de Groot Fund* (New York, M.M.A., 1977), front cover; see *Metropolitan Museum Journal*, 7 (1973), p. 155.

Baboon, Ptolemaic, in Toronto Mus. 972.51.1. MILLET in Royal Ontario Museum Toronto. *22nd Annual Report, July 1971–June 1972*, fig. on p. 18, cf. p. 17.

Two sphinxes, Ptolemaic. One, in Cairo Mus. JE 91303, EMERY in *J.E.A.* 56 (1970), pl. xiv [lower right] (called 4); other, headless, in Cambridge, Fitzwilliam Mus. E.11.1971, *Annual Report* (1971), pl. ii [upper] (restored), p. 9.

False-doors and stelae.

Lower part of false-door, Isbu [hieroglyphs], Overseer of oils in the Two Houses, etc., and wife Ḥenutemakhet [hieroglyphs], Prophetess of Neith, etc., on right jamb, and Ptaḥshepses and wife Khenut [hieroglyphs] on left jamb, Dyn. VI. [27]. Lintel-fragment of Isbu, [28].

Esḥaremwia [hieroglyphs], Elder of the hall of Ptaḥ foremost of the Two Lands in Thenent, son of Pedusiri, with Psammetikhos II before Ptaḥ and Isis. [158].

Irterau [hieroglyphs], two registers, **I,** adoring seated Osiris, with Western goddess behind, **II,** kneeling adoring Apis-bull, Late Period. [167].

Meresh [hieroglyphs], with hieroglyphic and Carian texts, Dyns. XXVI–XXVII. EMERY in *J.E.A.* 56 (1970), pl. xv [5], p. 8; MASSON and others, *Carian Inscriptions from North Saqqâra and Buhen*, pp. 20–1 [1], 58–60 [1] with pls. i [1], ii [1], xxxi [1].

Iresh [hieroglyphs], son of Nerseker [hieroglyphs], with hieroglyphic and Carian texts, Late Period, in Cairo Mus. JE 91387. Id. ib. pp. 25–6 [7], 86–7 [7] with pls. vi, xxxv [1].

Pasinu, son of ʿAnkh-ḥarmenḥap, with Apis-bull, Late Period. [166]; EMERY in *J.E.A.* 56 (1970), pl. xiv [lower left] (called 4).

Blocks.

Remains of three registers, **I,** butchers, **II,** sons Iynefertenptaḥ and Thesenptaḥ, both Inspectors of oils of King's adorners, and daughter Theset, Prophetess of Ḥatḥor, **III,** three offering-bringers, late Old Kingdom. [22].

Remains of personification and text mentioning Ramesses II. [124].

Offering-text of Pedubaste, Late Period. [292].

Various.

Offering-table of Amentefnakht, son of Irʿaḥeka and Tabes, Late Period. [261].

THE ISEUM. Burial-place of Isis Mother-of-Apis cows. Temp. Amasis to Ptolemy XV Caesar.

EMERY in *J.E.A.* 57 (1971), pp. 10–12, with plan, pl. xiii, and views, pls. xi, xii; SMITH (H. S.) in ib. 62 (1976), p. 17, with view, pl. vi [3]; id. *A Visit to Ancient Egypt*, pp. 37–41, with plan, fig. 7, and views, pl. ii [A, B]. Dates on hieratic and demotic stelae and graffiti, see id. in *Rev. d'Ég.* 24 (1972), pp. 176–87.

Wooden panel with painted procession of foreigners with bull and cow, Dyn. XXVII. EMERY, op. cit. fig. 3, pp. 10–11; MARTIN, *Ḥetepka*, No. 284.

Offering-table of Uzaḥor and ʿAnkhpekhrod, Late Period, in Oxford, Ashmolean Mus. 1971.135. Id. ib. No. 259.

IV. Miscellaneous

Statues.

Head in White Crown, probably Teti, in Louvre, A.F.2573. VANDIER, *Manuel*, iii, pl. vii [4], p. 574. See id. *Guide* (1973), p. 74.

Lower part of *ḥeb-sed* statuette of Pepy II, alabaster, in Brooklyn Mus. 16.80. Text, JAMES, *Corpus*, i, pl. xxvi [70], p. 29. See WIEDEMANN, *Ägyptische Geschichte* (1884), p. 215 with note 5; WILBOUR MSS. 2 C, 45; COONEY in *Rev. d'Ég.* 27 (1975), pp. 84 [bottom]–85 [top].

Small blue glass head, perhaps Amenophis III, in Cairo Mus. JE 4404. Id. *Glass Sculpture in Ancient Egypt* in *Journal of Glass Studies*, ii (1960), fig. 15, p. 24.

Divinities.

Horus, inscribed, green paste, Dyn. XXI, formerly in Allemant Colln., now in Antwerp, Mus. Vleeshuis, 79.1.234. CISELET in *Chron. d'Ég.* x (1935), pp. 320–1 with fig. See ALLEMANT, *Collection d'antiquités égyptiennes* [1878], No. 413; *A Catalogue . . . Collection of Egyptian Antiquities . . . Allemant*, Foster Sale Cat., London, May 9–10, 1878, No. 364; *Antwerp. Cat. de la Collection d'antiquités égyptiennes* (1881), pp. 36–7 [234]; *Oudheidkundige Musea. Vleeshuis, Cat. viii, Egypte*, p. 47 [230].

Isis suckling Horus, inscribed, alabaster, protected by vulture, bronze, Dyn. XXV–XXVI, formerly in N.Y. Hist. Soc. Colln., now in Brooklyn Mus. 37.400E. ROEDER, *Ägyptische Bronzefiguren*, Taf. 90 [c, d], p. 497 [669, c]; *Art of Ancient Egypt* (Emily Lowe Gallery,

Hofstra University, Hempstead, New York, Feb. 22–April 6, 1971), No. 10 with fig. (without vulture). See *N.Y.H.S. Cat.* p. 19 [291].

Osiris, dedicated by a son of Bintenduanūter (Theban tb.407), quartzite or basalt, Dyn. XXVI, in Louvre, N. 3952. Upper part, DE MEULENAERE and BOTHMER in *Kêmi*, xix (1969), pl. iii, pp. 11 with note 2, and 14 with note 7. Text on back pillar, MARIETTE, *Mastabas*, p. 448 [H 4]; id. *Mon. div.* pl. 77 [c].

Ptaḥ, dedicated by Meniuser [hieroglyphs], son of Nakht, basalt, Dyn. XIX, found in trench with animal bones, in Cairo Mus. CG 38432. DARESSY, *Statues*, pl. xxv, p. 117.

Ptaḥ, unfinished, with preliminary sketch, perhaps New Kingdom, in Cairo Mus. JE 45322. DE RACHEWILTZ, *L'Arte*, Tav. 12 [left], p. 16. Essen. *5000 Jahre*, No. 145 with Abb. See Brussels. *5000 ans*, p. 31 [79] (as Ptolemaic).

Tutu as sphinx, Roman, formerly in Abbott and N.Y. Hist. Soc. Collns., now in Brooklyn Mus. 37.1509E. COONEY, *Late Egyptian and Coptic Art*, pl. 8, p. 16; id. in *Brooklyn Mus. Bull.* x [3] (Spring 1949), fig. on p. 23; SAUNERON in *J.N.E.S.* xix (1960), pls. xi, xii, pp. 274 [50], 276. See BONOMI, *Cat. Colln. Abbott*, p. 4 [37]; *N.Y.H.S. Cat.* p. 9 [133].

Trial-pieces, etc. Late Period or Ptolemaic. In Cairo Museum.

Plaster-mask of a King, CG 1185. BORCHARDT, *Statuen*, iv, Bl. 166, p. 92.

Two royal heads, CG 33332, 33362. EDGAR, *Sculptors' Studies and Unfinished Works* (*Cat. Caire*), pls. ix, xvi, pp. 13–14, 40; PRISSE, *L'Art ég.* ii, *Sculpture*, 31st pl. [8, 2], 'Études de têtes' [etc.], *Texte*, p. 408.

Two royal heads, CG 33350, 33358. EDGAR, op. cit. pls. xiii, xv, pp. 30–1, 37–8; WEIGALL, *Anc. Eg. . . . Art*, 332 [lower]. CG 33350, PRISSE, op. cit. 31st pl. [3], *Texte*, p. 408.

Royal heads, CG 33331, 33333, 33348, 33351, 33353, 33356, 33359–61, 33363–4. EDGAR, op. cit. pls. ix, xiii–xvi, pp. 12–13, 14, 28–9, 31–3, 33–4, 36–7, 38–40, 40–2.

Royal head. PRISSE, op. cit. 31st pl. [4], 'Études de têtes' [etc.], *Texte*, p. 408.

Half royal head, CG 33352. Id. ib. 31st pl. [1], *Texte*, p. 408; EDGAR, op. cit. pl. xiii, p. 33. See MASPERO, *Guide*, p. 497 [4801].

Stelae.

Upper part, double-scene, King Ḥaremḥab before Osiris, probably from here, in Cairo Mus. Temp. No. 22.5.25.2. Text, DARESSY in *Ann. Serv.* xvii (1917), p. 85; HELCK, *Urk.* iv. 2129 [830], cf. *Übersetz.* (1961), p. 410; HARI, *Horemheb*, pl. xlix (from DARESSY), p. 293.

A Ptolemy (names erased) before bull-headed god [hieroglyphs] and Theban triad, in Cairo Mus. CG 22161. KAMAL, *Stèles Ptolémaïques et Romaines* (*Cat. Caire*), pl. xlix, pp. 146–7; LANZONE, *Diz.* Tav. cxxxv [lower]. Texts of gods, BRUGSCH, *Dictionnaire Géographique de l'Ancienne Égypte*, pp. 201–2 (as Mît Ghamr). See HABACHI in *Ann. Serv.* liii (1956), p. 462.

Paʿaḥaty [hieroglyphs] before Sēth, votive stela, faience, Ramesside. BAKRY in ib. lvii (1962), pp. 7–8 with fig.

Blocks, etc.

Pyramid-text fragment, end of Dyn. V or Dyn. VI, in Berlin Mus. 7727. Text, *Aeg. Inschr.* i, p. 4. See *Ausf. Verz.* p. 44.

Horus-name of Pepy I, in Basel, Mus. für Völkerkunde, III.5220. HORNUNG in *So lebten die Alten Ägypter* (Sonderausstellung 1976–7), fig. 3 on p. 12. See RÜTIMEYER,

Führer durch das Museum für Völkerkunde Basel, Alt-Ägypten (1930), p. 17; id. *Bericht* (1921) in *Verhandlungen der Naturforschenden Gesellschaft in Basel*, xxxiii, p. 3.

Block of Senbef [hieroglyphs], Prophet, Inspector of *sem*-priests of Sokari, son of Imes [hieroglyphs], Lector-priest, probably trial-piece, Dyn. VI (James) or Middle Kingdom (Simpson), formerly in Abbott and N.Y. Hist. Soc. Collns., now in Brooklyn Mus. 37.1355E. WILKINSON MSS. xli. 43 verso [bottom right]. Text, JAMES, *Corpus*, i, pl. xxv [65], p. 27. See BONOMI, *Cat. Colln. Abbott*, p. 2 [8]; *N.Y.H.S. Cat.* p. 14 [183]; SIMPSON in *A.J.A.* 79 (1975), p. 153 [65]; DE MEULENAERE in *Chron. d'Ég.* xlix (1974), p. 270.

Lintel of Ramesses III, in Brit. Mus. 1344. See *Guide* (*Sculpture*), p. 198 [717].

Trial-pieces, etc. Late Period or Ptolemaic. In Cairo Museum.

Winged goddess, head of jackal, Apis-bull, ram, man's head, CG 33413, 33425, 33437, 33444, 33489. EDGAR, *Sculptors' Studies and Unfinished Works* (*Cat. Caire*), pls. xxvi, xxviii, xxxii, xliii (excluding CG 33444), pp. 58, 61, 66, 69, 82. *Recto* of CG 33437, KATER-SIBBES and VERMASEREN, *Apis*, *I*, p. 12 [31] with pl. xxiii.

Forepart of ram, CG 33443. EDGAR, op. cit. pl. xxxiii, p. 69; PRISSE, *L'Art ég.* ii, *Sculpture*, 36th pl. [top], 'Animaux' [etc.]; MARIETTE, *Album du Musée de Boulaq* (1872), pl. 24 [683]; DE ROUGÉ, *Album photo.* pl. 137; WEIGALL, *Anc. Eg. . . . Art*, 329 [lower left]; CAPART, *Propos*, fig. 44 [left]; KEIMER in *Ann. Serv.* xxxviii (1938), fig. 39, p. 316.

Vessels.

Alabaster jar of Tuthmosis III, 21 hin, in Cairo Mus. CG 18734. VON BISSING, *Steingefässe* (*Cat. Caire*), Taf. iv, pp. 156–7; MARIETTE, *Mon. div.* pl. 100 [lower]. Text, LEGRAIN, *Répertoire*, No. 145; LUCAS and ROWE in *Ann. Serv.* xl (1940), pp. 87 [7], cf. 78–9 [vii]. See DARESSY in *Bull. Inst. Ég.* iii Sér. 8 (1897), p. 151 [1]; MASPERO, *Guide*, p. 542 [5510].

Alabaster vase of Tuthmosis III and Queen Siti'oḥ, 16 hin. Text, WILKINSON MSS. xxii. 38.

Others.

Alabaster model sistrum of Teti 'beloved of Ḥatḥor Mistress of Dendera', in New York, M.M.A. 26.7.1450. DAVIES (N. DE GARIS) in *J.E.A.* vi (1920), pl. viii, pp. 69–72; HAYES, *Scepter*, i, fig. 76; HICKMANN, *45 Siècles*, pl. lxxxviii [A, B]; FISCHER, *Dendera in the Third Millennium B.C.* [etc.], frontispiece, p. 37; HORNEMANN, *Types*, vi, pl. 1568; KAYSER, *Ägyptisches Kunsthandwerk*, Abb. 65; SÉE, *Naissance*, fig. on p. 203. Upper part, PIJOÁN, *Summa Artis*, iii (1945), fig. 214. See *Burlington Fine Arts Club. Catalogue of an Exhibition of Ancient Egyptian Art* (1922), p. 90 [39].

Two alabaster tablets from foundation deposit of Psammetikhos I, formerly in N.Y. Hist. Soc. Colln., now in Brooklyn Mus. 37.465E. See *N.Y.H.S. Cat.* p. 41 [646–7].

Weight of 300 deben in shape of cow's head, with cartouches of Sethos I, granite, in Cairo Mus. CG 31651. WEIGALL, *Weights and Balances* (*Cat. Caire*), pl. iii, p. 55; text, KITCHEN, *Ram. Inscr.* i. 125 [66]. See MASPERO, *Guide*, p. 542 [5512].

Terminal of handle of model axe with cartouche of Amenophis III, lapis lazuli, formerly in N.Y. Hist. Soc. Colln., now in Brooklyn Mus. 37.280E. Text, JAMES, *Corpus*, i, pl. lxxxix [252d], p. 111. See *N.Y.H.S. Cat.* p. 38 [592].

EL-ʿAZÎZÎYA

Offering-table of Tuthmosis IV, granite, in Cairo Mus. CG 23088. Text, KAMAL, *Tables d'offrandes* (*Cat. Caire*), p. 72; HELCK, *Urk.* iv. 1558 [493], cf. *Übersetz.* (1961), p. 149. See GAUTHIER in *Ann. Serv.* x (1910), p. 201 [upper].

Cylinder seal of Menkheperrēʿ (probably Tuthmosis III), showing Asiatic influence. CHASSINAT in *B.I.F.A.O.* viii (1911), fig. 1, pp. 145–8.

MÎT RAHÎNA

Map LXXI

Plan, L. *D.* i. 9, *Text*, i, pp. 202–4; PETRIE, *Memphis*, i, pl. i; DIMICK (J.) in ANTHES, *Mit Rahineh 1955*, map at end, pp. 81–3 (also published separately); WILKINSON MSS. xiii. 39; BURTON MSS. 25620, 9, with description, 25618, 82, 83, 84, 86, 88.

Northern Enclosure

PALACE OF APRIES.

KEMP in *Mitt. Kairo*, 33 (1977), pp. 101–8, with plan and sections, figs. 1, 2, and views, Taf. 28–30. Plan, PETRIE, *Memphis*, ii, pl. i. Views, including some showing palm-capitals, id. ib. ii, pls. x–xiii, pp. 1–5; DIMICK (M. T.), *Memphis, the City of the White Wall*, 13th–15th pls.; SÉE, *Naissance*, fig. on pp. 158–9.

Palm-capitals. (a) Copenhagen, Ny Carlsberg Glypt. Æ.I.N. 1045, MOGENSEN, *Coll. ég.* pl. cxi [A 747], p. 103; see KOEFOED-PETERSEN, *Cat. des bas-reliefs*, pp. 60–1 [81]. (b) Munich, Staatl. Samml. ÄS 79, VON BISSING in *Münchner Jahrb.* (1911), Abb. 13, p. 170 [19]; see WOLTERS, *Führer* (1923), p. 54 [82]; (1928), p. 55 [82].

Column-fragment with cartouche of Apries, in Bristol, City Mus. H 648. PETRIE, op. cit. ii, pl. xix [bottom right], pp. 3, 14. See GRINSELL, *Guide Catalogue to the Collections from Ancient Egypt* (1972), p. 59.

Blocks from thicknesses of gate in destroyed pylon, three registers on each side with unnamed king in *ḥeb-sed* ceremonies, Dyn. XXVI. PETRIE, op. cit. ii, pls. ii [1–3, 6, 7], iii–ix, pp. 5–11; iii, pl. xxxi [top right and upper middle right]. Left thickness: **I,** in Liverpool, Merseyside County Museums, 10.9.09.1, 2, see *Handbook and Guide to the Egyptian Collection* [etc.] (1932), p. 39 [5]; **II,** right side, in Oxford, Ashmolean Mus. 1909.1154 (for other blocks see right thickness, **II**); **III,** in Cairo Mus. JE 41436. Right thickness: **I,** in Copenhagen, Ny Carlsberg Glypt. Æ.I.N. 1046, MOGENSEN, *Coll. ég.* pl. cii [A 703], p. 95; CAPART, *Documents*, ii, pls. 88–9; id. *L'Art ég.* iii, pl. 593; KOEFOED-PETERSEN, *Cat. des bas-reliefs*, pl. lv [55], pp. 45–6; PIRENNE, *Hist. civ.* iii, pls. 32–3 after p. 140; head of king, PETRIE, *Arts and Crafts*, fig. 6 facing p. 14; **II,** new reconstruction, SÄVE-SÖDERBERGH, *On Egyptian Representations of Hippopotamus Hunting as a Religious Motive* in *Horae Soederblomianae*, iii (1953), fig. 13, pp. 49–53; KEES in *Studi Rosellini*, ii, Tav. xv, p. 149; block mentioning Festival of the White Hippopotamus, in Brussels, Mus. Roy. E.5036, DE WIT in *Chron. d'Ég.* xxxiii (1958), fig. 4, pp. 25–8; text, SPELEERS, *Rec. inscr.* p. 86 [320]; rest in New York, M.M.A. 09.183.1; **III,** two fragments in London, Univ. Coll. 15858–9.

Three fragments of texts, in Copenhagen, Ny Carlsberg Glypt. Æ.I.N. 1048–50. MOGENSEN, *Coll. ég.* pl. ci [A 701], pp. 94–5; two, PETRIE, op. cit. ii, pl. ii [4, 5], p. 5.

Bronze corner of door of Psammetikhos II, in Edinburgh, Roy. Scot. Mus. 1910.155. Id. ib. iii, pls. xxxii [3], xxxiii [13], p. 40; RUFFLE, *Heritage of the Pharaohs*, fig. 134 [upper].

Door-jamb of Thaiēsimu [hieroglyphs], Royal scribe, Royal herald, etc., *recto*, Thaiēsimu and text mentioning ꜥAḥmosi-sineit [hieroglyphs], Overseer of the antechamber, temp. Amasis to Dyn. XXVII, *verso*, Thaiēsimu suckled by goddess Semset, temp. Nektanebos I, re-used, in Cambridge, Fitzwilliam Mus. E.5.1909; PETRIE, op. cit. ii, pls. xvii, xxv [right], pp. 13, 20–1; Thaiēsimu on *recto*, id. *Arts and Crafts*, fig. 9 facing p. 20; PIRENNE, *Hist. civ.* iii, pl. 34 facing p. 141; see SCHARFF in *Ä.Z.* 74 (1938), p. 44, cf. Abb. 2. Companion-piece, in Brooklyn Mus. 56.152, see *infra*.

Blue glazed bowl fragment of Teos, in London, Univ. Coll. 15991. PETRIE, *Memphis*, ii, pl. xiv [bottom right], p. 12; id. *Scarabs and Cylinders*, pl. lvii [30.2].

Ivory inlay, man with birds, Late Period, in Edinburgh, Roy. Scot. Mus. X.294.3. Id. *Memphis*, ii, pl. xiv [middle right], p. 12; id. *Arts and Crafts*, fig. 126 facing p. 136.

Clay sealings. Id. *Memphis*, iii, pls. xxxv [1–21], xxxvi [1–21], xxxvii [42, 47–9], pp. 42–3.

'CAMP'. Plan of gate, PETRIE, *Memphis*, i, pl. xxx [left].

Two blocks from east of Palace, one of them with names of Ay, now in Boston Mus. 09.641, the other with Sekhmet and a king, perhaps same date, in Rochdale Mus. Id. ib. ii, pl. xix [top middle, and right], p. 14.

Embalming-bed of Amenḥotp, Chief steward, temp. Amenophis III (Ṣaqqâra tomb, see *supra*, pp. 702–3), alabaster, from south of Palace. HABACHI in *Mitt. Kairo*, 22 (1967), Taf. x, xi, figs. 1, 2, pp. 42–7.

Bronzes, including [Nos. 1–13 of Daressy] plaques with king or Nile-god offering and names of Tuthmosis III, Osorkon III, Kashta, Psammetikhos II, Amasis, Amenardais I, and Shepenwept I or II, [Nos. 14–16] three oval plaques dedicated by Weḥebrēꜥ-nebḳen [hieroglyphs], son of Psammethek-ꜥaneit [hieroglyphs], both Commanders of the army, temp. Psammetikhos II, Piamūn [hieroglyphs], son of Ḥarbes [hieroglyphs], and unnamed, [Nos. 17–22] mirrors, including [No. 17] Mutardais [hieroglyphs], daughter of Thai-pautitaui-imu [hieroglyphs] (mother), [No. 18] Irterau [hieroglyphs], daughter of Riri [hieroglyphs] and Taherib [hieroglyphs], [No. 19] Ḳeḳuiry [hieroglyphs], daughter of Menamenrēꜥ [hieroglyphs] (mother), [No. 20] Thesmutpert [hieroglyphs], daughter of Amen(em)ōpet [hieroglyphs], [No. 21] Esinḥertardais [hieroglyphs], daughter of Pedeḥarsemtu [hieroglyphs] and Heribi [hieroglyphs], mostly 3rd Int. Period or Dyn. XXVI, originally presumably from Thebes, found probably here, in Cairo Mus. JE 35107 (mirrors CG 44076–80), and Temp. Nos. 27.11.26.3, 4. DARESSY in *Ann. Serv.* iii (1902), pls. i–iii (some), pp. 139–50. Nos. 1, 2, 6, MASPERO, *Égypte*, figs. 560–2. Cartouches of Tuthmosis III on No. 7, LEGRAIN, *Répertoire*, No. 152. Incomplete top registers of Nos. 14 and 15, WAINWRIGHT in *Ann. Serv.* xxviii (1928), figs. 2, 3, p. 179; cloaked image, see DORESSE in *Rev. d'Ég.* 25 (1973), pp. 101–4 [15, 16], cf. fig. 1 (from DARESSY). Nos. 17–21, BÉNÉDITE, *Miroirs* (*Cat. Caire*), pls. xvi–xx, pp. 36–41; MUNRO in *Ä.Z.* 95 (1968–9), Taf. ii–vi (from BÉNÉDITE), pp. 92–3, 97–100. See MASPERO, *Guide*, pp. 457–8 [4340–51]; DANINOS PACHA in *Ann. Serv.* v (1904), pp. 142–3; KEMP in *Göttinger Miszellen*, No. 29 (1978), p. 61.

Ptaḥ Enclosure with Dependencies

TEMPLE OF PTAḤ. Ramesses II

Plan, PETRIE, *Memphis*, i, pl. ii; DARESSY in *Ann. Serv.* iii (1902), fig. 1, pp. 22–4; with sections, Haeny, *Basilikale Anlagen in der ägyptischen Baukunst des Neuen Reiches* in *Beiträge zur ägyptischen Bauforschung*, 9, Abb. 27a, b, pp. 69–70. Views, Petrie, op. cit. i, on pls. xxi–xxiii, pp. 5–6; Robichon and Varille, *En Égypte* (1937), pl. 32; (1955), pl. 27; Kees, *Das alte Ägypten* (1955), Abb. 28; (1958), Abb. 34; Eng. ed. *Ancient Egypt* (1961), pl. 16 [b]; Westendorf, *Das Alte Ägypten*, fig. on p. 167; James, *The Archaeology of Ancient Egypt*, fig. on p. 111; Dimick (M. T.), *Memphis, the City of the White Wall*, 2nd pl.; Tadema and Tadema Sporry, *De Pyramiden van Egypte*, pl. 1.

COLOSSI IN FRONT OF PYLON.

Fragments of statues of Ramesses II, red granite, alabaster, and limestone; Petrie, *Memphis*, i, pl. xxiii [top right, and middle], pp. 5, 9–10. Two red granite heads, in Cairo Mus. CG 643–4; Borchardt, *Statuen*, ii, Bl. 118, pp. 188–9; see Maspero, *Guide*, p. 182 [671–2]; id. and Roeder, *Führer*, p. 50 [612–13]. Texts of limestone colossus, Daressy, op. cit. p. 25 [near bottom].

Basalt base of colossus of Ramesses II with name-rings, standing in advance of Pylon. Petrie, op. cit. i, pl. xxiii [bottom], p. 10. See Daressy, op. cit. pp. 24 [bottom]–25 [top].

Found in front of Pylon.

Endowment stela of Ameny [hieroglyphs], Chief Justice and Vizier, granite, temp. Sesostris I. Part of text, Petrie, op. cit. i, pl. v, pp. 6–7, 17–18.

Three fragments of quartzite stela with coronation-text of Ḥaremḥab (for other copies see *Bibl.* ii^2. 6 and Turin Mus. Cat. 1379). Texts, Daressy, op. cit. pp. 27–8 [1–3]; Hari, *Horemheb*, pls. xxxviii, xxxix [upper] (from Daressy and Petrie), pp. 214–17. Fragment I, Petrie, op. cit. i, pl. vi, pp. 7, 18; Helck, *Urk.* iv. 2121–4 [826], cf. *Übersetz.* (1961), pp. 407–8; see Gardiner in *J.E.A.* 39 (1953), pp. 14, 28–31. Fragment III, Petrie, op. cit. i, pl. xxvi [2], pp. 10, 20. See Newberry in *Anc. Eg.* (1925), p. 4.

Two inscribed basalt blocks. Text, Daressy, op. cit. p. 28 [4]; Kitchen, *Ram. Inscr.* ii. 492 [190, 3]; of one, Petrie, op. cit. i, pl. xxiv [lower], p. 10.

Foundation deposit of Ramesses II and son Khaʿemwēset, in Manchester Mus. 4947–51; id. ib. i, pl. xix [lower left] (two objects not illustrated), p. 8; texts, Kitchen, *Ram. Inscr.* ii. 493 [190, 6]; see Gomaà, *Chaemwese* [etc.], pp. 82–3 [45], cf. Abb. 16 [a]. Sandstone block and faience plaque of Ramesses II and Khaʿemwēset, probably from here, in Brit. Mus. 48664, 49235; see Weinstein, *Foundation Deposits in Ancient Egypt*, p. 258 [89, B]; Gomaà, op. cit. p. 83 [46–7]; No. 48664, text, Shorter in *Studies Presented to F. Ll. Griffith*, p. 132; see *Guide, 4th to 6th*, p. 292 [61]. Faience plaque of Ramesses II, perhaps from here, in Brit. Mus. 49234.

PYLON.

Cartouches of Setnakht, Petrie, *Memphis*, i, pl. xxvi [7], p. 10; Kitchen, *Ram. Inscr.* v. 3 [4, e]; see Daressy, op. cit. pp. 25 [bottom]–26 [top].

Doorway. Jambs, outer, Ramesses II offering to Sekhmet and to Ptaḥ, inner, names and titles of the King; text, id. ib. p. 26 [near top and middle]; Kitchen, *Ram. Inscr.* ii. 488 [190, 1]. Bottom of one thickness, names and titles of Merneptaḥ and Ramesses III; Petrie, op. cit. i, pl. xxii [top], p. 9; Fischer in *Artibus Asiae*, xxiv [1] (1961), fig. 3 on p. 50; text, Daressy, op. cit. pp. 26 [bottom]–27 [top].

HYPOSTYLE HALL WITH NORTH AND SOUTH CORRIDORS. 'West Hall.'

Texts, Kitchen, *Ram. Inscr.* ii. 487–8 [189], 492–3 [190, 4].

Architectural elements of Ramesses II. Fragments of columns, PETRIE, *Memphis*, i, pls. xx [21], xxii [bottom right], p. 9; texts of two, DARESSY in *Ann. Serv.* iii (1902), p. 29 [7, 10]. Drums of granite columns, PETRIE, op. cit. i, pl. xxv [lower right], p. 10; SOGA, *The Nile*, fig. on p. 174 [right]; see DARESSY, op. cit. p. 29 [9]. Block with head of Ptaḥ and names of the King, granite, PETRIE, op. cit. i, pl. xxiv [upper], p. 10; cf. DARESSY, op. cit. p. 30 [15]. Texts of others, id. ib. pp. 28 [5], 30 [11–14, 16].

Column-fragments of Sethos II, quartzite. Texts, id. ib. pp. 30–1 [17].

False-door fragments of Ramesses II, granite. PETRIE, op. cit. i, pl. xx [22], pp. 8–9.

Finds

Statues.

Raʿy, Royal scribe, Overseer of the Two Granaries, etc., lower part, temp. Amenophis III, in Dublin, National Mus. 1908.514. PETRIE, *Memphis*, i, pl. xix [right], p. 8. See MURRAY, *General Guide to the Art Collections*, iii, *Egyptian Antiquities*, p. 65.

Two colossal statues of Ptaḥ dedicated by Ramesses II, sandstone, in Cairo Mus. CG 38429–30. DARESSY, *Statues*, pl. xxv, pp. 116–17; GRIFFITH INST. photo. 387 (*in situ*); MASPERO, *Guide* (1914), pp. 168–9 [662–3] with fig. 48; (1915), p. 268 [1295–6] with fig. 95 (both figs. CG 38429); id. and ROEDER, *Führer*, p. 50 [390–1] with Taf. 20 [a] (CG 38429). CG 38429, CAPART, *Memphis*, fig. 208; COOK in HAMMERTON, *Universal History of the World*, i, fig. on p. 645 [near right]; ROEDER, *Die ägyptische Götterwelt*, Taf. 2 [a]. CG 38430, MASPERO, *Égypte*, fig. 368. Texts, DARESSY in *Rec. Trav.* xiv (1893), p. 174 [lxviii]; KITCHEN, *Ram. Inscr.* ii. 493 [190, 5].

Votive stelae.

Texts of some, PETRIE, *Memphis*, i, pl. xv [bottom].

ʿAḥmosi, New Kingdom. (a) Bristol Mus. H 2218B, id. ib. i, pl. xvi [43], pp. 8, 20. (b) Hanover Mus. 1935.200.199, id. ib. i, pl. xvi [44], pp. 8, 20.

Beken[rēʿ], Custodian of the gate, with Tuthmosis I offering to Ptaḥ and Sekhmet, in Edinburgh, Roy. Scot. Mus. 1908.361. Id. ib. i, pl. vii [46], p. 7.

Ḥuy, Chariot-warrior, Dyn. XIX, in Edinburgh, Roy. Scot. Mus. 1908.360. Id. ib. i, pl. xvii, pp. 8, 20.

Ḳen and Merenptaḥ, Ramesside, in New York, M.M.A. 08.205.2C. Id. ib. i, pl. xv [40], p. 8.

Mer(y)rēʿ, Scribe of Memphis(?), Ramesside, in Philadelphia Mus. E 12509. Id. ib. i, pl. xiv [31], pp. 8, 19.

Nehia (woman), Dyn. XIX, in Manchester Mus. 4911. Id. ib. i, pls. vii [lower right], xvi [42], pp. 8, 20.

Raʿmosi, Head of serfs, temp. Tuthmosis IV. (a) Brussels, Mus. Roy. E.4499, id. ib. i, pls. vii [upper left], viii [4], p. 19; text, SPELEERS, *Rec. inscr.* p. 37 [134]; names of Ptaḥ and King, HELCK, *Urk.* iv. 1563 [502], cf. *Übersetz.* (1961), p. 152. (b) Hanover Mus. 1935.200. 229, PETRIE, op. cit. i, pls. viii [3], ix [lower middle right], pp. 7, 18–19. (c) Edinburgh, Roy. Scot. Mus. 1908.362, id. ib. i, pl. xv [36], pp. 8, 19.

Rēʿ, Dyn. XVIII, formerly in New York, M.M.A. 08.205.2A. Id. ib. i, pl. xiv [33], p. 8.

Name unknown, with King [Merneptaḥ] before Ptaḥ and Astarte, fragment, in London, Univ. Coll. 14392. Id. ib. i, pl. xv [37], pp. 8, 19; STEWART, *Eg. Stelae*, i, pl. 41 [2], p. 51; LECLANT in *Syria*, xxxvii (1960), fig. 1, pp. 10–13.

Others. Copenhagen, Ny Carlsberg Glypt. Æ.I.N. 1014–15, PETRIE, op. cit. i, pls. xvi [41], xiv [32], pp. 8, 20; MOGENSEN, *Coll. ég.* pls. cv [A 713], cviii [A 728], pp. 97, 100; SCHMIDT, *Choix* (1910), pl. xv [33–4], p. 29; Æ.I.N. 1014, KOEFOED-PETERSEN, *Ægyptens Guder*, pl. 18; Æ.I.N. 1015, id. *Les stèles égyptiennes*, pl. 39, p. 33. London, Victoria and Albert Mus. 423–4.1908, PETRIE, op. cit. i, pl. vii [lower left], viii [1], p. 7. London, Univ. Coll. 14396–7, id. ib. i, pls. xiv [35], xv [38], pp. 8, 19; STEWART, op. cit. pl. 29 [3, 5], p. 37. Philadelphia Mus. E 12508, PETRIE, op. cit. i, pl. xiv [34].

Ear-stelae.

Amenmosi, Ramesside, in Manchester Mus. 4906. PETRIE, *Memphis*, i, pls. ix [top near right], x [10], pp. 7, 19.

Iay, Head of quarrymen, and Ḥuy, Door-opener of the door of the tomb, Ramesside, in Brussels, Mus. Roy. E.4498. Id. ib. i, pl. xii [21], pp. 7, 19. Text, SPELEERS, *Rec. inscr.* p. 47 [167]. See DE MEULENAERE, *Het leven na de dood in het Oude Egypte* (Tentoonstelling van 21 juni tot 28 september 1969. Provinciaal Gallo-Romeins Museum—Tongeren), No. 69.

Ipy, Scribe of meat-offerings of Amūn, Ramesside, formerly in New York, M.M.A. 08.205.2E. PETRIE, op. cit. i, pl. xi [19], p. 7.

Maḥuia(?), Ramesside, in Brit. Mus. 1471. Id. ib. i, pl. xiii [30], pp. 7, 19. See *Guide (Sculpture)*, p. 304 [1171].

Ptaḥmosi, Head of sculptors, Ramesside, in Manchester Mus. 4909. PETRIE, op. cit. i, pls. ix [49], xiii [middle], pp. 7, 19.

Raʿmosi, Scribe of the Treasury of the Lord of the Two Lands, and wife Tentiunu, Ramesside. Id. ib. i, pl. xi [20], pp. 7, 19.

Others, Ramesside. Bristol Mus. H 2218A, id. ib. i, pl. xi [16]; see GRINSELL, *Guide Catalogue to the Collections from Ancient Egypt* (1972), p. 49. Brussels, Mus. Roy. unnumbered, PETRIE, op. cit. i, pls. ix [top right], xii [25], pp. 7, 25. Copenhagen, Ny Carlsberg Glypt. Æ.I.N. 1016–17, id. ib. i, pls. ix [top near left], xi [18], xiii [26], p. 19; MOGENSEN, *Coll. ég.* pl. cv [A 711–12], p. 97; SCHMIDT, *Choix* (1910), pl. xv [32, 31], pp. 29–30; KOEFOED-PETERSEN, *Les stèles égyptiennes*, pl. 40, p. 33. Dublin, National Mus. 1908.518–19, PETRIE, op. cit. i, pls. ix [upper middle left], x [12], xiii [29], p. 19; see MURRAY, *General Guide to the Art Collections*, iii, *Egyptian Antiquities*, p. 66. Edinburgh, Roy. Scot. Mus. 1908.363, PETRIE, op. cit. i, pl. xi [17]. Hanover Mus. 1935.200.204 (formerly The Hague, Scheurleer Mus.), id. ib. i, pl. viii [2], p. 7. Brit. Mus. 1472 and another, id. ib. i, pls. ix [upper middle near right and top left], x [14, 5], p. 7; see *Guide (Sculpture)*, p. 304 [1172]. London, Univ. Coll. 14398, 14394, 14393, 14395, PETRIE, op. cit. i, pls. ix [48], x [8, 9], xii [24], p. 7; STEWART, *Eg. Stelae*, i, pl. 29 [4, 6] (14398, 14395), pp. 37–8. Manchester Mus. 4905, 4907–8, PETRIE, op. cit. i, pls. x [6], xiii [27–8], p. 7. Philadelphia Mus. E 12506–7, id. ib. i, pls. x [11], ix [lower middle near left], xii [23], pp. 7, 19. Rochdale Mus., id. ib. i, pl. xi [15], pp. 7, 19. Formerly in New York, M.M.A. 08.205.2D, id. ib. i, pls. ix [lower middle near right], xii [22]; No. 08.205.2B, then Legg Colln., id. ib. i, pl. x [13].

Blocks. Re-used.

Five offering-bringers, Dyn. V–VI, in Brussels, Mus. Roy. E.5297. PETRIE, *Memphis*, i, pl. iii [left top], p. 6. See DE MEULENAERE, *Het leven na de dood in het Oude Egypte* (Tentoonstelling van 21 juni tot 28 september 1969. Provinciaal Gallo-Romeins Museum—Tongeren), No. 40.

Lintel and jambs of Neuserrēʿ, granite, from Sun-temple at Abû Ghurâb (*Bibl.* iii². 314–24), in Cairo Mus. Temp. Nos. 22.11.14.17–19. Lintel and one jamb, PETRIE, op. cit. i, pl. iii [middle and left bottom], p. 6.

Lintel of King Teti. Id. ib. i, pl. iii [right bottom], p. 6. Text, DARESSY in *Ann. Serv.* iii (1902), p. 29 [6].

God with shrine, Old Kingdom. PETRIE, op. cit. ii, pl. xviii [upper left], p. 13.

Jamb with remains of text mentioning Ramesses II, in Hanover Mus. 232. Id. ib. i, pl. xxvi [left], p. 10.

Three blocks, New Kingdom, (a) tree, in Brussels, Mus. Roy. E.7546, (b) upper part of god, in Rochdale Mus., (c) child on bull's head, in New York, M.M.A. 08.205.12. Id. ib. i, pl. xxvi [3–5], p. 10.

Offering-tables.

Waḥka [hieroglyph], Count, Overseer of prophets, early(?) Dyn. XII, granite. PETRIE, *Memphis*, i, pl. iv, p. 6.

Amenḥotp, Chief steward in Memphis, temp. Amenophis III (Ṣaqqâra tomb, see *supra*, pp. 702–3), in New York, M.M.A. 08.205.3. Id. ib. i, pls. ix [bottom right], xviii, p. 8, 20. Text, HELCK, *Urk.* iv. 1804 [646], cf. *Übersetz.* (1961), p. 264.

Various.

Model bark, granite, Dyn. XIX, in Cairo Mus. CG 4924. REISNER, *Models of Ships and Boats* (*Cat. Caire*), pl. xix, pp. 82–3; GÖTTLICHER and WERNER, *Schiffsmodelle im Alten Aegypten*, Taf. xvii [2]. See MASPERO, *Guide*, p. 168 [590].

Model bark with naos and statues of gods, incomplete, Dyn. XIX, in Cairo Mus. CG 4930. REISNER, op. cit. pls. xx, xxi, pp. 91–2. See MASPERO, op. cit. p. 168 [591].

EXTERIOR OF HYPOSTYLE HALL.

Base of north and south walls, geographical processions. North, MARIETTE, *Mon. div.* pl. 31; eight figures, BRUGSCH, *Dictionnaire Géographique de l'Ancienne Égypte*, p. 270; two, PETRIE, *Memphis*, i, pl. xxi [bottom left], p. 9; four names, BRUGSCH in *Ä.Z.* x (1872), p. 20; see YOYOTTE in *B.I.F.A.O.* lxi (1962), pp. 82–8, cf. 80–2. South, id. ib. pl. vii, pp. 88–9, cf. 80–2; three figures, PETRIE, op. cit. i, pl. xxi [near bottom left]; four names, DARESSY in *Ann. Serv.* iii (1902), p. 27 [middle]. Texts of both, KITCHEN, *Ram. Inscr.* ii. 488–92 [190, 2]. Sketch, possibly from here, WILKINSON MSS. xiii. 36 [lower]. Block re-used in Monastery of Apa Jeremias at Ṣaqqâra, see *supra*, p. 667.

Found nearby

Statue of Ramesses II and Ptaḥ-tatanen seated, granite, in Cairo Mus. CG 554. BORCHARDT, *Statuen*, ii, Bl. 93, pp. 101–2; HORNEMANN, *Types*, iv, pl. 1119; GRIFFITH INST. photo. 386. See MASPERO, *Guide*, p. 169 [597].

Bust, with scarab on head, probably Ramesses II (no text), granite, in Cairo Mus. CG 38104. See DARESSY, *Statues*, p. 35; MASPERO, *Guide*, p. 188 [731].

Headless sphinxes holding vase, of Ramesses II, sandstone. (a) PETRIE, *Memphis*, vi, pl. lviii [30], p. 33. (b) Cairo Mus. CG 1211, probably from here; BORCHARDT, *Statuen*, iv, Bl. 170, p. 110; text, KITCHEN, *Ram. Inscr.* ii. 497 [193, D]; see MASPERO, *Guide*, p. 161 [553].

ENCLOSURE WALL

NORTH GATE.

Lintel of Amenemḥēt III, quartzite. PETRIE, *Memphis*, v, pl. lxxvii [top], p. 32.

Colossal double-statue, Ramesses II and Ptaḥ, granite, in Copenhagen, Ny Carlsberg Glypt. Æ.I.N. 1483. Id. ib. v, pls. lxxvii [lower], lxxviii [middle right], p. 32; MOGENSEN, *Coll. ég.* pl. vii [A 14], p. 8; KOEFOED-PETERSEN, *Det gamle Ægypten* (1943), fig. on p. 18; id. *Ægyptisk Billedhuggerkunst* (1938), pl. 29; (1951), pl. 31; id. *Eg. Sculpture* (1951), pl. 33; (1962), pl. 35; id. *Cat. des statues*, pls. 68–9, pp. 34–5 [58]; CAPART in *Fra Ny Carlsberg Glyptotekets Samlinger* (1920), fig. 4, p. 46; MURRAY, *Sculpture*, pl. xxv [1]; *Capolavori*, i, No. 12 (1963), fig. on p. 185 [lower]; Eng. ed. fig. on p. 177 [lower]; upper part, FRANCESCHI and JOHANSEN, *Et hundrede fire og tyve fotografier*, pl. 17. Text, KITCHEN, *Ram. Inscr.* ii. 486–7 [188]. See BAGNOLD in *P.S.B.A.* x (1888), p. 458 [middle]; CHRISTOPHE in *Bull. Inst. Ég.* xxxvii (1954–5), p. 7 note 1.

Sphinx of Ramesses II, usurped by Merneptaḥ, granite, in Philadelphia Mus. E 12326. PETRIE, *Memphis*, v, pl. lxxviii [top], pp. 32–3; vi, pl. lvi [19, 20], p. 33; E. H. H[ALL] in *Penn. Mus. Journ.* v (1914), figs. 24–6, pp. 49–54; vi (1915), fig. 63 on p. 83; xvii (1926), figs. on pp. 107 [right], 115; RANKE in *Penn. Mus. Bull.* xv [2–3] (Nov. 1950), on fig. 59, pp. 101–2; RAINEY in ib. 18 [4] (Nov. 1954), on fig. on p. 26; O'CONNOR and SILVERMAN in *Expedition*, 21 [2] (Winter 1979), on fig. 64 on p. 42.

Scribe-statue (headless) of Amenḥotp, Chief steward, etc. (Ṣaqqâra tomb, see *supra*, pp. 702–3), quartzite, temp. Amenophis III, in Oxford, Ashmolean Mus. 1913.163. PETRIE, *Memphis*, v, pls. lxxviii [bottom right], lxxix, lxxx, pp. 33–6 (translation by Gardiner). Text, HELCK, *Urk.* iv. 1793–1801 [642], cf. *Übersetz.* (1961), pp. 259–63. See HAYES in *J.E.A.* 24 (1938), pp. 12 [P], 18–19, 20–1; BOTHMER in *Boston Mus. Bull.* xlvii (1949), pp. 48–9 with fig. 10 (from PETRIE). (The statue does not join Boston Mus. 29.729.)

Head, probably Late Period, in Copenhagen, Ny Carlsberg Glypt. Æ.I.N. 1480. PETRIE, *Memphis*, v, pl. lxxviii [middle left], p. 33.

SOUTH GATE.

Colossi.

Ramesses II, with daughter in relief by left leg, limestone, 'Abû el-Ḥôl'. L. *D.* i. 10 and iii. 142 [e–h], cf. *Text*, i, p. 204; ROSELLINI, *Mon. Stor.* lxxvi [1, 2]; BRUGSCH, *Recueil*, pl. i; PRISSE, *L'Art ég.* ii, *Sculpture*, 43rd pl., 'Colosse de Ramsès II', *Texte*, pp. 416–17; BONOMI in *Transactions of the Royal Society of Literature*, 2 Ser. ii (1847), pl. facing p. 304 [middle and right], cf. pp. 299–304; BAGNOLD in *P.S.B.A.* x (1887–8), pls. after p. 452, cf. pp. 452–5, 456 [lower]–457 [upper]; BÉCHARD and PALMIERI, *L'Égypte et la Nubie* (1887), pl. liii (reversed); HOREAU, *Panorama d'Égypte et de Nubie* (1841), pl. ix [lower]; MASPERO, *Hist. anc.* ii, fig. on p. 423; id. *Essais*, figs. 52–3; id. *Eg. Art*, pl. facing p. 140; EBERS, *Aegypten*, i, fig. on p. 143; Eng. ed. fig. on p. 124; VIOLLET and DORESSE, *Egypt*, pls. 164–5; HOREAU MSS. 4 [2]; GRIFFITH INST. photo. 380A (SEBAH, 177A); LUMLEY MSS. 16; BURTON MSS. 25634, 27–32, and 25618, 89; WILKINSON MSS. v. 52 [bottom], xiii. 35 [lower left], xxxvii. 52 [lower], cf. 53. Upper part, LANGE and HIRMER, *Aegypten. Architektur* (1955), pl. 229; (1957), pl. 242; (1967), pl. 240. Head or face, CHAMPOLLION in *Bibl. Ég.* xxxi, pl. iii, pp. 98–101; RANKE, *The Art of Ancient Egypt*, and BREASTED, *Geschichte Aegyptens* (1936), 159; LANGE, *Äg. Kunst*, pl. 102; id. *Ägyptische Bildnisse*, Taf. 28; BAIKIE, *Eg. Antiq.* pl. iii [right]; HERMANN, *Führer durch die Altertümer von Memphis und Sakkara*, frontispiece; *The*

Egyptian Education Bureau London. The Bulletin, No. 46 (July 1950), front cover; MONTET, *Lives of the Pharaohs*, pl. on p. 147; ANGIOLETTI and BIGONGIARI, *Testimone in Egitto* (1969), Tav. 32; MACQUITTY, *Island of Isis*, fig. on p. 26. Belt, dagger, and pectoral, EVERS, *Staat aus dem Stein*, ii, Taf. i [33]; and texts, CHAMPOLLION, *Mon.* x [3]. Dagger and cartouche on belt, ROSELLINI, *Mon. Civ.* cxxii [3]. Texts, KITCHEN, *Ram. Inscr.* ii. 494 [191, A]. See HÉKÉKYAN BEY MSS. 37458, 32, 44–8 (with plans and views); id. *A Treatise on the Chronology of Siriadic Monuments* (1863), pp. 17–19; HORNER in *Philosophical transactions of the Royal Society*, 148 (1858), pp. 55–7, 74, cf. 61–3.

Left fist of colossal statue, granite, probably from here, in Brit. Mus. 9. *Descr. Ant.* v, pls. 3, 4 [1]; BONOMI in *Transactions of the Royal Society of Literature*, 2 Ser. ii (1847), pl. facing p. 304 [bottom left]; LONG, *The Egyptian Antiquities in the British Museum*, i (1846), pp. 256–7 with fig. See SHARPE, *Eg. Antiq.* p. 57; *Guide* (*Sculpture*), p. 164 [597].

Found near South Gate

Statues.

Royal.

Amenemḥēt III, usurped by Merneptaḥ, granite, in Berlin (East) Mus. 1121. BRUGSCH, *Recueil*, pl. ii; *Aeg. und Vorderasiat. Alterthümer*, Taf. 11; *Ausf. Verz.* Abb. 14, p. 80; WEIGALL, *Anc. Eg. . . . Art*, 98 [lower]; VON BISSING, *Denkmäler*, *Text* to Taf. 39 [a] [fig.]; FECHHEIMER, *Plastik*, Taf. 52–3; BÉNÉDITE in *Gazette des Beaux-Arts*, 5 Pér. i (1920), fig. on p. 315; STRÖMBOM, *Egyptens Konst*, fig. 43; MURRAY, *Sculpture*, pl. xviii [3]; SCHÄFER, *Äg. Kunst*, fig. on p. 25 [9]; *Führer* (1961), Abb. 19, p. 53; HORNEMANN, *Types*, i, pl. 169; WENIG in *Forschungen und Berichte. Staatliche Museen zu Berlin*, 3/4 (1961), Abb. 4, p. 122; Museul de artă, Bucharest. *Egiptul antic* [etc.] (1975), No. 81 with fig. on p. 36; DEMBSKA and ŁYCZKOWSKA in *Przegląd Orientalistyczny*, 4 [104] (1977), 1st pl. after p. 342. Upper part, HAMMERTON, *Universal History of the World*, i, fig. on p. 429; GARDINER MSS. photo. 28.3. Texts, *Aeg. Inschr.* i, p. 144, and ii, p. 18. Cartouches, WILKINSON MSS. xiii. 76 [top].

Ramesses II holding standard with head of divinity, probably usurped by Ramesses VI. WILKINSON MSS. v. 37 [middle right], xxxvii. 54, cf. 55. Text, *L. D. Text*, i, p. 204 [α]; BURTON MSS. 25618, 90; LIEDER squeezes, 16.8. See CHRISTOPHE in *Bull. Inst. Ég.* xxxvii [1] (1954–5), pp. 26–7 [7].

Ramesses III. Name on back, LIEDER squeezes, 16.9. See BRUGSCH, *Reiseberichte*, p. 67.

Ramesses IV seated, with cartouche of Ramesses VI on bracelet. WILKINSON MSS. xiii. 31 (repr. CHRISTOPHE, op. cit. pl. vii, pp. 21–2 [3], 26 [3]).

Royal head, New Kingdom. WILKINSON MSS. xiii. 32 [upper left].

Shabataka seated, headless and fragmentary, granite, in Cairo Mus. CG 655. BORCHARDT, *Statuen*, iii, Bl. 121, p. 2; id. in *Ä.Z.* xxxvi (1898), Abb. 12, pp. 15–16 (as Karnak); VON BISSING, *Denkmäler*, *Text* to Taf. 60–1 [2nd fig.]; BOSSE, *Die menschliche Figur*, Taf. vii [142], p. 54; WILKINSON MSS. xiii. 37 [upper], 76 [bottom left]. Text, BRUGSCH, *Thes.* 1064 [7]; incomplete, MARIETTE, *Mon. div.* pl. 29 [e]. See MASPERO, *Guide*, p. 185 [680].

Private.

Minnakht (Theb. tb.87), lower part of seated statue, granite, temp. Tuthmosis III, in Vienna Mus. Inv.5802. Text, VON BERGMANN, *Hieroglyphische Inschriften*, Taf. i [lower], ii [upper]; REINISCH, *Miramar*, Taf. iv [D], xxxiii, pp. 97 [9], 249–52 [1]; SETHE, *Urk.* iv. 1188–9 [351]; LIEDER squeezes, 16.4. See BRUGSCH, *Reiseberichte*, p. 71 [vii].

Seated headless statue of a Hereditary princess (*rpꜥtt*), granite, Dyn. XVIII, in Vienna Mus. Inv.5769. Text, REINISCH, op. cit. Taf. xxx [C], p. 236 [23]. See BRUGSCH, op. cit. p. 71 [ix]; *Uebersicht* (1895), p. 36 [xxxvi]; (1923), p. 12 [xxxvi].

Amenmes(su) (Theb. tb.373), son of Penzerti and Iny (i.e. Mutemōnet), scribe-statue, granite, temp. Ramesses II, upper part (headless) in Manchester Mus. 5187, lower part in Vienna Mus. Inv.5749. Upper part, PETRIE, *Memphis*, iii, pls. xxx [2], xxxi [lower middle left], p. 39. Lower part, HABACHI in *Studies in Honor of George R. Hughes*, pp. 88–9 [6] with figs. 25–8, cf. 24 (upper part); REINISCH, *Miramar*, Taf. xxvii, pp. 225–8 [1]; BRUGSCH, *Monumens de l'Égypte* (1857), pl. xiii [lower]; list of feasts, id. *Thes.* 239–41; see id. *Reiseberichte*, p. 68 [i]; *Uebersicht* (1895), p. 34 [xvi]; (1923), p. 10 [xvi].

Khaꜥemwēset (son of Ramesses II), kneeling, incomplete, dedicated by son Raꜥmessu , granite, in Vienna Mus. Inv.5768. Text, BRUGSCH, *Recueil*, pl. v [1, 2]; REINISCH, *Miramar*, Taf. xxx [A], pp. 233–5 [21]; WRESZINSKI, *Aegyptische Inschriften aus dem K. K. Hofmuseum in Wien*, pp. 132–5; GOMAÀ, *Chaemwese* [etc.], Abb. 17, p. 83 [48]; three columns, LIEDER squeezes, 16.2; titles, BRUGSCH, *Thes.* 957 [upper].

Nezem , Royal messenger to every country, Overseer of the granaries of the Western Border, etc., block-statue with figure of Ptaḥ-tatanen at front, sandstone, temp. Ramesses II, in Boston Mus. 29.730. DUNHAM in *J.E.A.* xxi (1935), pl. xix, pp. 150–1. Text on back, MARIETTE, *Mon. div.* pl. 27 [f]; BRUGSCH, *Recueil*, pl. v [3]; LIEDER squeezes, 16.6. See BRUGSCH, *Reiseberichte*, p. 71 [vi].

Paser, Vizier (Theb. tb.106), temp. Sethos I to Ramesses II. (a) Kneeling with figure of Ptaḥ, cartouche of Ramesses II, granite, in Durham, Univ. Gulbenkian Mus. N.511; BIRCH, *Catalogue of the Collection of Egyptian Antiquities at Alnwick Castle*, pl. A [left], p. 72; *Gulbenkian Museum of Oriental Art and Archaeology*, pl. vii; RAWSON in *Apollo*, civ (1976), fig. 3 on p. 90; WILKINSON MSS. xxv. 51 verso; text, LIEDER squeezes, 16.1. (b) Standing holding figure of Ptaḥ, lower part, schist, in Cairo Mus. CG 630; BORCHARDT, *Statuen*, ii, Bl. 116, pp. 177–9; text, DARESSY in *Rec. Trav.* xiv (1893), pp. 172–4 [lxvii]; KITCHEN, *Ram. Inscr.* iii. 11–13 [5].

Upper part, head destroyed, with text on back pillar, temp. Ramesses II, in Cairo Mus. CG 870. BORCHARDT, *Statuen*, iii, p. 131 with fig. (as from the Serapeum at Ṣaqqâra); WILKINSON MSS. xviii. 42 [right] (provenance).

Ḥuy, kneeling, headless, holding Ḥatḥor-head, Ramesside, in Cairo Mus. JE 71897. WILKINSON MSS. xiii. 77 [lower right].

Roma , Chief steward in the Temple of Ptaḥ, kneeling with naos of Ptaḥ, fragmentary, Ramesside, sandstone, in Berlin (East) Mus. 2085. Texts, *Aeg. Inschr.* ii, pp. 80–2; some, LIEDER squeezes, 16.5. See *Ausf. Verz.* pp. 140–1; BRUGSCH, *Reiseberichte*, pp. 69–70 [iii].

Ḥarwoz , Greatest of the seers of Heliopolis, etc., son of [Ḥa]r[ua] and Nekhtubasterau , lower part of scribe-statue, granite, temp. Psammetikhos I, in Vienna Mus. Inv.5750. REINISCH, *Miramar*, Taf. xxviii, pp. 228–9 [2]. Text, VON BERGMANN, *Hieroglyphische Inschriften* [etc.], Taf. iii [upper]. Names and titles, LIEBLEIN, *Dict.* No. 2380; LEGRAIN in *Rec. Trav.* xxx (1908), pp. 20–1 [C]. See BRUGSCH, *Reiseberichte*, p. 70 [iv].

Uzaḥorresnet Neferebrēꜥ-nebpeḥti, Commander of troops, with naos of Osiris, fragmentary, granite, temp. Psammetikhos II–Apries, in Vienna Mus. Inv.5774 and Paris, Musée Rodin, 284. See id. ib. pp. 68–9 [ii]. Vienna Mus. Inv. 5774, see REINISCH, *Miramar*, p. 242 [29]. Paris, Musée Rodin, 284, see *Rodin collectionneur. Musée Rodin, Paris, 1967–1968*, No. 67.

Ḥarsemtuemḥēt [hieroglyphs], Prophet of Neith Mistress of Sais, etc., scribe-statue, upper part lost, sandstone, Dyn. XXVI, in Cairo Mus. CG 888. Text, BORCHARDT, *Statuen*, iii, pp. 139–40; DARESSY in *Mélanges Maspero*, i [1], pp. 86–8; on base, LIEDER squeezes, 16.7; WILKINSON MSS. xiii. 77 [upper]. See BRUGSCH, *Reiseberichte*, pp. 70–1 [v]. Another statue of same man, also probably from here, see *Bibl.* vii. 420 (as Ḥarkhebi in error).

Pefteuʿau-amūn [hieroglyphs] Psammethek-nūfer [hieroglyphs], Overseer of scribes of the council, etc., headless, kneeling with naos of Ptaḥ, diorite, Dyn. XXVI, in Turin Mus. Cat. 3020. HÉKÉKYAN BEY MSS. 37458, 49, 51, 52, 91 (provenance). Text, MASPERO in *Rec. Trav.* iv (1883), p. 150 [xliv]. Names and titles, BRUGSCH, *Thes.* 1431 [34]. See FABRETTI, etc., *R. Mus. di Torino*, pp. 409–10.

Iry [hieroglyphs], *waʿb*-priest of the Great Place of Ptaḥ, etc., son of Ḥarenḥap [hieroglyphs], headless block-statue, sandstone, Late Period, in Cairo Mus. CG 1106. Text, BORCHARDT, *Statuen*, iv, pp. 59–60; MARIETTE, *Mon. div.* pl. 27 [c]; BRUGSCH, *Thes.* 1062 [1]; DE ROUGÉ, *Inscr. hiéro.* pl. ciii [upper]; LIEDER squeezes, 16.3. See BRUGSCH, *Reiseberichte*, p. 71 [viii].

Basalt head and torso (no name), Late Period, in Brussels, Mus. Roy. E.4064 and 4618 (1st ed. incorrect). PETRIE, *Memphis*, iii, pls. xxx [1], xxix [1], p. 39; text of E.4618, SPELEERS, *Rec. inscr.* p. 86 [325].

telae.

Fragment with text naming Osorkon II, in Cairo Mus. JE 28582. Text, WILKINSON MSS. xiii. 76 [middle].

Blocks.

Blocks of Amenophis IV, re-used, one (= pl. 2 of NICHOLSON) in Sydney Univ. Nicholson Mus. of Antiquities, R.1143. NICHOLSON, *On some Remains of the Disk Worshippers* [etc.] in *Transactions of the Royal Society of Literature*, 2 Ser. ix (1870), pls. 1, 2, pp. 197–214 (repr. NICHOLSON, *Aegyptiaca*, pls. 1, 2, pp. 117–34); some, WILKINSON MSS. xiii. 78 [lower]–79; WILBOUR MSS. 3C, 239; two, NEWBERRY in *J.E.A.* xiv (1928), figs. 3, 4 (from NICHOLSON), pp. 8–9. Texts of two, SANDMAN, *Texts from the Time of Akhenaten*, p. 200 [cclxxxiii, cclxxxiv]. Block in Sydney, LÖHR in *Studien zur altägyptischen Kultur*, 2 (1975), Taf. iv [1], pp. 154–5; see REEVE, *Catalogue of the Museum of Antiquities of the Sydney University* (1870), p. 91 [1143].

Column-drum, Ramesses II offering to Ptaḥ, granite, in Copenhagen, Ny Carlsberg Glypt. Æ.I.N. 1147; MOGENSEN, *Coll. ég.* pl. cx [A 741], p. 102; KOEFOED-PETERSEN, *Cat. des bas-reliefs*, pl. lxxxiii [79], p. 60. Another, in Manchester Mus. See PETRIE, *Memphis*, iii, p. 39.

Ptaḥ in shrine, Dyn. XIX, re-used, in Copenhagen, Ny Carlsberg Glypt. Æ.I.N. 1510. Id. ib. vi, pl. lix [39], p. 33; KOEFOED-PETERSEN, *Cat. des bas-reliefs*, pl. xlii [42], p. 38.

Block of Shabataka. Cartouche, WILKINSON MSS. xiii. 76 [near bottom].

Names of Achoris, WILKINSON MSS. xiii. 76 [bottom right].

Various.

Fragments of altar-pedestal of Ramesses II, usurped by Ramesses III, VII, and IX, granite. See BRUGSCH, *Reiseberichte*, p. 67 [bottom] (possibly this). (a) Formerly in Fernandez Colln., now in Marseilles, Mus. d'archéologie, 205; text, WILKINSON MSS. xiii. 64 [lower right], 68 [lower]; WILBOUR MSS. iii. D. 11 [middle]; see MASPERO, *Catalogue du Musée Égyptien de Marseille*, p. 5 [5]. (b) Formerly in Palin Colln., now in Louvre, D 61;

LEPSIUS, *Auswahl*, Taf. xiv [bottom]; see DE ROUGÉ, *Notice des monuments* (1883), pp. 210–11; VANDIER, *Guide* (1948), p. 22; (1952), p. 23.

SUBSIDIARY BUILDINGS AND MONUMENTS

A. CHAPEL OF AMENOPHIS III. Along east to west axis of Temple of Ptaḥ.

Two quartzite blocks, the King before Sekhmet, in Boston Mus. 10.650 and Copenhagen, Ny Carlsberg Glypt. Æ.I.N. 1152. PETRIE, *Memphis*, iii, pl. xxix [2, 3], p. 39. Boston block, SIMPSON, *The Face of Egypt: Permanence and Change in Egyptian Art*, No. 38 with fig. Copenhagen block, MOGENSEN, *Coll. ég.* pl. cvii [A 723], p. 99; id. in *B.I.F.A.O.* xxx (1930), pl. i [1], pp. 457–8; KOEFOED-PETERSEN, *Cat. des bas-reliefs*, pl. xlvi [35], p. 32; the King, MYŚLIWIEC, *Le Portrait royal dans le bas-relief du Nouvel Empire*, pl. lxiii [147].

Quartzite head of Amenophis III, uninscribed, allegedly from here, in New York, M.M.A. 56.138. SCOTT in *M.M.A. Bull.* N.S. xv (Feb. 1957), fig. on p. 148, cf. p. 149; MÜLLER (H. W.) in *Encyclopedia of World Art*, iv, pl. 373.

B. CHAPEL OF AMASIS. Along east to west axis of Temple of Ptaḥ.

Quartzite blocks, including one, now in Edinburgh, Roy. Scot. Mus. 1910.154, with upper part of the King. PETRIE, *Memphis*, iii, pls. xxix [4, 5], xxxii [4–7], p. 39.

C. COLOSSUS OF RAMESSES II.

Colossal statue, with son Khaʿemwēset and daughter Bentʿanta in relief, usurped by Ramesses IV, granite, now set up in Cairo, Station Square. CHRISTOPHE in *Bull. Inst. Ég.* xxxvii [1] (1954–5), pls. i–iv, figs. 1–3, pp. 5–19; HABACHI, *Features of the Deification of Ramesses II*, pl. xiv, figs. 22 (= WILKINSON MSS. vii. 50), 23–4, pp. 35–7; WARD (J.), *Pyramids and Progress*, fig. on p. 47 [upper]; CAPART, *Memphis*, fig. 9; RICHER, *Le Nu*, fig. 100; PETRIE in WRIGHT (A.), *Twentieth Century Impressions of Egypt*, fig. 2 on p. 129 [lower]; LANGE, *Ägypten. Landschaft*, pl. 31; KUSCH, *Ägypten im Bild*, Abb. 58; DE MONTGON, *L'Égypte*, fig. on p. 89; WRIGHT (G. E.), *Biblical Archaeology*, fig. 31; *I.L.N.* Nov. 12, 1955, fig. on p. 823 [middle left]; DESROCHES-NOBLECOURT in *Bull. Soc. fr. d'Ég.* No. 23 (May 1957), pp. 15–18 with figs.; *Egypt Trav. Mag.* No. 17 (Dec. 1955), figs. on pp. 12–13; SOGA, *The Nile*, fig. on p. 142 [right]; MICHALOWSKI, *Art*, fig. 818; ELSTNER, *Egypt. The Gift of the Nile*, pl. 21; B. G. M[ERTZ] in *The New Encyclopaedia Britannica* (*Macropaedia*), 15th ed., vol. 11, fig. on p. 896; GRIFFITH INST. photos. 380, 3287; SOMERS CLARKE MSS. 19.4 (photo.); WILKINSON MSS. vii. 50 and xiii. 34 [bottom]. Hand, FEDDEN, *The Land of Egypt*, fig. 8. Upper part of Bentʿanta, BUTTLES, *The Queens of Egypt*, pl. xv; MURRAY, *Splendour*, pl. lxxvii [1]; id. *Sculpture*, pl. xxvii [2]; id. in *Anc. Eg.* (1925), pl. facing p. 97, cf. p. 102; head, PETRIE, *History*, iii, fig. 35; name, LIEBLEIN, *Dict.* No. 2098. Text, KITCHEN, *Ram. Inscr.* ii. 494 [191, B]. See BAGNOLD in *P.S.B.A.* x (1888), pp. 456 [upper], 457 [lower]–460; GOMAÀ, *Chaemwese* [etc.], p. 84 [50].

D. STELA OF APRIES.

Year 13, recording donation to Temple, sandstone. BRUGSCH, *Recueil*, pl. iii; MARIETTE, *Mon. div.* pl. 30 [b]; GUNN in *Ann. Serv.* xxvii (1927), pp. 211–37 with pl. Text, PIEHL in *A.Z.* xxviii (1890), p. 104; 1st line, WILKINSON MSS. xiii. 35 [top].

E. Colossal Alabaster Sphinx. Dyn. XVIII or Ramesses II.

Views[1] (some of details), Anthes, *Mit Rahineh 1956*, pls. 54–5, pp. 42–3; Montet, *Lives of the Pharaohs*, fig. on p. 69 (as Gîza); de Montgon, *L'Égypte*, figs. on pp. 23, 31; Robichon and Varille, *En Égypte* (1937), pl. 31; (1955), pl. 30; Laurent-Täckholm, *Faraos blomster*, pl. on p. 200; Fedden, *The Land of Egypt*, fig. 6; Cottrell, *Egypt*, fig. 25; Roeder, *Volksglaube im Pharaonenreich*, Taf. 6; Lange, *Ägypten. Landschaft*, pl. 32; id. *Äg. Kunst*, pl. 96; id. *Pyramiden, Sphinxe, Pharaonen*, pl. 18; id. and Hirmer, *Aegypten. Architektur* (1955 and 1957), pl. 114; (1967), pl. 122; Elstner, *Egypt. The Gift of the Nile*, frontispiece; Angioletti and Bigongiari, *Testimone*, Tav. 31; Kusch, *Ägypten im Bild*, Abb. 59; Wood and Drower, *Egypt in Colour*, pl. 18; Viollet and Doresse, *Egypt*, pl. 163; Dimick (M. T.), *Memphis. The City of the White Wall*, frontispiece; Siegner, *Ägypten. Ein Bildwerk*, pl. 148; Gilbert, *Couleurs de l'Égypte Ancienne*, pl. 14; Westendorf, *Das Alte Ägypten*, fig. on p. 166; Soga, *The Nile*, figs. on pp. 145 [upper], 174 [left]–175; Binder-Hagelstange, *Ägypten. Ein Reiseführer* (1966), fig. on p. 321; *Capolavori*, i, No. 11 (1963), fig. on p. 169 [bottom]; Eng. ed. fig. on p. 161 [bottom]; David, *The Egyptian Kingdoms*, figs. on pp. 9, 20; Fagan, *The Rape of the Nile*, fig. on p. 343. See *Chron. d'Ég.* xxviii (1953), p. 282; Evers, *Staat aus dem Stein*, ii, p. 85 [577].

F. Ḥathor-column capital. Not *in situ*.

Dimick (M. T.), *Memphis. The City of the White Wall*, 3rd pl. [lower].

G. Embalming House of Apis-bulls. Temp. Sesonchis I.

El Amir in *J.E.A.* 34 (1948), pp. 51–6, with views, etc., pls. xv–xvii; Dimick (J.) in Anthes, *Mit Rahineh 1955*, pp. 75–9, with plan, pl. 41, and views, etc., pls. 42–5; id. in *Archaeology*, 11 (1958), pp. 183–9, with reconstruction and view, figs. on pp. 183–4; see *J.E.A.* 27 (1941), p. 165. Position, cf. Petrie, *Memphis*, i, pl. xxx [lower right], pp. 12–13. View, Dimick (M. T.), *Memphis. The City of the White Wall*, 1st pl.

Embalming-tables with lion-bed in relief on sides, alabaster. (a) Dimick (J.) in Anthes, *Mit Rahineh 1955*, pl. 43 [a, 4], p. 77; id. in *Archaeology*, 11 (1958), on fig. on p. 186 [upper]; Posener, Sauneron, and Yoyotte, *Dict. civ.* fig. on p. 169; *Great Museums*, fig. on p. 214 [60]; James, *The Archaeology of Ancient Egypt*, fig. on p. 114; Cottrell, *Egypt*, fig. 24; el Amir, op. cit. pl. xv [2–4, 6], pp. 51, 54; Viollet and Doresse, *Egypt*, pls. 166–7; Desroches-Noblecourt, *Les Religions égyptiennes* in *L'Histoire générale des religions*, figs. on p. 309; Dimick (M. T.), *Memphis. The City of the White Wall*, on 5th pl. (b) Dimick (J.) in Anthes, *Mit Rahineh 1955*, pl. 45 [a], p. 77 [5]; id. in *Archaeology*, 11 (1958), fig. on p. 186 [lower]; Dimick (M. T.), *Memphis. The City of the White Wall*, 6th pl.; el Amir, op. cit. pls. xvi [3, 4], xvii [3], pp. 52, 55; Anthes in *Penn. Mus. Bull.* 20 [1] (March 1956), fig. 8, pp. 21–3.

Altar of Necho II, alabaster. El Amir, op. cit. pl. xv [5], p. 51; Dimick (J.) in Anthes, *Mit Rahineh 1955*, pl. 45 [e], p. 78 [bottom].

Table of 3 blocks, (a) south side, cartouches of Sesonchis I, and Anubis libating and Shedsunefertem, Greatest of the Directors of craftsmen, son of ʿAnkhefensekhmet, in Opening-the-Mouth ceremony, (b) north side, cartouches of Ramesses II and name of Apis. (a) Brugsch, *Thes.* 817, 948–9 [15]; Dimick (J.) in *Archaeology*, 11 (1958), fig. on p. 188, cf. p. 189; id. in Anthes, *Mit Rahineh 1955*, pl. 44 [a, 7], pp. 75, 78; Dimick (M. T.),

[1] Selected references.

Memphis. The City of the White Wall, 4th pl.; text, BRUGSCH in *Ä.Z.* xvi (1878), pp. 38–41; part, VERCOUTTER, *Textes*, p. 57. See PETRIE, *Memphis*, i, pp. 12–13; KEES in *Ä.Z.* 87 (1962), pp. 145–6 [2].

Block-stand of Amasis, alabaster, in Cairo Mus. JE 86757. EL AMIR, op. cit. on pl. xvi [5], pp. 52, 54.

Other finds.

Lower part of seated statuette of Shedsunefertem, Greatest of the Directors of craftsmen, etc., quartzite, temp. Sesonchis I, in Cairo Mus. JE 86758. Text, KEES in *Ä.Z.* 87 (1962), pp. 142–5.

Front part of statuette of bull, diorite. EL AMIR, op. cit. pl. xvii [1], p. 52.

Stelae showing Apis-bull in shrine being conveyed in bark on wheels, Ptolemaic or Roman. (a) and (b) Id. ib. pl. xvii [4], p. 52; see KATER-SIBBES and VERMASEREN, *Apis, I*, p. 20 [67–8] (No. 68 not in Cambridge), cf. pl. xlviii (= No. 67, from EL-AMIR). (c) Cambridge, Fitzwilliam Mus. E.74.1911; PETRIE, *Memphis*, iv, pl. xxxi [bottom right], p. 24; KATER-SIBBES and VERMASEREN, op. cit. p. 20 [71] with pl. xlix (as No. 68 in error). (d) Cairo Mus. JE 45044; MARIETTE, *Mon. div.* pl. 35 [top]; *Encycl. phot. Caire*, pl. 192; see MASPERO, *Guide*, p. 472 [4495]; KATER-SIBBES and VERMASEREN, op. cit. p. 21 [72], cf. pl. li (from MARIETTE). (e) Berlin Mus. 7494, probably from here; ERMAN, *Die ägyptische Religion* (1905), fig. 107; (1909), fig. 106; id. *Die Religion der Ägypter* (1934), fig. 133; SCHARFF, *Götter Ägyptens*, Taf. 15; KATER-SIBBES and VERMASEREN, op. cit. p. 19 [66] with pl. xlvii; see *Ausf. Verz.* p. 313. (f) Leipzig, Äg. Mus. Inv.1830, probably from here; MOND and MYERS, *The Bucheum*, iii, pl. cix [1]; i, p. 80; HAAS, *Bilderatlas zur Religionsgeschichte*, fig. 47; KATER-SIBBES and VERMASEREN, op. cit. p. 20 [70] with pl. l; F.E.R.E. photo. 5953; see KRAUSPE, *Ägyptisches Museum der Karl-Marx-Universität Leipzig* (1976), p. 63 [84/2]. (g) Hildesheim Mus. 1876, possibly from here; KATER-SIBBES and VERMASEREN, op. cit. p. 20 [69] with pl. l; see IPPEL and ROEDER, *Die Denkmäler des Pelizaeus-Museums zu Hildesheim*, p. 89. (Others, see *supra*, p. 573, where the date is to be corrected, and Ṣaqqâra, Serapeum, Apis-stelae not assigned to a particular Apis-bull.)

Measuring-vessel of Darius I, year 34, alabaster, in Cairo Mus. JE 86754. EL AMIR, op. cit. pl. xvii [2], pp. 52, 54; LUCAS in *Ann. Serv.* xlii (1943), figs. 30–1, pp. 165–6.

H. CHAPEL OF SABACON.

Plan and view, PETRIE, *Memphis*, i, pls. xxvii [upper left], xxv [bottom left], p. 10.

I. TEMPLE OF TUTHMOSIS IV.

Foundation deposit, in Manchester Mus. 4938–46; PETRIE, *Memphis*, i, pl. xix [upper left], p. 8; texts, HELCK, *Urk.* iv. 1561 [498], cf. *Übersetz.* (1961), p. 151. Another, in Cairo Mus. JE 35174; see DARESSY in *Ann. Serv.* iii (1902), p. 25 [upper].

Found in this area.

Seated royal statues, Old Kingdom. Khephren, alabaster, in Cairo Mus. CG 41; Menkaurēʿ, diorite, CG 42; Neuserrēʿ, granite, CG 38; Menkauḥor, alabaster, CG 40; another, uninscribed, alabaster, CG 39. BORCHARDT, *Statuen*, i, Bl. 10, 11, pp. 36–9; VANDIER, *Manuel*, iii, pls. iii [2], v [2], vi [1, 3, 5], p. 558; MASPERO, *Guide*, figs. 12–14 (CG 42, 38–9), pp. 53–5 [111–15]; id. in GRÉBAUT, *Le Musée Égyptien*, i, pls. viii–xii, pp. 9–12; see BORCHARDT in *Ä.Z.* xxxvi (1898), p. 17. CG 38, BOTHMER in *Kêmi*, xxi (1971), pl. ii, pp. 14–15; incomplete, id. in *Mitt. Kairo*, 30 (1974), Taf. 45 [a, b], p. 165 with note 3; PETRIE, *History*, i

(1899), fig. 45; (1923), fig. 58 (= PETRIE GÎZA photo. 515). CG 38–9, 41–2, MASPERO, *Hist. anc.* i, figs. on pp. 390, 364, 372, 374; BUDGE, *A History of Egypt*, ii, figs. on pp. 73, 44, 48, 53. CG 39, upper part, VON BISSING, *Äg. Kunstgeschichte*, Taf. li [343], *Text*, i, p. 86. CG 39, 42, GOSSE, *The Civilization of the Ancient Egyptians*, fig. 79. CG 40–1, HORNEMANN, *Types*, iii, pls. 766, 686. CG 41, VON BISSING, *Denkmäler*, i, Taf. 9; WEIGALL, *Anc. Eg. . . . Art*, 28; SCHÄFER and ANDRAE, *Kunst* (1925), 220; (1930 and 1942), 230; RAGAI, *L'Art*, pl. 35 [62]; HAMMERTON, *Universal History of the World*, i, fig. on p. 425 [right]; *Encycl. phot. Caire*, pl. 11; PIJOÁN, *Summa Artis*, iii (1945), fig. 135; MONTET, *Eternal Egypt*, pl. 21; DONADONI, *Egyptian Museum Cairo*, pl. on p. 33 [left]; SUZUKI, *Sculpture of the World*, 3, *Egypt*, pl. 3; LECLANT and others, *Le temps des Pyramides*, fig. 183. CG 41–2, MASPERO, *Égypte*, figs. 143, 27. CG 42, id. *Eg. Art*, pl. facing p. 38 [upper]; id. *Essais*, fig. 1, pp. 20–2; incomplete, PETRIE GÎZA photo. 514.

Statue-base(?) imitating façade, alabaster, Dyn. II–III, in Cairo Mus. CG 57001 (JE 27851). MASPERO in GRÉBAUT, *Le Musée Égyptien*, i, pl. vii [lower], p. 9; BORCHARDT in *Ä.Z.* 41 (1904), Abb. 1, p. 85; LAUER, *Pyr. à deg.* i, fig. 69, pp. 87–8. See MASPERO, *Guide*, p. 79 [176].

Stela-fragment, double-scene, Amenophis III led by Sekhmet receives life from Ptaḥ, in Cairo Mus. JE 34558 (quoted in error in *Bibl.* ii². 446). Id. in GRÉBAUT, op. cit. pl. vii [upper], pp. 8–9. Heads of the King, MYŚLIWIEC, *Le Portrait royal dans le bas-relief du Nouvel Empire*, pls. lxv [153], lxvii [156]. See BOGOSLOVSKAYA in *Tutankhamon i ego vremya* (1976), p. 55, cf. fig. on p. 56.

J. CHAPEL OF SETHOS I.

HABACHI in ANTHES, *Mit Rahineh 1956*, p. 60.

Doorway, with lintel with double scene, a King before Ptaḥ. Id. in *Göttinger Miszellen*, No. 31 (1979), on pl. i on p. 55, cf. pp. 49–50.

Blocks of Sabacon and Taharqa, re-used (former in Berlin (West) Mus. 39/66). See LECLANT in *Orientalia*, N.S. 20 (1951), p. 346. Block of Sabacon, HABACHI in *Göttinger Miszellen*, No. 31 (1979), on pl. i on p. 55; KAISER, *Äg. Mus. Berlin* (1967), p. 96 [957] with Abb.

Three seated statues, Ptaḥ (headless) between Isis and Nephthys, both nursing Sethos I. PERKINS in *A.J.A.* liii (1949), pl. ix [A], p. 41; DESROCHES-NOBLECOURT in *Bull. Soc. fr. d'Ég.* No. 1 (June 1949), fig. on p. 10 [upper], cf. pp. 14, 17; LECLANT, op. cit. pls. xxxiii–xxxiv [16–18], pp. 345–6 [6]; Ptaḥ and Nephthys, *Jaarbericht Ex Oriente Lux*, No. 13 (1953–4), pl. lxiii [upper], p. 304 [49].

Stela, Merneptaḥ before Ptaḥ, with text mentioning building enclosure wall. HABACHI in ANTHES, *Mit Rahineh 1955*, pl. 9 [a], p. 5; text, KITCHEN, *Ram. Inscr.* iv. 32 [14].

K. TEMPLE OF RAMESSES II.

ANTHES, *Mit Rahineh 1956*, pp. 4–17, with plans, sections, and views, pls. 1–15; id. in *Penn. Mus. Bull.* 20 [1] (March 1956), pp. 12–14, with plan and views, on figs. 1, 2, 4; 21 [2] (June 1957), pp. 3–7, with plan and views, on figs. 1–3. Plan, id. *Mit Rahineh 1955*, on pl. 1.

Pylon.

HABACHI in ANTHES, *Mit Rahineh 1956*, pp. 60–5; JACQUET in ib. *1955*, pl. 10 [b], pp. 13–14.

North wing. Texts, KITCHEN, *Ram. Inscr.* ii. 495–6 [192, B].

Outer face. Remains of [King] before goddess, offering milk, and before Ptaḥ below; HABACHI in *Mit Rahineh 1956*, pls. 20 [b], 21, 23 [b], fig. 4 [E 1, 3, 4, frag. 1], pp. 61, 64.

Thickness. King offers image of Maʿet to Ptaḥ, id. ib. pl. 20 [a], fig. 4 [S 1–6], pp. 61, 63.

Inner face. Two registers, King before god, and before Ptaḥ, with name of door below, and block with heads of Ptaḥ and King receiving *ḥeb-sed*; id. ib. pls. 22, 23 [a], fig. 4 [W 1–5, frag. 3], pp. 63, 65.

Re-used block with bowing courtier, temp. Amenophis IV. Id. ib. pl. 23 [c, left], p. 65.

Sanctuary.

Views, ANTHES, *Mit Rahineh 1955*, pl. 10 [a], pp. 65–6; DIMICK (M. T.), *Memphis. The City of the White Wall*, 7th and 8th pls.; DESROCHES-NOBLECOURT, *Les Religions égyptiennes* in *L'Histoire générale des religions*, fig. on p. 249 [left]; BADAWI in *Ann. Serv.* xliv (1944), pls. xxiii, xxiv, p. 205.

King before Ptaḥ, on right side of façade, HELCK, *Ägypten* in HAUSSIG, *Götter und Mythen im Vorderen Orient*, Taf. v [10] after p. 406.

Re-used block of Amenophis III. See ANTHES, *Mit Rahineh 1956*, p. 5 [upper].

Names of Sethos II at base of walls and pillars. See id. ib. p. 8 [top].

Finds from Temple and neighbourhood

Statues.

Head, granite, probably Middle Kingdom. ANTHES, *Mit Rahineh 1956*, pl. 38 [a, b], p. 100 [40].

Head and shoulders of prostrate man, quartzite, probably end of Dyn. XVIII. Id. ib. pl. 38 [g, h], pp. 100–1 [42].

Amenḥotp [hieroglyphs] Ḥuy [hieroglyphs], Chief Governor in Memphis, Steward, middle part, sandstone, temp. Ramesses II. BADAWI in *Ann. Serv.* xliv (1944), pl. xxii, pp. 202–5.

Mutemwia [hieroglyphs] (woman), seated, lower part, Ramesside. ANTHES, *Mit Rahineh 1956*, pl. 35 [f, g], fig. 14 [a, b], p. 98 [37].

ʿAḥmosi [hieroglyphs], seated, headless, New Kingdom. BAKRY in ib. *1955*, pl. 22, fig. 13 [142], p. 41.

Roy [hieroglyphs], kneeling, lower part, New Kingdom. Id. ib. pl. 23, fig. 13 [143], p. 41.

Head, New Kingdom. ANTHES, *Mit Rahineh 1956*, pl. 35 [a–c], p. 100 [41].

Torso, quartzite, probably Dyn. XXVI. Id. ib. pl. 35 [d, e], fig. 14 [39], p. 100.

Uzaḥorresnet [hieroglyphs], Greatest of the physicians, temp. Amasis to Darius I, dedicated by Minardais(?) [hieroglyphs] (?) [hieroglyphs], son of Weḥebrēʿ [hieroglyphs] and Sems(et) [hieroglyphs], fragment, granite, probably Dyn. XXXI. Id. ib. pls. 36, 37 [a–c], fig. 13, pp. 98–100 [38]; see id. in *Penn. Mus. Bull.* 21 [2] (June 1957), p. 14.

Headless sphinx, probably Late Period. Id. *Mit Rahineh 1956*, pl. 40 [a], p. 101 [43].

Royal head, sculptor's model, Late Period or Ptolemaic. BAKRY in ib. *1955* pl. 24 [c, d], p. 41 [144].

Fragmentary statuettes of Tuēris, probably Dyn. XIX. ANTHES, *Mit Rahineh 1956*, pl. 27 [b–i], p. 78 [5–8].

Ramesside blocks. Mostly re-used in intrusive burials of 3rd Int. Period.

ANTHES, *Mit Rahineh 1955*, pp. 67–9, with position on pl. 1; id. ib. *1956*, pp. 17–20, with position on pl. 1.

Jamb-fragment mentioning Inenay [hieroglyphs], Head of physicians in the Temple of Ptaḥ, and Paḥatiʿa [hieroglyphs], with former kneeling. Bakry in ib. *1955*, pl. 25 [d], fig. 13 [148], p. 43. Title of Inenay, Van de Walle and De Meulenaere in *Rev. d'Ég.* 25 (1973), pp. 77–8.

Five blocks of Iyiry [hieroglyphs], Greatest of the Directors of craftsmen, temp. Sethos II (Ṣaqqâra tomb, see *supra*, p. 704). Anthes, *Mit Rahineh 1956*, pls. 27 [a], 28, 29 [a], figs. 7, 8, pp. 79–85 [Ba]; id. in *Penn. Mus. Bull.* 21 [2] (June 1957), frontispiece, figs. 8–11, pp. 12–13, 28–33; deceased and wife, with children below, Leclant in *Orientalia*, N.S. 27 (1958), pl. iii [4], p. 83.

Jambs of Neḥesi [hieroglyphs], Commander of the army of the Lord of the Two Lands, etc., with 3 columns of hymn to King's *ka* on each. Anthes, *Mit Rahineh 1956*, pl. 29 [b, c], fig. 9, pp. 85–7 [Bb]; see id. in *Penn. Mus. Bull.* 21 [2] (June 1957), p. 13 [lower].

Five blocks, one of them originally of the end of Dyn. XVIII; id. *Mit Rahineh 1956*, pl. 30 [a–e], fig. 10, pp. 87–8 [Bc]; blocks with Osiris seated and man before Anubis, id. ib. *1955*, pl. 12 [a], p. 67 note 11. Three blocks, including jamb-fragment of a Chief steward in the Temple of Ramesses II, id. ib. *1956*, pl. 32 [a, d, c], fig. 11 [19, 21], pp. 88–9 [Bd]. Two blocks, lower part of seated man and of seated couple, id. ib. pl. 33 [b–d], p. 91 [Be].

Other blocks.

Fragment of text of Ḥaremḥab (less likely Amenophis I). Anthes, *Mit Rahineh 1956*, pl. 39 [a, 57], fig. 14 [57], p. 104.

Fragment of topographical list, probably Dyn. XVIII. Id. ib. pl. 39 [a, 56], fig. 14 [56], p. 104.

Royal head, trial-piece, perhaps New Kingdom. Id. ib. *1955*, pl. 24 [a], p. 43 [150].

Various fragments, id. ib. pls. 25 [a, c], 26 [a], pp. 43 [154, 152, 153].

Column-fragment of Ramesses II. Petrie, *Memphis*, i, on pl. xxv [middle left], pp. 10, 12.

Lintel with Ptaḥ-khaʿ [hieroglyphs] and father ʿAshakhet [hieroglyphs], both God's fathers and Secretaries of the Temple of Ptaḥ, etc., kneeling before cartouches of Psusennes I, and jambs with offering-texts. Anthes, *Mit Rahineh 1956*, pl. 31, fig. 12 [26–8], pp. 92–5 [Cb]; see id. in *Penn. Mus. Bull.* 21 [2] (June 1957), pp. 13–14 (as Kha).

Upper part of jamb with offering-text to Sekhmet, Dyn. XXI. Id. *Mit Rahineh 1956*, pl. 30 [f], fig. 12 [29], p. 96 [Cc].

Other finds.

Votive stela, man before Ptaḥ, and fragments of others, New Kingdom. Anthes, *Mit Rahineh 1956*, pls. 39 [f, c–e], 40 [c], fig. 14 [53], pp. 102–4 [52, 51, 53–5].

Offering-basin with [statue] of Amenemḥēt [hieroglyphs], Scribe of the dockyard, son of Nebwaʿwi [hieroglyphs], Dyn. XIX. Id. ib. pls. 24, 25 [a–c], fig. 5, pp. 73–5; id. in *Penn. Mus. Bull.* 21 [2] (June 1957), fig. 5, pp. 5–7, 25; Leclant in *Orientalia*, N.S. 27 (1958), pl. iv [5], p. 83; Jacquet and Wall-Gordon in *Mitt. Kairo*, 16 (1958), Taf. xii, xiii, pp. 161–75 with figs.; O'Connor and Silverman in *Expedition*, 21 [2] (Winter 1979), fig. 49 on p. 32.

Faience tower-tile, inscribed on four faces, dedicated by Paḳebeḥ [hieroglyphs], Head of the making (*wdḥ*) of faience (*mfkȝt*), with offering-scene at top, Dyn. XIX. Anthes, *Mit Rahineh 1956*, pl. 26 [a, b], fig. 6 [2], pp. 75–6.

Jar-fragment of Ḥatshepsut, alabaster. Id. ib. *1955*, pl. 26 [d], fig. 14 [155], p. 44.

L. Temple of Ramesses II.

El-Sayed Mahmud, *A New Temple for Hathor at Memphis*, p. 1 [top], with position on fig. 1.

Colossal statues of Ramesses II, two standing and two seated, granite. One standing, DAVID, *The Egyptian Kingdoms*, fig. on p. 49 [upper]; RUFFLE, *Heritage of the Pharaohs*, fig. 72. See LAUER in *Bull. Soc. fr. d'Ég.* No. 33 (March 1962), p. 16; LECLANT in *Orientalia*, N.S. 32 (1963), p. 86 [12].

M. TOMBS OF HIGH PRIESTS OF MEMPHIS OF DYNASTY XXII.

EL-AMIR in *The Egyptian Education Bureau London. The Bulletin*, No. 40 (Nov.–Dec. 1949), p. 19; *Chron. d'Ég.* xxi (1946), pp. 56–7.

SHESHONḲ [hieroglyphs], Greatest of the Directors of craftsmen, etc. Temp. Osorkon II.

Parents, Osorkon II and Keramama.
BADAWI in *Ann. Serv.* liv (1957), pp. 157–77, with views, Taf. i–iii [A].

Burial Chamber. In Cairo Mus. JE 88131.

Outer lintel of doorway, re-used block, right, Ḥaremḥab followed by deceased kneels before Sokari and Ḥatḥor, left, similar scene before Osiris. Right of door, deceased before Anubis, and two large figures of Ptaḥ. Left of door, deceased before Horus, and large figure of Sokari.

Id. ib. Taf. iv, pp. 159–60. Re-used block, HABACHI in *Glimpses of Ancient Egypt. Studies in Honour of H. W. Fairman*, p. 35 with pl. ii, fig. 2 (suggests originally Tutʿankhamūn's).

Inner lintel of doorway, re-used block, double-scene, Sethos I running towards seated goddess. On each side of doorway, two Sons of Horus.

BADAWI, op. cit. Taf. v (lintel), pp. 161–2. Text of lintel, KITCHEN, *Ram. Inscr.* i. 124–5 [65].

West wall. Texts and scenes from Book of the Dead.

BADAWI, op. cit. Taf. vi, vii, Abb. 2, pp. 162–8.

North wall. Left, *zad*-pillar before Atum and Ḥatḥor seated, right, *zad*-pillar held by Isis and Nephthys.

Id. ib. Taf. viii, p. 168.

East wall, right to left. Upper register, **1**, deceased before bark dragged by Souls of Pe and Nekhen, **2**, bending Nut upheld by Shu, assisted by ram-headed gods on each side, with others adoring, **3**, serpent-headed goddess, serpent, Osiris seated followed by Maʿet and another god. Lower register, texts and scenes from Book of the Dead.

Id. ib. Taf. ix–xi, Abb. 1, pp. 168–76.

Finds

Four canopic-jars, alabaster, in Cairo Mus. JE 86764. Id. ib. Taf. xii [A], p. 176.
Gold bracelet, inscribed. Id. ib. Taf. xv [A], p. 177.

Burial above Burial Chamber.

Stela of Amenophis II, with account of Asiatic campaigns of years 7 and 9, quartzite, re-used, in Cairo Mus. JE 86763. Id. in *Ann. Serv.* xlii (1943), pl. i, pp. 1–23; EDEL in *Zeitschrift des Deutschen Palästina-Vereins*, 69 (1953), Taf. 3–5, pp. 103, 113–36; EL-AMIR in *The Egyptian Education Bureau London. The Bulletin*, No. 46 (July 1950), fig. on p. 31, cf. pp. 29–30. King offering to Amen-rēʿ, MYŚLIWIEC, *Le Portrait royal dans le bas-relief du Nouvel Empire*, pl. xliii [100]. Text, HELCK, *Urk.* iv. 1299–1309 [375, A], cf. *Übersetz.* (1961), pp. 32–40; discussion of parts, Vikentiev in *Bull. Inst. Ég.* xxx (1947–8), pp. 251–307 with figs. 6, 9; Drioton in *Ann. Serv.* xlv (1947), pp. 57–64, 99–106; Grdseloff in ib. pp. 107–20. See *Descr. somm.* No. 6301.

Sarcophagus-lid of woman Taʿashakhet, Dyn. XXII. See el-Amir in *The Egyptian Education Bureau London. The Bulletin*, No. 40 (Nov.–Dec. 1949), p. 19.

Thekerti, Great Chief of the Ma, Greatest of the Directors of craftsmen.[1] Probably temp. Sesonchis III.

Father, Sheshonḳ[1] (tomb, see above).

See Badawi in *Ann. Serv.* liv (1957), p. 157 [bottom].

Pedēsi, Great Chief of the Ma, Greatest of the Directors of craftsmen.[1] Temp. Pemu or later.

Parents,[1] Thekerti (tomb, see above) and Thesubasteper(t).

See id. ib. xliv (1944), p. 181.

Outer sarcophagus of Amenḥotp Ḥuy, Chief Governor in Memphis, etc., granite, temp. Ramesses II, re-used. Id. ib. pls. xvi–xx, pp. 182–202.

Anthropoid coffin, silver. Id. ib. pl. xxi, p. 185 note 1.

Another burial, probably from same or adjoining tomb.

Anthropoid sarcophagus of Amenḥotp Ḥuy (same as above), granite, re-used, in Cairo Mus. JE 59128. Hamada in ib. xxxv (1935), pls. i, ii, pp. 122–31; Hornemann, *Types*, iii, pl. 799; see Badawi, op. cit. xliv (1944), p. 182 note 1.

Ḥarsiēsi, Great Chief of the Ma, Greatest of the Directors of craftsmen.[1] Temp. Pemu or later.

Father, Thekerti (Badawi) or Pedēsi (tombs of both, see above).

See Badawi in *Ann. Serv.* xliv (1944), p. 181 note 2; liv (1957), pp. 157 [bottom]–158 [top].

Finds from Ptaḥ Enclosure and Dependencies

Statues.

Royal.

Sesostris II kneeling, fragment, sandstone, in Cairo Mus. CG 387. Borchardt, *Statuen*, ii, Bl. 61, pp. 6–7. Text, Mariette, *Mon. div.* pl. 27 [a]; Brugsch, *Thes.* 1063 [4].

Lower part of seated King, New Kingdom. Petrie, *Memphis*, vi, pl. lvi [21], p. 33.

Private.

ʿAnkhu, Scribe of the Great Prison, son of Itneferu (mother), squatting, headless, granite, Middle Kingdom, in Cairo Mus. CG 410. Text, Mariette, *Mon. div.* pl. 27 [b]; Brugsch, *Thes.* 1062 [3]; Borchardt, *Statuen*, ii, p. 21.

Ptaḥwēr, Chief steward, etc., son of ʿAmet (mother), granite, Middle

[1] Not mentioned in tomb.

Kingdom, in Berlin (East) Mus. 8808. Texts, *Aeg. Inschr.* i, p. 146; BRUGSCH, *Thes.* 1062 [2]; KAYSER, *Die Tempelstatuen ägyptischer Privatleute im mittleren und im neuen Reich*, pp. 14–15; on front, MARIETTE, op. cit. pl. 27 [d]. See *Ausf. Verz.* pp. 82–3.

Amenḥotp, Chief [steward], etc. (Ṣaqqâra tomb, see *supra*, pp. 702–3), scribe-statue, granite, temp. Amenophis III, in Cairo Mus. CG 1169. Text, BORCHARDT, *Statuen*, iv, p. 88; HELCK, *Urk.* iv. 1801 [643], cf. *Übersetz.* (1961), p. 263.

Nefertemḥotp, block-statue with four female relatives in high relief on sides, Ramesside, in Bristol Mus. H 395. PETRIE, *Memphis*, ii, pl. xviii [lower left], p. 14 (as Cambridge).

Ptaḥmosi, Royal scribe, Ramesside. Text, MARIETTE, *Mon. div.* pl. 28 [e].

Tenro [hieroglyphs], Scribe of the Temple of Ptaḥ, block-statue with naos at front, sandstone, Ramesside, in Cairo Mus. CG 1210. Text, id. ib. pl. 27 [h]; BORCHARDT, *Statuen*, iv, p. 109.

A Fan-bearer on the right of the King, Prophet of Amūn at Karnak, etc., Ramesside. Text, MARIETTE, op. cit. pl. 28 [a].

Papu [hieroglyphs], Overseer of cattle, Steward of Ptaḥ, etc., squatting, fragment, New Kingdom (?), in Cairo Mus. CG 671. See BORCHARDT, *Statuen*, iii, pp. 17–18 (text); text, MARIETTE, op. cit. pl. 28 [b].

Ḥarsiēsi [hieroglyphs], Greatest of the Directors of craftsmen, etc., holding naos of Ḥatḥor, dedicated by son ʿAnkhefensekhmet [hieroglyphs], same title, fragment, sandstone, temp. Sesonchis V, in Cairo Mus. CG 1212. BORCHARDT, *Statuen*, iv, Bl. 170, pp. 110–11. Text, MARIETTE, op. cit. pl. 27 [g].

Neferebrēʿ-sineit [hieroglyphs], Overseer of singers of the Great House, etc., son of Merib [hieroglyphs], kneeling with naos, lower part, schist, temp. Psammetikhos II or later, in Berlin (East) Mus. 8809. SCHÄFER and ANDRAE, *Kunst* (1925), 415 [1]; (1930), 431 [1]; (1942), 436 [1]; WORRINGER, *Ägyptische Kunst*, Abb. 29. Text, MARIETTE, op. cit. pl. 28 [d]; BRUGSCH, *Thes.* 1063 [6]; PIEHL in *P.S.B.A.* x (1888), pp. 536–7 [11], cf. xi (1889), p. 77. See *Ausf. Verz.* p. 256.

Pef[teuʿauneit], Greatest of physicians of Upper and Lower Egypt, etc., middle part, basalt, temp. Apries. BAKRY in *Oriens Antiquus*, ix (1970), Tav. xxxv–xxxvii, fig. 1, pp. 325–33.

ʿAksonb [hieroglyphs], First prophet of Amen-rēʿ Lord of Diospolis Inferior, etc., lower part of squatting statue, early Dyn. XXVI, in Cairo Mus. CG 915. Text, BORCHARDT, *Statuen*, iii, pp. 151–2; part, BRUGSCH, *Thes.* 1063 [5]; id. *Dictionnaire Géographique de l'Ancienne Égypte*, p. 1327 [top].

Head, sandstone, Dyn. XXV–XXVI, in Brit. Mus. 37883. PRISSE, *L'Art ég.* ii, *Sculpture*, 33rd pl. 'Fragments de statues iconiques' [etc.] [1], *Texte*, p. 409; BUDGE, *A History of Egypt*, iii, fig. on p. 131; WEIGALL, *Anc. Eg. . . . Art*, 320 [upper left]; HALL in *J.E.A.* xiii (1927), pls. xi, xii, pp. 27–9, 265–6; id. in HAMMERTON, *Universal History of the World*, ii, fig. on p. 1022 [left]; id. in *Encyclopaedia Britannica*, 14th ed. (1929), pl. x [9]; *The Cambridge Ancient History. Plates*, i (1927), pl. on p. 269 [a]; *Guide, 3rd and 4th*, fig. on p. 95, cf. p. 96 [186]; *Guide, 4th to 6th*, fig. on p. 123, cf. p. 124 [39]; *Guide, Eg. Collns.* (1930), fig. 92, p. 171; (1964), fig. 70, p. 185; ROSS, *The Art of Egypt*, pl. on p. 227; BOSSE, *Die menschliche Figur*, Taf. xi [201], p. 73; POULSEN (F.), *Ægyptens Kunst* (1933), fig. 81; WOLF, *Kunst*, Abb. 632; id. *Hochkulturen*, Abb. 55; WOLDERING, *Götter*, Abb. 96; VANDERSLEYEN, *Das Alte Ägypten*, Abb. 214; JAMES, *An Introduction to Ancient Egypt*, fig. 79.

Man (name lost) holding naos, fragment, slate, Dyn. XXVI, in Cairo Mus. CG 673. BORCHARDT, *Statuen*, iii, Bl. 123, p. 20. Text, MARIETTE, *Mon. div.* pl. 29 [c]; BRUGSCH, *Thes.* 1065 [9].

Head, granite, Late Period, in Copenhagen, Ny Carlsberg Glypt. Æ.I.N. 1505. Petrie, *Memphis*, vi, pl. lv [15], p. 33; Mogensen, *Coll. ég.* pl. xviii [A 75], p. 20; Koefoed-Petersen, *Cat. des statues*, pl. 122, p. 66 [114].

Divinities.

Upper part of bull-headed Apis, Dyn. XII. Petrie, *Memphis*, vi, pl. liii [4], p. 32. See Vandier, *Manuel*, iii, pp. 197 note 2, 605.

Osiris seated, headless, dedicated by Irʿaḥor Neferebrēʿ-nūfer (Ṣaqqâra tb. LS 23), basalt, temp. Necho II to Apries, in Cairo Mus. CG 38236. Daressy, *Statues*, pl. xiv, pp. 69–70. Text, Mariette, *Mon. div.* pl. 29 [a]; Piehl in *Ä.Z.* xxv (1887), pp. 120–1 [xlv]. See Maspero, *Guide*, p. 204 [828].

Lower part of statue of Osiris, dedicated by ʿAnkhpekhrod, granite, Dyn. XXVI, in Cairo Mus. CG 38233. Text, Mariette, op. cit. pl. 28 [c]; Daressy, op. cit. pp. 68, cf. 67 (as Ṣaqqâra).

Stelae.

Amenophis II before Ptaḥ, in Cairo Mus. CG 34020. Lacau, *Stèles*, pl. xii, pp. 40–1.

Tuthmosis IV smiting enemy before Ptaḥ. Petrie, *Memphis*, vi, pl. lv [12], p. 33.

Amenḥotp, Steward, temp. Amenophis III (Ṣaqqâra tomb, see *supra*, pp. 702–3), and son Piay, Scribe, in Manchester Mus. 5050. Id. ib. ii, pls. xviii [lower right], xxv [lower left], pp. 14, 21. Text, Helck, *Urk.* iv. 1804–6 [647], cf. *Übersetz.* (1961), pp. 264–5.

Wenent, son of Irterau(?), ear-stela, Dyn. XVIII(?). Petrie, *Memphis*, vi, pl. lv [13], p. 33.

Raʿmosi, Goldworker, with representation of Pylon of Temple of Ptaḥ, Dyn. XIX, in Cairo Mus. Temp. No. 16.3.25.12. Mariette, *Mon. div.* pl. 30 [a]; Bruyère, *Mert Seger à Deir el Médineh*, fig. 30, p. 50 note 1. See Yoyotte, *Les Pèlerinages dans l'Égypte ancienne* in *Sources Orientales*, iii, pp. 44, 70 [81] (as Temp. No. 14.3.25.12).

[Man] before Ptaḥ and Sekhmet, fragment, Dyn. XIX, in Copenhagen, Ny Carlsberg Glypt. Æ.I.N. 1516. Petrie, *Memphis*, vi, pl. lviii [34], p. 33; Mogensen, *Coll. ég.* pl. cvi [A 717], p. 98; Koefoed-Petersen, *Les Stèles égyptiennes*, pl. 38, pp. 32–3.

Unnūfer, God's father of Osiris, Scribe of accounts, etc., dedicated by son Shedsuḥori, Scribe of the temple, etc., fragment, Ramesside. Text, Mariette, *Mon. div.* pl. 29 [b].

. . . ḥotp before Reshef, Ramesside, in London, Univ. Coll. 14400. Petrie, *Memphis*, iii, pl. xxxix [5], p. 39; Leibovitch in *Ann. Serv.* xl (1940), fig. 60, p. 491; Stewart, *Eg. Stelae*, i, pl. 35 [2], p. 44.

Hawk and ibis, Late Period or Ptolemaic, in Cairo Mus. Petrie, *Memphis*, vi, pl. lx [44], p. 34.

Blocks.

Man with staff, Dyn. IV–V, re-used. Petrie, *Memphis*, vi, pl. liii [3], p. 32.

Cornice of a Hereditary prince, etc., Old Kingdom(?). Id. ib. vi, pl. liv [5], p. 32.

Remains of texts, Old Kingdom. Id. ib. vi, pl. liii [1, 2], p. 32.

Column, probably temp. Amenophis III, in Brussels, Mus. Roy. E.4987. Id. ib. ii, pl. xix [upper left], pp. 14, 18; *Bruxelles. Mus. Roy. Département égyptien. Album* (1934), pl. 2. Text, Speleers, *Rec. inscr.* p. 38 [141].

Blocks of Amenophis IV. Fragment of rewarding scene, with collars, PETRIE, op. cit. vi, pl. liv [6], p. 32; see LÖHR in *Studien zur altägyptischen Kultur*, 2 (1975), Taf. v [2] (from PETRIE), p. 161. Fragment of boat scene, in Cambridge, Fitzwilliam Mus. E.19.1913, PETRIE, op. cit. vi, pl. liv [7], p. 32; detail showing animal skin, DAVIES MSS. 2.30 [middle]; see LÖHR, op. cit. Taf. iv [3] (from PETRIE), pp. 160–1. Offering-scene, in Brussels, Mus. Roy. E.7636, PETRIE, op. cit. vi, pl. liv [8], p. 32; LÖHR, op. cit. Taf. iv [2], p. 160. Upper part of Queen Nefertiti, in London, Univ. Coll. 73, PETRIE, op. cit. vi, pl. liv [9], p. 32; SAMSON, *Amarna*, pl. 21 (as 037); STEWART, *Eg. Stelae*, i, pl. 9 [2], p. 17; see LÖHR, op. cit. Taf. iii [2] (from PETRIE), p. 159 (as 037). Chariot and men before altars, formerly in von Bissing Colln. and The Hague, Scheurleer Mus., PETRIE, op. cit. vi, pl. liv [10], p. 32; COHEN, *Egypte en Voor-Azië*, pl. 14; see LÖHR, op. cit. Taf. v [1] (from PETRIE), pp. 159–60. All blocks, see ROEDER, *Amarna-Reliefs aus Hermopolis*, ii, pp. 362–3 [d].

Remains of text, temp. Amenophis IV, possibly in Cairo Mus. MARIETTE, *Mon. div.* pl. 27 [e]. Text, LEGRAIN, *Répertoire*, No. 298.

Block with cartouche of Ḥaremḥab, in Chicago, Or. Inst. 9169; PETRIE, *Memphis*, vi, pl. lv [17], p. 33. Another, id. ib. vi, pl. lv [16], p. 33.

Lintel of Ramesses II. Id. ib. vi, pl. lix [36], p. 33.

Jamb with two registers, Ramesses II offering image of Maʿet, and censing and libating, before Ptaḥ, quartzite. Id. ib. vi, pl. lvi [18], p. 33.

Ramesses II before Ptaḥ. Sketches, WILBOUR MSS. 2 E, 19.

Head of King, perhaps Ramesses II, granite, in Copenhagen, Ny Carlsberg Glypt. Æ.I.N. 1513 (moved here from *Bibl.* iv. 86). PETRIE, *Memphis*, vi, pl. lix [37], p. 33; MOGENSEN, *Coll. ég.* pl. cix [A 738], p. 102 (as Ṭarkhân); KOEFOED-PETERSEN, *Cat. des bas-reliefs*, pl. xli [41], p. 38; head, MYŚLIWIEC, *Le Portrait royal dans le bas-relief du Nouvel Empire*, pl. cviii [239].

King, perhaps Ramesses II, embraced by Ptaḥ, granite. PETRIE, op. cit. vi, pl. lix [38], p. 33.

Part of double-scene, Khaʿemwēset (son of Ramesses II) and men performing ceremony, in Cambridge, Fitzwilliam Mus. E.59.1914. Id. ib. vi, pl. lvi [22], p. 33; see GOMAÀ, *Chaemwese* [etc.], p. 82 [44].

Name of Merneptaḥ-Siptaḥ altered to Sethos II. PETRIE, op. cit. vi, pl. lvii [23], p. 33.

Lintel of Iny [hieroglyphs], Royal scribe, Chief lector-priest, Dyn. XIX, in Philadelphia Mus. E 12279. Id. ib. iii, pl. xxxi [bottom].

Column-fragments of Ramesses III. Id. ib. i, on pl. xxv [middle left], p. 10; ii, pl. xxiii [middle left, bottom left], pp. 14, 19.

Cornice of Ramesses VI, in Copenhagen, Ny Carlsberg Glypt. Æ.I.N. 1148. Id. ib. iii, pl. xxxi [lower middle right], pp. 39–40. See KOEFOED-PETERSEN, *Cat. des bas-reliefs*, p. 60 [80].

Upper part of King's *ka*, probably New Kingdom. PETRIE, *Memphis*, vi, pl. lviii [31], p. 33.

Two blocks, priests before King(?), and upper part of Ptaḥ, granite, probably New Kingdom. Id. ib. vi, pl. lviii [32–3], p. 33.

Apis-bull running towards Mert, basalt, probably New Kingdom. Id. ib. iii, pl. xxx [3], p. 39.

Remains of King Amenemōpet before Sekhmet, in Cairo Mus. Temp. No. 3.7.24.11. Texts, GAUTHIER in *Ann. Serv.* xxii (1922), pp. 204–5.

Column of Shedsunefertem [hieroglyphs], Chief Governor of Memphis, etc., with cartouches of Siamūn, and Ptaḥ and Ḥatḥor. PETRIE, *Memphis*, ii, pl. xxiii [right], p. 14.

Cornice-fragment of Sesonchis I. Id. ib. vi, pl. lvii [24], p. 33.

[King] before bark of Sokari, sandstone, Dyn. XXVI, about 30 metres south-east of Pylon of the Temple of Ptaḥ. Text, Daressy in *Ann. Serv.* iii (1902), p. 31 [19].

Trial-piece, hawk, quartzite, Dyn. XXVI, in Copenhagen, Ny Carlsberg Glypt. Æ.I.N. 1512. Petrie, *Memphis*, vi, pl. lxi [50], p. 34; Mogensen, *Coll. ég.* pl. lxxxv [A 647], p. 82; id. *Modeller og Øvelsesstykker* [etc.] in *Fra Ny Carlsberg Glyptoteks Samlinger* (1920), fig. 30, p. 36.

Cartouche of Nektanebos I, in London, Univ. Coll. 14538; Petrie, *Memphis*, vi, pl. lvii [25], p. 33. Another, id. ib. iii, pl. xxxii [1].

Blocks of Nektanebos II, re-used in tank or vat between Hypostyle Hall of the Temple of Ptaḥ and Embalming House of Apis-bulls. Texts, Daressy in *Ann. Serv.* ii (1901), pp. 241–2.

Two inscribed blocks, Late Period. Brugsch, *Thes.* 1061 [bottom].

Three Souls of Pe, Late Period, in Copenhagen, Ny Carlsberg Glypt. Æ.I.N. 1511. Petrie, *Memphis*, vi, pl. lv [11], p. 32; Mogensen, *Coll. ég.* pl. cviii [A 733], p. 101; Koefoed-Petersen, *Cat. des bas-reliefs*, pl. li [51], pp. 42–3.

Trial-piece, vulture, Late Period, in London, Univ. Coll. 15507. Petrie, op. cit. v, pl. lxxviii [bottom left], p. 33; von Bissing in *Bull. Antieke Beschaving*, v [1] (June 1930), fig. 3 on pl. facing p. 6 (as Cairo).

Various.

Sarcophagus of cat, dedicated by Ḏḥutmosi (son of Amenophis III), in Cairo Mus. CG 5003. Borchardt in *Ä.Z.* 44 (1907), p. 97 with fig.; Wildung in *Die Kunst*, 90 [6] (June 1978), fig. 5 on p. 335; id. and Grimm, *Götter, Pharaonen* (1978), No. 28; Fischer in *Metropolitan Museum Journal*, 12 (1977), fig. 5, p. 178 with note 33. Texts, Daressy in *Rec. Trav.* xiv (1893), pp. 174–5 [lxix]; Reisner, *Canopics*, pp. 392–4. See Maspero, *Guide* (1902), p. 75 [232].

Kôm el-Nawa

Lintel-fragments of Amenemḥēt II, granite. L. D. *Text*, i, p. 203 [middle]; Petrie, *Memphis*, ii, pl. xxiii [top], p. 14.

Block of Amasis, granite. Id. ib. ii, pl. xxiii [left lower middle], p. 14.

Block with head of Ptaḥ, quartzite, Dyn. XVIII. *Sotheby Sale Cat.* Nov. 11, 1963, No. 89 with fig.

Lower part of Horus on crocodiles stela, granite, Dyn. XXVI, in Cairo Mus. CG 9411. Text, Daressy, *Textes et dessins magiques* (*Cat. Caire*), pp. 26–7; part, Klasens, *A Magical Statue Base* [etc.], pp. 37–8 [C 4].

Kôm el-Arbaʿîn

Fragments of statue-base of Ḥori, Governor of the town, Vizier, etc., son of Ḥori, Greatest of the Directors of craftsmen, sandstone, temp. Merneptaḥ-Siptaḥ to Ramesses III, one formerly in New York Hist. Soc. Colln., now in Brooklyn Mus. 37.1920E, other in Cairo Mus. CG 1174. Brooklyn Mus. fragment, De Meulenaere in *Annuaire de l'Institut de Philologie et d'Histoire Orientales et Slaves*, xx (1968–72), pls. i, ii, pp. 191–6; Černý MSS. photos. 2.186; see *N.Y.H.S. Cat.* p. 8 [126]. Text of Cairo fragment, Borchardt, *Statuen*, iv, p. 90.

Remains of double-statue, lower part of seated god probably crowning kneeling Ḥaremḥab (only feet left), quartzite. See SIMPSON in *J.E.A.* 42 (1956), pp. 118–19.

Kôm el-Fakhry

CEMETERY. 1st Int. Period or early Middle Kingdom.

Tombs with decorated burial chambers, see EL HITTA in *La Revue du Caire*, xxxiii [175] (1955), pp. 50–1; LILYQUIST in *J.A.R.C.E.* xi (1974), pp. 27–30 (several men called Impy and woman Impyʿankh [hieroglyphs], Prophetess of Ḥatḥor, etc.), with views, etc., pls. i–iii.

Re-used blocks from tombs of Dynasty XXX.

Neferseshem-psammethek [hieroglyphs], Scribe of divine books, etc., in Cairo Mus. See YOYOTTE in *Chron. d'Ég.* xxix (1954), p. 278. (a) Presentation of jewellery, with deceased seated on left, JE 10978; MARIETTE, *Mon. div.* pl. 35 [middle]; MASPERO, *Le Musée Égyptien*, ii, pls. xxxv [upper], xxxvi, pp. 79–80; id. *Égypte*, fig. 520; id. *Guide* (1914), fig. 61, p. 203 [870]; (1915), fig. 73, p. 210 [870]; BORCHARDT, *Das Grabdenkmal des Königs S'aꜣḥu-reʿ*, ii, Abb. 10, p. 63; SCHMIDT, *Levende og Døde*, fig. 892; TERRACE and FISCHER, *Treasures*, pp. 173–6 with pls.; DEVÉRIA squeezes, 6165, i. 51; couples with jewellery, *Encycl. phot. Caire*, pl. 191; Brussels. *5000 ans*, fig. 44, p. 30 [72]; London. *5000 Years*, pl. xxiii, p. 21 [78]; Louisiana. *5000 års*, No. 204 with fig.; Zürich. *5000 Jahre*, Abb. 70, p. 76 [215]; head of 2nd girl from right, HEMELRIJK in *Bull. Antieke Beschaving*, xxxviii (1963), fig. 1, pp. 31–2; 1st and 2nd couples from right, DRIOTON in *Studies Presented to F. Ll. Griffith*, pl. 46 [c], pp. 293–4; 2nd, ALDRED, *Jewels of the Pharaohs*, pl. 149; 2nd and 3rd, WEIGALL, *Anc. Eg. . . . Art*, 324; see MARIETTE, *Notice des principaux monuments . . . à Boulaq* (1864), pp. 75–6 [49]. (b) Offering-bringers before deceased seated on left, JE 10976; MARIETTE, *Mon. div.* pl. 35 [bottom]; MASPERO, *Le Musée Égyptien*, ii, pls. xxxii [top], xxxiii; PERROT and CHIPIEZ, *Hist. de l'Art*, i, figs. 485–6; SPRINGER, *Die Kunst des Altertums* (1923), Abb. 128; BUHL in *Fra Nationalmuseets Arbejdsmark* (1948), fig. 2, pp. 49–50; 1st to 4th offering-bringers with children, *Encycl. phot. Caire*, pl. 189; 4th to 6th, HAMANN, *Äg. Kunst*, Abb. 326; see MASPERO, *Guide*, p. 200 [801].

Upper parts of offering-bringers before deceased seated on right, JE 10977. MASPERO, *Le Musée Égyptien*, ii, pl. xxxviii [top], pp. 81–2.

Miscellaneous.

Bust, perhaps Tutʿankhamūn or Ḥaremḥab, in Cairo Mus. JE 55032. See *Descr. somm.* No. 6183.

Lower part of statue of King Petubastis (Seḥetepibrēʿ) seated, granite. HABACHI in *Ä.Z.* 93 (1966), Taf. v [b, c], figs. 1–3, pp. 70–1.

Fragment of statue of kneeling captive attacked by lion, slate, Late Period, in Cairo Mus. Temp. No. 16.9.30.12. HORNEMANN, *Types*, v, pl. 1333.

Kôm el-Rabîʿa

TEMPLE OF ḤATḤOR. Temp. Ramesses II.

EL-SAYED MAHMUD, *A New Temple for Hathor at Memphis*, passim, with plan, fig. 2, diagrams of scenes, fig. 3, and views, pls. 1–4, 6. View, BAKRY in *Mitt. Kairo*, 28 (1972),

Taf. xxii [left upper], p. 77. Names of Ḥatḥor, KITCHEN, *Ram. Inscr.* ii. 496 [192, C]. See LECLANT in *Orientalia*, N.S. 41 (1972), p. 254 [13]; 42 (1973), p. 403 [25, b].

Pylon.

Doorway, west thickness. Remains of top register, with King before [a god], scene with [Ptaḥ], and royal names.

EL-SAYED MAHMUD, op. cit. pls. i and 5, p. 7 (references to pls. in text incorrect, passim).

West part, inner face. From east, remains of top two registers, **I, 1,** King offering incense to Ptaḥ, **2,** before a seated god, **3,** kneeling on *ḥeb*-sign before a seated god, with a goddess behind him. **II, 1,** King before a lioness-headed goddess, **2,** preceded by standards, **3,** purified by Horus and Thoth before Ptaḥ, **4,** offering collar to Ḥatḥor.

Id. ib. pls. ii–x and 11, 12, 15, 16, pp. 7–8. **4,** BAKRY, op. cit. Taf. xxii [left lower], p. 77.

Court.

West wall. Remains of register **II** (**I** lost), from north, **1,** King in foundation ceremony before Sefkhet-ʿabu, **2,** before Min-Amūn, **3,** with *ḥes*-vase before Ḥatḥor Mistress of Ḥetept, **4,** before [a god], **5,** [before a lion-headed goddess].

EL-SAYED MAHMUD, op. cit. pls. xi–xix and 13, 14, pp. 8–11.

Pillars with Ḥatḥor capitals and scenes of king before gods (including Amen-rēʿ) and royal names.

Id. ib. pls. 7–10, p. 11, with texts of one column on fig. 4; BAKRY, op. cit. Taf. xxii [right], p. 77.

BUILDING OF SIAMŪN.

Plan, PETRIE, *Memphis*, i, pl. xxx [upper right], p. 12.

Monuments of ʿAnkhefenmut.

Lintel, Siamūn in double-scene, right, followed by ʿAnkhefenmut [hieroglyphs], God's father, Secretary of Ptaḥ, etc., son of Ḥatiay [hieroglyphs], before Ptaḥ and Sekhmet, left, followed by Neterkheperrēʿ-mer(y)ptaḥ [hieroglyphs] Paupau [hieroglyphs], Greatest of the Directors of craftsmen of Ptaḥ, etc., before Ptaḥ and Ḥatḥor, and left jamb with offering-texts of ʿAnkhefenmut, in Copenhagen, Ny Carlsberg Glypt. Æ.I.N. 1012. Id. ib. ii, pl. xxiv [top and right], pp. 14–15, 19–20; MOGENSEN, *Coll. ég.* pl. cxi [A 746], pp. 102–3; SCHMIDT, *Choix* (1910), pls. xvii [43], xviii [45], pp. 31–2; id. *Levende og Døde*, figs. 484–5; KOEFOED-PETERSEN, *Cat. des bas-reliefs*, pls. lxvii–lxxii, pp. 54–5 [71], 74–5. Texts, id. *Rec. inscr.* pp. 84–5. Names and titles, see DE MEULENAERE in *Bibliotheca Orientalis*, xiv (1957), p. 72 [71].

Lintels, double-scene, ʿAnkhefenmut as fan-bearer kneeling before names of Siamūn. (a) Philadelphia Mus. E 14345; PETRIE, *Memphis*, ii, pl. xxiv [upper middle], pp. 15, 20; RANKE in *Penn. Mus. Bull.* xv [2–3] (Nov. 1950), fig. 26, p. 46. (b) Manchester Mus. 4933; texts, PETRIE, op. cit. ii, pl. xxiv [left lower middle]. (c) Pittsburgh, Museum of Art, Carnegie Institute, 3755; texts, id. ib. ii, pl. xxiv [right lower middle]. (d) Brit. Mus. 1470; texts, id. ib. ii, pl. xxiv [left bottom]; see *Guide* (*Sculpture*), pp. 303–4 [1170] (with royal names).

Fragments of lintel and jamb, similar to last (name lost), re-used near Enclosure Wall of Ptaḥ. ANTHES, *Mit Rahineh 1956*, pls. 32 [b], 33 [a], fig. 11 [24–5], p. 92.

Lintel, Siamūn followed by ʿAnkhefenmut before Amen-rēʿ and Mut, in Cairo Mus. JE 40033. PETRIE, *Memphis*, i, pl. xxxi [top and middle right], p. 13; ii, pl. xix [left bottom] (omitting ʿAnkhefenmut), p. 18; upper part of Siamūn, id. *Egypt and Israel*, fig. 32; see MASPERO, *Guide* (1915), p. 181 [663].

Two jamb-fragments of ʿAnkhefenmut (another name of father was Khaʿemwēset [hieroglyphs]), in Bristol, City Mus. H 3568–9. See GRINSELL, *Guide Catalogue to the Collections from Ancient Egypt* (1972), p. 57. Texts of one, PETRIE, *Memphis*, ii, pl. xxiv [middle bottom], pp. 15, 20.

Two jamb-fragments of ʿAnkhefenmut, in Brussels, Mus. Roy. E.4979, and Manchester Mus. 5106. Id. ib. ii, pl. xxiii [middle and right of middle lower], pp. 14, 19. Text of Brussels E.4979, SPELEERS, *Rec. inscr.* p. 81 [308].

Other finds.

Fragmentary lintel, left part of double-scene, [Osorkon I] followed by Zeptaḥefʿankh, Overseer of cattle of the Temple of Ptaḥ, etc., before Bubastis and Horus, in Munich, Staatl. Samml. Gl.78. VON BISSING in *Münchner Jahrb.* (1911), Abb. 11, p. 166 [12]; *Äg. Sammlung* (1966), Abb. 64; *Staatl. Sammlung* (1972), pl. 45 [lower], p. 82; EGGEBRECHT *Schlachtungsbräuche im Alten Ägypten* [etc.], Taf. xiv [C]. See PETRIE, *Memphis*, ii, p. 14; WOLTERS, *Illus. Kat.* p. 13 [34c]; id. *Führer*, p. 13 [70]; *Staatl. Sammlung* (1976), p. 147.

Two fragments of texts mentioning Temple of Osiris, probably 3rd Int. Period, re-used. PETRIE, *Memphis*, i, pl. xxxii [left], p. 13.

Block with remains of biographical text, 3rd Int. Period. Id. ib. ii, pl. xxiii [upper middle], pp. 14, 19.

Statue (head and feet lost) of Thaiḥepimu [hieroglyphs], brother of Teos and father of Nektanebos II, breccia, in New York, M.M.A. 08.205.1. Id. ib. i, pls. xxxi [upper left], xxxii [right], pp. 13, 20–1; SCOTT, *Egyptian Statues* (1945), 28th pl. (as quartzite); *Guide to the Collections. Egyptian Art* (1962), fig. 49. See *A Handbook of the Egyptian Rooms* (1911), pp. 133–4; DE MEULENAERE in *Ä.Z.* 90 (1963), p. 91.

Ramesside temple-blocks. From foundations of church south-west of Building of Siamūn.

PETRIE, *Memphis*, iv, pls. xxvii–xxx, pp. 23–4. Libyan(?) figures and cartouches of Ramesses II (= pl. xxviii [top right]) and offerings (= pl. xxix [4th from top right]), in Cambridge, Fitzwilliam Mus. E.63 and 75.1911. Parts of 4 hieroglyphs from name of Ramesses II (= pl. xxviii [on top left]), in Chicago, Or. Inst. 9160. Arm with censer, and smaller figure of man below (= pl. xxix [middle bottom]), in Copenhagen, Ny Carlsberg Glypt. Æ.I.N. 1421; MOGENSEN, *Coll. ég.* pl. c [A 693], pp. 93–4; KOEFOED-PETERSEN, *Cat. des bas-reliefs*, pl. xlviii [49], p. 42. Names of Ramesses II (= pl. xxviii [top left]), in Evanston (Ill.), Hibbard Memorial Library, 4. Palimpsest texts (= pl. xxx [2nd from top right]), in Manchester Mus. 5375.

Kôm el-Qalʿa

Map LXXII [1]

ANTHES, *Mit Rahineh 1956*, pp. 35–8, with plan, figs. 2, cf. 1.

TEMPLE OF PTAḤ. Merneptaḥ.

PETRIE, *Memphis*, i, pp. 3–4, 11–12, with plan, pl. xxvii.

Outer court.

Doorway. Lintel, double-scene, King seated in kiosk, and smiting foes before Ptaḥ;

Quibell in *Ann. Serv.* viii (1907), pp. 120–1 with pl.; Petrie, *Memphis*, ii, pl. xxi, pp. 18–19.

Re-used lotus-capitals, probably Dyn. V. One, in Manchester Mus. 5107, id. ib. i, pl. iii [right top], p. 6; Petrie, *Egyptian Architecture*, pl. xviii [94]; Spanton in *Anc. Eg.* (1917), fig. 47, p. 19. Another two, in Manchester Mus. 5102 and Cairo Mus.; one, Petrie, *Memphis*, ii, pl. xviii [upper right], pp. 13–14; Spanton, op. cit. fig. 46, p. 19.

Re-used column-fragment of Khaʿemwēset (son of Ramesses II), in Edinburgh, Roy. Scot. Mus. 1908.364; Petrie, *Memphis*, i, pl. xxv [top left], pp. 10, 11; Gosse, *The Civilization of the Ancient Egyptians*, fig. 107; Gomaà, *Chaemwese* [etc.], Abb. 15, p. 82 [42]. Text of another, presumably from here, Petrie, *Memphis*, ii, pl. xxv [upper left], pp. 15, 20; see Gomaà, op. cit. p. 82 [43], cf. Abb. 16 [b] (from Petrie).

Inscribed column with rope-pattern binding, probably from here; Petrie, *Memphis*, i, pls. xxv [upper right], xxvi [6], pp. 10, 20.

Inner doorway.

Left jamb with names of the King and Nile-gods at bottom, in Brit. Mus. 1469; id. ib. i, pl. xxix [right], p. 11; see *Guide* (*Sculpture*), p. 303 [1169].

Finds

Two colossal negro heads, Dyn. XIX, in Bristol, City Mus. H 799, and Copenhagen, Ny Carlsberg Glypt. Æ.I.N. 1047. Petrie, *Memphis*, ii, pl. xx [top and middle], p. 14. Bristol H 799, Grinsell, *Guide Catalogue to the Collections from Ancient Egypt* (1972), fig. 29, p. 52. Copenhagen Æ.I.N. 1047, Mogensen, *Coll. ég.* pl. xviii [A 76], p. 20; Koefoed-Petersen, *Cat. des statues*, pl. 92, p. 50 [80].

Stela-fragment with head of Sēth, Ramesside. Petrie, op. cit. ii, pl. xx [bottom], p. 14.

Two stelae with Ḥatḥor-cow, one dedicated by woman Tanenuny, Nurse of the King's son, Ramesside, in Manchester Mus. 4910, 4914. Id. ib. i, pl. xxviii [21–2], p. 12.

Pylon. Merneptaḥ.

C. S. F[isher] in *Penn. Mus. Journ.* viii (1917), pp. 226–8. View, ib. vi (1915), fig. 61 on p. 81.

Two papyrus-columns, King before gods, in Philadelphia Mus. E 13576–7. *Penn. Mus. Journ.* xvii (1926), fig. on p. 111 [left, right]; Ranke in *Penn. Mus. Bull.* xv [2–3] (Nov. 1950), on fig. 63, p. 104; part of text, Fischer in *Metropolitan Museum Journal*, 12 (1977), p. 177.

Outer doorway, in Philadelphia Mus. E 13575, and two blocks E 13568–9. (a) and (b) Jambs. Four registers, **I,** King before Ptaḥ, **II,** receives *ḥeb-sed* from Ptaḥ in kiosk, **III,** receives ☥ from Nefertem, **IV,** smites foes. Base, *sma*-symbol bound by Nile-gods, with two kneeling captives, and names of Ramesses IV below. (c) and (d) Thicknesses. Ptaḥ in kiosk before names of the King. Base, four geographical personifications, and names of Ramesses IV below.

(a) and (b) Omitting **I,** *Penn. Mus. Journ.* xvii (1926), fig. on p. 109 [left, right]. (a) **IV** and base, Ranke in *Penn. Mus. Bull.* xv [2–3] (Nov. 1950), fig. 62, pp. 102–4; Nile-gods, Capart in *Chron. d'Ég.* xxxii (1957), fig. 78, p. 235 (repr. as *Causeries sur l'Art égyptien*, fig. 68, p. 77). (b) Two blocks E 13568–9, see Ranke, op. cit. p. 105 [near top]. **II,** C. S. F[isher] in *Penn. Mus. Journ.* viii (1917), fig. 84, p. 226; **IV** and base, Christophe in *Bull. Inst. Ég.* xxxvii [1] (1954–5), pl. vi, p. 21 [2, b]. (d) Bottom register and base, id. ib. pl. v, pp. 20–1 [2, a]; base, Anthes, *Mit Rahineh 1956*, pl. 53, pp. 14, 36–7, 38.

PALACE. Merneptah.

Plan LXXII [2]

C. S. F[ISHER] in *Penn. Mus. Journ.* viii (1917), pp. 211–25, with plan, fig. 79, and views, figs. 77–8, 80–1, 83. View, ib. vi (1915), fig. 60 on p. 81. Reconstruction, O'CONNOR and SILVERMAN in *Expedition*, 21 [2] (Winter 1979), fig. 36 on p. 25 (by Fisher).

Outer Vestibule. 20 of Fisher.

Columns and bases of Merneptah, in Philadelphia Mus. E 13558–9. E 13558B, *Penn. Mus. Journ.* xvii (1926), fig. on p. 107 [left].

Court. 19 of Fisher.

(1) Lintel, in Philadelphia Mus. E 13557.

Inner Vestibule. 18 of Fisher.

Column of Ramesses II, re-used by Merneptah, granite, in Philadelphia Mus. E 636. RANKE in *Penn. Mus. Bull.* xv [2–3] (Nov. 1950), on fig. 59, p. 100; O'CONNOR and SILVERMAN in *Expedition*, 21 [2] (Winter 1979), on fig. 64 on p. 42.

Throne Room. 7 of Fisher.

C. S. F[ISHER] in *Penn. Mus. Journ.* xii (1921), pp. 30–4 with pl. iii (reconstruction); xv (1924), pp. 93–100. Model, ib. xvii (1926), fig. on p. 113.

(2) Doorway. Lintel, double-scene, King seated receiving *ḥeb-sed* from Horus and Sēth standards, and before Ptaḥ, jambs, names with Nile-gods at bottom.

FISHER in ib. xv (1924), fig. on p. 92, cf. pp. 97–8; PHILAD. photos. 33989–91.

Dais of throne, bows and foreigners. C. S. F[ISHER] in *Penn. Mus. Journ.* viii (1917), fig. 82, p. 218; KUHLMANN, *Der Thron im alten Ägypten*, Taf. v [12].

Window, in Philadelphia Mus. E 13565. FISHER in *Penn. Mus. Journ.* xv (1924), fig. on p. 96, cf. p. 97; see RANKE in *Penn. Mus. Bull.* xv [2–3] (Nov. 1950), pp. 104–5.

Room 14 (of Fisher).

(3) Doorway. Block from outer left jamb with remains of text and King with lion smiting foreigners, in Philadelphia Mus. E 17527.

Philadelphia E 17527, PIJOÁN, *Summa Artis*, iii (1945), fig. 554; see RANKE in *Penn. Mus. Bull.* xv [2–3] (Nov. 1950), p. 105.

Room 12 (of Fisher).

(4) Doorway, in Philadelphia Mus. E 13560.

Private Apartments behind Throne Room.

Window, in Philadelphia Mus. E 13564. FISHER in *Penn. Mus. Journ.* xv (1924), fig. on p. 99; RANKE in *Penn. Mus. Bull.* xv [2–3] (Nov. 1950), fig. 64, p. 104; CAPART in *Chron. d'Ég.* xxxii (1957), fig. 32, p. 185; id. *Causeries sur l'Art égyptien*, fig. 22, p. 30.

Hall. 5 of Fisher.

EDGAR in *Ann. Serv.* xv (1915), pp. 97–104, with plan, views, and sketch of decoration, figs. 1, 2, and pl.

Columns. Texts, id. ib. pp. 100–1.

Doorways, names of the King on lintels and jambs (one doorway in Cairo Mus. JE 45029, and another, formerly in Cairo Mus. Temp. No. 3.2.21.1, now in Philadelphia Mus. E 13552). Texts, id. ib. pp. 102–4.

Bedroom. 10 of Fisher.

(5) Doorway, in Philadelphia Mus. E 13553–4. Lintel and jambs, royal names; FISHER in *Penn. Mus. Journ.* xv (1924), fig. on p. 94; ib. xvii (1926), fig. on p. 111 [middle].

Finds from the South Pylon and Palace areas

In Cairo Museum.

Statues.

Head,[1] variously identified but probably Nefertiti, quartzite, ʿAmârna Period, in Cairo Mus. JE 45547. *Penn. Mus. Journ.* vi (1915), fig. 62 on p. 82; C. S. F[ISHER] in ib. viii (1917), fig. 88, p. 228; CAPART, *Documents*, i, pl. 30; id. *L'Art ég.* ii, pl. 346; *Encycl. phot. Caire*, pl. 102; DRIOTON and SVED, *Art ég.* fig. 82; LANGE, *Ägyptische Bildnisse*, pl. 20; BILLE-DE MOT, *Die Revolution des Pharao Echnaton*, Abb. 77; ROEDER in *Ä.Z.* 83 (1958), Taf. iv [a], pp. 62–3; PETERSON in *Medelhavsmuseet Bulletin*, 4 (1964), fig. 8, p. 25; ALDRED, *N.K. Art* (1951), pl. 130; (1961), pl. 135; id. *Akhenaten*, pl. 8; id. *Akhenaten and Nefertiti*, fig. 37, p. 61; GILBERT in *Chron. d'Ég.* xxxvi (1961), figs. 10, 11, pp. 40–5; Paris. *Toutankhamon et son temps*. Petit Palais, 1967, Exhib. Cat. No. 12 with figs.; Brussels. *5000 ans*, fig. 25, p. 25 [34]; Vienna. *5000 Jahre*, No. 104 with Abb.; Stockholm. *5000 år*, No. 78 with fig.; London. *5000 Years*, pl. xxii, p. 18 [59]; Essen. *5000 Jahre*, No. 97 with Abb.; Amsterdam. *5000 jaar*, fig. 22 [59]; Louisiana. *5000 års*, No. 155 with fig.; MICHALOWSKI, *Art*, fig. 455; BRINKMANN in *Jahrbuch der Staatlichen Kunstsammlungen in Baden-Württemberg*, iv (1967), fig. 7, p. 14; PAVLOV in *Vestnik Drevney Istorii*, 1972, No. 4 (122), fig. 2, p. 90; PERC, *Spomeniki starega Egipta* (1974), No. 26 with fig.; *Le Règne du Soleil. Akhnaton et Nefertiti.* Exposition . . . Bruxelles, 17 janvier–16 mars 1975, No. 18; *Echnaton, Nofretete, Tutanchamun.* Ausstellung . . . Wien, 23. April–29. Juni 1975, No. 18; *Solens rike. Aknaton, Nefertiti, Tut-ank-Amon.* Utstillingen . . . Oslo, 16. juli–16. september 1975, No. 18 with pl. 6; *Echnaton och Nefertiti.* Utställning . . . Stockholm, 16 oktober–7 december 1975, No. 18 with pl. 6; *Nofretete, Echnaton.* Ausstellung . . . München, 17. Januar–21. März 1976, No. 54; *Nofretete, Echnaton.* Ausstellung . . . Berlin, 10. April–16. Juni 1976, No. 54; *Echnaton, Nofretete, Tutanchamun.* Ausstellung . . . Hildesheim, 15. Juli–26. September 1976, No. 54; FATON in *Archeologia*, No. 80 (March 1975), fig. on p. 63 [upper]; HARRIS in *Gutenberghus Årsskrift*, 1976, fig. on p. 11; *Akhnaton og Nefertiti* in *Louisiana Revy*, 17 [1] (Oct. 1976), fig. on p. 1 [54]. See *Descr. somm.* No. 6212.

Small glass head, possibly of Merneptaḥ, JE 46416. COONEY, *Glass Sculpture in Ancient Egypt* in *Journal of Glass Studies*, ii (1960), figs. 20–1, p. 28.

May [hieroglyphs], Overseer of works in the Temples of Rēʿ and Ptaḥ, son of Bekenamūn [hieroglyphs] and Takertia [hieroglyphs], squatting, with cartouches of Merneptaḥ on shoulders, granite, JE 67878. HABACHI in *Chron. d'Ég.* xxix (1954), figs. 27–8, pp. 213–16; *Ramsès le Grand* (Galeries Nationales du Grand Palais, Paris, 1976), Cat. xiii; *Bible et Terre Sainte*, No. 185 (Nov. 1976), fig. 8. Text and notes, GRDSELOFF MSS. 3.5.

[1] Selected references.

Stelae.

Lower part of stela of year 24 (of Ramesses III) concerning presenting statue of Ramesses III to the Temple of Merneptaḥ (Excav. No. 2882). SCHULMAN in *J.N.E.S.* xxii (1963), pl. vii, pp. 177–84. Text, KITCHEN, *Ram. Inscr.* v. 249–50 [74]. See HELCK in *J.N.E.S.* xxv (1966), pp. 32–41.

Ramesses III censes three barks on stands, JE 45548. PHILAD. photo. 34078.

Ramesses IX kneels with wine before Ptaḥ, year 13, JE 45567. Ib. 34073.

Rebaḥi [hieroglyphs] (or Baḥi?) before two figures of Amen-rēʿ and Mut(?), upper part, Ramesside, JE 45557. SCHULMAN in *J.N.E.S.* xxiii (1964), pl. iii [upper], pp. 278–9.

Others, Ramesside, JE 45535, 45543, 45550, 45552. JE 45543, PHILAD. photo. 34037.

Lower part of donation-stela, Petubastis I before god, year 6, with text mentioning Yewerhen [hieroglyphs], Leader of foreign troops, etc., JE 45530. SCHULMAN in *J.A.R.C.E.* v (1966), pl. xiii [2], pp. 33–9. Text, DARESSY MSS. E.30 [6]. Localities Per-ḥenu and Per-sekhemkheper, see YOYOTTE in *Rev. d'Ég.* 13 (1961), pp. 93–4 [b]; 15 (1963), p. 90.

Ḥatḥor Mistress of Aphroditopolis before Ptaḥ, dedicated by Pinezem [hieroglyphs], Dyn. XXI, JE 45539.

Late Period stela, JE 45549. PHILAD. photo. 34049.

Blocks, etc.

Jamb with remains of text of Ramesses III, sandstone, JE 45570. GABALLA in *J.E.A.* 59 (1973), pl. xxxvii [2], fig. 3, p. 113 [3]; text, KITCHEN, *Ram. Inscr.* v. 230 [62].

Offering-texts mentioning Queen Tausert, JE 45568. GABALLA in *B.I.F.A.O.* 71 (1972), pl. xxvi, fig. 4, p. 134.

Lintel-fragment of Shedsunefertem, Prophet of Ptaḥ, etc., kneeling before names of Siamūn, JE 45569.

In Philadelphia, University Museum.

Statues.

Sebkḥotp-ḥenku [hieroglyphs], Greatest of the Directors of craftsmen, etc., son of Ressonb [hieroglyphs], *waʿb*-priest of Neith, and Neitnub [hieroglyphs], seated, headless, granite, Middle Kingdom, E 13647.

Senusert [hieroglyphs], son of Ḥetep, squatting, lower part, granite, Middle Kingdom, No. 29.75.484.

Werbauptaḥ [hieroglyphs], squatting in cloak, fragment, basalt, Middle Kingdom, No. 29.75.502.

Amenophis IV, fragment of back pillar, sandstone, E 13644. LÖHR in *Studien zur altägyptischen Kultur*, 2 (1975), pp. 149–50 with fig.

A Scribe of Ptaḥ, son of Teti [hieroglyphs], Scribe, and Raʿres [hieroglyphs], kneeling, sandstone, Dyn. XIX, No. 29.75.525.

Merysekhmet [hieroglyphs], Mayor, holding stela with statuette of Ptaḥ, granite, Ramesside, E 13652.

An Overseer of the harîm, fragment of block-statue, Ramesside, No. 29.75.551.

Royal bust (name lost) holding inscribed staff, granite, New Kingdom(?), E 13653.

Khaʿemwēset [hieroglyphs], *waʿb*-priest of Ptaḥ, etc., squatting, headless, dedicated by son Werkherp-ḥemut [hieroglyphs], Scribe, sandstone, New Kingdom, E 12038.

Neferronpet [hieroglyphs], Scribe of the fields of Amūn, block-statue, headless, sandstone, New Kingdom, E 13645.

Ptaḥwēr [hieroglyphs], Fashioner of gods of the Mansion of Gold, seated, lower part, New Kingdom, E 13661.

Upper part of seated statuette, granite, New Kingdom, E 13646.

Pain [hieroglyphs], son of Zeptaḥefʿankh [hieroglyphs], scribe-statue, headless, Dyn. XXI, E 13648. C. S. F[ISHER] in *Penn. Mus. Journ.* viii (1917), fig. 86, p. 228; PHILAD. photo. 34078.

Statue-base, inscribed, granite, Dyn. XXII–XXV, No. 29.75.544.

Foreign soldier, Dyn. XXVII or later, No. 29.75.499.

Seated man, Dyn. XXX–XXXI, No. 29.75.533.

An Overseer of the royal harîm, holding Ḥatḥor-head, fragment of block-statue, probably Late Period, No. 29.75.531.

Woman seated, lower part with remains of text, Late Period, No. 29.75.454.

Royal head, sculptor's model, Late Period or Ptolemaic, E 13658. *Penn. Mus. Journ.* vi (1915), fig. 64 on p. 84.

Statuettes of Ptaḥ. (a) Dedicated by Paḥemneter [hieroglyphs], fragment, New Kingdom, No. 29.75.511. (b) Dedicated by a Chief royal scribe of the Lord of the Two Lands, alabaster base and feet, New Kingdom, E 13655. (c) Wearing feathered robe, headless, inscribed, faience, probably Dyn. XVIII, No. 29.84.482; *The Pennsylvania Gazette*, 77 [5] (March 1979), fig. on p. 33 [lower left].

Stelae.

Top of stela, Tuthmosis III seated, E 13623. PHILAD. photo. 34067.

Inḥertmosi [hieroglyphs], Outline-draughtsman, probably Dyn. XVIII, E 13595.

Ramesside stelae. Titles of some, SCHULMAN in *J.A.R.C.E.* vi (1967), p. 154 note 4.

Amenemōpet [hieroglyphs], Mayor of Hermonthis and Dendera, King's son in the Wâdi Naṭrûn, etc., with wife Ipa [hieroglyphs], granite, E 13608. PHILAD. photo. 34045.

Amenḥotp, E 13614.

Kauemperptaḥ [hieroglyphs], Sailor of the bark of Ptaḥ, E 13609. PHILAD. photo. 34075.

Kharu [hieroglyphs], Servant (*bꜣk*) of the Temple of Ptaḥ, E 13598.

Khaʿemwēset [hieroglyphs], Governor of the Town and Vizier, Greatest of the Directors of craftsmen, etc., before Ptaḥ and Maʿet, faience, temp. Ramesses IX, E 13578. SCHULMAN in *Expedition*, 2 [4] (Summer 1960), fig. on p. 32, cf. p. 33.

Khaʿy [hieroglyphs], Infantryman of the Residence, E 13613. PHILAD. photo. on 34070.

Mosi, E 13597.

Neferronpet [hieroglyphs], Servant (*sdm-ʿš*), upper part, E 13602.

Neḥeḥ [hieroglyphs], No. 29.75.561. PHILAD. photo. 34051.

Paserpanub [hieroglyphs], E 13612. See VANDIER in *Rev. d'Ég.* 17 (1965), p. 94 [D. cxiv].

Pashensekhmet [hieroglyphs], Overseer of works of Ptaḥ, and wife Tentnamenesh [hieroglyphs], fragment, E 13618. PHILAD. photo. 34066.

Payneferptaḥ [hieroglyphs], Servant (*sdm*) of Ptaḥ, re-used basin, granite, E 13628.

Pedeḥenutpet [hieroglyphs], E 13624.

Ptaḥmay [hieroglyphs], *waʿb*-priest, with wife Nubemwaskhet [hieroglyphs], Songstress of Amūn, and family, E 13610. C. S. F[ISHER] in *Penn. Mus. Journ.* viii (1917), fig. 85, p. 227.

Puipeḥ(?) [hieroglyphs](?), E 13627.

Puy [hieroglyphs], Songstress, E 13592. PHILAD. photo. 33919.

Raʿmeses-sauemyunu [hieroglyphs], Royal butler, E 13625. Ib. 34074.

Suemʿankhef [hieroglyphs], Scribe . . ., No. 29.75.565.

Ptaḥ and god Neḥi as bird, E 13621. SCHULMAN in *J.N.E.S.* xxiii (1964), pls. i, iii [fig. 1], pp. 275–6, 279.

Osiris seated, E 13589. Id. in *J.A.R.C.E.* vi (1967), pl. ii [8], p. 156 [8].

Head of ram of Amen-rēʿ, E 13631. Id. ib. pl. i [4], p. 155 [4].

Others, E 13579–80, 13582–3, 13585–6, 13588, 13590–1, 13593–4, 13596, 13599–601, 13603–7, 13611, 13615–17, 13619–20, 13622, 13626, 13629–30, 13632, 13641, 13651, and Nos. 29.75.554, 557–8, 560, 563–4, 566–7, 574, 29.84.76, 742, 29.85.732. E 13605 and 13607, on PHILAD. photo. 34070; E 13630, ib. 33921, 34050.

ʿAnkhefensekhmet [hieroglyphs], Incense-bearer of Ptaḥ, son of Ababsunūter-nehktef [hieroglyphs], Late Period, E 13581. PHILAD. photo. 34043.

Blocks, etc.

Lintel of Sethos I, E 13573. See RANKE in *Penn. Mus. Bull.* xv [2–3] (Nov. 1950), p. 100.

[Ramesses II] offers image of Maʿet to Ptaḥ, No. 29.75.555.

Lintel, Ramesses II kneels before Amen-rēʿ as ram, E 13572. PHILAD. photos. 34011–12. See RANKE, op. cit. p. 100.

Lintel-fragment of Setau, Viceroy of Kush, etc., adoring names of Ramesses II, E 13566. SCHULMAN in *The Society for the Study of Egyptian Antiquities Journal*, viii (1978), pl. iv, pp. 42–5 (as E 13655); PHILAD. photo. 34115. Text, KITCHEN, *Ram. Inscr.* iii. 111 [65] (as E 13655). See RANKE, op. cit. pp. 99–100.

Lintel-fragment(?), Ramesses III kneels with image of Maʿet before Ptaḥ in kiosk, E 13570.

Lintel, double-scene, Neferronpet [hieroglyphs], Governor of the Town and Vizier, etc., kneels before cartouches of Ramesses VI, E 13567. CHRISTOPHE in *Bull. Inst. Ég.* xxxvii [1] (1954–5), pl. viii, pp. 24–5 [2]. See RANKE, op. cit. p. 100.

Offering-table cut out from block of Paḥemneter [hieroglyphs], New Kingdom, E 13684.

Trial-piece(?), male head, Late Period, E 13643. C. S. F[ISHER] in *Penn. Mus. Journ.* viii (1917), fig. 87, p. 228; *MASCA Journal*, 1 (Dec. 1978), fig. on p. 3 [right].

Trial-piece, *recto*, man holding lion, *verso*, hawk, uraeus, and altar, Late Period, E 13634.

Other finds.

Lower part of niche with statuette of Tyerneḥeḥ [hieroglyphs], Fan-bearer on the right of the King, with deceased kneeling adoring on sides, granite, New Kingdom, E 13662.

Location unknown. Some possibly in Cairo Mus.

Statues.

Bust with cartouche of Ramesses III on shoulder, granite.

Penmeḥyt holding headless figure of Ptaḥ, New Kingdom (Excav. No. 2218).

Amenardais [hieroglyphs], Director of the Palace, Scribe of the royal documents in the presence, statue-base, Dyn. XXVI (Excav. No. 11821).

Stelae. Ramesside unless stated.

ʿAnkh-ptaḥ [hieroglyphs], Carrier of the offering-table of Ptaḥ, before Ptaḥ and Sekhmet (Excav. No. 2906). PHILAD. photo. 34029.

Ḥatnūfer [hieroglyphs] adores Amen-rēʿ, Ptaḥ, lion-headed goddess and Amenōpet (Excav. No. 3634). Ib. 34041.

Nezem, upper part (Excav. No. 3201).

Paker . . . (?), with Reshef at top. PHILAD. photo. 34054.

Sᶜankh, Field-worker of the Temple of Ptaḥ, with two figures of Ptaḥ (Excav. No. 2766). SCHULMAN in *J.N.E.S.* xxiii (1964), pl. ii, pp. 278–9 [2].

Sᶜankh adores Sobk (Excav. No. 2673).

Small stelae, Ptaḥ seated, Ḥatḥor-head, etc., on re-used blocks. SCHULMAN in *J.A.R.C.E.* vi (1967), pls. i [1–3], ii [5–7], pp. 154–6 [1–3, 5–7].

Others, Excav. Nos. 1689, 2090, 2774, 2786, 2840–2, 2907, 2992, 3108, 4696. Excav. Nos. 1689, 2907, 3108, PHILAD. photos. 34106, 34069, 34058.

Pedeneit, son of Neitemḥēt (mother), followed by brother ᶜAnkh-weḥebrēᶜ, Dyn. XXVI (Excav. No. 1802). PHILAD. photos. 34046–7.

Tawertemḥab (woman) seated, Dyn. XXVI (Excav. No. 2795).

Jambs, lintels, blocks, etc.

Sethos I (Excav. No. 2667).

Ramesses II, (a) and Merneptaḥ (Excav. No. 4350); PHILAD. photo. 34080; (b) usurped by Setnakht (Excav. No. 4373).

Merneptaḥ, (a) Excav. No. 4353; (b) offers image of Maᶜet to Ptaḥ in kiosk; PHILAD. photo. 34022; (c) between Thoth and Horus; ib. 34021.

Ramesses III (Excav. No. 4372); PHILAD. photo. 34082.

Ramesses IX holding two ointment-jars (Excav. No. 9348).

Ramesses XI (Excav. No. 6773).

Others, New Kingdom unless stated. Amenemōnet, First prophet of Amūn; PHILAD. photo. 38723. Amenemōpet, Overseer of the granary, etc., temp. Ḥaremḥab, re-used; ib. 38718–19. Bekenamūn, Greatest of the Directors of craftsmen(?); ib. 38722. Ḥēt, Overseer of prophets of all the gods of Panopolis, First prophet of Min. Ḥori, Governor of the town and Vizier, adores names of Setnakht; ib. 38605. Khaᶜemwēset (Excav. No. 7182). Ptaḥmosi, Greatest of the Directors of craftsmen (Excav. No. 4370). Raᶜmosi, Scribe, Director of all works before His Lord; ib. 38371–2, 38688. To, Vizier, temp. Ramesses III. King near building with two columns (Excav. No. 2903). Three kneeling Libyans, Dyn. XVIII (Excav. No. 2889).

MISCELLANEOUS FROM KÔM EL-QALᶜA

Statues.

Semtu-tefnakht, Overseer of crews of royal boats, etc., squatting with left knee up, headless, granite, temp. Psammetikhos I, in Cairo Mus. CG 653. BORCHARDT, *Statuen*, ii, Bl. 120, p. 197. Text, MARIETTE, *Mon. div.* pl. 34 [g]; DARESSY in *Ann. Serv.* xviii (1919), pp. 30, cf. 29; WILBOUR MSS. 3 C. 74.

Neferebrēᶜ-nūfer (*i.e.* Irᶜaḥor, Ṣaqqâra tb. LS 23), holding naos of Ptaḥ, faience, temp. Psammetikhos II, in Cairo Mus. CG 807. BORCHARDT, op. cit. Bl. 149, pp. 104–5. Texts, MARIETTE, op. cit. pl. 34 [a]; PIEHL, *Inscr. hiéro.* 3 Sér. lxxi–lxxii [I]; part, DE ROUGÉ, *Inscr. hiéro.* pls. xlv, xlvi. See MASPERO, *Guide*, p. 448 [4238].

Ḥor, son of Penen, block-statue, face destroyed, slate, Dyn. XXVI, in Boston Mus. 29.731. DUNHAM in *J.E.A.* xv (1929), pl. xxxiii, p. 165. Parts of text, BRUGSCH, *Recueil*, pl. iv [6]; MARIETTE, op. cit. pl. 34 [b]; MÜLLER (W. Max) in *Rec. Trav.* xxvi (1904), pp. 33 [top], cf. 32.

Pikhaʿs [hieroglyphs], General of the Residence, etc., son of ʿAnkh-ḥap [hieroglyphs] and Ḥatḥor-emakhet [hieroglyphs], headless, holding figure of Apis, schist, Dyn. XXX or Ptolemaic, in Cairo Mus. CG 1085. BORCHARDT, *Statuen*, iv, Bl. 162, pp. 49–50. Text, MARIETTE, op. cit. pl. 34 [c]; DARESSY in *Rec. Trav.* xv (1893), p. 157 [5].

Hawk protecting King, Late Period(?), in Cairo Mus. JE 33262. HORNEMANN, *Types*, v, pl. 1309. See *Bull. Inst. Ég.* iii Sér. 9 (1898), p. 413.

Man holding naos of Harpocrates, Ptolemaic, in Cairo Mus. JE 33266. MASPERO, *Égypte*, fig. 485. See id. *Guide*, p. 226 [973]; *Bull. Inst. Ég.* iii Sér. 9 (1898), p. 413.

Stelae.

Pakharu [hieroglyphs], Door-keeper of the Temple of Ptaḥ, son of ʿAnkh-khons [hieroglyphs] and Heresibnes [hieroglyphs], Horus on crocodiles, Dyn. XXVI, in Cairo Mus. CG 9405. DARESSY, *Textes et dessins magiques* (*Cat. Caire*), pls. v, vi, pp. 15–17.

Fragment with trilingual decree (of year 6) of Ptolemy IV Philopator, granite, in Cairo Mus. CG 31088. KAMAL, *Stèles Ptolémaïques et Romaines* (*Cat. Caire*), pl. lxxiv (as 21088 in error), pp. 218–19; SPIEGELBERG, *Die demotischen Inschriften*, Taf. ii, pp. 14–20; PERDRIZET in *Bulletin de Correspondance Hellénique*, xxxv (1911), pl. ii, pp. 122–3. Ptolemy on horseback, MASPERO, *Égypte*, fig. 503. See MASPERO, *Guide*, p. 232 [995].

Ptolemy VI Philometor in double-scene before divinities of Tanis and Thebes, with line of demotic below, in Cairo Mus. CG 22189. KAMAL, op. cit. pl. lxiv, pp. 187–8. Text, DARESSY in *Rec. Trav.* xxiv (1902), p. 166 [cciii].

Stela of Paʿrʿashthereth [hieroglyphs] or Paʿri [hieroglyphs], son of Shemrebi [hieroglyphs] (mother), Horus on crocodiles, with hieroglyphic and Phoenician texts, greywacke, on limestone pedestal with offering-basin, Ptolemaic, in Cairo Mus. CG 9402. DARESSY, *Textes et dessins magiques* (*Cat. Caire*), pls. ii, iii, pp. 3–11; LACAU in *Mon. Piot*, xxv (1921–2), pl. xvi, figs. 4–6, pp. 195–6, 199–201. *Recto*, BORCHARDT, *Works of Art*, pl. 29; DE WIT, *Oud-Egyptische Kunst*, fig. 142 facing p. 225 (with pedestal); ROEDER, *Der Ausklang der ägyptischen Religion* [etc.], Taf. 10 (with pedestal), Abb. 6, p. 162; LEIBOVITCH, *Anc. Eg.* fig. 139; LOUKIANOFF in *Bull. Inst. Ég.* xiii (1930–1), pl. iii [14] (as CG 9404), p. 79; xxi (1938–9), pl. vi, p. 261; PICARD in *Société Royale d'Archéologie, Alexandrie. Bulletin*, N.S. x [1] [No. 32] (1938), fig. 3, p. 14; DRIOTON, *La magie dans l'Égypte des Pharaons* in *Formes et Couleurs*, xi [1] (1949), 4th fig.; PIRENNE, *Hist. civ.* iii, pl. 107 facing p. 392; SEELE in *J.N.E.S.* vi (1947), pl. iii [B], pp. 43, 48. Parts of text, KLASENS, *A Magical Statue Base* [etc.], pp. 37–8, 46–50 [C 3]. See MASPERO, *Guide*, p. 490 [4751].

Blocks.

Block (perhaps stela) with cartouches of the Aten and Amenophis IV on three sides, in Cairo Mus. MARIETTE, *Mon. div.* pl. 34 [e]. Text, SANDMAN, *Texts from the Time of Akhenaten*, p. 161 [clxxvii]; LEGRAIN, *Répertoire*, No. 299. See LÖHR in *Studien zur altägyptischen Kultur*, 2 (1975), pp. 151–2 with fig. (from MARIETTE).

Ramesses II holds captives, in Cairo Mus. JE 46189. BRUYÈRE, *Rapport sur les fouilles de Deir el Médineh (1935–1940)*, iii, fig. 5, p. 63; MITRY, *Illus. Cat.* No. 769; FORMAN (W. and B.) and VILÍMKOVÁ, *Eg. Art*, pls. 85–6; DE RACHEWILTZ, *Vita nell'antico Egitto*, Tav. v [lower]; upper part of King, MYŚLIWIEC, *Le Portrait royal dans le bas-relief du Nouvel Empire*, pl. cx [244]. See *Descr. somm.* No. 769.

Others.

Offering-table of Amenemḥēt I, granite, in Cairo Mus. Text, MARIETTE, *Mon. div.* pl. 34 [f].

Sistrum of Darius I, faience, in Cairo Mus. CG 69324. HICKMANN, *Instruments de Musique* (*Cat. Caire*), pl. lviii, p. 85; id. in *Bull. Inst. Ég.* xxxvi (1953–4), fig. 5, p. 591. Text, MARIETTE, *Mon. div.* pl. 34 [d]; POSENER, *La Première Domination Perse* [etc.], pp. 153–4 [102].

Bolt with lion, bronze, probably Ptolemaic, in Cairo Mus. JE 37765. DARESSY in *Ann. Serv.* vi (1905), pl. ii, pp. 237–8; PILLET in ib. xxiv (1924), fig. 3, p. 192 [2]; see VARILLE in ib. liii (1956), p. 86 with fig. 1 (from DARESSY).

Miscellaneous from Mît Rahîna

Statues.

Royal.

Upper part of Sesostris I, diorite, in Berlin (East) Mus. 1205. EVERS, *Staat aus dem Stein*, i, Taf. 45; HAMANN, *Äg. Kunst*, Abb. 170. Head, L. *D.* iii. 301 [82] (as Nektanebos I). See *Ausf. Verz.* p. 247 (as Nektanebos I); *Führer* (1961), p. 49.

Colossal head wearing White Crown, perhaps Sesostris I, granite, in Brit. Mus. 615. BUDGE, *Egyptian Sculptures in the British Museum*, pl. x. See *Guide* (*Sculpture*), p. 39 [137].

Bust, perhaps of Sesostris II, granite, in Copenhagen, Ny Carlsberg Glypt. Æ.I.N. 659. SCHMIDT (V.) in *P.S.B.A.* xxviii (1906), pp. 268–9 with pl.; id. *Den Æg. Sam.* (1908), pp. 81–4 with fig. [E.40]; id. *Choix* (1910), pl. vi [10], pp. 19–20; id. *Levende og Døde*, fig. 256; EVERS, *Staat aus dem Stein*, i, Taf. 69; MOGENSEN, *Coll. ég.* pl. ii [A 3], pp. 5–6; KOEFOED-PETERSEN, *Cat. des statues*, pl. 21, pp. 15–16 [19]; id. *Ægyptisk Billedhuggerkunst*, pl. 11; id. *Eg. Sculpture* (1951), pl. 11; (1961), pl. 15; ALDRED, *M.K. Art*, pl. 42.

Colossal head, perhaps of Amenophis II, in Cairo Mus. CG 641. BORCHARDT, *Statuen*, ii, Bl. 118, pp. 187–8. See VANDIER in *Mon. Piot*, xliii (1949), p. 8 with fig. 6 [d] (from BORCHARDT).

Headless kneeling statue of Amenophis III with offering-table, cartouche erased, quartzite, in Cambridge, Fitzwilliam Mus. E.82.1913.

Fragment of back pillar with Aten cartouches, perhaps from statue of Amenophis IV, quartzite, in Copenhagen, Ny Carlsberg Glypt. Æ.I.N. 1144. MOGENSEN, *Coll. ég.* pl. iii [A 7], p. 6; id. in *B.I.F.A.O.* xxx (1930), pl. i [2], p. 458; KOEFOED-PETERSEN, *Cat. des statues*, pl. 52, p. 28 [45] (as granite). Text, SANDMAN, *Texts from the Time of Akhenaten*, p. 184 [bottom]. See LÖHR in *Studien zur altägyptischen Kultur*, 2 (1975), pp. 148–9 with fig. (after MOGENSEN).

Sethos I (or II). Text on back, BRUGSCH, *Thes.* 1066 [9].

Seated god, with [Sethos I] between knees, granite, in Cairo Mus. CG 1293. HORNEMANN, *Types*, iv, pl. 1127. Text, BORCHARDT, *Statuen*, iv, pp. 151, cf. 150; KITCHEN, *Ram. Inscr.* i. 124 [64].

Colossus of Ramesses II wearing Blue Crown and holding standards of Ptaḥ and Thoth, granite, found at Ḥod el-Wissada. EL-AMIR in *Ann. Serv.* xlii (1943), pls. xxi, xxii, pp. 359–63; KINROSS, *Portrait of Egypt*, 3rd pl. after p. 16; WILDUNG, *Egyptian Saints. Deification in Pharaonic Egypt*, fig. 10. Texts, KITCHEN, *Ram. Inscr.* ii. 496 [193, A]; of standards, ČERNÝ Notebook, 118, p. 1. See *Chron. d'Ég.* xxi (1946), pp. 55–6.

Statue-base with names of Ramesses II and Queen Merytamūn. DARESSY MSS. E.30 [8].

Statue-base of Ramesses II. WILKINSON MSS. xiii. 36 [upper].

Ramesses II holding standard, fragments, granite, in Cairo Mus. Temp. No. 31.12.38.1.

Texts, DARESSY in *Ann. Serv.* xx (1920), pp. 167–8 [1]; KITCHEN, *Ram. Inscr.* ii. 494–5 [192, A].

Adoring baboon protecting King, probably Sethos II, granite, in Vienna Mus. Inv.5782. DEMEL, *Ägyptische Kunst*, Abb. 23; *Meisterwerke. Führer durch das Kunsthistorische Museum*, 1 (1958 and 1968), fig. 14; MICHALOWSKI, *Art*, fig. 539; VANDIER, *Manuel*, iii, pl. cxxx [4] (from DEMEL), p. 645. See REINISCH, *Miramar*, p. 243 [59].

Statue-base(?) of Ramesses III, usurped by Ramesses IV and VI. BRUGSCH, *Recueil*, pl. iv [2]. See CHRISTOPHE in *Bull. Inst. Ég.* xxxvii [1] (1954–5), pp. 22–3 [4].

Ramesses VI, head and legs lost, granite, in Berlin (East) Mus. 7701. Muzeul de artă, Bucharest. *Egiptul antic* [etc.] (1975), No. 71 with fig. on p. 38. Texts, *Aeg. Inschr.* ii, p. 85. See *Ausf. Verz.* p. 120.

Fragment of seated statue, granite, New Kingdom(?), in Cairo Mus. CG 1206. See BORCHARDT, *Statuen*, iv, p. 107.

Fragment of statue of Apries kneeling with figure of Ptaḥ, alabaster, in Cairo Mus. CG 1052. Text, BORCHARDT, *Statuen*, iv, p. 39.

Head, perhaps of Amasis, schist, in Louvre, E.25480. VANDIER in *Ä.Z.* 90 (1963), Taf. xi, xii, pp. 115–18. See id. in *La Revue du Louvre*, xii (1962), p. 294 with note 14.

Royal head (sculptor's model), Dyn. XXVII, in Budapest, Szépművészeti Múzeum, 60.17. VARGA in *Bulletin du Musée National Hongrois des Beaux-Arts*, 18 (1961), fig. 2, pp. 3–7; id. *Egyiptomi kiállítás. Vezető* (1976), pl. 47; id. and WESSETZKY, *Egyiptomi kiállítás* (1961), pl. xv [2]; (1964), pl. xvi [2]; id. *Az ókori Egyiptom. Kiállításvezető* (1970), pl. 28.

Achoris kneeling, lower part, diorite, in Cairo Mus. CG 681. BORCHARDT, *Statuen*, iii, Bl. 124, p. 25.

Ptolemy XII Neos Dionysos, granite, in Berlin (East) Mus. 8810. See *Ausf. Verz.* p. 324 (as Ptolemy X, *i.e.* IX Soter II); BOTHMER in *La Revue des Arts*, ix (1959), p. 107 note 26.

Private.

Ḥetepdief [hieroglyphs] kneeling, with names of Kings Ḥetepsekhemui, Raʿneb and Ninūter, granite, late Dyn. II or Dyn. III, in Cairo Mus. CG 1. BORCHARDT, *Statuen*, i, Bl. 1, pp. 1–2; WEIGALL, *Anc. Eg. . . . Art*, 13 [left]; JÉQUIER in DE MORGAN, *Recherches*, ii, pl. iv, fig. 852; PETRIE, *History*, i (1894), fig. 18; (1923), figs. 19–20 (= PETRIE GÎZA photo. 501); VON BISSING, *Äg. Kunstgeschichte*, Taf. lxiv [391], *Text*, i, p. 39; id. in *Rev. Arch.* 4 Sér. xv (1910), fig. 35, p. 259; MASPERO, *Égypte*, fig. 137; id. in GRÉBAUT, *Le Musée Égyptien*, i, pl. xiii, figs. 1, 2, pp. 12–13; CAPART, *Les Débuts de l'art en Égypte*, fig. 180; id. *Primitive Art in Egypt*, fig. 196; CAROTTI, *L'Arte*, fig. 36; MITRY, *Illus. Cat.* No. 3072; BYVANCK, *De Kunst* (1947), pl. xiv [49]; SMITH, *Hist. Eg. Sculp.* pl. 2 [b], p. 16; HORNEMANN, *Types*, iii, pl. 557; SHOUKRY, *Privatgrabstatue*, Abb. 1; GIEDION, *The Eternal Present*, ii, figs. 219–20; WOLF, *Kunst*, Abb. 33, pp. 60–1; id. *Die Kultur Ägyptens*, Abb. 52; LANGE and HIRMER, *Ägypten. Architektur* (1967), pl. 7; TERRACE and FISCHER, *Treasures*, pp. 25–8 with pls.; *Great Museums*, pls. 12, 13; WESTENDORF, *Das Alte Ägypten*, fig. on p. 26; MICHALOWSKI, *Art*, fig. 183; VANDERSLEYEN, *Das Alte Ägypten*, Abb. 122, fig. 62 on p. 220; SUZUKI, *Sculpture of the World*, 3, *Egypt*, pl. 29; LECLANT and others, *Le temps des Pyramides*, fig. 173. Royal names, MORET in *Mélanges Maspero*, i [2], fig. 1, p. 624. See MASPERO, *Guide*, p. 300 [3072].

Kawaʿb, King's son of his body (of Khufu), Chief Justice and Vizier (Gîza tb. G 7110+7120), seated, restored by Khaʿemwēset (son of Ramesses II), lower part, diorite, in Cairo Mus. JE 40431. GOMAÀ, *Chaemwese* [etc.], Taf. iv, Abb. 19, p. 84 [51].

Menkheperraᶜsonb [hieroglyphs], Overseer of foreign countries, Chief of the Meza, etc., son of Neferkhaut [hieroglyphs] and Riuresti [hieroglyphs], block-statue, granite, temp. Tuthmosis III, in Cairo Mus. CG 547. BORCHARDT, *Statuen*, ii, Bl. 91, pp. 92–4; HORNEMANN, *Types*, ii, pl. 446. Text, SETHE, *Urk*. iv. 991–4 [291].

Neferweben [hieroglyphs], Chief Justice and Vizier, seated, headless, granite, temp. Tuthmosis III, in Brussels, Mus. Roy. E.7333. CAPART in *Bull. Mus. Roy*. 3 Sér. x (1938), fig. 21, pp. 114–16.

Sebkḥotp, Overseer of the seal (Theb. tb. 63), seated on cushion reading, sandstone, fragment, temp. Tuthmosis IV, in Cairo Mus. CG 1090. BORCHARDT, *Statuen*, iv, Bl. 162, p. 51. Text, HELCK, *Urk*. iv. 1585 [519], cf. *Übersetz*. (1961), p. 164.

Ḥaremḥab (later King) as scribe,[1] granite, in New York, M.M.A. 23.10.1. WINLOCK in *M.M.A. Bull*. Pt. ii, Oct. 1923, pp. 3–4 with figs. on pp. 1, 5, 9, 13; id. in *J.E.A*. x (1924), pls. i–iv, pp. 1–5; id. *Egyptian Statues and Statuettes* (1937), fig. 19; ROSS, *The Art of Egypt*, pl. on p. 176; KEES, *Ägyptische Kunst*, Abb. 37; ROSTOVTZEFF, *A History of the Ancient World*, i, pl. xxx [1]; STEINDORFF, *Die Blütezeit des Pharaonenreichs* (1926), Abb. 190; id. and SEELE, *When Egypt Ruled the East*, fig. 95; SCHÄFER and ANDRAE, *Kunst* (1930 and 1942), 354–5; PILLET, *Thèbes. Palais et Nécropoles*, fig. 70; BOREUX in *Mon. Piot*, xxxiii (1933), fig. 1, p. 14; HAMMERTON, *Universal History of the World*, i, fig. on p. 668 (as Cairo Mus.); *A Guide to the Collections*, i (1934), fig. on p. 13; (1936 and 1937), fig. on p. 17; (1939 and 1940), fig. on p. 19; RANKE, *The Art of Ancient Egypt*, and BREASTED, *Geschichte Aegyptens* (1936), 141; HAMANN, *Äg. Kunst*, Abb. 273; HOYNINGEN-HUENE and STEINDORFF, *Egypt* (1943), fig. on p. 123; (1945), fig. on p. 128; CAPART, *L'Art ég*. ii, pl. 360; id. *Limites*, pl. iii [4], p. 44; SCOTT, *Egyptian Statues* (1945), 20th pl.; PIJOÁN, *Summa Artis*, iii (1945), figs. 455–6; CID PRIEGO, *El Arte Egipcio*, pl. facing p. 164 [upper]; WILSON, *The Burden of Egypt*, fig. 26a; ALDRED, *N.K. Art* (1951), pl. 169; (1961), pl. 171; id. *Akhenaten*, pl. 56; TAYLOR in *M.M.A. Bull*. N.S. x (April 1952), fig. on p. 221; BENDOW, *Stormaktstidens Egypt*, pl. facing p. 112 [right lower]; LANGE and HIRMER, *Aegypten. Architektur* (1955), pls. 196–7; (1957), pls. 198–9; (1967), pls. 202–3; WOLF, *Kunst*, Abb. 445; HAYES, *Scepter*, ii, fig. 190; HARI, *Horemheb*, figs. 4, 5, pl. vii, pp. 42–5; SMITH, *Art . . . Anc. Eg*. pl. 140, p. 207; DONADONI in *Enciclopedia dell'Arte Antica Classica e Orientale*, iii, fig. 329; PRITCHARD, *Anc. Near East*, fig. 418; *Guide to the Collections. Egyptian Art* (1962), fig. 39; MICHALOWSKI, *Art*, fig. 372; POULSEN (V.), *Ägyptische Kunst. Neues Reich und Spätzeit*, pl. on p. 61; GILES, *Ikhnaton: Legend and History*, pl. xiii [upper]; GROENEWEGEN-FRANKFORT and ASHMOLE, *Art of the Ancient World*, fig. 67 (as diorite); VANDERSLEYEN, *Das Alte Ägypten*, Abb. 201 [a]. Upper part or head, *A Brief Guide to the Egyptian Collection* (1946), fig. on p. 21; MÜLLER (H. W.) in *Münchner Jahrb*. 3 Ser. xviii (1967), Abb. 13, pp. 22–3 (as diorite). Text, HELCK, *Urk*. iv. 2089–94 [804], cf. *Übersetz*. (1961), pp. 393–5.

Teti, Head of *waᶜb*-priests, statue-group, Dyn. XVIII, in Cairo Mus. JE 44673.

Piay [hieroglyphs], Servant (*sḏm-ᶜš*), son of Pawēr [hieroglyphs], block-statue with Ḥatḥor-emblem at front, schist, temp. Ramesses II, in Husson Colln. CLÈRE in *J.E.A*. 54 (1968), pls. xxii, xxiii, fig. 2, pp. 138–41, 145–8.

Raᶜmeses-smakhaset [hieroglyphs], Chief steward in the Temple of the *ka* of Ptaḥ, etc., bust, granite, temp. Ramesses II, in Hildesheim Mus. 423. HABACHI in *Studia Aegyptiaca*, i (*Recueil . . . Wessetzky*), figs. 6–9, pp. 139–42. See IPPEL and ROEDER, *Die Denkmäler des Pelizaeus-Museums zu Hildesheim*, pp. 81–2.

Iyiry [hieroglyphs], Greatest of the Directors of craftsmen, block-statue with naos of

[1] Selected references.

Ptaḥ-Sokari, temp. Sethos II, in Louvre, A 71 [N.72]. CLARAC, *Musée de Sculpture* [etc.], v, pl. 997 [2558E], *Texte*, v, p. 302; VANDIER, *Manuel*, iii, pl. cliii [3], p. 672; ARCHIVES phot. E.7–LE–21. Texts, DEVÉRIA squeezes, Gal. Nat. Londres, 14. Name and titles, PIERRET, *Rec. inscr.* i, p. 10. See DE ROUGÉ, *Notice des monuments* (1883), pp. 37–8; VANDIER, *Guide* (1948), p. 14; (1952), p. 15; (1973), p. 23.

A Second prophet of Ptaḥ, head, granite, Dyn. XIX, in Harrow School Mus. 956. See BUDGE, *Cat. of the Egyptian Antiquities . . . of . . . Sir Gardner Wilkinson*, p. 86.

Female head, Dyn. XIX, in Dublin, National Mus. 1908.516. See MURRAY, *General Guide to the Art Collections*, iii, *Egyptian Antiquities*, p. 65.

Neferronpet [hieroglyphs], Royal scribe in the Temple of Ptaḥ, son of Nebt-taui [hieroglyphs] (mother), lower part of kneeling statue with two small figures on either side, sandstone, New Kingdom, in Cairo Mus. JE 41642. HORNEMANN, *Types*, v, pl. 1367.

Granite torso (with recently added name of Amenophis I), New Kingdom, in Copenhagen, Ny Carlsberg Glypt. Æ.I.N. 32. See SCHMIDT, *Den Æg. Sam.* (1899), p. 108 [A.77]; (1908), pp. 150–1 [E.86].

A Fan-bearer on the right of the King, etc., probably New Kingdom. Text, BRUGSCH, *Thes.* 1065 [8].

Seated double-statue, Dyn. XVIII, usurped by Shedsunefertem, Greatest of the Directors of craftsmen, son of ʿAnkhefensekhmet [hieroglyphs], same title, and wife Tashepenēsi [hieroglyphs], temp. Sesonchis I, granite, in Cairo Mus. CG 741. BORCHARDT, *Statuen*, iii, Bl. 137, pp. 67–9; WILDUNG and GRIMM, *Götter, Pharaonen* (1978), No. 52. Text, DARESSY in *Rec. Trav.* xviii (1896), pp. 46–9 [i]. Name and titles of wife, GRDSELOFF in *Ann. Serv.* xlvii (1947), p. 212. See KEES in *Ä.Z.* 87 (1962), pp. 140–2 [a].

Niche, dedicated by ʿAnkh-sheshonḳ [hieroglyphs], God's father, etc., with 6 statuettes of his ancestors, (a) ʿAnkh-sheshonḳ, Head of the Heads of craftsmen of the Temple of Ptaḥ, etc., son of Iufʿa [hieroglyphs], (b) probably his wife Tapert [hieroglyphs], daughter of Pedēsi [hieroglyphs], Great chief of the Ma, etc., (c) probably their son Thaenab [hieroglyphs], Head of craftsmen of the Temple of Ptaḥ, etc., (d) his wife Esmerptaḥ [hieroglyphs], (e) their son ʿAnkh-sheshonḳ, Head of craftsmen, etc., (f) his wife Nekhtubasterau [hieroglyphs], sandstone, probably Dyn. XXV, in Cairo Mus. JE 36728. VERNUS in *B.I.F.A.O.* 76 (1976), pls. v, vi, pp. 3–15. Text, LEGRAIN in *Rec. Trav.* xxix (1907), pp. 174–8.

ʿAnkhemthenent [hieroglyphs], with name of father(?) Irefʿaenptaḥ [hieroglyphs], bust, quartzite, Dyn. XXV, formerly in Cairo Mus. JE 29878, now in New York, M.M.A. 07.228.47. HOYNINGEN-HUENE and STEINDORFF, *Egypt* (1945), fig. on p. 168; BOTHMER, *Eg. Sculp.* pl. 10 [23–5], pp. 11–12 [10].

Pedēsi [hieroglyphs] Ḥarkhebi [hieroglyphs], block-statue, Dyn. XXV–XXVI, in Cairo Mus. CG 659. See BORCHARDT, *Statuen*, iii, pp. 7–8 (text).

Amen(em)ōpetemḥēt [hieroglyphs], Overseer of singers of Amūn of Ōpet, etc., son of Iḥsetpep [hieroglyphs] (mother), kneeling (headless) holding Ḥatḥor-head, schist, temp. Psammetikhos I, in New York, M.M.A. 24.2.2. FISCHER in *Apollo*, lxxxii (1965), fig. 8, p. 173; DE MEULENAERE in *Metropolitan Museum Journal*, 8 (1973), figs. 1–4, pp. 27–32; RUSSMANN in ib. figs. 1–3, pp. 33–46.

Nekht-ḥarḥebi [hieroglyphs] Neferebrēʿ-sineit [hieroglyphs], Royal herald, etc., son of Pede[neit], kneeling with naos of Ptaḥ, lower part, schist(?), temp. Psammetikhos II or later, in Berlin (East) Mus. 11332. See *Ausf. Verz.* pp. 256–7.

Pedubaste [hieroglyphs] Weḥebrēʿ [hieroglyphs], Royal scribe, etc., son of Usirinakht, kneeling with offering-table, fragment, granite, temp. Apries, in Marseilles Mus. 210 (formerly attached to upper part of another statue). WILBOUR MSS. iii. D. 15–16. Some names, LIEBLEIN, *Dict.* No. 2339. See MASPERO, *Catalogue du Musée Égyptien de Marseille*, pp. 9–10 [10].

ʿAḥ[mosi] (i.e. ʿAḥmosi-sineit), Overseer of the antechamber, etc., kneeling with naos of Ptaḥ, lower part, slate, temp. Amasis to Dyn. XXVII, in Cairo Mus. CG 666. Text, BORCHARDT, *Statuen*, iii, p. 14; DARESSY in *Rec. Trav.* xi (1889), p. 93 [xliii] (as basalt). (Head in Moscow Mus. I.1.a.5740 may join.)

Uzaḥorresnet, Greatest of the physicians, fragment of probably naophorous statue, granite, temp. Amasis to Darius I, in Michaelidis Colln. MICHAELIDIS in *Ann. Serv.* xliii (1943), figs. 34–5, pp. 101–2 [vii].

Upper part of scribe-statue, schist, early Dyn. XXVI, in New York, M.M.A. 25.2.1. WINLOCK, *Egyptian Statues and Statuettes* (1937), fig. 22; SCOTT, *Egyptian Statues* (1945), 27th pl.; BOTHMER, *Eg. Sculp.* pl. 20 [46], pp. 24–5 [21]; *Treasures from the Metropolitan* (Indianapolis Museum of Art, Oct. 25, 1970–Jan. 3, 1971), No. 58 with fig. (as Dyn. XXV).

Ḥarenḥap, Judge of the Great Place of the Temple of Ptaḥ-Sokari-Apis, son of Ipi and Zeubastesʿankh, kneeling, probably Dyn. XXVI, in Berlin (East) Mus. 10289. See *Ausf. Verz.* p. 258; *Führer* (1961), p. 77.

Ipy, Greatest of the Six, etc., son of Pedēsi, kneeling with naos, lower part, basalt, Dyn. XXVI, formerly in Turaev Colln., now in Leningrad, State Hermitage Mus. 2961. LAPIS and MAT'E, *Drevneegipetskaya skul'ptura v sobranii Gosudarstvennogo Ermitazha*, fig. 73, pl. iii [117], pp. 109–10. Text, TURAJEFF in *Ä.Z.* 48 (1910), p. 163 [iv]; WILBOUR MSS. 2 Q, 5 (giving provenance).

Ptaḥḥotp, Overseer of the Treasury, etc., head and feet lost, holding [naos], schist, temp. Darius I, in Brooklyn Mus. 37.353. COONEY in *Brooklyn Mus. Bull.* xv [2] (Winter 1953), figs. 1–5, pp. 2–16; BOTHMER, *Eg. Sculp.* pls. 60–1 [151–3], pp. 76–7 [64].

Psammethek-sineit, Director of all craftsmen of the King in silver and gold, son of Zeptaḥefʿankh and Tagemirēsi, kneeling with naos of Osiris, greywacke, Dyn. XXVII, in Cairo Mus. CG 726. BORCHARDT, *Statuen*, iii, Bl. 134, pp. 60–2; CAPART, *L'Art ég.* (1909), pl. 86; (1911), pl. 187 (upper part); id. *L'Art ég.* ii, pls. 385–6; ROEDER, *Altägyptische Erzählungen und Märchen*, Taf. 11; BOSSE, *Die menschliche Figur*, Taf. vi [125], p. 49; LEIBOVITCH, *Anc. Eg.* fig. 93; TULLI in *Miscellanea Gregoriana*, fig. 6, p. 217; BOTHMER, *Eg. Sculp.* pls. 61–2 [154–7], pp. 78–9 [65]; id. in *The Connoisseur Year Book 1962*, fig. 7, p. 37; HORNEMANN, *Types*, iii, pl. 615; TERRACE and FISCHER, *Treasures*, pp. 169–72 with pls.; PERC, *Spomeniki starega Egipta* (1974), No. 36 with fig. Upper part or head, OFFORD in *P.S.B.A.* xxi (1899), pl. facing p. 80; SPIEGELBERG, *Geschichte*, Abb. 77; VON BISSING, *Denkmäler*, *Text* to Taf. 108 [a] [figs.]; PIRENNE, *Hist. civ.* iii, pl. 39 facing p. 161; RICHTER in *The Journal of Roman Studies*, xlv (1955), pl. iv [14], p. 43 with note 32. See MASPERO, *Guide*, p. 203 [824]; BRUGSCH in *Bull. Inst. Ég.* iii Sér. 7 (1897), p. 144.

Psammethek-sonb, Vizier, etc., son of ʿAnkh-psammethek, God's father, *imy-iwnt*, kneeling with naos of Atum, Dyn. XXIX, in Cairo Mus. CG 682. BORCHARDT, *Statuen*, iii, Bl. 124, pp. 26–7; GRDSELOFF in *Ann. Serv.* xl (1940), fig. 28, p. 189. Text, DARESSY in *Rec. Trav.* xiv (1893), pp. 177–8 [lxxii]; id. MSS. E.30 [8]. See YOYOTTE in *B.I.F.A.O.* liv (1954), pp. 93–4 [Doc. 6, b].

Esmiḥos, Overseer of the royal harîm, etc., son of Pedemiḥos, Prophet, kneeling with naos of Ptaḥ, fragment, granite, Late Period, in Naples, Museo Nazionale, 1063. Text, WIEDEMANN in *Rec. Trav.* viii (1886), p. 68 [10]. Names and titles, LIEBLEIN,

Dict. No. 2363. See MARUCCHI in RUESCH, *Guida illustrata del Museo Nazionale di Napoli* (1911), p. 139 [425]; YOYOTTE in *B.I.F.A.O.* lii (1953), p. 184 note 2.

Pedepep [hieroglyphs], God's father, *sem*-priest, headless block-statue, Late Period, in Cairo Mus. CG 595. Text, BORCHARDT, *Statuen*, ii, p. 149.

Block-statue, Late Period, in Cairo Mus. CG 727. Id. ib. iii, Bl. 134, p. 62.

Head, faience, Late Period, in Cairo Mus. CG 808. Id. ib. iii, Bl. 149, p. 106; MARIETTE, *Album du Musée de Boulaq* (1872), on pl. 25; COTTRELL, *Egypt*, fig. 75.

Lower part of statue of daughter of Ḥarḥap [hieroglyphs] (mother), dedicated by brother Pedekhons [hieroglyphs], *waʿb*-priest of the gods of Memphis, etc., Ptolemaic, in Cairo Mus. JE 35351. Text, DARESSY in *Rec. Trav.* xiv (1893), p. 184 [lxxxiii]; xxiv (1902), p. 161 [cxciv].

Head ('Brooklyn Black Head'), with remains of text on back pillar, diorite, late Ptolemaic, in Brooklyn Mus. 58.30. BOTHMER, *Eg. Sculp.* frontispiece and pls. 123–4 [329–31], pp. 172–3 [132]; BRENDEL in *A.J.A.* 71 (1967), pl. 120 [7], p. 408; CHARBONNEAUX in *Mélanges d'archéologie et d'histoire offerts à André Piganiol* (ed. CHEVALLIER), i (1966), fig. 12, p. 418; *Handbook* (1967), pl. on p. 96; *Brief Guide* (1970 and 1974), fig. on p. 90; WESTENDORF, *Das Alte Ägypten*, fig. on p. 228; WOLF, *Hochkulturen*, Abb. 58; FAZZINI, *Images for Eternity*, Cat. No. 117; *Ägyptische Kunst aus dem Brooklyn Museum* (Berlin, Ägyptisches Museum, 4. Sept.–31. Okt. 1976), No. 84; VANDERSLEYEN, *Das Alte Ägypten*, Abb. 236; *Égypte Éternelle. Chefs-d'œuvre du Brooklyn Museum* (Palais des Beaux-Arts, Bruxelles, 9 décembre 1976–20 février 1977), No. 84.

Part of head, basalt, Ptolemaic, in Brooklyn Mus. 57.42. BOTHMER, *Eg. Sculp.* pl. 98 [263], p. 136; FAZZINI, *Images for Eternity*, Cat. No. 115; *Ägyptische Kunst aus dem Brooklyn Museum* (Berlin, Ägyptisches Museum, 4. Sept.–31. Okt. 1976), No. 81; *Égypte Éternelle. Chefs-d'œuvre du Brooklyn Museum* (Palais des Beaux-Arts, Bruxelles, 9 décembre 1976–20 février 1977), No. 81.

Pedusiri [hieroglyphs], Prophet of Khem Lord of Letopolis, etc., son of Ḥar-ʿashakhet [hieroglyphs] and Ēsiwert [hieroglyphs], schist, Roman, formerly in Huber Colln., now in Cairo Mus. CG 696. BORCHARDT, *Statuen*, iii, Bl. 128, pp. 38–9; MASPERO, *Égypte*, fig. 484; id. *Guide*, fig. 78, p. 225 [971]; id. and ROEDER, *Führer*, Taf. 42 [a], p. 62 [720] (as granite); *Encycl. phot. Caire*, pl. 216; *Great Museums*, fig. 7 on p. 127; DONADONI, *Egyptian Museum Cairo*, pls. on pp. 156–7. Upper part, DRIOTON and SVED, *Art ég.* fig. 147; MICHALOWSKI, *Art*, fig. 695. Text, BRUGSCH, *Recueil*, pl. vii [2]; DARESSY in *Rec. Trav.* xv (1893), p. 159 [7].

Divinities, animals, sphinxes.

Torsos of two female sphinxes with name of Amenemḥēt III, granite, in Vienna Mus. Inv.5753–4. REINISCH, *Miramar*, p. 230 [5, 6] with Taf. xxix [2] (one). Inv.5753, EVERS, *Staat aus dem Stein*, ii, Taf. xiv [68], p. 113; VON BISSING, *Äg. Kunstgeschichte*, Taf. lxxii [481], *Text*, ii, pp. 140 note 6, 147; KEIMER in *Ann. Serv.* xxxv (1935), pl. iv [b] (from EVERS), pp. 185, 190 [2], 191 [4]; SCHWEITZER, *Löwe und Sphinx im alten Ägypten*, Taf. ix [5], p. 44. See *Uebersicht* (1895), p. 33 [III]; (1923), p. 9 [III].

Ptaḥ seated, fragment, dedicated by Merneptaḥ (son of Ramesses II, later King), diorite, in Berlin (East) Mus. 7553. Text, *Aeg. Inschr.* ii, p. 85; KITCHEN, *Ram. Inscr.* ii. 496–7 [193, B]. See *Ausf. Verz.* p. 122.

Ptaḥ, diorite, dedicated by Ramesses II, in Berlin (East) Mus. 2274. Text, *Aeg. Inschr.* ii, p. 86; KITCHEN, *Ram. Inscr.* ii. 497 [193, C]. See *Ausf. Verz.* pp. 121–2.

Lion devouring captive, temp. Ramesses II, in Cairo Mus. JE 37647. HAMZA in *Ann. Serv.* xxx (1930), fig. 6, p. 48; HORNEMANN, *Types*, v, pl. 1329.

Thoth, faience statue-base, dedicated by Bek(en)amūn, Overseer of foreign countries, New Kingdom, in Cairo Mus. JE 30139. See *Bull. Inst. Ég.* iii Sér. 3 (1892), p. 281.

Osiris, dedicated by Kharkhons, Door-opener, son of (U)serken, granite, 3rd Int. Period, in Blacas Colln. Texts, BLACAS in *Revue Égyptologique*, N.S. i (1919), pp. 39, 40–6.

Head of Neith, granite, Dyn. XXVI, in Brit. Mus. 659. See *Guide (Sculpture)*, p. 238 [872].

Head, probably of Ḥatḥor, Late Period, formerly in von Bissing Colln. PETRIE, *Memphis*, i, pl. xxxiii [lower middle], p. 13.

Colossal head, perhaps of Imḥōtep, Late Period, in Copenhagen, Ny Carlsberg Glypt. Æ.I.N. 1384. MOGENSEN, *Coll. ég.* pl. xix [A 77], p. 20; KOEFOED-PETERSEN, *Cat. des statues*, pl. 121, p. 66 [113].

Sphinx, Ptolemaic or Roman, in Cairo Mus. CG 1175. BORCHARDT, *Statuen*, iv, Bl. 165, p. 90.

Sphinx, Ptolemaic, in Baltimore, Johns Hopkins Univ. Mus. 9210. POOLE in *Art News*, xlvii [9] (Jan. 1949), fig. on p. 38 [upper].

Cache of bronze statuettes. Dyn. XXII or later. All formerly in Posno Colln.

Hôtel Drouot Sale Cat. May 22–6, 1883, Nos. 524, 468, 190, 266 with pls. vi, v, iii, iv. See *Antiquités égyptiennes . . . Collection de M. Gustave Posno* (1874), Nos. 524, 468, 190, 266; STERN in *Zeitschrift für die gebildete Welt*, iii (1883), pp. 285–7.

(a) Bepeshes, Child of the Chief of a foreign country, in Louvre, E.7693. LONGPÉRIER in *Gazette Archéologique*, viii (1883), pl. 13, pp. 95–6; PERROT and CHIPIEZ, *Hist. de l'Art*, i, fig. 435; MASPERO, *L'Arch. ég.* (1887), fig. 272; (1907), fig. 296; VON BISSING in *Mitteilungen des Kaiserlich Deutschen Archäologischen Instituts, Athenische Abteilung*, xxxviii (1913), Abb. 8, pp. 253–7; FECHHEIMER, *Kleinplastik der Ägypter*, Taf. 105; BÉNÉDITE in *La Revue de l'Art ancien et moderne*, xliii (1923), fig. 6, p. 171; BOREUX, *Guide*, ii, pl. lvi [left], pp. 409–10; SCHMIDT, *Levende og Døde*, fig. 897; BOSSE, *Die menschliche Figur*, Taf. i [18], p. 18; MICHALOWSKI, *Art*, fig. 593; VANDIER, *Guide* (1948), pl. xv [2], p. 71; (1952), pl. xv [2], p. 73; (1973), pl. xix [1], p. 122; ARCHIVES phot. E.65. Name and title, YOYOTTE in *B.I.F.A.O.* lvii (1958), pp. 81–9 with fig. 1; REVILLOUT in *Revue Égyptologique*, iii (1885), p. 47 [bottom].

(b) Man, in Louvre, E.7692. LONGPÉRIER in *Gazette Archéologique*, viii (1883), pl. 12, pp. 94–6; PERROT and CHIPIEZ, *Hist. de l'Art*, i, fig. 434; VON BISSING in *Mitteilungen des Kaiserlich Deutschen Archäologischen Instituts, Athenische Abteilung*, xxxviii (1913), Abb. 7, pp. 253, 257–8; MASPERO, *Égypte*, fig. 538; RICHER, *Le Nu*, fig. 152; SCHMIDT, *Levende og Døde*, fig. 896; *Encycl. phot. Louvre*, i, pl. 108; CHARBONNEAUX, *Les Merveilles du Louvre*, i, pl. on p. 139 [left]. See BOREUX, *Guide*, ii, p. 333.

(c) Horus[1] pouring libation, in Louvre, E.7703. PERROT and CHIPIEZ, *Hist. de l'Art*, i, fig. 44; MASPERO, *Égypte*, fig. 539; id. *L'Arch. ég.* (1887), fig. 271; (1907), fig. 295; id. *Hist. anc.* i, fig. on p. 100; RICHER, *Le Nu*, fig. 153; STRÖMBOM, *Egyptens Konst*, fig. 213; BÉNÉDITE in *La Revue de l'Art ancien et moderne*, xliii (1923), fig. 5, p. 171; BOREUX, *Guide*, ii, pl. lvi [right], pp. 565–6; id. *L'Art ég.* pl. lviii; GAUCH in *Bulletin des Musées de France*, v (1933), fig. on p. 119; *Encycl. phot. Louvre*, i, pls. 120–1; DESROCHES, *L'Art égyptien au Musée du Louvre* (1941), fig. on 27th p. [upper]; RANKE, *The Art of Ancient Egypt*, and BREASTED, *Geschichte Aegyptens* (1936), 176; PIJOÁN, *Summa Artis*, iii (1945), fig. 274;

[1] Selected references.

Charbonneaux, *Les Merveilles du Louvre*, i, pl. on p. 134; Sainte Fare Garnot, *L'Égypte*, fig. on p. 96 [upper]; Vandier and Sougez, *La Sculpture égyptienne au Musée du Louvre*, 24th pl.; *Egyptian Mythology*, fig. on p. 44; Pirenne, *Hist. civ.* iii, pl. 60 between pp. 228–9; Soga, *The Nile*, fig. on p. 69 [left]; Westendorf, *Das Alte Ägypten*, fig. on p. 209; Leca, *Médecine*, fig. 12. See Vandier, *Guide* (1948), p. 71; (1952), pp. 72–3.

(d) Sēth made over into ram-headed Amūn, in Copenhagen, Ny Carlsberg Glypt. Æ.I.N. 614 (previously in Hoffmann Colln.). Arndt, *La Glyptothèque Ny-Carlsberg* (1896), pl. 198; Maspero, *Hist. anc.* i, fig. on p. 133 [right]; Schmidt, *Den Æg. Sam.* (1908), pp. 116–20 [E.62] with fig.; Mogensen, *Coll. ég.* pl. xxiv [A 99], pp. 26–7; Pijoán, *Summa Artis*, iii (1945), fig. 519; Koefoed-Petersen, *Cat. des statues*, pls. 95–7, p. 51 [83]; id. *Eg. Sculpture* (1951), pls. 34–5; (1962), pl. 37; id. *Ægyptens Guder*, pls. 26–7; id. *Det gamle Ægypten* (1943), fig. on p. 33; Pritchard, *Anc. Near East*, fig. 553; Poulsen (V.), *A Guide to the Collections* (1953), fig. on p. 12; (1972), fig. on p. 8; id. *Führer durch die Sammlungen* (1969), fig. on p. 10; Michalowski, *Art*, fig. 532; Rachet (G. and M. F.), *Dictionnaire de la civilisation égyptienne*, fig. on p. 236. Upper part, Franceschi and Johansen, *Et hundrede fire og tyve fotografier*, pl. 21. Head, Legrain in *Rec. Trav.* xvi (1894), fig. 2, pp. 167–8.

Stelae.

Royal.

Raᶜneb, granite, originally probably from Ṣaqqâra, in New York, M.M.A. 60.144. *I.L.N.* April 1, 1961, fig. on p. 545 [middle left]; Fischer in *Artibus Asiae*, xxiv [1] (1961), figs. 2, 10, pp. 45, 48, 53, 55–6; Edwards in *The Cambridge Ancient History*, Plates to Vols. i and ii (1977), 28 [a].

Ḥaremḥab, upper part with 5 lines of text, in London, Univ. Coll. 14391. Hari, *Horemheb*, fig. 82, pl. l [upper middle], pp. 300–2 [9]; Stewart, *Eg. Stelae*, i, pl. 1 [2], pp. 5–6. Text, Helck, *Historisch-biographische Texte*, p. 143 [152]. See Petrie, *History*, ii (1904), pp. 242, 252; *Handbook of Egyptian Antiquities* (1915), No. 530 [last item].

Amasis, year 29, upper part, sandstone, in Cairo Mus. JE 37494. Text, Daressy in *Ann. Serv.* xxiii (1923), pp. 47–8 (as JE 37974).

Amasis before Ptaḥ, in Cairo Mus. JE 34741 (= JE 35182).

Private.

Merymery, Royal scribe, record of land transaction, temp. Tutᶜankhamūn, in Cairo Mus. CG 34186. Text, Lacau, *Stèles*, pp. 232–3; Daressy in *Rec. Trav.* xvi (1894), p. 123 [cvii]; Helck, *Urk.* iv. 2078 [798], cf. *Übersetz.* (1961), p. 389; parts, Legrain, *Répertoire*, No. 312.

A Scribe of the Treasury of the Lord of the Two Lands, with Tutᶜankhamūn censing to Ptaḥ in upper register, in London, Univ. Coll. 14470. Stewart, *Eg. Stelae*, i, pl. 41 [1], pp. 50–1.

Amenemōpet with wife Nefertere and son before Ptaḥ, Dyn. XVIII, in London, Univ. Coll. 14467. Id. ib. pl. 28 [1], p. 36.

Mer(y)sekhmet, with hymns, and [Ptaḥ and Sekhmet above], lower part, sandstone, late Dyn. XVIII or early Dyn. XIX, in Copenhagen, Ny Carlsberg Glypt. Æ.I.N. 897. Koefoed-Petersen, *Les stèles égyptiennes*, pl. 37, pp. xxxiv, 31–2; Mogensen, *Coll. ég.* pl. cvi [A 719], p. 98; id. in *P.S.B.A.* xxxv (1913), pl. ii, pp. 37–40; Schmidt, *Choix* (1910), pl. xii [24], p. 28; id. *Levende og Døde*, fig. 508. Lower part, id. *Den Æg. Sam.* (1908), pl. 14, pp. 172–4 [E.106]; Pijoán, *Summa Artis*, iii (1945), fig. 1. Text, Platt in *P.S.B.A.* xxxv (1913), pl. xxxi, pp. 129–32; Koefoed-Petersen, *Rec. inscr.* p. 57 [897].

Two men Ḥori [hieroglyphs], each Greatest of the Directors of craftsmen, the 1st son of Khaʿemwēset (son of Ramesses II), the 2nd father of Vizier Ḥori, and Khaʿemwēset (father of 1st Ḥori), before Ptaḥ and Sekhmet, with relatives before Ḥatḥor below, sandstone, late Dyn. XIX to early Dyn. XX, in Michaelidis Colln. MAYSTRE in *Ann. Serv.* xlviii (1948), pl. i, pp. 449–55.

Paḥemneter [hieroglyphs], Greatest of the Directors of craftsmen, etc., before Ptaḥ, granite, probably Dyn. XIX, in Cairo Mus. JE 27322. Text, DARESSY in *Rec. Trav.* x (1888), p. 150 [xiii].

Roma [hieroglyphs], Door-keeper, with paralysed leg, and wife Imaia [hieroglyphs] and son, dedicated to Astarte, Dyn. XIX, in Copenhagen, Ny Carlsberg Glypt. Æ.I.N. 134. MADSEN in *Ä.Z.* 41 (1904), pp. 114–15 with fig.; MOGENSEN, *Coll. ég.* pl. cvii [A 724], p. 99; SCHMIDT, *Den Æg. Sam.* (1908), pp. 180–3 [E.111] with fig.; id. *Choix* (1910), pl. xiv [29], pp. 28–9; *Levende og Døde*, fig. 493; SLOMANN in *Bulletins et Mémoires de la Société d'Anthropologie de Paris* (1927), fig. 8, p. 76; DAWSON, *Magician and Leech*, pl. i (frontispiece), p. 107; RANKE in *Studies Presented to F. Ll. Griffith*, pl. 66, pp. 413–14; PIJOÁN, *Summa Artis*, iii (1945), fig. 605; WOLF, *Die Welt der Ägypter*, Taf. 107; KOEFOED-PETERSEN, *Les stèles égyptiennes*, pl. 44, pp. xxxv, 35–6, 74; WATERMANN, *Bilder aus dem Lande des Ptah und Imhotep*, Abb. 20, p. 44; SIGERIST, *A History of Medicine*, i, pl. viii [20]; RIAD, *La Médecine au temps des Pharaons*, fig. 56; HARRISON in *The Biblical Archaeologist*, xvi (1953), fig. 14, p. 89; MAZAR, *Views*, ii, pl. 167; GHALIOUNGUI, *Magic and Medical Science* (1973), pl. 21; BRUNNER-TRAUT, *Die Alten Ägypter*, Taf. 48; LECA, *Médecine*, pl. ix; WELLS, *Bones, Bodies and Disease*, pl. 44. Deceased, TOLSTOÏ, *Étude des Représentations Pathologiques dans l'Art Égyptien*, fig. 7, pp. 78–80. Texts, KOEFOED-PETERSEN, *Rec. inscr.* p. 59 [134].

Seba [hieroglyphs], Overseer of the cattle of Ptaḥ, and wife Wert-khenr(eti) [hieroglyphs], three registers, **I,** deceased and two female relatives before Osiris and Sons of Horus, **II,** deceased and wife kneeling before Apis-bull, **III,** Mosi [hieroglyphs], Craftsman of the Place of Truth, and his wife Ēsinefer(t) [hieroglyphs], kneeling before Ḥatḥor-cow, incomplete, Dynasty XIX, in Florence Mus. 2541. BEREND, *Principaux monuments*, pl. vii, pp. 52–3; SPIEGELBERG, *Ägyptologische Mitteilungen* in *Sitzungsberichte der Bayerischen Akademie der Wissenschaften*, Philos.-philol. und hist. Kl. (1925), 2. Abhand. Taf. iv (from BEREND), pp. 20–1, 22–4; BOSTICCO, *Le stele egiziane del Nuovo Regno*, fig. 53, pp. 59–61; ALINARI photo. 43809 [left]; MARBURG INST. photo. 628883. Apis-bull, LANZONE, *Diz.* Tav. cci [1], p. 530. Names and titles, LIEBLEIN, *Dict.* Nos. 785, 2074. See ROSELLINI, *Breve Notizia degli Oggetti di Antichità Egiziane* [etc.] (1830), p. 93 [106]; SCHIAPARELLI, *Mus. Arch. Firenze*, pp. 360–2 [1624] (text); MASPERO in *Rec. Trav.* ii (1880), p. 179 [xxxix]; MIGLIARINI, *Indication*, p. 16.

Names lost, with Ptaḥ and Termuthis in upper register, Dyn. XIX, in London, Univ. Coll. 14572. STEWART, *Eg. Stelae*, i, pl. 28 [2], p. 36.

Khaʿ [hieroglyphs], Barber, before Ptaḥ, Ramesside, in London, Univ. Coll. 14427. Id. ib. pl. 29 [1], p. 36.

Fragment, two faces, (a) two men (one a General, Overseer of a fortress, etc.) adoring, (b) Ptaḥ and Sekhmet, quartzite, Ramesside, in London, Univ. Coll. 14578. Id. ib. pl. 29 [8], p. 38.

Name much effaced, with Tuthmosis IV smiting enemies before Ptaḥ, probably Ramesside, in Hanover, Kestner-Mus. 1935.200.230. MUNRO in *Städel-Jahrbuch*, N.F. 3 (1971), p. 35 [32] with fig.

Paḥu [hieroglyphs], Tallow-chandler, before Ptaḥ, New Kingdom, in Berlin (West) Mus. 9427. Text, *Aeg. Inschr.* ii, p. 216. See *Ausf. Verz.* p. 133.

Shedsunefertem and (father) ʿAnkhefensekhmet, both Greatest of the Directors of craftsmen, adoring figure of Ptaḥ in high relief, with genealogy and mention of (son) Esptaḥ, God's father, fragment, temp. Sesonchis I or a little later, in Berlin (East) Mus. 8169. Text, *Aeg. Inschr.* ii, pp. 232–4; BRUGSCH, *Thes.* 811–13, with sketch. See *Ausf. Verz.* p. 231.

Donation-stela of year 17 of Apries, in Berlin (East) Mus. 15393. GARDINER MSS. photo 28.232. Text, ČERNÝ Notebook, 47, p. 42.

Pashenmut, Head of trumpeters, son of Uzaḥor-khat(?), same title, and Taḥyb, Dyn. XXVII, in London, Univ. Coll. 14510. PETRIE, *Memphis*, i, pl. xxxiii [upper left], p. 13.

Kaḥa[ishutef?], *ỉmy-st*, *ḥsk*-priest of Thoth, top part, Late Period, in Leyden Mus. F.1934/2.1.

Irtḥarerau, son of Thaiḥepimu and Heribesnes, Late Period or Ptolemaic, in Cairo Mus. CG 31082. SPIEGELBERG, *Die demotischen Inschriften*, pp. 9–10 with figs.

Blocks, etc.

Names of Pepy I. WILKINSON MSS. xiii. 32 [upper right].

Cartouches of the Aten, temp. Amenophis IV, in Brussels, Mus. Roy. E.4491. Text, SPELEERS, *Rec. inscr.* p. 100 [419].

Upper part of prince offering ointment, Dyn. XVIII, in Munich, Staatl. Sammlung, Gl.93. VON BISSING in *Münchner Jahrb.* (1911), Abb. 8, pp. 164–6 [10]; *Staatl. Sammlung* (1976), p. 88 with fig. See WOLTERS, *Illus. Kat.* p. 14 [39c]; id. *Führer*, p. 13 [74]; *Äg. Sammlung* (1966), No. 48; *Staatl. Sammlung* (1972), p. 73 [60].

Upper part of Ramesses II offering incense, formerly in Mansoor Colln., now in Detroit, Institute of Arts, 65.2. *Ancient Egyptian Art*, Parke-Bernet Galleries, Sale Cat. Jan. 30–1, 1952 (MANSOOR Colln.), No. 130 with fig.; PECK in *J.N.E.S.* 31 (1972), fig. 1, pp. 11 with note 1, 15; id. in *The Connoisseur*, clxxv (1970), fig. 5 on p. 270. See DARESSY in *Ann. Serv.* xx (1920), p. 168 [2]; *Bulletin of the Detroit Institute of Arts*, xlv (1966), p. 17; KITCHEN in *J.N.E.S.* 32 (1973), pp. 483–4.

Block with names of Ramesses II and son Raʿmeses-userpeḥti, alabaster. Text, DARESSY, op. cit. p. 169 [4].

Ptaḥ writing name of Ramesses II on persea-leaf. See id. ib. p. 169 [3].

Column-fragment of Ramesses II, in Bristol Mus. H 649. See GRINSELL, *Guide Catalogue to the Collections from Ancient Egypt* (1972), pp. 50–1.

Texts of Ramesses II on block from a door-jamb and column. BRUGSCH, *Recueil*, pl. iv [1, 5].

Lotus-column of Ramesses II, granite, in Cairo Mus. JE 38576 (also JE 48837). MASPERO, *Guide*, on fig. 64, p. 192 [754].

Block with names of Merneptaḥ. WILKINSON MSS. xiii. 32 [lower left].

Name and title of Raʿmessu, King's son (perhaps son of Khaʿemwēset and grandson of Ramesses II). L. *D. Text*, i, on p. 204 [bottom].

Name of Sethos II altered to Merneptaḥ-Siptaḥ, in Cairo Mus. JE 30174. See *Bull. Inst. Ég.* iii Sér. 3 (1892), p. 283.

Column-fragment with names of Sethos II and Merneptaḥ-Siptaḥ, in Bristol, City Mus. H 647. See GRINSELL, op. cit. p. 53.

Block, 5 columns of text of a King's son on front and one on side, probably Dyn. XIX, in Chicago, Or. Inst. 9170.

Pillar with Horus-name of Ramesses III. Text, BRUGSCH, *Recueil*, pl. iv [4].

Column, Ḥori [hieroglyphs], Greatest of the Directors of craftsmen, etc., son of Ptaḥmosi [hieroglyphs], before Ptaḥ and before Mut, probably Ramesside, in Cairo Mus. Temp. No. 20.1.25.4. Text, DARESSY in *Rec. Trav.* xi (1889), p. 81 [xxiv]. Names and titles, LIEBLEIN, *Dict.* No. 2042.

Titles of a Prophet of Iʿoḥ, Saḥurēʿ, and Astarte, etc., with a Ramesside(?) cartouche. BRUGSCH, *Recueil*, pl. iv [3].

Two fragments of column-base of a Greatest of the Directors of craftsmen, etc., with cartouches of Sesonchis I, granite. DARESSY in *Rec. Trav.* xxii (1900), p. 143 [clxxvii].

Two blocks, Sesonchis III and Thekerti [hieroglyphs], Greatest of the Directors of craftsmen, etc., before Sekhmet, and remains of similar scene before Ptaḥ and Sekhmet below, in Cairo Mus. JE 46915. Texts, id. in *Ann. Serv.* xx (1920), pp. 169–70 [5].

Remains of a goddess, with text mentioning Zeubastesʿankh [hieroglyphs], Chief of the harîm of Ptaḥ, etc., Dyn. XXII. Texts, id. ib. pp. 170–1 [6].

Block with dramatic mythological text, basalt, temp. Sabacon, in Brit. Mus. 498. SHARPE, *Eg. Inscr.* 1 Ser. 36–7 [top], 38; READ and BRYANT in *P.S.B.A.* xxiii (1901), pl. facing p. 160, cf. pp. 160–87; BREASTED in *Ä.Z.* xxxix (1901), Taf. i, ii, pp. 39–54; WILLIAMS rubbings, iv. 125–6; SEYFFARTH MSS. xii. 9768–72 (rubbings). Text, ERMAN, *Ein Denkmal memphitischer Theologie* in *Sitzungsb. Berlin*, xliii (1911), pp. 924–45, cf. 916–24, 946–7; SETHE, *Das „Denkmal memphitischer Theologie“* [etc.] in *Dramatische Texte* [etc.] (*Untersuchungen zur Geschichte und Altertumskunde Aegyptens*, 10), pp. 20–77, cf. 1–19, 78–80; line 2, DE ROUGÉ in *Mélanges archéologiques*, i (1873), pp. 20–1 (repr. in *Bibl. Ég.* xxvi, pp. 281–2); lines 3–48, JUNKER, *Die politische Lehre von Memphis* in *Abhandlungen der Preussischen Akademie der Wissenschaften*, Phil.-hist. Kl. (1941), No. 6, Taf. 1, pp. 7–77; parts, SANDMAN HOLMBERG, *The God Ptah*, pp. 3*–5* [1–4], cf. 19–22 (from JUNKER). Cartouche and sketch, YORKE and LEAKE in *Transactions of the Royal Society of Literature of the United Kingdom*, i, Pt. i (1827), pl. x [26] (repr. as *Remarks on some Egyptian Monuments in England*). See JUNKER, *Die Götterlehre von Memphis* (*Schabaka-Inschrift*) in *Abhandlungen der Preussischen Akademie der Wissenschaften*, Phil.-hist. Kl. (1939), No. 23, pp. 3–77; DRIOTON in *Arts Asiatiques*, i (1954), pp. 96–7; SHARPE, *Eg. Antiq.* p. 89 [135*]; *Guide* (*Sculpture*), pp. 220–1 [797]; *Guide, Eg. Collns.* (1964), pp. 61, 132; JUNGE in *Mitt. Kairo*, 29 (1973), pp. 195–204.

Fragments of the so-called 'Palermo Stone', with list of kings, etc., probably a Dyn. XXV copy of earlier document, basalt. GIUSTOLISI, *La 'Pietra di Palermo' e la cronologia dell'Antico Regno* in *Sicilia archeologica*, i [4] (1968), pp. 5–14 with figs.; ii [5] (1969), pp. 38–55 with figs.; ii [6] (1969), pp. 21–38. Texts of kings of Dynasties IV and V, SETHE, *Urk.* i. 235–49 [10 (150)]. See GODRON in *Chron. d'Ég.* xxvii (1952), pp. 17–22; HELCK in *Mitt. Kairo*, 26 (1970), pp. 83–5.

(a) Palermo, Museo Nazionale; PELLEGRINI, *Nota sopra un'iscrizione egizia* [etc.] in *Archivio Storico Siciliano*, N.S. xx (1896), Tav. i, ii, pp. 297–316; SCHÄFER, *Ein Bruchstück altägyptischer Annalen* (repr. from *Anhang zu den Abhandlungen der königl. Preuss. Akademie der Wissenschaften zu Berlin*, 1902), Taf. i, ii, pp. 1–41; NAVILLE in *Rec. Trav.* xxv (1903), pls. i, ii, pp. 64–81; GREGORIO, *Détails historiques et fac-simile en photographie de la 'Pierre de Palerme'*; DARBY, GHALIOUNGUI, and GRIVETTI, *Food: The Gift of Osiris*, i, figs. 1. 20–1. *Recto*, BREASTED, *History*, fig. 29; DONADONI in *Enciclopedia dell'Arte Antica Classica e Orientale*, ii, fig. 1216, p. 956; BRENTJES, *Von Schanidar bis Akkad*, pl. 90; ROUSSEAU-LIESSENS, *Le Dossier secret du Nil et la Pierre de Palerme*, fig. 21; bottom part, PETRIE in HAMMERTON, *Universal History of the World*, i, fig. on p. 24. Names of estates of Neferirkarēʿ, JACQUET-GORDON, *Domaines*, p. 151 [3R5]. Boats, HASSAN, *Gîza*, vi [1], fig. 33, pp.

77–8. Palaeographical notes, CHEREZOV in *Festschrift Golenishchev* (*Drevniy Egipet. Sbornik statey.*), pp. 262, cf. 261–72.

(b)–(d) Cairo Mus. JE 39734–5, 44859, said to have been found at el-Minya, see *Bibl.* iv. 133.

(e) Cairo Mus. JE 44860; GAUTHIER in MASPERO, *Le Musée Égyptien*, iii, pl. xxxi, pp. 29, 50–3; text, DARESSY in *B.I.F.A.O.* xii (1916), pp. 173–4.

(f) Cairo Mus.; DE CENIVAL in *Bull. Soc. fr. d'Ég.* No. 44 (Dec. 1965), pp. 13–17 with fig.

(g) London, Univ. Coll. 15508; STEWART, *Egyptian Stelae, Reliefs and Paintings from the Petrie Collection*, ii, pl. 3 [1], p. 6 [17]; *recto*, PETRIE in *Anc. Eg.* (1916), fig. on p. 119, cf. pp. 115, 120; *verso*, REEVES in *Göttinger Miszellen*, No. 32 (1979), pp. 47–51 with figs.

Jamb with Amasis wearing Red Crown, quartzite; text, DARESSY in *Ann. Serv.* xx (1920), p. 171 [7]. Companion-piece (White Crown) in Memphis (Tennessee), at entrance to Zoological Garden.

Names of Amasis, WILKINSON MSS. xiii. 32 [lower right]. Others, L. *D. Text*, i, on p. 204 [bottom].

Door-jamb of Thaiēsimu (companion-piece in Cambridge, Fitzwilliam Mus. E.5.1909, see *supra*), *recto*, Thaiēsimu and text, *verso*, Thaiēsimu embraced by goddess Semset [hieroglyphs], temp. Nektanebos I, in Brooklyn Mus. 56.152. BOTHMER, *Eg. Sculp.* pls. 70–1 [181–4], pp. 92–4 [74]; upper part of Thaiēsimu, BRECKENRIDGE, *Likeness. A Conceptual History of Ancient Portraiture*, figs. 32–3.

Names of Ptolemy I Soter. L. *D. Text*, i, on p. 204 [bottom].

Various.

Shrines.

Osiris and Min, dedicated by Siamūn [hieroglyphs], Scribe of the Great Prison, son of Sery [hieroglyphs] and Sitip [hieroglyphs], Middle Kingdom, in Berlin Mus. 1624. Texts, *Aeg. Inschr.* i, pp. 151–2. See *Ausf. Verz.* p. 85.

Ptaḥ, with statuette, dedicated by Amenemōnet [hieroglyphs], Overseer of work on the pylon, cartouche of Ramesses II, quartz, in London, Univ. Coll. 14490.

Block, probably from shrine, Ramesses II offering(?), quartzite, in Munich, Staatl. Sammlung, Gl.124. *Äg. Sammlung* (1966), Abb. 59; *Staatl. Sammlung* (1976), p. 7 with fig.; head of King, MYŚLIWIEC, *Le Portrait royal dans le bas-relief du Nouvel Empire*, pl. cvi [235]. See WOLTERS and VON BISSING in *Münchner Jahrb.* (1913), p. 162 [533]; *Staatl. Sammlung* (1972), p. 5.

Termuthis, dedicated by Amenḥotp Ḥuy [hieroglyphs], Servant (*sḏm-ʿš*), Dyn. XIX, formerly in Descotil Colln. (quoted in error in *Bibl.* iv. 5). *Descr. Ant.* v, pl. 47 [6–8]; DENON, *Voyage dans la Basse et la Haute Égypte* (Paris, 1802), pl. 124 [4–6]; *Histoire scientifique et militaire de l'Expédition française en Égypte. Atlas*, pls. 269–70 [4–6].

Neith, dedicated by Amasis, granite, in Cairo Mus. CG 70010. ROEDER, *Naos* (*Cat. Caire*), Taf. 8 [a], pp. 37–8; FECHHEIMER, *Plastik* (1914), on Taf. 98; (1923), on Taf. 108. See MASPERO, *Guide*, p. 212 [879].

Vessels.

Apophis II (ʿAḳenenrēʿ), fragment, granite, in Berlin Mus. 20366. LABIB, *Die Herrschaft der Hyksos in Ägypten und ihr Sturz*, Taf. 4, p. 29 [1]. Text, *Aeg. Inschr.* i, p. 269; HELCK, *Historisch-biographische Texte*, p. 56 [78].

Sethos I, faience, in Cairo Mus. JE 87784.

Chalice with gods, etc., in relief, inscribed for Sheshonḳ [hieroglyphs], son of (Osorkon II and) Keramama, incomplete, faience, in Berlin (West) Mus. 4563. WALLIS, *Egyptian Ceramic Art* (1900), fig. 38, p. 25; VON BISSING in *Nachr. Göttingen* (1941), Taf. ii [1], p. 119; TAIT in *J.E.A.* 49 (1963), pl. xxi [1], fig. 6, pp. 123–4 [xxxii]; KAISER, *Äg. Mus. Berlin* (1967), Abb. 814c, p. 80; KAYSER, *Ägyptisches Kunsthandwerk*, Abb. 119; *Meisterwerke altägyptischer Keramik.* Höhr-Grenzhausen, 16. Sept. bis 30. Nov. 1978, No. 349 with fig. Rim with text, TAIT in *Apollo*, lxxviii (1963), fig. 1, p. 200. See *Ausf. Verz.* p. 445.

Seven inscribed ointment-jars, faience, Late Period, formerly in Hilton Price and MacGregor Collns., now in Brooklyn Mus. 49.52.1–7. *Sotheby Sale Cat.* (MACGREGOR), June 26–July 6, 1922, pl. vii [290], p. 40; RIEFSTAHL, *Ancient Egyptian Glass and Glazes in the Brooklyn Museum* (1968), fig. 64, p. 108; HILTON PRICE in *P.S.B.A.* xxv (1903), pp. 326–7 with pl. (one); *Sotheby Sale Cat.* (HILTON PRICE), July 12–21, 1911, No. 713 with pl. xvii (one). Texts, HILTON PRICE, *A Catalogue of the Egyptian Antiquities* [etc.], ii (1908), p. 88 [4791].

Others.

Mirror of Ḥetep-ḥatḥor [hieroglyphs], Prophetess of Ḥatḥor, etc., bronze, late Old Kingdom or early Middle Kingdom, in Cairo Mus. CG 44075 (JE 30065). LILYQUIST, *Ancient Egyptian Mirrors* [etc.], fig. 11, p. 14 with note 142; BÉNÉDITE, *Miroirs* (*Cat. Caire*), pp. 34–5 with fig. 8. See KAPLONY, *Beschriftete Kleinfunde in der Sammlung Georges Michailidis*, p. 25 [60, 1].

Weight of 270 debens of Taharqa, basalt, in Cairo Mus. CG 31652. WEIGALL, *Weights and Balances* (*Cat. Caire*), pls. v, vi, p. 10. See MASPERO, *Guide*, p. 542 [5511].

Sistra of Amasis, faience. (a) Fragment, Reading, Ure Museum of Greek Archaeology, E.63.18. (b) Cairo Mus. CG 69334; HICKMANN, *Instruments de Musique* (*Cat. Caire*), pl. lix [A, B], p. 93; id. *Ägypten*, Abb. 27 [right].

Faience fragment of King Senkamaniskeñ, in Cairo Mus. JE 41293. See DARESSY in *Ann. Serv.* x (1910), pp. 183–4.

Plaque mentioning Temple of Sethos I, faience, probably from foundation deposit, in New York, M.M.A. 17.194.2333. Text, BRUGSCH, *Thes.* 1223 [lower middle] (perhaps this); KITCHEN, *Ram. Inscr.* i. 124 [63, b]. See HAYES, *Scepter*, ii, p. 332.

Plaque of Ramesses III, faience, in Cairo Mus. JE 30082. See *Bull. Inst. Ég.* iii Sér. 3 (1892), p. 278.

Menat-fragment with cartouche of Psammetikhos II, faience, in Munich, Staatl. Sammlung, ÄS 5464.

Cylinder-seal with Horus-name Sekhemkhaᶜu (probably Shepseskarēᶜ), bronze, in Cairo Mus. JE 45495. Text, DARESSY in *Ann. Serv.* xv (1915), p. 94 [upper] (as JE 45041).

Clay sealing with cartouches of Amasis, in London, Univ. Coll. 17061. PETRIE, *Scarabs and Cylinders with Names*, pl. lviii [26.5.1].

EL-BADRASHEIN

Stela, To [hieroglyphs], Pastry-cook, with wife Iay [hieroglyphs] and others before Ptaḥ and Sekhmet, Dyn. XX, in Cairo Mus. JE 34208. MASPERO in GRÉBAUT, *Le Musée Égyptien*, i, pl. xlvi [right], p. 44.

PYRAMID-FIELD OF DAHSHÛR

Maps LXXIII, LXXIV

Plan, L. *D.* i. 34 [left]–35; DE MORGAN, *Dahchour*, i, plan at the beginning; ii, pl. i; id. *Carte de la Nécropole Memphite*, 1–4; FAKHRY, *Sneferu*, i, fig. 3 (adapted from DE MORGAN); and view, PERRING, *Pyramids*, iii, pl. xiii [bottom right and 15]; VYSE, *Operations*, iii, pl. facing p. 56. Plan of southern part, ARNOLD and STADELMANN in *Mitt. Kairo*, 31 (1975), Abb. 3 on p. 172. Views (mostly pyramids), FRITH, *Cairo, Sinai, Jerusalem* [etc.] (1860), 8th pl. = id. *Lower Egypt and Thebes*, 14th pl.; SÉE, *Naissance*, fig. on pp. 164–5 (with south Ṣaqqâra); YOYOTTE, *Treasures*, pl. on p. 18. MICHAŁOWSKI, *Pyramidy i mastaby*, pl. 27. Views of Pyramids, with plan and sections of interior of the Red Pyramid, POCOCKE, *A Description of the East*, i (1743), pl. xix facing p. 52. General accounts of de Morgan's excavations, DARESSY in *Bull. Inst. Ég.* iii Sér. 5 (1894), pp. 193–205; DE MORGAN in *Comptes rendus* (1895), pp. 169–79; id. in *Bull. Inst. Ég.* iii Sér. 7 (1897), pp. 131–3.

I. Pyramids

A AND B. PYRAMID-COMPLEXES OF SNEFRU

'PYRAMID-TOWN'.

BORCHARDT in *Ä.Z.* 42 (1905), p. 1, with position, Abb. 1.

Protective decree of Pepy I, year of 21st census, found near south-east corner of building, in Berlin (East) Mus. 17500. Id. ib. Taf. i, ii, pp. 2–11; WEILL, *Les Décrets Royaux* [etc.], pl. iii [1], pp. 43–52; MORET in *Journal Asiatique*, 11e Sér. x (1917), pls. iv, v, pp. 387–427; GOEDICKE, *Königliche Dokumente aus dem Alten Reich*, Abb. 5, pp. 55–77. Text, SETHE, *Urk.* i. 209–13 [45 (136)]. See FAKHRY, *Sneferu*, i, p. 9; *Führer* (1961), p. 47.

A. NORTHERN COMPLEX

MARAGIOGLIO and RINALDI, *L'Architettura*, iii, pp. 124–39, with plans and sections, Tav. 18, 19.

CAUSEWAY.

See FAKHRY, *Sneferu*, i, p. 33.

PYRAMID. Lepsius, XLIX; Red Pyramid.

L. *D. Text*, i, pp. 206–7. Description, plans, and section, BURTON MSS. 25618, 9–10; 25620, 137. Plans, sections, and view, PERRING, *Pyramids*, iii, pl. xiv; VYSE, *Operations*, iii, pls. facing pp. 64, 65 [1st pl.], 58 [upper], cf. pp. 63–5. Vertical aerial view, GRINSELL, *Eg. Pyramids*, pl. xiii [a] facing p. 157; id. *Barrow, Pyramid and Tomb*, fig. 68. Views (some also showing interior), CAPART, *Memphis*, figs. 37–8; GILBERT, *Le Classicisme de l'architecture égyptienne*, fig. 3; VARILLE, *À propos des pyramides de Snefrou*, fig. 1, pp. 3–4; FAKHRY, *The Pyramids*, figs. 56, 58, pp. 95–7; id. in *The Egyptian Education Bureau London. The Bulletin*, No. 65 (May–June 1952), fig. on p. 31 [lower]; LAUER, *Mystère*, pl. ix [a]; VANDERSLEYEN, *Das Alte Ägypten*, Abb. 26 [b], 27 [a]; MENDELSSOHN, *The Riddle of the Pyramids*, pls. 29, 30; LECLANT and others, *Le temps des Pyramides*, figs. 87, 291; of interior, MENDELSSOHN in *Science Journal*, 4 [3] (1968), fig. on p. 51.

Masons' graffiti, on casing blocks on south side. L. *D.* ii. 1 [f, g], and *Text*, i, p. 206.

B. SOUTHERN COMPLEX

(perhaps also [hieroglyphs])

MARAGIOGLIO and RINALDI, *L'Architettura*, iii, pp. 54–123, with plans and sections, Tav. 8–17.

Plan, FAKHRY, *Sneferu*, i, fig. 5; id. in *Ann. Serv.* lii (1954), fig. 1 on p. 567; id. *The Pyramids*, fig. 43.

LOWER CAUSEWAY.

ARNOLD and STADELMANN in *Mitt. Kairo*, 31 (1975), p. 173 [2], with view, Taf. 111 [c].

LOWER TEMPLE.

Plan LXXIII (inset)

FAKHRY, *Sneferu*, i, pp. 27–9, 33, and 106–17 (by Ricke), with plans, reconstruction, and views, pls. iv [B], xlvi, xlvii, xlviii [A], xlix–li, figs. 60–2; id. ib. ii, Pt. 1, passim, with plans, reconstruction, and views, pls. i–iii [A], v–xi, figs. 1, 3–6; id. ib. ii, Pt. 2, passim; id. in *Ann. Serv.* lii (1954), pp. 569–93, with plan and views, pls. i [A], iv, v [A], vi, vii, fig. 3; RICKE in ib. pp. 610–16, 618–23, with plans and views, pls. iv–vi [a], Abb. 4, 6. Plan and reconstruction, FAKHRY, *The Pyramids*, fig. 44. Plan, reconstruction, and view, SMITH, *Art . . . Anc. Eg.* pl. 25 [A], figs. 12, 13, pp. 39–41. Views, LECLANT in *Orientalia*, N.S. 21 (1952), pls. xxx [5], xxxii [7], p. 237.

Fragments of two stelae with names of Snefru (originally one at each corner). FAKHRY, *Sneferu*, ii, Pt. 1, pls. iii [B], iv, pp. 1, 3; see id. in *Ann. Serv.* lii (1954), pp. 573–4 [A].

Central Hall and Court.

(1), (2)–(5), (6), (7) Base. Processions of nomes and estates, of Upper Egypt at (1)–(5), and of Lower Egypt at (6) and (7).

FAKHRY, *Sneferu*, ii, Pt. 1, pls. xii–xv, xxvii [C], figs. 9–34, cf. 8, pp. 17–58; id. in *Ann. Serv.* lii (1954), pls. v [B], viii–x, figs. 4–6, pp. 572, 573, 577–83. Parts, id. *The Pyramids*, figs. 42, 45; LECLANT in *Orientalia*, N.S. 21 (1952), pl. xxxi [6], p. 237; EDWARDS, *Pyramids* (1961), pl. 10 [b]; WOLF, *Kunst*, Abb. 172; SMITH, *Art . . . Anc. Eg.* pl. 26 [B]; HELCK, *Geschichte des Alten Ägypten*, Taf. i [3]; LAUER, *Mystère*, pl. 12 [a]. Names, JACQUET-GORDON, *Domaines*, pp. 125–37 [1R4], cf. figs. 1, 2.

Pillars.

Relief-fragments, the King alone or with gods (including Ptaḥ, Min, and Seshet), in *ḥeb-sed* ceremonies, and inspecting cattle-stalls of oryxes, Nile-gods bringing offerings, and fowling-scenes. FAKHRY, *Sneferu*, ii, Pt. 1, pls. xviii [A], xix [A, B left], xxiii–xxvii [A, B], xxix [A], cf. xxx–xxxii, figs. 35–118, pp. 59–110; id. in *Ann. Serv.* lii (1954), pls. xi [A], xii [B], xiv [A], xv [A], xvi, pp. 584–7 [1, 4, 8, 9, 11].

Six Chapels.

Relief-fragments, the King and names. Id. *Sneferu*, ii, Pt. 1, pls. xx–xxii, xxviii [B], xxix [B], cf. xxx–xxxii, figs. 119–37, pp. 111–22; id. in *Ann. Serv.* lii (1954), pls. xi [B], xiii, xiv [B], fig. 7, pp. 573, 585–7 [2, 5–7]. Two, RICKE in ib. pl. vi [b, c], Abb. 5, pp. 622–3.

Fragments of three statues of the King, originally attached to rear walls of niches of

Chapels. FAKHRY, *Sneferu*, ii, Pt. 2, pls. xxxiii–xxxvii, pp. 3–4 [A]; id. in *Ann. Serv.* lii (1954), pls. xviii, xix, pp. 575 [2], 588. Head and hand, id. *The Pyramids*, fig. 47.

Relief-fragments, original position uncertain.

The King, gods, and names. FAKHRY, *Sneferu*, ii, Pt. 1, frontispiece, pls. xvi, xvii, xviii [B], xix [B right], xxviii [A], xxix [C, D], cf. xxx–xxxii, figs. 138–282, pp. 125–65; id. in *Ann. Serv.* lii (1954), pls. xii [A], xv [B], xvii, pp. 585 [3], 587 [10], 588; heads of the King and lion-headed goddess, id. *The Pyramids*, fig. 46; SMITH, *Art . . . Anc. Eg.* pl. 26 [A], p. 41; DE RACHEWILTZ, *L'Arte*, Tav. 17, p. 30.

Statues

Old Kingdom.

ʿAḥauka [hieroglyphs], [King's son] of his body (probably of Snefru), Lector-priest, squatting, fragmentary. FAKHRY, *Sneferu*, ii, Pt. 2, pl. xlvi [A], p. 10 [2].

Duarēʿ (tomb, see *infra*), temp. Saḥurēʿ or later. Two fragmentary scribe-statues, id. ib. ii, Pt. 2, pls. xlvi [B, C], xlvii, figs. 285–6, pp. 10–11 [3, 4]; id. in *Ann. Serv.* lii (1954), pl. xxii [A] (one only), p. 589.

Nefermaʿet [hieroglyphs], Treasurer of the King of Lower Egypt, lower part of squatting statue, diorite. Id. *Sneferu*, ii, Pt. 2, fig. 287, p. 12 [5].

Wemtet[ka] [hieroglyphs], King's daughter of his body, squatting, Dyn. IV–V. Id. ib. ii, Pt. 2, pls. xliii, xliv, fig. 284, p. 9 [1]. Text, id. in *Ann. Serv.* lii (1954), p. 590 [top].

A Prophet of Snefru, Secretary, squatting with arms crossed on breast, headless, Dyn. V. Id. *Sneferu*, ii, Pt. 2, pl. xlv, p. 12 [6]; id. in *Ann. Serv.* lii (1954), pl. xxii [B] after p. 594.

Fragment of seated statue, with text mentioning Khufu, granite. Id. *Sneferu*, ii, Pt. 2, fig. 288, p. 13 [8].

Fragments of sandstone statuettes, one with text mentioning Snefru. Id. ib. ii, Pt. 2, fig. 288, pp. 12 [7], 13 [9].

Middle Kingdom.

Ameny-snefru [hieroglyphs], son of Iʿakhu [hieroglyphs], fragment. FAKHRY, *Sneferu*, ii, Pt. 2, fig. 307, p. 31 [43].

Faiḥezui [hieroglyphs], Inspector of prophets of the southern Pyramid of Snefru, etc., son of Snefruemsasi [hieroglyphs] (mother), block-statue, headless. Id. ib. ii, Pt. 2, pls. li, lii, figs. 289–90, pp. 15–16 [2]; see id. in *Ann. Serv.* lii (1954), p. 590; BOTHMER in *Brooklyn Museum Annual*, ii–iii (1960–2), p. 32 [xviii].

Iḳer [hieroglyphs], Guardian of the chamber, seated, fragment. FAKHRY, *Sneferu*, ii, Pt. 2, fig. 311, p. 32 [49].

Iti [hieroglyphs], Recipient from the ruler's table, son of Ameny-waḥ [hieroglyphs] and Kerḥi [hieroglyphs], statue-base with family in relief. Id. ib. ii, Pt. 2, pls. lxi, lxii, figs. 340–2, pp. 41–4 [1]; id. in *Ann. Serv.* lii (1954), pl. xxvi [B], p. 590.

Khentiuka [hieroglyphs], Chief lector-priest, fragment. Id. *Sneferu*, ii, Pt. 2, fig. 337, p. 38 [70].

Khent[iuka], Overseer of the cabinet, son of Si-ḥatḥor [hieroglyphs] and Sit-ḥatḥor [hieroglyphs], statue-base. Id. ib. ii, Pt. 2, pls. lxiii, lxiv, figs. 343–6, pp. 47–50 [4].

Meket [hieroglyphs], statue-base fragment, basalt. Id. ib. ii, Pt. 2, fig. 301, p. 28 [34].

Meket [hieroglyphs], fragmentary statue-base with family in relief. Texts, id. ib. ii, Pt. 2, pp. 45–6 [2].

Meketʿankh [hieroglyphs], Director of boats, and a Chief lector-priest of Snefru, seated, fragment of double-statuette, granite. Texts, id. ib. ii, Pt. 2, p. 21 [9].

Nakht-snefru [hieroglyphs], statuette-base and feet. Id. ib. ii, Pt. 2, pl. lx [B], fig. 299, p. 27 [30].

Neteruʿankh(?) [hieroglyphs], *waʿb*-priest, son of Ḥatḥoriyti [hieroglyphs] (mother), and wife(?) Sepenmut [hieroglyphs], daughter of Meri [hieroglyphs], seated double-statuette, incomplete. Id. ib. ii, Pt. 2, pl. lvii [A], figs. 295–6, pp. 19–20 [7]; see Bothmer in *Brooklyn Museum Annual*, ii–iii (1960–2), p. 33 [xx] (as two men).

Ptaḥpuwaḥ [hieroglyphs] Renefso(n)b [hieroglyphs], . . . of the Pyramid of Snefru, Keeper of the chamber of the Great House, son of Sit-ḥatḥor [hieroglyphs] (mother), statue-base with scenes in relief. Fakhry, *Sneferu*, ii, Pt. 2, pls. lxvi [D], lxvii, figs. 350–3, pp. 53–5 [6].

Raʿḥotp [hieroglyphs], Steward, fragments. Id. ib. ii, Pt. 2, pl. lxxvii [A, left], figs. 303–6, p. 30 [40–2].

Renesʿankh [hieroglyphs], seated, much damaged. Id. ib. ii, Pt. 2, pl. lvi [A], fig. 294, p. 19 [5].

Si-ḥatḥor [hieroglyphs], *waʿb*-priest [of Snefru], son of Mek(et) [hieroglyphs], headless block-statue dedicated by son Min-snefru-sheri [hieroglyphs]. Id. ib. ii, Pt. 2, pls. liii, liv, figs. 291–3, pp. 17–18 [3]; id. in *Ann. Serv.* lii (1954), pl. xxiv [A], p. 590; see Bothmer in *Brooklyn Museum Annual*, ii–iii (1960–2), pp. 32–3 [xix].

Snefru-ḥirkhent [hieroglyphs], Lector-priest, statue-base with relatives in relief. Fakhry, *Sneferu*, ii, Pt. 2, pls. lxv, lxvi [C], figs. 347–9, pp. 51–2 [5]; id. in *Ann. Serv.* lii (1954), pl. xxvi [A], p. 590.

Snefruḥotp [hieroglyphs], Chief lector-priest and Inspector of prophets in the Pyramid of Snefru, ebony. Id. *Sneferu*, ii, Pt. 2, pl. l, p. 15 [1]; id. in *Ann. Serv.* lii (1954), pl. xxiii, p. 590.

. . . rer [hieroglyphs] . . . [hieroglyphs] Snefru, son of Khent[iuka]. Fragments, granite; id. *Sneferu*, ii, Pt. 2, figs. 316, 318, pp. 34 [58], 36 [62].

A Scribe, Inspector of prophets, statuette-base fragment with name of Sesostris II, granite. Id. ib. ii, Pt. 2, fig. 339, p. 39 [72].

Two inscribed double-statuettes, man and woman, and two women, basalt and alabaster, fragments. See id. ib. ii, Pt. 2, p. 22 [10, 11].

Statue-bases, inscribed and some with relatives in relief, mostly fragments. Id. ib. ii, Pt. 2, figs. 354–84, pp. 46–7 [3], 55–61 [7–22].

Inscribed fragments, limestone, basalt, and granite. Id. ib. ii, Pt. 2, pl. lxxvi [C], figs. 297–8, 300, 302, 308–10, 312–15, 317, 319–36, 338, pp. 24 [20], 26 [25], 27–8 [31–2], 29 [35–6], 31–2 [44–8], 32–3 [50–1], 33–4 [53–7], 35 [59–61], 36 [63], 37–8 [64–9], 39 [71].

Uninscribed statues and fragments, limestone, basalt, alabaster, granite, diorite, and sandstone. Id. ib. ii, Pt. 2, pls. lv, lvi [B], lvii [B], lviii, lix, lx [A, C, D], pp. 19 [4, 6], 21 [8], 22–4 [12–19], 25 [21–4], 26–7 [26–9], 28 [33], 29 [37–9], 33 [52]; four, id. in *Ann. Serv.* lii (1954), pls. xxiv [B], xxv [A] and [B] (= No. 27), p. 590; one, Leclant in *Orientalia*, N.S. 21 (1952), pl. xxxiii [8], p. 237.

Other finds

Old Kingdom and 1st Int. Period.

Stela of Neterʿaperef [hieroglyphs], King's son, Prophet of Snefru foremost of the *ḫʿ*-Pyramid, etc., with three estates at bottom, middle Dyn. V or later, found re-used, in Cairo Mus. JE 89290. Fakhry, *Sneferu*, ii, Pt. 2, pls. xxxviii–xl, fig. 283, pp. 4–8 [B]; id. in *Ann. Serv.* lii (1954), pl. xxi, pp. 591–2; H. Br[unner] in *Archiv für Orientforschung*, xvi (1952–3), Abb.

20, pp. 162–3; FISCHER, *Dendera in the Third Millennium B.C.*, pl. i, pp. 8–9. Names of estates, JACQUET-GORDON, *Domaines*, pp. 434–5 [2D4], cf. figs. 187–8. Dating, SCHMITZ, *Untersuchungen zum Titel s3-njśwt 'Königssohn'*, pp. 152–4 [VI].

Incomplete stela of woman Khons [hieroglyphs], 1st Int. Period. FAKHRY, *Sneferu*, ii, Pt. 2, pl. lxxiii [B], fig. 402, pp. 84–5 [3].

Clay sealings of Neferirkarēʿ. See id. ib. ii, Pt. 2, pp. 13–14 [C].

Middle Kingdom.

Stela-fragment mentioning Ipi [hieroglyphs], Chief lector-priest. FAKHRY, *Sneferu*, ii, Pt. 2, fig. 409, p. 87 [11].

Family-stela of an Outline draughtsman, Lector-priest (name erased). Id. ib. ii, Pt. 2, pls. lxxii, lxxiii [A], pp. 79–83 [1].

Inscribed stela-fragments. Id. ib. ii, Pt. 2, pls. lxxvii [A, middle and right], figs. 401, 403–8, 412, pp. 83–4 [2], 85–7 [4–10], 88 [15].

Inscribed fragments. Id. ib. ii, Pt. 2, figs. 410–11, 413–26, pp. 87–8 [12–14], 88–90 [16].

Pedestal and offering-table of Snefru, Overseer of *waʿb*-priests of the temple, etc., son of Meket [hieroglyphs] (mother). Id. ib. ii, Pt. 2, pl. lxx, figs. 390–3, 427, pp. 69–74 [2], 91–2 [17]; see id. in *Ann. Serv.* lii (1954), p. 591 [11].

Offering-table of Sebkḥotp Petety [hieroglyphs], Lector-priest, son of Renesʿankh [hieroglyphs] Ḥezert [hieroglyphs] (mother). Id. *Sneferu*, ii, Pt. 2, pl. lxxiv [A], fig. 428, p. 92 [18].

Offering-table of Meket [hieroglyphs], Director of recruits, son of Sitmeseḥ [hieroglyphs] (mother), and wife Sitamūn. Id. ib. ii, Pt. 2, pl. lxxv [A], fig. 429, p. 93 [19].

Offering-table with remains of texts and scenes, unfinished. Id. ib. ii, Pt. 2, pl. lxxiv [B], p. 94 [22].

Naos of Snefru, *waʿb*-priest, son of Ipet [hieroglyphs] (mother), fragments. Id. ib. ii, Pt. 2, pl. lxxi, figs. 397–400, pp. 75–7 [5].

Naos-fragments with remains of scenes and texts. Id. ib. ii, Pt. 2, figs. 394–6, pp. 74–5 [3, 4].

Shrine for torch of Seshenu [hieroglyphs], Overseer of the Temple, Overseer of sculptors, son of Kerḥi [hieroglyphs] (mother), with 'text of the torch', and relatives. Id. ib. ii, Pt. 2, pls. lxviii, lxix, figs. 385–9, pp. 63–9 [1].

Trial-piece, *recto*, cartouche of Amenemḥēt II, *verso*, hand holding pigeons, and foxes mating. See id. ib. ii, Pt. 2, p. 99 [16].

Fragment of limestone lid of box for documents concerning appointment of temple officials, years 1, 5, 11, 15. Id. ib. ii, Pt. 2, pl. lxxvi [B], fig. 430, p. 96 [6].

Two fragmentary inscribed pestles, sandstone and basalt. Texts, id. ib. ii, Pt. 2, p. 97 [9, 10].

Cylinder seal with Horus-name of Snefru, faience. See id. ib. ii, Pt. 2, p. 95 [1].

UPPER CAUSEWAY.

FAKHRY, *Sneferu*, i, pp. 36–9, with views, pls. iii, iv [A], and RICKE in ib. pp. 105–6, with plans and section, fig. 59; RICKE in *Ann. Serv.* lii (1954), pp. 609–10, with plans and views, pls. ii [b], iii, Abb. 3; JÉQUIER, *Douze ans*, pp. 11–12, with plan, fig. 2.

UPPER TEMPLE.

FAKHRY, *Sneferu*, i, pp. 75–87, 98–104 (latter by Ricke), with plans, sections, views, and reconstruction, pls. xxvii–xxxi and frontispiece, figs. 4, 42–5, 57–8; id. in *Ann. Serv.* li (1951), pp. 513–21, with plan and views, pl. ii [B], figs. 1, 2; lii (1954), pp. 564–5, and RICKE in ib.

pp. 605–8, with plans and views, pls. i, ii [a], Abb. 1, 2. Plan, FAKHRY, *The Pyramids*, fig. 48; SMITH, *Art . . . Anc. Eg.* fig. 11, p. 39. View, LECLANT in *Orientalia*, N.S. 21 (1952), pl. xxix [4], p. 237; HELCK, *Geschichte des Alten Ägypten*, Taf. i [2].

Fragments of two stelae with names of the King. FAKHRY, *Sneferu*, i, figs. 38–41, p. 75.

Two altars, both of Snefrusonb-nezes [hieroglyphs], Great *wa'b*-priest, Regulator of a phyle, son of Ip [hieroglyphs] (mother), and probably his father Snefru(sonb), same titles, Dyn. XII. Id. ib. i, pls. xxxii–xxxvi, figs. 47–52, pp. 84–7; id. in *Ann. Serv.* li (1951), pls. iii, iv, figs. 3–5, pp. 518–21; one, LECLANT, op. cit. pl. xxxiii [9], p. 237.

PYRAMID. Lepsius, LVI. Blunted, Bent, False, or Rhomboidal Pyramid.

L. *D. Text*, i, p. 208; BURTON MSS. 25618, 11–12, with plan, 25620, 138; PETRIE, *A Season in Egypt*, pp. 26–32, with plans and section, pl. xxiv; FAKHRY, *Sneferu*, i, pp. 25–6, 32, 40–59, 65–73 (by MUSTAPHA), with plans, sections, views, etc., pls. ii, v, vi, viii–xv, xxvi, figs. 16–24, 33–6; ii, Pt. 2, p. 102 with fig. (by RINALDI); id. in *Ann. Serv.* li (1951), pp. 509–13, with views, pls. i, ii [A]; id. *The Pyramids*, pp. 88–94, with plan, sections, views, etc., figs. 50–5; MUSTAPHA in *Ann. Serv.* lii (1954), p. 599, with plans, sections, views, etc., pls. 2–6, fig. 4. Plan, sections, and view, PERRING, *Pyramids*, iii, pls. xv [1, 2, 4–6, 9], xvi; VYSE, *Operations*, iii, pls. facing pp. 65 [2nd pl.], 66, 67, 68, 69 [1–3].

Vertical aerial view, GRINSELL, *Eg. Pyramids*, pl. xiii [b] facing p. 157; id. *Barrow, Pyramid and Tomb*, fig. 67. Aerial view, SAMIVEL and AUDRAIN, *The Glory of Egypt*, pl. 19. Views[1] (some including interior), FRITH, *Cairo, Sinai, Jerusalem* [etc.] (1860), 20th pl.; CAPART, *Memphis*, fig. 33; id. *L'Art ég.* i, pl. 10; SCHÄFER and ANDRAE, *Kunst* (1925), 201 [lower]; (1930 and 1942), 208 [lower]; PIJOAN, *History of Art*, i, fig. 73; id. *Summa Artis*, iii (1945), fig. 93; BORCHARDT and RICKE, *Egypt*, pl. 96; STEINDORFF, *Kunst*, 110; VARILLE, *À propos des pyramides de Snefrou*, fig. 2, pp. 4–8; HAMANN, *Äg. Kunst*, Abb. 117; DE WIT, *Oud-Egyptische Kunst*, fig. 10 facing p. 24; DESROCHES-NOBLECOURT, *L'Art ég.* fig. 7; GARNONS WILLIAMS in *I.L.N.* March 22, 1947, fig. 1 on p. 303; FAKHRY in *The Egyptian Education Bureau London. The Bulletin*, No. 65 (May–June 1952), fig. on p. 31 [upper], cf. pp. 28, 33; SPIEGEL, *Hochkultur*, Taf. 6 [b]; COTTRELL, *Egypt*, fig. 78; BAROCAS, *Egypt*, fig. 3; *Great Museums*, fig. on p. 192 [20]; MENDELSSOHN, *The Riddle of the Pyramids*, pls. vii, 25–7; id. in *Science Journal*, 4 [3] (1968), fig. on p. 50 [upper right]; MICHAŁOWSKI, *Piramidy i mastaby*, pls. 23–4; SOGA, *The Nile*, figs. on pp. 50 [upper], 60; MONTET, *Lives of the Pharaohs*, fig. on p. 19; DAVID, *The Egyptian Kingdoms*, fig. on p. 37 [top]; LAUER, *Mystère*, pls. viii, 11 [b]; VANDERSLEYEN, *Das Alte Ägypten*, Abb. 26 [a]; LECLANT and others, *Le temps des Pyramides*, figs. 85–6, 289–90; HAY MSS. 29812, 92–4; of interior, GARNONS WILLIAMS in *I.L.N.* March 22, 1947, figs. 3–10 on pp. 304–5; EDWARDS, *Pyramids* (1961), pl. 10 [a], 11 [a]; SMITH, *Art . . . Anc. Eg.* pl. 25 [B], p. 39; RUFFLE, *Heritage of the Pharaohs*, fig. 133.

Masons' graffiti and marks, including two with names of Snefru (one from Upper Burial Chamber, the other from north-east corner of Pyramid). FAKHRY, *Sneferu*, i, pls. xvi–xx, figs. 25–9, p. 59; name of Snefru at north-east corner, GARNONS WILLIAMS in *I.L.N.* April 5, 1947, figs. 2, cf. 1, on p. 344; see VARILLE, *À propos des pyramides de Snefrou*, pp. 6–7.

Two visitors' graffiti, of Pairptaḥ [hieroglyphs], God's father of Ptaḥ, son of Penamūn [hieroglyphs], and of Neferḥer [hieroglyphs], *wa'b*-priest, Late Period, in Northern Entrance Passage. FAKHRY, *Sneferu*, i, figs. 14, 15, pp. 46–7; PERRING, *Pyramids*, iii, pl. xv [7, 8]; VYSE, *Operations*, iii,

[1] Selected references.

pl. facing p. 69 [4], cf. p. 76; MARIETTE, *Mastabas*, p. 576; PETRIE, *A Season in Egypt*, pl. xix [695–6]; id. in SAYCE MSS. 14d; WILKINSON MSS. v. 46 [lower]; HAY MSS. 29833, 79 [right top]; BURTON MSS. 25618, 13, 16, and 25620, 133, 134 (squeezes).

SUBSIDIARY PYRAMID. Lepsius, LVII.

FAKHRY, *Sneferu*, i, pp. 89–96, 104–5 (latter by RICKE), with plans, sections, and views, pls. xxxvii–xxxix, xliv, xlv, figs. 55–6; id. in *Ann. Serv.* lii (1954), pp. 565–8, with views, pls. ii [A], cf. i [B]. Section, PERRING, *Pyramids*, iii, pl. xv [3]; MARIETTE, *Mastabas*, p. 582, cf. pp. 579–82. Views, GARNONS WILLIAMS in *I.L.N.* April 5, 1947, figs. 4, 5 on p. 344. Measurements, VYSE, *Operations*, iii, p. 70.

Masons' graffiti. FAKHRY, *Sneferu*, i, pls. xxi–xxiv, p. 94.

Two stelae with names of the King (lower part of the northern only, the southern in Cairo Mus. JE 89289). FAKHRY, *Sneferu*, i, pls. xl–xliii, figs. 53–4, pp. 89–90, 104 (last by Ricke). Cairo JE 89289, FAKHRY in *Ann. Serv.* lii (1954), pls. ii [B], iii, p. 566; EDWARDS, *Pyramids* (1961), pl. 11 [b]; King seated, FAKHRY, *The Pyramids*, fig. 49; MENDELSSOHN, *The Riddle of the Pyramids*, pl. 47.

C. PYRAMID-COMPLEX OF SESOSTRIS III

Plan LXXV

CAUSEWAY.

JÉQUIER in *Ann. Serv.* xxv (1925), pp. 56–61, with plan and section, fig. 1; id. *Douze ans*, pp. 134–8, with view, fig. 38.

Block, two registers of Nubian archers, in Cairo Mus. JE 51978; id. ib. fig. 39, p. 136; MÜLLER, *Äg. Kunst*, Abb. 71; FISCHER in *Kush*, ix (1961), pl. xiv [c], pp. 72–3; see GUNN in *Ann. Serv.* xxix (1929), p. 93. Another two blocks, in Cairo Mus. JE 51958 (stolen), 51959. Sea-going boats, see JÉQUIER in *Ann. Serv.* xxv (1925), p. 59; id. *Douze ans*, pp. 136–7.

UPPER ENCLOSURE

Plan, DE MORGAN, *Dahchour*, i, fig. 105 between pp. 48–9; ii, pl. xv; id. in *Le Monde Moderne*, Jan. 1895, p. 71.

MORTUARY TEMPLE.

Reliefs. Names of the King, id. *Dahchour*, i, figs. 111–12, p. 51; another, fig. on p. 47 [top], cf. p. 165. Fragments of cartouche, offering-list, offering-bringers, offerings, butchers, priests, etc., PERRING, *Pyramids*, iii, pl. xiii [4–12]; VYSE, *Operations*, iii, pls. facing pp. 60 and 63 [3–10], cf. pp. 72–6 (BIRCH) (repr. DE MORGAN, *Dahchour*, i, fig. 1 [lower], p. 3).

PYRAMID. Lepsius, XLVII.

DE MORGAN, *Dahchour*, i, pp. 47–50, 84–5, with sections, etc., figs. 106–9, and views, pls. ii, iii, xii–xiv; ii, figs. 132–6, cf. 131 (sarcophagus), pp. 87–97. View, in *Le Monde Moderne*, Jan. 1895, fig. on p. 68. Section and view, PERRING, *Pyramids*, iii, pl. xiii [1, 14]; VYSE, *Operations*, iii, on pls. facing pp. 60, 58 [lower], cf. pp. 57–63. Description, BURTON MSS. 25618, 17.

Visitors' graffiti, hieratic, probably Ramesside (one [= fig. 183] in Cairo Mus. CG 25377), DE MORGAN, *Dahchour*, i, figs. 183–6, p. 77; transcription of Cairo CG 25377, DARESSY,

Ostraca (*Cat. Caire*), p. 98. Another two, PERRING, op. cit. iii, pl. xiii [2, 3]; VYSE, op. cit. iii, pl. facing p. 60 [1, 2] (repr. DE MORGAN, *Dahchour*, i, fig. 1 [upper]).

NORTH GALLERIES AND MASTABAS OF PRINCESSES.

DE MORGAN, *Dahchour*, i, pp. 53–75, with plans and sections, figs. 119–21, 124, 128, 163, cf. pls. xv–xxv (jewellery); id. in *Comptes rendus* (1894), pp. 113–17, with plan on p. 115. View, id. in *Le Monde Moderne*, Jan. 1895, fig. on p. 72.

Two inscribed pottery jars, Middle Kingdom. Id. *Dahchour*, i, figs. 164–5, p. 73.

Upper gallery with four mastabas above.

Fragments with titles of a queen, id. ib. i, fig. 182, p. 77.

I (from west). Fragments of statue of Nesumontu, Chief steward, etc., diorite, Dyn. XII. Text, id. ib. i, fig. 116, p. 53.

II. Sarcophagus of Nefert-ḥenut, King's wife (of Sesostris III), etc. Id. ib. i, figs. 117–18, p. 53.

Lower gallery.

Sarcophagi of Ment and Sent-senbetes, both King's daughters (of Sesostris III). Texts, id. ib. i, figs. 122–3, p. 56.

Two fragmentary canopic-jars of Ment, alabaster, in Cairo Mus. CG 4005–6. Texts, id. ib. i, fig. 126, p. 57; REISNER, *Canopics*, pp. 3–4; id. in *Ä.Z.* xxxvii (1899), pp. 62 [8], cf. 64 [I, a].

Granite chest, uninscribed, in Cairo Mus. CG 4046, originally containing inscribed gold-leaf covered wooden canopic-box of a princess. Text of box, DE MORGAN, *Dahchour*, i, fig. 125, p. 57. Cairo CG 4046, REISNER, *Canopics*, pl. lxxx, pp. 25–7; see MASPERO, *Guide*, p. 110 [307].

1st 'cache' of jewellery. With scarab of Sit-ḥatḥor, King's daughter (of Sesostris II).

Pectoral[1] of Sesostris II, gold and coloured stones, in Cairo Mus. CG 52001. DE MORGAN, *Dahchour*, i, p. 60 [1] with pls. xv [1], xvi [1], xxi [upper right]; VERNIER, *Bijoux et orfèvreries* (*Cat. Caire*), pl. i, pp. 1–4; id. *La Bijouterie et la joaillerie égyptiennes*, pl. ix [1, 3], p. 115; MÖLLER, *Die Metallkunst der alten Ägypter*, Taf. 7; BOREUX, *L'Art ég.* pl. lxii [a]; WILKINSON (A.), *Ancient Egyptian Jewellery*, pl. xv, p. 85. *Recto*, DE MORGAN in *Le Monde Moderne*, Jan. 1895, fig. on p. 73 [lower]; BORCHARDT, *Works of Art*, pl. 41 [top]; WEIGALL, *Anc. Eg. . . . Art*, 92 [upper]; SCHÄFER and ANDRAE, *Kunst* (1925), 296 [upper left]; (1930 and 1942), 309 [upper left]; WOLF in BOSSERT, *Geschichte des Kunstgewerbes*, iv, fig. 2 on p. 115; MITRY, *Illus. Cat.* No. 3983; CAPART, *L'Art ég.* iv, pl. 634 [lower]; *Encycl. phot. Caire*, pl. 73; SMITH, *Art . . . Anc. Eg.* pl. 80 [A, top], p. 111; PIRENNE, *Hist. civ.* ii, pl. 17 facing p. 64; PIJOÁN, *Summa Artis*, iii (1945), fig. 296 [upper left]; LEIBOVITCH, *Anc. Eg.* fig. 118; LANGE and HIRMER, *Ägypten. Architektur* (1967), pl. xiv [top]; Amsterdam. *5000 jaar*, fig. 20 [48]; Brussels. *5000 ans*, fig. 17, p. 24 [26]; MICHALOWSKI, *Art*, fig. 791; ALDRED, *Jewels of the Pharaohs*, pl. 33; LECLANT and others, *Le temps des Pyramides*, figs. 220, 232. *Verso*, PETRIE, *Arts and Crafts*, fig. 97 facing p. 88; WARD (J.), *The Sacred Beetle*, fig. on p. 34 [lower]; id. in *P.S.B.A.* xxii (1900), fig. on p. 310; STEINDORFF, *Kunst*, 292 [upper right]. See MASPERO, *Guide*, p. 424 [3983]; EVERS, *Staat aus dem Stein*, ii, pp. 66–8 [447 (7), 454]; FEUCHT-PUTZ, *Die königlichen Pektorale*, p. 161 [1], cf. Taf. iv.

[1] Selected references.

2nd 'cache' of jewellery. With scarabs of Mereret [hieroglyphs] (or Meryt [hieroglyphs]), King's daughter (of Sesostris III and probably Khnemt-neferḥezet [hieroglyphs]).

Pectoral[1] of Sesostris III, gold and coloured stones, in Cairo Mus. CG 52002. DE MORGAN, *Dahchour*, i, p. 64 [1] with pls. xix [1], xxi [upper left]; VERNIER, *Bijoux et orfèvreries* (*Cat. Caire*), pl. i, p. 4; id. *La Bijouterie et la joaillerie égyptiennes*, pl. ix [4, 5], pp. 93, 115; WEIGALL, *Anc. Eg. . . . Art*, 93 [upper]; MÖLLER, *Die Metallkunst der alten Ägypter*, Taf. 8; CAPART, *L'Art ég.* iv, pl. 635; id. *L'Art ég.* (1909), pl. 50; BOREUX, *L'Art ég.* pl. lxii [b]; WILKINSON (A.), *Ancient Egyptian Jewellery*, pl. xvii and col. pl. ii, pp. 85–6. *Recto*, DE MORGAN in *Le Monde Moderne*, Jan. 1895, fig. on p. 73 [upper]; MASPERO, *Guide*, fig. 121, pp. 423–4 [3970]; SCHÄFER and ANDRAE, *Kunst* (1925), 296 [upper right]; (1930 and 1942), 309 [upper right]; BORCHARDT, *Works of Art*, pl. 41 [bottom]; PIJOÁN, *Summa Artis*, iii (1945), fig. 296 [upper right]; LANGE and HIRMER, *Ägypten. Architektur* (1967), pl. xiv [middle]; SMITH, *Art . . . Anc. Eg.* pl. 80 [A, bottom], p. 111; KAYSER, *Ägyptisches Kunsthandwerk*, col. pl. xiii facing p. 224; MÜLLER, *Äg. Kunst*, Abb. 76 [upper]; *Great Museums*, pl. 57; YOYOTTE, *Treasures*, pl. on p. 55 [upper]; ALDRED, *Jewels of the Pharaohs*, pl. 41; VILÍMKOVÁ, *Chefs-d'œuvre*, pl. 9; VANDERSLEYEN, *Das Alte Ägypten*, Abb. lvi [a]; WESTENDORF, *Das Alte Ägypten*, fig. on p. 97; DEMISCH, *Die Sphinx*, Abb. 65; LECLANT and others, *Le temps des Pyramides*, fig. 234. *Verso*, PETRIE, *Arts and Crafts*, fig. 98 facing p. 88; WARD (J.), *The Sacred Beetle*, fig. on p. 117; id. in *P.S.B.A.* xxii (1900), fig. on p. 311; STEINDORFF, *Kunst*, 292 [upper left]; ALDRED, *M.K. Art*, pl. 72. See EVERS, *Staat aus dem Stein*, ii, pp. 68–70 [458–66], cf. i, Abb. 20 on p. 79 (from VERNIER); FEUCHT-PUTZ, *Die königlichen Pektorale*, p. 163 [4], cf. Taf. iv.

Pectoral[1] of Amenemḥēt III, gold, coloured stones, and faience(?), in Cairo Mus. CG 52003. DE MORGAN, *Dahchour*, i, p. 64 [2] with pls. xx [2], xxi [lower]; VERNIER, *Bijoux et orfèvreries* (*Cat. Caire*), pl. ii, p. 5; id. *La Bijouterie et la joaillerie égyptiennes*, pl. xi [4, 5], pp. 93, 115; WEIGALL, *Anc. Eg. . . . Art*, 105; ALDRED, *Jewels of the Pharaohs*, pls. 42, 76; WILKINSON (A.), *Ancient Egyptian Jewellery*, pl. xviii, pp. 86–7. *Recto*, DE MORGAN in *Le Monde Moderne*, Jan. 1895, fig. on p. 74 [upper]; MITRY, *Illus. Cat.* No. 3971; *Encycl. phot. Caire*, pl. 74; SCHÄFER and ANDRAE, *Kunst* (1925), 296 [lower right]; (1930 and 1942), 309 [lower right]; ROSENBERG, *Aegyptische Einlage in Gold und Silber*, figs. 12–14, pp. 5–7; id. *Geschichte der Goldschmiedekunst. Zellenschmelz*, figs. 4, 5, pp. 5, 6; KISA, *Das Glas im Altertume*, i, Abb. 26, p. 147; PIJOÁN, *Summa Artis*, iii (1945), fig. 296 [lower right]; WOLDERING, *Götter*, Taf. xv; WOLF in BOSSERT, *Geschichte des Kunstgewerbes*, iv, fig. 3 on p. 115; RIESTERER, *Kunstschätze . . . Kairo*, pl. 22 (as el-Lâhûn); MICHALOWSKI, *Art*, fig. 793; LANGE and HIRMER, *Ägypten. Architektur* (1967), pl. xiv [bottom]; MÜLLER, *Äg. Kunst*, Abb. 76 [lower]; *Great Museums*, pl. 56; YOYOTTE, *Treasures*, pl. on p. 55 [lower]; VILÍMKOVÁ, *Chefs-d'œuvre*, pl. 10; WILDUNG and GRIMM, *Götter, Pharaonen* (1978), No. 19. *Verso*, ALDRED, *M.K. Art*, pl. 73; KAYSER, *Ägyptisches Kunsthandwerk*, Abb. 153. See MASPERO, *Guide*, p. 424 [3971]; EVERS, *Staat aus dem Stein*, ii, pp. 70–1 [467–71]; FEUCHT-PUTZ, *Die königlichen Pektorale*, pp. 163–4 [5], cf. Taf. iv.

Two bracelet slides of Amenemḥēt III, gold and coloured stones, in Cairo Mus. CG 52026–7. DE MORGAN, *Dahchour*, i, p. 66 [15, 16] with pl. xx; ALDRED, *Jewels of the Pharaohs*, on pl. 46. See VERNIER, *Bijoux et orfèvreries* (*Cat. Caire*), p. 21; MASPERO, *Guide*, p. 423 [3968–9].

[1] Selected references.

Two shafts north of Mastaba I. D and F of de Morgan.

Two uninscribed alabaster sarcophagi, Old Kingdom, in Cairo Mus. CG 28102–3. LACAU, *Sarcophages*, pl. xiv (CG 28102), p. 80. See DE MORGAN, *Dahchour*, i, pp. 75–6; FIRTH [etc.], *Step Pyr.* i, p. 42 note; LAUER in *Ann. Serv.* xxxiii (1933), pp. 165–6; DONADONI ROVERI, *Sarcofagi egizi*, pp. 110–11 [B 6, 7]; MASPERO, *Guide*, pp. 11 [30], 28 [40].

Fragment with names of Sesostris III, from shaft D. DE MORGAN, *Dahchour*, i, fig. 127, pp. 57, 165; id. in *Le Monde Moderne*, Jan. 1895, fig. on p. 70.

SOUTH MASTABAS.

Relief-fragments, perhaps from here. Offering-lists, id. *Dahchour*, i, figs. 178–80, p. 76.

SOUTH-EAST COURT.

Visitors' graffiti, hieratic, Ramesside (column-fragments with some [= figs. 190–1, 194] in Cairo Mus. CG 25378–9). Id. ib. i, figs. 190–5, p. 78; transcription of Cairo CG 25378–9, DARESSY, *Ostraca* (*Cat. Caire*), pp. 98–100.

Fragment of votive stela, deceased before statue of deified Sesostris I, New Kingdom. DE MORGAN, *Dahchour*, i, fig. 83bis on p. 42, cf. p. 165.

Shaft H. Paneit [hieroglyphs], Head of police, son of Pedusiri and Taimḥōtep, Ptolemaic.

Names and titles, id. ib. i, fig. 200, p. 78.

Lower part of statuette of Senbebu(?) [hieroglyphs], Door-keeper of the temple, Middle Kingdom, intrusive. Id. ib. i, fig. 175bis, p. 165.

BOAT-BURIALS. Some in a brick-built vaulted chamber.

DE MORGAN, *Dahchour*, i, pp. 81–3, with plans, sections, and views, including wooden boats and sled, pls. xxviii–xxxi, figs. 201–4. View, WARD (J.), *Pyramids and Progress*, figs. on p. 56 [upper, cf. lower right].

Boats. (a) and (b) Two (also fragment of rudder and sled), in Cairo Mus. CG 4925–6 (with CG 4927–8); see REISNER, *Models of Ships and Boats* (*Cat. Caire*), pp. 83–9, with details; MASPERO, *Guide*, p. 7 [6, 9] (as Sesostris II); view of one boat, CLARKE and ENGELBACH, *Ancient Egyptian Masonry*, fig. 34; MITRY, *Illus. Cat.* No. 6; hawk-heads on rudder-posts, DAVIES MSS. 2.14. (c) Chicago, Field Mus. Nat. Hist. A.31760; BREASTED, *History*, fig. 82; LANDSTRÖM, *Ships of the Pharaohs*, figs. 274, cf. 275, 277–82, pp. 90–3. (d) Pittsburgh, Museum of Art, Carnegie Institute, 1842.

D. PYRAMID-COMPLEX OF AMENEMḤĒT II

Plan LXXIV (inset)

UPPER ENCLOSURE

DE MORGAN, *Dahchour*, ii, pp. 29–39, with plans and sections, pl. ii, figs. 63, 77–83.

Inscribed temple relief-fragments with names of Amenemḥēt II (one = fig. 93, formerly in Paris, Mus. Guimet, 4849, now in Louvre, E.22348), and of intrusive private monuments of Si-ipy [hieroglyphs], Regulator of a phyle, son of ʿAmet [hieroglyphs] (mother), Senbebu [hieroglyphs], Great *waʿb*-priest of Ptaḥ, and others, Middle Kingdom, from eastern part. Id. ib. ii, figs. 86–94, pp. 37–9.

PYRAMID. Lepsius, LI, White Pyramid.

Masons' graffiti and marks. Id. *Dahchour*, ii, figs. 64–76, 85, pp. 31, 36.

Fragment of statue of Sebkemḥēt [hieroglyphs], Chief steward, son of Sitwerut [hieroglyphs] (mother), diorite, Middle Kingdom, intrusive. Text, id. ib. ii, fig. 84, p. 36.

TOMBS IN WEST PART OF ENCLOSURE

ITI [hieroglyphs] and KHNEMT [hieroglyphs], King's daughters (presumably of Amenemḥēt II).[1]

DE MORGAN, *Dahchour*, ii, pp. 40–68, with plan, section, and view, figs. 96–8. Date, see WILLIAMS (B.) in *Serapis*, 3 (1975–6), pp. 41–55 (as Dyn. XIII).

Masons' graffiti. DE MORGAN, op. cit. ii, figs. 99–104, p. 44.

Wooden rectangular coffins. Iti, id. ib. ii, figs. 105, 109, pp. 46–8 (texts). Khnemt; texts, id. ib. ii, pp. 57–8.

Canopic chest of Khnemt, wood(?). Texts, id. ib. ii, p. 68.

Two sets of alabaster ointment jars, eight each, and another jar, in Cairo Mus. CG 18643–50 (with wooden box, CG 18642), 18652–9 (box, CG 18651), 18661. VON BISSING, *Steingefässe* (*Cat. Caire*), pp. 136–9, 140 with Taf. A. Texts, DE MORGAN, *Dahchour*, ii, figs. 108, 110, pp. 49, 56.

Lower part of false-door of Amenemḥēt‘ankh [hieroglyphs], King's son (probably of Amenemḥēt II), etc., re-used in offering-chamber of Khnemt, in Cairo Mus. CG 1488 (panel, see *infra*). Id. ib. ii, fig. 111, p. 68; text, BORCHARDT, *Denkmäler*, i, pp. 189–90.

AMENḤOTP, Overseer of the seal, etc., temp. Amenemḥēt II, and KEMINUB [hieroglyphs], King's wife (of Amenemḥēt II).

DE MORGAN, *Dahchour*, ii, pp. 68–71, with plan, fig. 112.

Fragments of inscribed wooden coffin of Amenḥotp. Id. ib. ii, figs. 113–15, p. 70.

Fragments of wooden coffin with Chapter 30B of Book of the Dead and canopic-chest of Keminub. Id. ib. ii, figs. 116–17, p. 70.

ITIWERT[2] [hieroglyphs], King's daughter (presumably of Amenemḥēt II), and SIT-ḤAT(ḤOR)-MER(T) [hieroglyphs], temp. Amenemḥēt II.

DE MORGAN, *Dahchour*, ii, pp. 71–7, with plan and section, figs. 118–19.

Masons' graffiti. Id. ib. ii, figs. 120–2, p. 71.

Wooden coffins. Itiwert; texts, id. ib. ii, pp. 73–4. Sit-ḥat(ḥor)-mer(t), in Cairo Mus. CG 28101; texts, id. ib. ii, pp. 75–6; LACAU, *Sarcophages*, ii, pp. 77–9, cf. 80; Coffin-texts, DE BUCK, *Coffin Texts*, vii, Da 1 C.

Canopic-chests, wood(?). Iti(wert); text, DE MORGAN, op. cit. ii, p. 74. Sit-ḥat(ḥor)-mer(t); text, id. ib. ii, p. 76 [lower].

Two sets of alabaster ointment jars, in Cairo Mus. CG 18662–9 (probably these), 18670–7. Texts, VON BISSING, *Steingefässe* (*Cat. Caire*), pp. 140–3; of jars of Sit-ḥat(ḥor)-mer(t), DE MORGAN, op. cit. ii, fig. 126, p. 76.

Statue of swan, wood, from offering-chamber of Itiwert, in Cairo Mus. Temp. No. 24.6.25.4. Id. ib. ii, fig. 123, p. 74; VANDIER D'ABBADIE in *Rev. d'Ég.* 25 (1973), pl. 2, pp. 38–41 with fig. 4.

[1] Uninscribed jewellery of Iti and Khnemt is in Cairo Museum.
[2] Jewellery in Cairo Museum.

E. PYRAMID-ENCLOSURE PROBABLY OF DYNASTY XIII

Lepsius, LIV

Fakhry, *The Pyramids*, p. 217; Arnold and Stadelmann in *Mitt. Kairo*, 31 (1975), p. 174 [4], with view, Taf. 112 [b].

F. PYRAMID-COMPLEX OF AMENEMḤĒT III

Arnold in *Archiv für Orientforschung*, xxv (1974–7), pp. 321–2 [2–5], cf. Abb. 8; id. and Stadelmann in *Mitt. Kairo*, 31 (1975), pp. 170–3 [1], cf. Taf. 110 [b].

Valley Temple.

Arnold and Stadelmann in *Mitt. Kairo*, 33 (1977), pp. 15–17 [2], with plan, Abb. 1, and views, Taf. 1 [b], 2 [a].

Limestone model of interior of a pyramid, late Dyn. XII or Dyn. XIII. Id. ib. Taf. 3 [b], p. 16.

Causeway.

De Morgan, *Dahchour*, ii, pp. 99–100, with sections, figs. 143–4.

Upper Enclosure

Plan, de Morgan, *Dahchour*, i, fig. 205; ii, pls. xvii, cf. xvi (as Amenemḥēt II); Arnold and Stadelmann in *Mitt. Kairo*, 31 (1975), Abb. 1 facing p. 170.

Mortuary Temple.

De Morgan, *Dahchour*, i, pp. 116–17; ii, p. 98.

Fragment of text, id. ib. i, fig. 271, p. 117; ii, fig. 142, p. 98; Arnold and Stadelmann in *Mitt. Kairo*, 31 (1975), Taf. 111 [b], p. 170.

Fragment of offering-list, probably from here, in Heidelberg, Äg. Inst. 27. Evers, *Staat aus dem Stein*, i, Taf. 110; Otto (E.), *Aus der Sammlung des Ägyptologischen Institutes der Universität Heidelberg* (1964), Abb. 11, p. 91.

Hieratic graffito of Mery-inḥer(t), Administrator of the ruler's table(?), son of Sonb, Dyn. XII or 2nd Int. Period, in Cairo Mus. CG 25380. De Morgan, *Dahchour*, i, fig. 272, p. 117. Transcription, Daressy, *Ostraca* (*Cat. Caire*), p. 100.

Wooden statuette, Middle Kingdom, in Cairo Mus. CG 515. De Morgan, op. cit. i, figs. 270, 274, p. 117; Borchardt, *Statuen*, ii, Bl. 88, p. 78.

Pyramid. Lepsius, LVIII; Black Pyramid.

Arnold and Stadelmann in *Mitt. Kairo*, 33 (1977), pp. 18–20 [4], with section and view of interior, Abb. 3 and Taf. 3 [a]; *L. D. Text*, i, p. 209; Vyse, *Operations*, iii, pp. 70–1; de Morgan, *Dahchour*, i, pp. 87–8; ii, pp. 102–5; Burton MSS. 25618, 14. Section, Perring, *Pyramids*, iii, pl. xiii [13]. View, Frith, *Cairo, Sinai, Jerusalem* [etc.] (1860), 23rd pl.; Mariette, *Mastabas*, fig. on p. 575; de Morgan, *Dahchour*, i, pls. xxxii, xl; id. in *Le Monde Moderne*, Jan. 1895, fig. on p. 76; Ward (J.), *Pyramids and Progress*, fig. on p. 54 [lower]; Evers, *Staat aus dem Stein*, i, Taf. 108; Borchardt and Ricke, *Egypt*, pl. 97; Helck, *Geschichte des Alten Ägypten*, Taf. iii [9]; Mendelssohn, *The Riddle of the Pyramids*, pl. 44;

D'ERME, *Egiziani costruttori*, fig. on p. 32 [upper]; of entrance, ARNOLD in *Archiv für Orientforschung*, xxv (1974–7), Abb. 9 on p. 322; id. and STADELMANN in *Mitt. Kairo*, 31 (1975), Taf. 111 [a], cf. Abb. 2 facing p. 170 (section).

Pyramidion of Amenemḥēt III, granite, in Cairo Mus. JE 35133 (also JE 35745). E and N faces (of Maspero), and all texts, MASPERO in *Ann. Serv.* iii (1902), pp. 206–8 with pl.; E and usually one other face, id. *Égypte*, fig. 182; BREASTED, *History*, fig. 94; id. *The Dawn of Conscience*, fig. 6 facing p. 58; PIER, *Inscriptions of the Nile Monuments*, fig. 3; EVERS, *Staat aus dem Stein*, i, on Taf. 109; MITRY, *Illus. Cat.* No. 626; VAN DER LEEUW, *De Godsdienst van het oude Aegypte*, pl. 14 facing p. 36; GIEDION, *The Eternal Present*, ii, fig. 287; BRUNNER-TRAUT, *Die Alten Ägypter*, Taf. 33; VANDERSLEYEN, *Das Alte Ägypten*, Abb. 56; RUFFLE, *Heritage of the Pharaohs*, fig. 42; *Ancient Egypt: Discovering its Splendors*, fig. on p. 78 [right]; TEICHMANN, *Der Mensch und sein Tempel. Ägypten*, Abb. 4. 2nd line of text on W face (of Maspero), FISCHER, *The Orientation of Hieroglyphs*, i, fig. 60, p. 56. See SCHÄFER in *Ä.Z.* 41 (1904), pp. 84–5; MASPERO, *Guide*, p. 176 [626].

Masons' graffiti, in burial chamber. DE MORGAN, *Dahchour*, ii, fig. 152, p. 104.

Fragment of canopic-jar of Ḥatḥor-ḥotpet [hieroglyphs], King's daughter, in Cairo Mus. JE 59175. Id. ib. ii, fig. 154, p. 105.

TOMBS IN NORTH PART OF ENCLOSURE

1. King AWIBRĒʿ I [cartouche] ḤOR [cartouche] (or [cartouche]). Dyn. XIII.

DE MORGAN, *Dahchour*, i, pp. 88–106, with plans and sections, figs. 206, 208, 211, 242 (on p. 89)–244bis; id. in *Le Monde Moderne*, Jan. 1895, pp. 77–80, with section, fig. on p. 79 [left]; id. in *Comptes rendus* (1894), pp. 171–2.

Two alabaster stelae, with offering-text, and with 14 columns of Pyramid-texts, in Cairo Mus. JE 30952, 30951. Texts, id. *Dahchour*, i, figs. 218, 217, pp. 94 [4, 3], 165.

Circular offering-table, in Cairo Mus. JE 30953. Text, id. ib. i, fig. 219, p. 95 [5].

Wooden rectangular coffin (gold leaf with texts, in Cairo Mus. CG 28106, and fragment with *uzat*-eyes, CG 28100). Id. ib. i, pl. xxxvi [bottom], figs. 241, 241bis, p. 101. CG 28100 and 28106, LACAU, *Sarcophages*, ii, pl. xix (CG 28100), pp. 77, 84–5. Texts, DE BUCK, *Coffin Texts*, vii, Da 4 C. CG 28100, see MASPERO, *Guide*, p. 331 [3298].

Mummy-mask, wood, in Cairo Mus. CG 28107. DE MORGAN, *Dahchour*, i, fig. 229, p. 98; id. in *Le Monde Moderne*, Jan. 1895, fig. on p. 79 [right]; see LACAU, op. cit. ii, p. 85.

Canopic-chest, wood with gold leaf (fragments in Cairo Mus. JE 51266), with clay sealing of Amenemḥēt III. DE MORGAN, *Dahchour*, i, pls. xxxvi [middle right], xxxvii, figs. 245–6, pp. 102, 104–5.

Four canopic-jars, alabaster, in Cairo Mus. CG 4019–22. REISNER, *Canopics*, pl. iv, pp. 11–14; EVERS, *Staat aus dem Stein*, i, Taf. 134 [upper]. Texts, DE MORGAN, *Dahchour*, i, fig. 247, p. 106. See REISNER in *Ä.Z.* xxxvii (1899), pp. 62 [12], cf. 64 [I, b]; MASPERO, *Guide*, p. 328 [3280].

Wooden *ka*-statue,[1] in Cairo Mus. CG 259 (with fragment of *ka*-sign, CG 1159), found in wooden naos, CG 70035 (fragments of inscribed gilded plaster, formerly in Hilton Price Colln., now in Copenhagen, Ny Carlsberg Glypt. Æ.I.N. 1382). DE MORGAN, *Dahchour*, i, pls. xxxiii–xxxv, figs. 212–16, pp. 91–2 [1, 2]. CG 259 and 1159, BORCHARDT, *Statuen*, i, Bl. 56 (CG 259), p. 166, and iv, Bl. 164, p. 84. CG 259 and 70035, CAPART, *L'Art ég.* ii, pl. 288; GUIMET in *Revue de l'Histoire des Religions*, lxviii (1913), figs. 1, 2, pp.

[1] Selected references.

12–13; Ross, *The Art of Egypt*, pl. on p. 138 [2]; Schweitzer, *Das Wesen des Ka*, Taf. iii [b]; Lange and Hirmer, *Aegypten. Architektur* (1955 and 1957), pls. 112–13; (1967), pls. 120–1; Smith, *Art . . . Anc. Eg.* pl. 65 [A], pp. 100, 102; Montet, *Eternal Egypt*, pl. 45; Hayes in *The Cambridge Ancient History*, Plates to Vols. i and ii (1977), 70; Shurinova, *Iskusstvo Drevnego Egipta*, pl. 51; Maspero, *Guide*, fig. 37 (CG 259), pp. 101–2 [280–1]; *Descr. somm.* No. 280 with pl. CG 259, de Morgan in *Le Monde Moderne*, Jan. 1895, figs. on pp. 80, 81; Capart, *L'Art ég.* (1909), pl. 40; von Bissing, *Denkmäler*, i, Taf. 40A [left], and *Text* [1st fig.]; Tarchi, *L'Architettura*, Tav. 17 [upper right]; Bulle, *Der schöne Mensch im Altertum*, Taf. 11, 12; Weigall, *Anc. Eg. . . . Art*, 113–14; Steindorff, *Kunst*, 204; Breasted, *History*, fig. 88; Murray, *Sculpture*, pl. xviii [4]; Schäfer and Andrae, *Kunst* (1925), 273; (1930 and 1942), 285; Pijoán, *Summa Artis*, iii (1945), fig. 247; Aldred, *M.K. Art*, pl. 79; Donadoni, *Egyptian Museum Cairo*, pl. on p. 80; *Great Museums*, pl. 50 and fig. on p. 88; Michałowski, *Piramidy i mastaby*, pls. 25–6; Suzuki, *Sculpture of the World*, 3, *Egypt*, pl. 76 and fig. on p. 140; incomplete, Daumas, *Civ. de l'Ég.* pl. 124; Vandier, *Eg. Sculpture*, pl. 55; James, *Egyptian Sculptures*, pl. 9; Wolf, *Kunst*, Abb. 275; Michalowski, *Art*, fig. 330; Westendorf, *Das Alte Ägypten*, fig. on p. 96. CG 70035, Roeder, *Naos* (*Cat. Caire*), Taf. 40 [a], pp. 121–2. Copenhagen Æ.I.N. 1382, Koefoed-Petersen, *Catalogue des sarcophages et cercueils égyptiens*, pl. xix, p. 14 [4]; parts of texts, Hilton Price, *A Catalogue of the Egyptian Antiquities* [etc.], i (1897), p. 454 [3819].

Wooden gold-leaf covered *ka*-statuette (fragments of probably this statuette in Cairo Mus. CG 1163), originally in wooden naos. Text on base, de Morgan, *Dahchour*, i, fig. 209, pp. 90, 95 [7], cf. fig. 220. Cairo CG 1163, Borchardt, *Statuen*, iv, Bl. 164, p. 86.

Two libation-vases, alabaster, fragmentary (now restored), in Cairo Mus. CG 4028–9. Reisner, *Canopics*, pl. vi, pp. 17–18 (lids not belonging). Text, de Morgan, op. cit. i, fig. 210, pp. 90, 95 [6].

2. Nubḥetepti-khred, King's daughter. Dyn. XIII.

De Morgan, *Dahchour*, i, pp. 107–15, with plans, figs. 249–50; id. in *Le Monde Moderne*, Jan. 1895, pp. 80–2, with plan on p. 82; id. in *Comptes rendus* (1894), pp. 172–5.

Wooden rectangular coffin (gold leaf with texts, in Cairo Mus. CG 28104). De Morgan, *Dahchour*, i, pl. xxxvi [top], figs. 263, cf. 264, p. 110. Texts of Cairo CG 28104, Lacau, *Sarcophages*, ii, pp. 81–2; de Buck, *Coffin Texts*, vii, Da 2 C.

Canopic-chest, wood with gold leaf (in Cairo Mus. JE 51268). De Morgan, *Dahchour*, i, pl. xxxvi [middle left], fig. 268, p. 115.

Four canopic-jars, alabaster, in Cairo Mus. CG 4007–10. Reisner, *Canopics*, pl. i, pp. 4–7. Texts, de Morgan, *Dahchour*, i, fig. 269, p. 115. See Reisner in *Ä.Z.* xxxvii (1899), pp. 62 [12], 64 [II], cf. fig. 3 [right] (CG 4010); Maspero, *Guide*, p. 328 [3281].

Seven inscribed ointment-jars, alabaster, in Cairo Mus. CG 18722–8, in wooden box, CG 18721, sealed by Senebtifi, Real royal acquaintance. De Morgan, *Dahchour*, i, figs. 258–62, pp. 109–110. CG 18721–8, see von Bissing, *Steingefässe* (*Cat. Caire*), pp. 153–5 (texts).

Building north of causeway.

De Morgan, *Dahchour*, ii, p. 100, with plan and section, figs. 145–6. View, Arnold and Stadelmann in *Mitt. Kairo*, 31 (1975), Taf. 110 [a], pp. 171, 173.

Fragments of false-door and offering-table of Khnemt-neferḥezet-ʿat, King's wife (of Amenemḥēt III), etc. De Morgan, *Dahchour*, ii, figs. 147–8, p. 100.

REMAINS OF BUILDING SOUTH OF CAUSEWAY. Plan, id. ib. ii, fig. 150, p. 102.

Sandstone jamb-fragment of Amenemḥēt III. Id. ib. ii, fig. 149, p. 102.

G AND H. PYRAMIDS PROBABLY OF DYNASTY XIII

ARNOLD and STADELMANN in *Mitt. Kairo*, 31 (1975), p. 174 [3].

I. PYRAMID OF AMENY-ḲEMAU [cartouche]. Dyn. XIII

MARAGIOGLIO and RINALDI in *Orientalia*, N.S. 37 (1968), pp. 325–38, with plans and sections, pls. li, lii, and views, pls. liii–lx [1–21]; LECLANT in ib. N.S. 27 (1958), pp. 81–2 [10] with note 7; H. BR[UNNER] in *Archiv für Orientforschung*, xviii (1957–8), pp. 479–80; GABRA, *Chez les derniers adorateurs du Trismegiste*, p. 205; ARNOLD and STADELMANN in *Mitt. Kairo*, 31 (1975), p. 174 [3], with view, Taf. 112 [a], and position, on Abb. 3.

Inscribed canopic-jar fragments, in Cairo Mus. Temp. Nos. 25.11.60.1–4.

II. Necropolis

Maps LXXIII, LXXIV

A. EAST OF THE NORTHERN PYRAMID OF SNEFRU

NORTHERN PART (SOUTH-EAST OF THE ENCLOSURE OF SESOSTRIS III)

5. Probably Dyn. IV.

DE MORGAN, *Dahchour*, i, p. 9, with plan, fig. 6.

Reserve-head, probably female, in Cairo Mus. CG 519. Id. ib. i, fig. 7; SMITH, *Hist. Eg. Sculp.* pl. 6 [a], p. 27 [29]; SIMPSON in *M.M.A. Bull.* N.S. vii (June 1949), fig. on p. 289 [left]. See BORCHARDT, *Statuen*, ii, p. 79.

7. Mastaba-group. Probably Dyn. V.

DE MORGAN, *Dahchour*, i, pp. 11–13, with plan, fig. 9. Dating as late Old Kingdom, SCHMITZ, *Untersuchungen zum Titel sꜣ-njśwt 'Königssohn'*, pp. 150–1 [IV].

Male statue, headless, from Tomb a. DE MORGAN, op. cit. i, fig. 10.

Offering-table of Niʿankhrēʿ [hieroglyphs], Royal acquaintance, from Tomb b. Name, id. ib. i, p. 12.

Fragments of false-door of Kaʿaḥaf [hieroglyphs], King's son of [his body], Overseer of the expedition, Prophet of Snefru, etc. (four fragments in Cairo Mus. CG 1381–3, 1672). Id. ib. i, figs. 12, 13. Texts of CG 1381–3, 1672, BORCHARDT, *Denkmäler*, i, pp. 41–2; ii, p. 129.

SOUTHERN PART (NORTH OF THE ENCLOSURE OF AMENEMḤĒT II)

Plan LXXIV (inset)

Plan, DE MORGAN, *Dahchour*, ii, pl. ii.

1. SESHEMNŪFER [hieroglyphs], Scribe of the royal documents in the presence. 2nd half of Dyn. V or Dyn. VI.

DE MORGAN, *Dahchour*, ii, pp. 2–3, with plan, fig. 2.

Fragments of north false-door. Deceased carried in palanquin, in Berlin (East) Mus. 15790; id. ib. ii, fig. 3; Szépművészeti Múzeum, Budapest. *Egyiptomi művészet* [etc.] (1975), No. 13 with fig. 2; see *Führer* (1961), p. 44. Offering-bringers, DE MORGAN, op. cit. ii, fig. 4.

South brick-built false-door. Men bringing unguents, painted, in Cairo Mus. CG 1783, 1785. Id. ib. ii, fig. 5; BORCHARDT, *Denkmäler*, ii, Bl. 109, pp. 203, 204.

Painted scenes of carpenters and butchers, latter in Cairo Mus. CG 1781. DE MORGAN, op. cit. ii, figs. 6, 7; Cairo CG 1781, BORCHARDT, op. cit. ii, Bl. 108, p. 202.

2. IN-SNEFRU-ISHTEF [hieroglyphs], Inspector of tenants of the Great House, etc. Dyn. V–VI.

DE MORGAN, *Dahchour*, ii, pp. 4–7, with plan, on fig. 8, and section of shaft, fig. 12. Date, BALCZ in *Ä.Z.* 67 (1931), pp. 9–15.

False-door, in Dundee, Mus. and Art Gallery, 66.222. DE MORGAN, op. cit. ii, fig. 9.

Wall-paintings, in Cairo Mus. CG 1769–80. All, BORCHARDT, *Denkmäler*, ii, Bl. 102–7, pp. 188–202. CG 1769, remains of two registers, **I,** men carrying [palanquin], **II,** freight-boats; DE MORGAN, op. cit. ii, pl. xx; boats, WRESZ., *Atlas*, i. 411; boat on right, KÖSTER, *Das antike Seewesen*, Taf. 5. CG 1770, two registers, **I,** bringing donkeys, piling up sheaves, winnowing, **II,** rowing-boats; DE MORGAN, op. cit. ii, pl. xxi; piling up sheaves, id. *Recherches*, i, fig. 522; boats, WRESZ., op. cit. i. 409. CG 1771, remains of registers before [deceased] and attendants, presenting fowl in **I,** and unloading fish in **II;** unloading fish, id. ib. i. 413; DE MORGAN, *Recherches*, i, fig. 519; FARINA, *La Pittura egiziana*, Tav. xi (from WRESZ.). CG 1772, netting fish; DE MORGAN, *Dahchour*, ii, pl. xxiii; WRESZ., op. cit. i. 412 (reversed). CG 1773, two sailing-boats; DE MORGAN, *Dahchour*, ii, pl. xix; WRESZ., op. cit. i. 410; boat on right, JÉQUIER in *B.I.F.A.O.* ix (1911), pl. iii [1], p. 58 note 2. CG 1774, registers, **I** (lower part only), bringing cattle before deceased and wife, **II,** estates; DE MORGAN, *Dahchour*, ii, pl. xviii; WRESZ., op. cit. i. 415; names, JACQUET-GORDON, *Domaines*, pp. 440–1 [4D6], cf. figs. 191–2. CG 1775, lower part of two scenes, deceased and family spearing fish and fowling; DE MORGAN, *Dahchour*, ii, pl. xxiv. CG 1776, registers of funeral scenes, **I** (almost completely lost), men dragging sledge, **II,** rowing-boats towing boat with shrine, **III,** men towing boat towards embalming-house, with butchers; id. ib. ii, pl. xxii; **III,** JUNKER in *Mitt. Kairo* 9 (1940), Abb. 2, pp. 10–12; embalming-house and lector-priest, BORCHARDT, *Ägyptische Tempel mit Umgang* in *Beiträge zur ägyptischen Bauforschung*, 2, Abb. 7, pp. 24–5; see WERBROUCK, *Pleureuses*, pp. 79–80. CG 1777, deceased seated, with monkey under chair, and [man] making bed under canopy. CG 1778, lady guest, and two registers of female dancers and musicians from banquet scene; DE MORGAN, *Dahchour*, ii, pl. xxv; HICKMANN, *45 Siècles*, pls. lxi, cii; id. in *Bull. Inst. Ég.* xxxv (1952–3), pl. ii, p. 320; dancers and musicians, WRESZ., op. cit. i. 414. CG 1779–80, lower part of deceased seated and offerings, with offering-bringers below.

Wall-paintings, perhaps also from here, but more likely from another tomb. Lower part of two scenes, deceased and family (including son Nikau[p]taḥ [hieroglyphs], Inspector of tenants of the Great House) spearing fish and fowling (canoe with fish from fishing scene in Cairo Mus. CG 1782 and 1786); DE MORGAN, *Recherches*, i, fig. 516; CG 1782 and 1786,

BORCHARDT, *Denkmäler*, ii, Bl. 108, 109, pp. 203, 205; CG 1786, GALASSI, *L'arte del più antico Egitto* [etc.] in *Rivista dell'Istituto Nazionale d'Archeologia* [etc.], N.S. iv (1955), fig. 63, p. 62; DAVIES (NINA), *Ancient Egyptian Paintings*, i, pl. iv; SMITH, *Hist. Eg. Sculp.* pl. 51 [b], pp. 205–6 note 2; DAVIES MSS. photo. 1.328. Two registers before deceased (lower part only) and son, netting fowl, and cattle crossing water, with herdsmen in canoe (right part of latter, with stern of canoe and cattle, in Cairo Mus. CG 1784); DE MORGAN, *Recherches*, i, fig. 517; Cairo CG 1784, BORCHARDT, *Denkmäler*, ii, Bl. 109, p. 204; CAPART, *Memphis*, fig. 374; id. *L'Art ég.* iii, pl. 420; part, MÜLLER (H. W.) in *Encyclopedia of World Art*, iv, pl. 328 [lower].

Lower part of pair-statue. DE MORGAN, *Dahchour*, ii, fig. 13.

7. NEFERIRTNES [hieroglyphs], Inspector of tenants of the Great House. Dyn. VI.

DE MORGAN, *Dahchour*, ii, pp. 10–11, with plan, fig. 21.

Offering table of woman Khenti [hieroglyphs], in Corridor. Id. ib. ii, fig. 25.

False-door, from Offering-room, in Cairo Mus. CG 1393. Id. ib. ii, fig. 22; text, BORCHARDT, *Denkmäler*, i, p. 54.

8. NIʿANKH-SNEFRU [hieroglyphs] FEFI [hieroglyphs], Judge and Inspector of scribes, etc. Probably Dyn. VI.

DE MORGAN, *Dahchour*, ii, pp. 11–12, with plan, on fig. 26.

False-door, in Cairo Mus. CG 57122. Id. ib. ii, fig. 27.

Drum with names and title, in Cairo Mus. CG 1489. Text, BORCHARDT, *Denkmäler*, i, p. 190.

Small false-door and lintel of Shepy [hieroglyphs], Chief of the estate, Lector-priest, etc. Texts, DE MORGAN, op. cit. ii, figs. 28–9.

11. NEFERḤER-SNEFRU [hieroglyphs], King's son. Probably Dyn. V or VI.

DE MORGAN, *Dahchour*, ii, p. 14, with plan, on fig. 26.

Drum of doorway with name and title, in Cairo Mus. CG 1487. Text, id. ib. ii, fig. 32; BORCHARDT, *Denkmäler*, i, p. 189.

12. UZAU [hieroglyphs], Overseer of the department of tenants of the Great House, Overseer of interpreters, etc. Dyn. VI.

DE MORGAN, *Dahchour*, ii, pp. 14–15, with plan, fig. 33.

Lintel of doorway with offering-text, in Berthoud (Burgdorf), Sammlung für Völkerkunde, 7613. Id. ib. ii, fig. 34.

24. Probably Dyn. VI.

DE MORGAN, *Dahchour*, ii, pp. 18–21, with plan, on fig. 43.

Statuettes from serdab. All wood. Numbers are those of Cairo Mus.

Woman grinding corn, CG 504. Id. ib. ii, fig. 44, p. 18 [1]; id. *Recherches*, i, fig. 325;

BORCHARDT, *Statuen*, ii, Bl. 86, p. 73; CHAMPDOR, *Thèbes aux Cent Portes*, fig. on p. 32. See BREASTED (Jr.), *Eg. Servant Statues*, p. 21 [e, 4].

Rower, and kneeling man. DE MORGAN, *Dahchour*, ii, figs. 45–6, p. 18 [2, 3].

Two female offering-bringers with basket on head, CG 509–10. Id. ib. ii, fig. 47 (one), pp. 18–20 [4, 5]; BORCHARDT, op. cit. ii, Bl. 87 (CG 509), pp. 75–6; one, see BREASTED (Jr.), op. cit. p. 61 [4].

Man seated, CG 517. DE MORGAN, *Dahchour*, ii, fig. 48, p. 20 [6]; BORCHARDT, op. cit. ii, Bl. 88, p. 78.

Two, man standing (one CG 503). DE MORGAN, *Dahchour*, ii, fig. 49 (CG 503), p. 20 [7, 8]. CG 503, BORCHARDT, op. cit. ii, Bl. 85, p. 73.

Two groups, originally four 'servants of the estate of Shepy' (cf. *supra*, tb.8) each (only three of each left), CG 511–12. DE MORGAN, *Dahchour*, ii, pl. iii (CG 511), pp. 20–1 [9, 10]; BORCHARDT, op. cit. ii, Bl. 87–8, pp. 76–7. CG 511, TARCHI, *L'Architettura*, Tav. 17 [upper left]. See BREASTED (Jr.), op. cit. p. 60 [17].

Two seated and four standing statuettes. See DE MORGAN, *Dahchour*, ii, p. 21 [11–16].

Four standing statuettes, CG 505, 516, 514, 506. Id. ib. ii, pl. iv, p. 21 [17–20] (misreading title as name); BORCHARDT, op. cit. ii, Bl. 86 (CG 505–6), pp. 73–4, 77, 78. CG 506, see BOREUX in *Revue de l'Art ancien et moderne*, lxxi (1937), p. 212, cf. fig. 3 (from BORCHARDT).

Other statuettes, some fragmentary. See DE MORGAN, *Dahchour*, ii, p. 21 [21–30].

27. ḲEDSHEPSES [hieroglyphs], King's son of his body, Prophet of Snefru, etc. Probably Dyn. V or later.

DE MORGAN, *Dahchour*, ii, p. 22, with plan, on fig. 50. Dating as late Dyn. VI or 1st Int. Period, SCHMITZ, *Untersuchungen zum Titel sꜣ-njśwt 'Königssohn'*, p. 149 [III].

False-door jamb, with names and titles of deceased and sons, in Cairo Mus. CG 1390. Texts, DE MORGAN, op. cit. ii, fig. 51; BORCHARDT, *Denkmäler*, i, p. 51.

28. KANŪFER [hieroglyphs], King's eldest son of his body, Overseer of the Pyramid of Snefru, etc.[1] Advanced Dyn. IV or later.

Wife, Khunesu [hieroglyphs], King's adorner, etc.

DE MORGAN, *Dahchour*, ii, p. 23, with plan, fig. 52. Dating as end Dyn. VI to Dyn. VIII, SCHMITZ, *Untersuchungen zum Titel sꜣ-njśwt 'Königssohn'*, pp. 145–9 [II].

South niche in east façade, with false-door. DE MORGAN, op. cit. ii, pl. xxvi, fig. 53. Central part of false-door, in Brit. Mus. 1324; *Hiero. Texts*, i, pl. 4; i², pl. x [1], p. 10; *Guide* (*Sculpture*), pl. i, p. 4 [8] (as Gîza); *Wall Decorations of Egyptian Tombs*, fig. 1; dedication of eldest son Kawaʿb [hieroglyphs], Royal acquaintance, SETHE, *Urk.* i. 227 [5 (145), A]. Niche, in Louvre, E.11286; see BOREUX, *Guide*, i, p. 230; VANDIER, *Guide* (1948 and 1952), p. 8; (1973), p. 12.

Offering-table, dedicated by son Kanūfer, in Brit. Mus. 1345. DE MORGAN, *Dahchour*, ii, fig. 54; *Hiero. Texts*, i, pl. 5 [9]; i², pl. ix [2], p. 9; see *Guide* (*Sculpture*), p. 5 [9] (as Gîza).

Drum, perhaps from here, in Louvre, C 155 [E.3908]. WILKINSON MSS. xviii. 43 [right]. Name and titles, PIERRET, *Rec. inscr.* ii, p. 56. See DE ROUGÉ, *Notice des monuments* (1883), p. 134; BOREUX, *Guide*, i, p. 236.

[1] Also Chief Justice and Vizier, in unclear context.

B. EAST OF THE SOUTHERN PYRAMID OF SNEFRU

IYNŪFER [hieroglyphs], King's son, etc. Early Dyn. IV.

BARSANTI in *Ann. Serv.* iii (1902), pp. 198–201 [I], with plans, sections, and elevations, figs. 1–6; MASPERO, *Trois années de fouilles* [etc.] in *Mém. Miss.* i, pp. 189–90 [1].

Lower parts of two niches, with estates on thicknesses, in Cairo Mus. CG 57121, 57120 (JE 38563–4). BARSANTI, op. cit. pls. i, ii, pp. 198–9. Jambs and rear wall of CG 57120, and upper part of deceased from rear wall of CG 57121, STAEHELIN, *Tracht*, Taf. vi [10], xv [23]. Right jamb of CG 57120, SMITH, *Hist. Eg. Sculp.* pl. 36 [b], p. 150; id. *Art . . . Anc. Eg.* pl. 28 [A], p. 41. Names of estates, JACQUET-GORDON, *Domaines*, pp. 430–3 [1D4], cf. figs. 183–6, with pl. i facing p. 201 (estate No. 14, from CG 57120). Hieroglyph of ram in name of estate No. 1 (of JACQUET-GORDON) on CG 57121, KEIMER in *Ann. Serv.* xxxviii (1938), pl. xl, p. 299. Texts of CG 57120, WILBOUR MSS. 2 G, 62 [top]. See MASPERO, *Guide*, p. 39 [75A, B].

DUARĒʿ [hieroglyphs], Overseer of the two Pyramids of Snefru, Prophet of Rēʿ in the Sun-temple of Userkaf,[1] *waʿb*-priest of the Pyramid of Userkaf,[1] etc. Temp. Saḥurēʿ or later.

Wife, Mertiotes [hieroglyphs], Royal acquaintance.

MASPERO, *Trois années de fouilles* [etc.] in *Mém. Miss.* i, pp. 190–1 [2], with plan. Some texts, WILBOUR MSS. 2 G, 63, 64 [lower]. Names, titles, and names of two estates, LIEBLEIN, *Dict.* No. 1379.

Outer Room.

False-door of deceased and eldest son ʿAnkhmaʿrēʿ [hieroglyphs], Overseer of the southern Pyramid of Snefru, etc., in Cairo Mus. CG 1389. BORCHARDT, *Denkmäler*, i, Bl. 12, pp. 49–51, cf. ii, Bl. 58 [1552A, lintel]; some texts, MASPERO, op. cit. p. 190; names and some titles, LIEBLEIN, *Dict.* No. 1363.

Offering-basins, in Cairo Mus. Deceased, CG 1375; text, BORCHARDT, op. cit. i, p. 34. ʿAnkhmaʿrēʿ, CG 1325; id. ib. i, Bl. 4, p. 11.

Inner Room.

Doorway, lintel, and jambs with names and titles, and thicknesses, registers, **I, III, IV,** estates, **II,** bringing oryx, in Cairo Mus. CG 1552. Id. ib. ii, Bl. 58 (lintel belongs to CG 1389), pp. 9–13; texts of thicknesses, MASPERO, op. cit. pp. 190–1; names of estates, JACQUET-GORDON, *Domaines*, pp. 436–9 [3D5], cf. figs. 189–90.

KAWEZʿANKH [hieroglyphs], Boundary official of a frontier district, Overseer of the phylai of Upper Egypt, etc. Middle Dyn. V.

Parents, Nesutnūfer (not mentioned here) and Khentetka Khent [hieroglyphs] (Gîza tb. G 4970, *Bibl.* iii². 143–4).

MASPERO, *Trois années de fouilles* [etc.] in *Mém. Miss.* i, p. 191 [3], with name and title from lintel of doorway; cf. FISCHER in *J.A.O.S.* 74 (1954), pp. 27–8.

False-door, in Brit. Mus. 1223. *Hiero. Texts*, i, pl. 15 [65]; i², pl. viii [2], p. 8; part of text, WILBOUR MSS. 2 G, 62 [middle].

[1] On offering-basin Cairo CG 1375 only.

NEFERMAʿET [hieroglyphs], Overseer of the phylai of Upper Egypt, etc. Middle Dyn. V.

Parents, Nesutnūfer and Khentetka Khent (latter not mentioned here) (Gîza tb. G 4970, *Bibl.* iii². 143–4).

BARSANTI in *Ann. Serv.* iii (1902), pp. 203–4 [IV, V] (probably same tomb); cf. FISCHER in *J.A.O.S.* 74 (1954), pp. 26–9.

Lintel and drum of false-door, mentioning deceased and father, in Cairo Mus. CG 57143. Texts, BARSANTI, op. cit. p. 204 [V]; WILBOUR MSS. 2 G, 62 [bottom]; of lintel, MASPERO, *Trois années de fouilles* [etc.] in *Mém. Miss.* i, p. 191 [4, 1st text].

Relief-fragments. (a) Deceased and wife at table. (b) Two registers with four people seated, including brothers of deceased Kaemib [hieroglyphs], Sole companion, and Kaḥersetef [hieroglyphs], Inspector of boats, in Cairo Mus. CG 57142. (c) Lintel or drum with name and titles. (d) Couple standing. Texts of all, BARSANTI, op. cit. pp. 203–4 [IV]; of (c), MASPERO, op. cit. p. 191 [4, 2nd text].

ITHI [hieroglyphs], Overseer of the chamber of dancers, etc. Dyn. IV–V.

Wife, Wesenptaḥ(?) [hieroglyphs], *mìtrt*.

Deceased and wife seated, with two sons and two daughters. Texts, MASPERO, *Trois années de fouilles* [etc.] in *Mém. Miss.* i, p. 191 [5]; some names and titles, LIEBLEIN, *Dict.* No. 1372.

THENTI [hieroglyphs], Prophet of Snefru, etc. Old Kingdom.

Name and titles from lintel of doorway, MASPERO, *Trois années de fouilles* [etc.] in *Mém. Miss.* i, p. 191 [6].

KAEMḲED [hieroglyphs], Prophet of Snefru(?), Secretary [of the King in] all his places, etc. Probably Dyn. V.

Mother, Nefertnesut [hieroglyphs], King's daughter, Prophetess of Snefru and Ḥatḥor Mistress of the Sycamore, etc.

Lower part of false-door, in Cairo Mus. JE 37953. Texts, BARSANTI in *Ann. Serv.* iii (1902), pp. 202–3 [III]; WILBOUR MSS. 2 G, 64 [upper]. Dating as late Old Kingdom, SCHMITZ, *Untersuchungen zum Titel s3-njśwt 'Königssohn'*, pp. 151–2 [V].

KARES [hieroglyphs], Prophet of Snefru, etc. Old Kingdom.

Wife, Meresʿankh [hieroglyphs], Prophetess of Ḥatḥor Mistress of the Sycamore, etc.

Lower part of false-door. Texts, BARSANTI in *Ann. Serv.* iii (1902), pp. 201–2 [II].

FINDS

Two standing statues, headless, Old Kingdom. GABRA, *Chez les derniers adorateurs du Trismegiste*, fig. on p. 209, cf. p. 205.

C. NORTH OF THE ENCLOSURE OF SESOSTRIS III

Plan LXXV

Plan and views, DE MORGAN, *Dahchour*, i, pls. iv, v, fig. 18.

2. KHNEMḤOTP, Chief Justice and Vizier, etc. Probably temp. Sesostris III.

DE MORGAN, *Dahchour*, i, pp. 18–23, with plan and section, figs. 20–1.

Frieze with offering-texts, from exterior (fragment formerly in Likhachev Colln. and Leningrad, Institute of Books, Documents and Manuscripts of the Academy of Sciences of U.S.S.R., now in Leningrad, State Hermitage Mus. 18230, and another in Marschall Colln.). Id. ib. i, fig. 24. Leningrad 18230 (= fig. 24, C, 2nd line right), PEREPELKIN, *Fragment d'une inscription égyptienne de la 12e dynastie* [etc.] in *Comptes Rendus de l'Académie des Sciences de l'U.R.S.S.*, 1929, fig. on p. 20 (in Russian); LANDA and LAPIS, *Egyptian Antiquities in the Hermitage*, pl. 19. Marschall Colln. block (= fig. 24, A, 2nd line left), ALTENMÜLLER in HORNBOSTEL and others, *Kunst der Antike* (1977), No. 8 with fig.

Fragments with titles, remains of autobiographical text, etc., including one mentioning deified Amenemḥētʿankh (perhaps son of Amenemḥēt II). DE MORGAN, op. cit. i, figs. 22–3, 25–6.

Canopic-chest, sandstone, in Cairo Mus. CG 4048. REISNER, *Canopics*, pl. lxxxi, pp. 28–32; texts, DE MORGAN, op. cit. i, fig. 28; see MASPERO, *Guide*, p. 110 [308].

6. Middle Kingdom.

DE MORGAN, *Dahchour*, i, p. 25, with plan and sections, fig. 33.

Offering-table of Temʿa, daughter of Sit-ḥatḥor (mother). Id. ib. i, fig. 34.

8. NAME UNKNOWN. Middle Kingdom.

Mother, Sit-ḥatḥor.

DE MORGAN, *Dahchour*, i, pp. 25–6, with plan and section, fig. 37.

Fragment of false-door. Id. ib. i, fig. 36.

11. KHENTEKHTAIEMSAF, Embalmer. Temp. Sesostris III or later.

Mother(?), Sent. Wife, Sit-ḥatḥor.

DE MORGAN, *Dahchour*, i, pp. 27–30, with plans, section, and views, pls. vi–ix, figs. 41–3. View, id. in *Le Monde Moderne*, Jan. 1895, fig. on p. 69.

Fragments of reliefs and inscriptions, deceased and wife at tables, etc., from exterior, in Cairo Mus. CG 1468–77. Id. *Dahchour*, i, figs. 44–53; BORCHARDT, *Denkmäler*, i, Bl. 37 (CG 1477), pp. 158–64.

Offering-table, against east face. Text, DARESSY in *Rec. Trav.* xxiv (1902), p. 163 [cxcvii].

Canopic-chest, in Cairo Mus. CG 4049. REISNER, *Canopics*, pl. lxxix, pp. 32–3; DE MORGAN, *Dahchour*, i, figs. 54–5; see MASPERO, *Guide*, p. 116 [361] (as Dyn. XIII).

17. SEBKEMḤĒT [hieroglyphs], Chief Justice and Vizier, etc. Probably temp. Sesostris III.

DE MORGAN, *Dahchour*, i, pp. 31–3, with plan, section, etc., figs. 61–3; cf. SIMPSON in *J.E.A.* 43 (1957), pp. 26–9.

Fragments of reliefs with offering-bringers and titles. DE MORGAN, op. cit. i, figs. 65–7.

Fragments of offering-table. Id. ib. i, fig. 64.

18. NAME UNKNOWN, Hereditary prince, Count, etc. Temp. Sesostris III.

DE MORGAN, *Dahchour*, i, pp. 33–4.

Relief-fragments with [deceased] at table, offering-bringers and butchers. Id. ib. i, figs. 68–9.

19. Probably late Dyn. XII.

DE MORGAN, *Dahchour*, i, pp. 34–5, with plan and section, figs. 70–1.

Fragments of squatting statuette, diorite or granite (head formerly in Cairo Mus. CG 828 and von Bissing Colln., now in The Hague, Gemeente Museum voor Oude Kunst, 1952). Head and text, id. ib. i, figs. 72, 72a; head, VAN GELDER in *Mededeelingen van den Dienst voor Kunsten en Wetenschappen der Gemeente 's-Gravenhage*, v (1938), fig. 5, p. 9; SCHEURLEER in *Jaarbericht Ex Oriente Lux*, No. 7 (1940), pl. xvi, p. 550 [20]; see BORCHARDT, *Statuen*, iii, pp. 115–16.

22. Middle Kingdom.

DE MORGAN, *Dahchour*, i, pp. 35–6.

Texts of wooden coffin, id. ib. i, fig. 73 (by Daressy).

24. IPITI [hieroglyphs], Overseer of the department, etc. 2nd half of Dyn. XII.

DE MORGAN, *Dahchour*, i, p. 37, with section, fig. 77.

Stela, with Khaʿkheperrēʿ-sonb [hieroglyphs], Embalmer of the temple, before deceased, and uninscribed offering-table, in Cairo Mus. CG 1486. Id. ib. i, pl. xi, p. 165; BORCHARDT, *Denkmäler*, i, Bl. 41, pp. 187–8; see MASPERO, *Guide*, p. 113 [324].

25. KHNEMḤOTP [hieroglyphs], Regulator of a phyle. Middle Kingdom.

Mother(?), Mereryt [hieroglyphs].

DE MORGAN, *Dahchour*, i, p. 38.

False-door, in Cairo Mus. CG 1478. Id. ib. i, fig. 79; BORCHARDT, *Denkmäler*, i, Bl. 38, p. 165.

27. NENI [hieroglyphs], Nubian (woman). Middle Kingdom.

DE MORGAN, *Dahchour*, i, pp. 38–9.

Stela, in Cairo Mus. CG 1481. Id. ib. i, fig. 80; BORCHARDT, *Denkmäler*, i, Bl. 38, pp. 168–9.

28. NEN... (woman). Middle Kingdom.

DE MORGAN, *Dahchour*, i, p. 40.

Stela. Id. ib. i, fig. 81.

D. SOUTH OF THE ENCLOSURE OF AMENEMḤĒT II

SIĒSI, Overseer of the seal, etc. Dyn. XII.

'Pyramid' LV of Lepsius.

DE MORGAN, *Dahchour*, ii, pp. 78–86.

Four relief-fragments, in Cairo Mus. Temp. Nos. 24.5.28.1–4. MASPERO, *Guide*, pp. 112 [319–20] with fig. 42 (one relief), 115 [334–5]. (a) *Sem*-priest, etc., before deceased at table, DE MORGAN, op. cit. ii, pl. xiv; MASPERO and ROEDER, *Führer*, Taf. 21 [a], p. 33 [224]; VANDERSLEYEN, *Das Alte Ägypten*, Abb. 276; head of deceased, MASPERO, *Égypte*, fig. 198. (b) Head of deceased, PIRENNE, *Hist. civ.* ii, pl. 31 facing p. 101.

Pyramid-texts, from walls of Burial Chamber. DE MORGAN, op. cit. ii, pp. 78–85 (by Legrain).

FINDS

Panel of false-door of Amenemḥētʿankh, King's son (probably of Amenemḥēt II) (lower part, see *supra*), probably intrusive, and relief-fragment with two squatting men (including 'his brother' Amenemḥētʿankh, Regulator of a phyle). DE MORGAN, op. cit. ii, fig. 128.

Stela and offering-table of Senuʿankh, Boat-builder, son of Ḥetep-ḥatḥor Ḥetept (mother), Middle Kingdom, in Cairo Mus. CG 20528–9. Id. ib. ii, figs. 129–30; texts, LANGE and SCHÄFER, *Grab- und Denksteine des Mittleren Reichs* (*Cat. Caire*), ii, pp. 129–31.

III. Miscellaneous

Old Kingdom.

Seated (headless) and standing statues, Dyn. V, in Cairo Mus. CG 507–8. BORCHARDT, *Statuen*, ii, Bl. 87 (CG 508), pp. 74–5.

Head, granite, in Cairo Mus. CG 1249. See id. ib. iv, p. 129.

False-door of Ismet, Noblewoman of the King, Prophetess of Ḥatḥor, Dyn. VI or later, in Cairo Mus. CG 1395. Id. *Denkmäler*, i, Bl. 14, pp. 55–6; VANDIER, *Manuel*, ii, fig. 278 [lower right], p. 404.

Offering-table of Sethu, Judge and Overseer of scribes, Dyn. V–VI, in Cairo Mus. CG 1330. BORCHARDT, *Denkmäler*, i, Bl. 5, p. 14; MARIETTE, *Mon. div.* pl. 94; CAPART, *Memphis*, fig. 221; VANDIER, *Manuel*, ii, fig. 308 [bottom left], pp. 526–8 [3]; PETRIE GÎZA photo. 555.

Offering-table 'of King Kakai (Neferirkarēʿ)', in Cairo Mus. JE 37951.

Obelisk of Snefru... Ḥetep, Overseer of commissions, Overseer of the five... of the Great House, Dyn. VI, found south of the Red Pyramid, in Cairo Mus. CG 1315. BORCHARDT, *Denkmäler*, i, Bl. 2, p. 8; text, KUENTZ, *Obélisques* (*Cat. Caire*), pp. 6–7.

Bowl of King Khaʿba, diorite, said to come from here, formerly in Robinow Colln., now in Manchester Mus. 5373. ARKELL in *J.E.A.* 44 (1958), p. 120 with figs.; KAPLONY in *Mitt. Kairo*, 20 (1965), Taf. vi [57], p. 27 [57]; see *The Museums Journal*, 59 (1959–60), p. 111.

Ink-slab of Zadkarēᶜ (Isesi), flint, bought in Cairo, said to come from here, in London, Univ. Coll. 11771. PETRIE, *History*, i (1894), fig. 48; (1923), fig. 61; id. *Objects of Daily Use*, pl. lvi [9], p. 63; id. KOPTOS photos. 30–1; text, id. *Scarabs and Cylinders*, pl. ix [5.8(3)]; see *Burlington Fine Arts Club* (1922), p. 89 [35].

Middle Kingdom.

Statuette of Khentiuka [hieroglyphs], son of Khentiuka, with offering-text invoking Snefru and Ptaḥ-Sokari, diorite, probably temp. Sesostris III, probably from here, formerly in Benzion Colln. and Meyers (G. H.) Colln., Washington (D.C.), 7.2, now in New York, M.M.A. 62.77. HAYES in *M.M.A. Bull.* N.S. xxi (Oct. 1962), fig. on p. 68, cf. p. 69; F.E.R.E. photo. 17647; see *Benzion Collection Sale Cat.* (Cairo, March 14, 1947), No. 186.

Upper part of seated statuette, grey hard stone, in Cairo Mus. CG 518. HORNEMANN, *Types*, iii, pl. 738. See BORCHARDT, *Statuen*, ii, pp. 78–9.

Seated statuette, wood, in Cairo Mus. CG 513. See id. ib. ii, p. 77.

Block(?) with texts of Senebsumaᶜ [hieroglyphs], Overseer of the seal, etc. Text, MARIETTE, *Mastabas*, p. 583.

Gold leaf from coffin of woman Sitsobk [hieroglyphs], in Cairo Mus. CG 28105. Coffin-texts, LACAU, *Sarcophages*, ii, p. 83; DE BUCK, *Coffin Texts*, vii, Da 3 C.

Late Period.

Coffin of woman Ḥartesnakht [hieroglyphs]. Text, MARIETTE, *Mastabas*, p. 584.

ADDENDA

The following notes complete the information on some monuments included in this volume, but do not attempt to add to the cited works or list all new material which has come to our notice since the publication of Fascicle 1 in 1978. Most of them are based on published or personal communications of other Egyptologists, in particular R. S. Bianchi, E. Brovarski, W. V. Davies, E. Edel, H. G. Fischer, R. Gillam, L. Limme, H. De Meulenaere, D. A. Pendlebury, B. J. Peterson, and A. Roccati. The footnotes on pages 420, 501, and 547 are to be disregarded.

Page

451 Tomb No. 9 [B 4], Ipi. Thicknesses, in Ungar Colln., are on loan to Zürich, Rietbergmuseum.

452 Tomb No. 14 [D 43], Smenkhuptaḥ Itwesh. Delete Inv. 1841 of Vienna, Kunsthistorisches Museum.

463 Tomb No. 47 [E 3], Sabu Thety, is dated temp. Pepy II or later.

481 (2) Relief with geese and cranes, from 4th register, is in Turin Mus. Sup. 1257.

482 Tomb No. 73 [D 13], Shepsi. Father, Peḥnuika (tomb D 70 [LS 15]); wives of father, Zefatsen and Ḥetepḥeres. Date, probably middle Dyn. V.

491 (4) Zefatsen is Peḥnuika's wife.

503 Tomb of Unnūfer. Reliefs in Louvre, E. 3065, quoted on p. 760, should be moved here.

505 Sarcophagus of Zeḥo is the same as New York, M.M.A. 11.154.7, quoted on p. 765, so the entry should be deleted here.

506 Stela of Khaʿḥap. Delete Phoenician.

506 n. 1 Head of marble sarcophagus probably does not belong to the stela, and should be deleted.

507 Sarcophagus of Ḥarkhebi. Correct the name to Ḥaremḥab.

558 Tomb of Raʿwēr. Now published by el-Fikey, *The Tomb of the Vizier Rēʿ-wer at Saqqara*, and the date should be corrected to probably temp. Pepy I or later.

561 Shaft No. 289, Khenu and Ipiemsaf. Khenu is a Scribe and Treasurer of the God of the Pyramid of Merykarēʿ, Regulator of a phyle of the Pyramid of Teti, etc., so the dating probably is 1st Int. Period.

562 Statue of Thauineb-ḥezet. Correct the name of father to Khnemnakht.

570 Block of Meḥi. Part is in Amsterdam, Allard Pierson Mus. 8752 (formerly Zandee Colln.).

571 Ointment-slab of Sekhemptaḥ Sekhemu. Correct the title to Inspector of manicurists of the Great House.

589 Another two blocks are at Wildenstein Art Center, Houston (Texas).

638 Tomb of Akhtiḥotp. One wooden statue (No. 4 of Batrawi) is in Cairo Mus. JE 93167.

661 Tomb of Iurokhy. Correct the date to temp. Ramesses II.

691 Tomb of Inpukhaʿ. Lower part of false-door is in Wellcome Colln.

695 n. 1 This relief is now Brooklyn Mus. 79.176. Another relief was seen with Ede (dealer in London) in 1980.

698–9 Tomb of Tepemʿankh. This man is the same as Tepemʿankh quoted in *Bibl.* iii². 109, and the whole entry should be moved there.

Page

706 Tomb of Neferronpet. A relief-fragment is at Wildenstein Art Center, Houston (Texas).

707 Tomb of Nia. Lid of double ushabti-coffin of deceased and wife is in Boston Mus. 1977.717.

726 See note to p. 755.

732 See note to p. 757.

755 Four pillars of Khaʿy, perhaps the same man as that mentioned on p. 726, are probably in Cairo Mus.

757 Lintel of Meru, the same man as that mentioned on p. 732, is in Dresden, Skulpturensammlung, Inv. Aeg. 753.

760 See note to p. 503.

762 The lintel-fragment of a Prophet of the Sun-temple of Userkaf is in Kristianstad Mus.

763 Sarcophagus-fragment of Unnūfer, Prophet, Royal scribe, son of Nebt-ḥyt (mother), Ptol., formerly Amherst and Kahn Collns., is in Bryn Athyn (Pa.), Museum of the Academy of the New Church. This is the same man as the owner of the lid in Cairo Mus. CG 29310, quoted on p. 764.

764 See preceding note.

773 Canopic-jars of Weḥebrēʿ. The name of the mother should be read Webennesiʿoḥ. Ṣaqqâra as the provenance of the piece is in doubt.

APPENDIXES

A. CLASSIFICATION OF SELECTED SCENES IN OLD KINGDOM PRIVATE TOMBS

Numbers refer to pages

SUMMARY OF SECTIONS

Division into sections retained from *Bibl.* iii², Part 1

1. Deceased and family in marshes

(*a*) **Fowling**
467 (7), 495 (2), 520 (2), 522 (13), 526 (12), 583 (2), 595, 596, 616 (2), 620 (5), 628 (5), 631 (12), 634 (6)–(7), 639 (4), 642 (4), 643 (22), 644 (4), 645 (3), 646, 696, 891, 891.

(*b*) **Spearing fish**
518 (3), 522 (13), 527 (15), 583 (2), 594 (8), 595, 596, 614 (4), 616 (2), 620 (7), 624 (2), 626 (4), 631 (12), 634 (6)–(7), 642 (4), 643 (22), 644 (4), 645 (3), 891, 891. The same, but not performed by the tomb-owner, 534 (81), 639 (4).

(*c*) **Pulling papyrus from raft**
471 (23), 534 (81).

(*d*) **Other or unspecified activities**
476 (45), 522 (9), 617 (2) and (4), 624 (4).

2. Palanquin scenes

(*a*) **Deceased in palanquin**
460 (3), 470 (6)–(7), 496 (13), 497 (2), 520 (3), 523 (22), 532 (74), 535 (108), 536 (115), 536 (116)–(117), 596, 603 (20), 643 (18), 647, 671, 891, 891. On donkeys, 642 (11).

(*b*) **Men or women carrying empty palanquin**
527 (14), 535 (94).

2A. Deceased painting seasons

509 (13), 526 (10).

2B. Deceased and wife playing draughts

533 (79).

3. Agriculture

(*a*) **General**
Including ploughing, hacking ground, issuing seed, sowing, animals treading grain, reaping corn, binding sheaves, filling and tying sacks with sheaves, bringing donkeys, donkeys carrying produce, heaping sheaves, threshing with donkeys, sheep, or cattle, piling up, sifting, winnowing and measuring corn, filling granaries, stacking straw. Flute-player, singer, and men with resonant sticks in harvest scenes, *see* Sect. 12*a*.
447 (4), 454 (2), 467 (2), 472 (34), 476 (46), 481 (2), 486 (2), 487 (2), 491 (3), 494, 496 (13), 498, 512 (2), 533 (80), 546, 569, 578, 584 (8), 585, 594 (7), 595, 597 (15), 599 (4), 620 (9), (10), and (13), 623 (6), 624 (3) and (9), 628 (9), 635 (3), 637 (2), 640 (1)–(2), 643 (17) and (18), 644 (2), 645 (2), 647, 654, 671, 694, 699 (2), 753, 755, 756, 758, 891.

(*b*) **Flax-harvest**
Including pulling flax and tying up bundles. 454 (2), 467 (2), 472 (34), 496 (13), 520 (8), 533 (80), 578, 584 (8), 594 (7), 628 (9), 635 (3), 643 (18), 644 (2), 645 (2), 694, 699 (2), 755.

(*c*) **Various**
Picking fruit (mostly figs), 495 (7)–(8), 525, 533 (78), 584 (7), 616, 620 (14), 624 (6), 637 (2), 642 (10). Catching birds (not the same as netting fowl in marshes, Sect. 8*e*), including putting birds into cages, 473 (36), 495 (9), 533 (78) and (80), 546, 584 (7), 594 (6), 635 (3), 637 (2), 642 (7). Felling trees, including carrying and dressing logs, 628 (10), 640 (3), 642 (7). Filling water-pool, 628 (10).

3A. Gardening

527 (13), 616, 622 (31), 637 (2), 642 (7), 694.

3B. Poultry-yard

Including scenes of feeding fowl.
469 (1), 470 (10), 516 (9), 518 (4), 523 (20), 529 (33), 536 (117), 631 (8), 750.

4. Vintage

Including watering, picking grapes, bringing baskets of grapes, treading grapes and pressing must, filling and sealing wine-jars, but omitting bringing wine. Men with resonant sticks, *see* Sect. 12*a*.
473 (36), 495 (7)–(8), 531 (66), 584 (7), 599 (1)–(2), 601 (17), 624 (7), 628 (10), 637 (2), 640 (1)–(2), 642 (7), (9), and (10), 750.

5. Herdsmen and herds

Butchers, *see* Sect. 7.

(*a*) **General**
Mostly cattle, but also goats. Including feeding, milking, calving, cow suckling calf, bull mounting cow, men overthrowing bull and lassoing cow. Omitting scenes of bringing cattle, etc.
454 (1), 467–8 (8), 469 (1), 470 (9), 475 (44), 476 (46), 488 (6), 494, 495 (10), 518 (4), 520 (4), 522 (12), 523 (20), 535 (93), 570, 575 (3), 594 (6) and (8), 599 (1)–(2), 599 (6), (7), and (10)–(11), 602 (18), 607 (3), 608, 614 (3), 617 (7), 620 (8), 624 (9) and (11), 631 (6), 635 (2) and (3), 637 (1), 640 (1)–(2), and (3), 642 (7), 643 (22), 644 (5), 646, 653 (3), 753, 754, 754, 761.

(*b*) **Crossing water**
Including herdsmen in papyrus rafts reciting charm against crocodiles.
438, 467 (8), 475 (44), 476 (46), 482 (5), 487 (7), 494 (1), 495 (2), 512 (2), 520 (4), 522 (12), 527 (13), 594 (8), 599 (5), 601 (17), 617 (7), 620 (13), 635 (2), 639 (4), 640 (1)–(2), 643 (22), 646, 758, 892.

(*c*) **Cooking or drinking**
454 (1), 575 (3), 594 (8), 640 (1)–(2), 643 (22), 644 (5), 754.

(*d*) **Mat making**
475 (44), 522 (12), 594 (8), 643 (22), 644 (5), 754. *See also* Sect. 9*h*.

(*e*) **Special details**
Skinning goat, 640 (1)–(2). Feeding puppy, 522 (12).

6. Rendering accounts by chiefs of estates, herdsmen, etc.

461 (1), 467 (2), 474 (37), 484 (5), 486 (2), 495 (10) and (11), 509 (15), 518 (4), 522 (11), 528 (23), 617 (3), 618 (8), 631 (13), 635 (3), 637 (1), 640 (1)–(2), 643 (17), 645 (2), 699 (2), 756.

7. Butchers

447 (1), 448 (7), (9), (10), (12), and (13), 454 (1) and (3), 455, 455 (2), 456 (6), 460 (3), 461 (6) and (7), 468 (8), 468, 470 (4), 471 (24), 475 (38) and (41), 481, 481 (1), 483, 483, 484 (6) and (7), 485 (6) and (7), 486 (1), 487 (1), 488 (5), 492 (7), 493 (3), 495 (12), 497 (4), 498, 499, 506, 510 (30) and (36), 513 (16), 516 (11), 518, 518 (9), 519 (2)–(3), 520 (8), 524 (35), 529 (35) and (39), 531 (62), 535 (97) and (109), 536 (121), 539, 541, 558, 569, 570, 575 (3), 576 (5), 577, 579, 581, 581 (5), 582 (5), 583 (3), 594 (7) and (8), 595, 596, 597 (15), 599 (7), 600 (16), 603 (19), 607 (5), 609, 609, 614 (2), 615 (3), 616 (12), 618 (20), 619 (21) and (24), 621 (17), (19), and (25), 625 (21) and (23), 627 (2), 628 (8), 629 (16), 631 (18), 634 (6)–(7), 634 (1), 636 (5), 639 (2)–(3), 640 (4), 642 (2) and (3), 642 (4), 644 (25) and (26), 646, 653 (7), 671, 696, 696, 699 (4) and (6), 762, 827, 891, 891.

8. Marsh-scenes

Deceased fowling, fishing, etc., *see* Sect. 1. Herdsmen with cattle crossing water, *see* Sect. 5*b*.

(*a*) **Papyrus harvest, with men pulling or carrying bundles of papyrus**
443, 467 (7), 476 (46), 494, 599 (6), 601 (17), 617 (7), 623 (5), 628 (9) and (10), 635 (2), 637 (2), 640 (1)–(2), 644 (3) and (5), 695.

(*b*) **Making papyrus-rafts (sometimes with men making ropes)**
467 (7), 476 (46), 522 (12), 594 (8), 599 (6), 601 (17), 613, 617 (7), 628 (9), 635 (2), 640 (1)–(2), 644 (3) and (5), 695, 761.

(*c*) **Netting fish**
468 (8), 475 (44), 482 (5), 487 (7), 492 (4), 498, 501 (1), 520 (4), 522 (9), 523 (21), 529 (26) and (36), 535 (93), 569, 583 (2), 585, 594 (8), 607 (4), 616 (4)–(5), 617 (4), 620 (13), 627 (3), 628 (9), 631 (1), 635 (2), 639 (4), 640 (1)–(2), 642 (9), 644 (4), 695, 700 (8), 754, 891. With small net/hand-net/dip-net/clap-net, 467 (7), 522 (13), 529 (26), 599 (5), 605, 617 (2), (4), and (7), 642 (9); with baskets, 469 (1), 476 (46), 523 (21), 529 (26), 642 (9), 753. Spearing fish, *see* Sect. 1*b*.

(*d*) **Angling**
476 (45), 515 (6), 522 (9) and (13), 529 (26), 594 (8), 599 (6), 617 (4) and (7).

(*e*) **Netting fowl**
Including making/mending and setting up clap-net, waiting for birds to enter net, pulling rope, taking birds out of net and putting into cages, but omitting men bringing fowl.
454 (2), 468 (8), 475 (44), 482 (5), 484, 488 (5), 492 (4), 513 (8), 516 (9), 523 (20), 579, 583 (2), 585, 594 (8), 597 (15), 599 (3), 601 (17), 614 (3), 619 (3), 620 (13), 623 (5), 635 (2), 639 (4), 640 (1)–(2), 642 (9), 644 (5), 646, 699 (2), 754, 892.

(*f*) **Hippopotamus-hunt**
476 (45), 494, 522 (13), 527 (15), 579, 617 (7), 635 (2).

(*g*) **Boatmen jousting**
454 (2), 467 (8), 476 (46), 570, 594 (8), 599 (5), 601 (17), 606 (1), 614 (3), 618 (17), 635 (2), 640 (1)–(2), 643 (22), 695, 753, 753.

(*h*) **Various**
Cutting out roes of fish/cutting open fish/ preparing botargo, 475 (44), 482 (5), 488 (6), 492 (4), 498, 518 (7), 523 (21), 583 (2), 594 (8), 601 (17), 607 (3), 608, 628 (9), 631 (5), 635 (2), 644 (3), 695, 753, 754. Fishing from boats (unspecified), 623 (5). Unloading fish, 891. Plucking lotus-flowers from rafts, 614 (3).

(*i*) **Unspecified**
Could also be Sect. 1.
509 (22), 519 (2)–(3), 608, 616 (13).

9. Crafts

(*a*) **Metal-workers**
Including men with blowpipes, weighing, beating metal, pouring molten metal into mould, etc.
473 (36), 484 (5), 486 (2), 513 (7), 522 (14), 528 (20), 620 (11), 631 (9), 643 (19).

(*b*) **Carpenters**
Including bending poles, sawing, making bed, coffin, door-bolt, wooden column, etc.
473 (36), 484 (5), 486 (2), 528 (20), 640 (3), 643 (19), 891.

(*c*) **Boat-builders**
471 (26)–(27), 473 (35), 495 (6), 532 (76), 640 (3), 642 (7). Making papyrus-rafts, *see* Sect. 8*b*.

(*d*) **Jewellers (usually dwarfs)**
486 (2), 513 (7), 528 (20), 600 (16), 631 (9), 640 (1)–(2), 643 (19).

(*e*) **Leather-workers**
473 (36), 513 (7).

(*f*) **Makers of stone vessels**
473 (36), 486 (2), 499, 513 (7), 528 (20).

(*g*) **Sculptors**
473 (36), 486 (2), 513 (7), 528 (20), 631 (9), 643 (19). *See also* Sect. 13*c*.

(*h*) **Others**
Pottery-making, 472 (32), 496. Seal-maker, 473 (36). Mat-making, 498; *see also* Sect. 5*d*. Spinning, 546. Unspecified, 754.

10. Baking and cooking

Herdsmen cooking, *see* Sect. 5*c*.

(*a*) **Bread or cakes**
Also preparing for brewing. Including issuing corn, grinding corn on quern, sifting flour, kneading dough, shaping loaves, heating pots, pouring dough into pots, testing bread with stick, and baking cakes on fire.
472 (32), 486 (2), 488 (6), 498, 509 (15), 512 (5), 583 (2), 584 (8), 594 (5), 616 (1), 620 (8), 642 (6), 753, 753, 760.

(*b*) **Fowl or meat**
Including plucking, cleaning, cooking, or roasting fowl, and cutting up and cooking meat.
448 (11), 488 (5), 516 (9), 594 (7), 607 (3), 620 (8), 628 (7), 631 (5).

(*c*) **Unspecified**
443, 483 (1), 605, 760.

11. Brewing

Baking bread, *see* Sect. 10*a*. Including grinding corn in mortar, treading pieces of bread in vat, straining beer, cleaning, filling, and sealing beer-jars.
472 (32), 486 (2), 488 (6), 509 (15), 510, 512 (5), 594 (5), 620 (8), 642 (6), 745, 753.

12. Music, singing, and games

(*a*) **Musicians (mainly flutists and harpists), including scenes with wife or daughter playing the harp, and singers**
471 (25), 475 (38), 486 (4), 488, 495 (7)–(8), 498, 501 (4), 530 (50), 541, 580 (4), 582 (6), 584 (6), 585, 594 (7), 600 (16), 607 (4), 614 (3), 616 (6), 621 (17), 623, 628 (7), 631 (7), 636 (5), 640 (5), 643 (20), 644 (7), 646, 697, 699 (6), 761, 762, 891. Flute-player in harvest-scene, 533 (80), 584 (8), 620 (10), 694; with singer, 472 (34). Men with resonant sticks in harvest-scene, 584 (8); in vintage-scene, 531 (66), 637 (2), 640 (1)–(2), 750.

(*b*) **Male or female dancers/acrobats and/ or clappers**
471 (25), 487 (2), 488, 495 (7)–(8), 498, 514 (23), 522 (15), 530 (53), 535 (100), 577, 579, 580 (4), 584 (6), 585, 605, 607 (4), 621 (17), 628 (7), 636 (5), 640 (1)–(2), 643 (20), 699 (6), 891. Female clappers and dancers in funeral-scene, *see* Sect. 13*d*; mirror-dance, *see* Sect. 12*d*.

(*c*) **Playing *meḥen*-game (snake-game) and/ or *senet*-game (draughts)**
495 (7)–(8), 496, 498, 584 (6), 585, 628 (7), 631 (7).

(*d*) **Children playing games**
Including mirror-dance.
498, 509 (16), 533 (78), 595 (8), 601 (17), 602 (18).

13. Funerary scenes and rites

(*a*) **Coffin or sarcophagus**
Carried or dragged, 514 (22), 532 (70), 605, 618 (9), 628 (8), 891. Transported in boat, 532 (70), 618 (9), 628 (8), 653 (4)–(5), 891. Men before canopy with coffin(?), 653 (4)–(5).

(*b*) **Chest(s) with feathers on top**
619, 653 (4)–(5); being dragged, 524 (30) and (32), 599 (7), 616 (3), 623 (6), 642 (5).

(*c*) **Statue(s) of deceased**
Dragged to tomb (but also in connection with sculptors), including censing, 447 (1), 460 (3), 471 (24), 487 (1), 495 (9), 523 (18), 528 (20), 583 (1), 593 (2) and (3), 605, 616 (3), 617 (5), 627 (2), 634 (1), 642 (2), (3), and (5), 654 (9), 695. Transported in boat, 470 (4), 593 (3), 642 (2) and (3). Offering to, sometimes with censing, 508 (12), 519 (4), 528 (24), 531 (54), 642 (2) and (3). Others, 452.

(*d*) **Dancers and clappers**
Dancers, 605, 618 (9), 628 (8); accompanying statues, 634 (1). Female dancers and clappers, 532 (70), 593 (3), 653 (4)–(5).

(*e*) **Buildings**
Purification-tent or embalming house, 532 (70), 628 (8), 891. House of deceased, 514 (22). Tomb, 532 (70).

14. Estates

Concordance with H. K. Jacquet-Gordon, *Les Noms des domaines funéraires sous l'Ancien Empire égyptien* (1962). The list includes estates in royal complexes, on other monuments, or named only, and all those in Part 1 of *Top. Bibl.* iii².

Jacquet-Gordon	*Bibl. iii²*
1 R 4	877
1 R 5	398
2 R 5	330 (16), 332
3 R 5	873
4 R 5	337
5 R 5	314
6 R 5	424
7 R 5	418
1 R 6	426 (5) and (6)
1 A 4	7
1 G 4	134
2 G 4	189 (7) and (9)
3 G 4	196 (2)
4 G 4	194
5 G 4	139
6 G 4	140
7 G 4	204 (2) and (3)
8 G 4	202 (3)
9 G 4	232 (3)
10 G 4	198 (9)
11 G 4–5	234 (3)
12 G 4–5	231 (4), 232 (8)
13 G 4–5	71 (3)
14 G 4–5	244 (1)
15 G 4–5	256 (2)
16 G 4–5	219
17 G 4–5	145
18 G 5	142 (2) (= lower half of page)
19 G 5	77 (2)–(3)
20 G 5	146 (9)
21 G 5	278
22 G 5	78 (3)–(4)
23 G 5	150 (6)
24 G 5	142 (2) (= upper half of page)
25 G 5	144 (6)
26 G 5	208 (4)–(5)
27 G 5	52
28 G 5	66
29 G 5	266 (6), 267
30 G 5	154 (6)
31 G 5	171 (5)
32 G 5	190 (3)
33 G 5	283 (1) and (2)
34 G 5	263 (7), 264 (8)
35 G 5	206 (2)
36 G 5	205
37 G 5	245
38 G 5	86 (8) and (13)
39 G 5	88–9 (8)
40 G 5	95 (3)
41 G 5–6	164 (3)
42 G 6	102 (3)
43 G 6	225 (15)
44 G 6	87
45 G 6	227
46 G 6	51 (1) and (2)
47 G 6	149 (3)
48 G 6	167
49 G 6	106 (2)
50 G 6	179
1 S 4	493 (1)
2 S 4	453 (4)
3 S 4	453 (5)
4 S 4	502 (3) and (4)
5 S 4	443
6 S 5	694
7 S 5	578
8 S 5	582 (2)
9 S 5	580 (2) and (3)
10 S 5	483 (1)
11 S 5	583 (1)
12 S 5	637 (5)
13 S 5	488 (1) and (3)
14 S 5	652
15 S 5	487 (2)
16 S 5	608
17 S 5	469 (1), 477 (44)–(46)
18 S 5	491–2 (3) and (4)
19 S 5	495 (6)
20 S 5	455 (2)
21 S 5	497 (3)
22 S 5	693
23 S 5	692
24 S 5	597 (16) and (17)
25 S 5	599 (1)–(2) and (5)–(6)
26 S 5	623 (4)
27 S 5	763
28 S 5–6	603 (19)
29 S 5–6	652
30 S 6	627 (2)
31 S 6	595
32 S 6	512 (3)
33 S 6	543
34 S 6	491
35 S 6	529 (32)

Jacquet-Gordon	*Bibl. iii*[2]
36 S 6	535 (99)
37 S 6	460 (3)
38 S 6	620 (10)
39 S 6	615 (1)
40 S 6	631 (2)
1 D 4	894
2 D 4	880
3 D 5	894
4 D 6	891

Others (mostly no names), 74 (5), 75 (3), 96 (1), 136 (3), 186 (5), 192 (5), 255 (6) and (7), 263 (5), 264 (10) and (11), 493 (5), 585, 614 (3), 624 (10), 642 (11), 643 (19), 678.

15. Special or less common scenes

Hunting-scene, 473 (35), 487 (3), 491 (4), 493 (4), 528 (18), 536 (112), 599 (1)–(2), 601 (17), 605, 619, 628 (10), 642 (10). Rewarding scene, 647; rewarding weavers with jewellery, 634 (1), 653 (1); putting necklaces in boxes, 496 (13). Servants preparing bed, 530 (51), 607 (3), 616 (10), 621 (16), 624 (16), 639 (1), 645 (1), 752, 891; and chair, 699 (2). Market-scenes, 473 (36), 484 (5), 512 (6), 523 (22), 642 (7). Surgical operations, 514 (21). Circumcision, 514 (21). Manicure and pedicure, 509 (16), 642 (7). Fattening hyenas, 523 (20), 532 (76). Inspection of linen, 496. Boat or raft transporting cattle, 593 (4), 618 (15); corn, 623 (6); oils, 642 (10). Men tied to whipping-post, 509 (15), 528 (23). Siege of a fortified settlement, 542 (5).

16. Special or unusual people

Barbers, 642 (7). Fishmonger, 642 (7). Swimmers, 532 (70). Dwarfs with dog(s) and/or monkey, 470 (6)–(7), 475 (44), 501 (4), 513 (8), 523 (22), 532 (74), 584 (8), 696, 696; as attendant, 624 (8); with box, 510 (38), 518 (3); holding palette, 640 (4); making jewellery, *see* Sect. 9*d*.

17. Less common animals, birds, insects

Only when specifically mentioned in the text.
Baboon, 460 (3), 484 (5), 613, 640 (1)–(2) and (3).
Civet-cat, 619.
Eel, 608.
Frog, 527 (12), 583 (2).
Grasshopper, 527 (12).
Hare, 473 (35), 576 (4).
Hedgehog, 515 (7), 519 (8).
Hoopoe, 481, 593 (1).
Hyena, 523 (20), 532 (76), 602 (18).
Ichneumon, 526 (12), 527 (15), 579, 594 (8), 620 (5), 623 (5).
Leopard, 602 (18).
Lion, 473 (35), 519 (8), 536 (112), 602 (18), 605.
Monkey, 501, 513 (8), 523 (22), 529 (27), 535 (108), 600 (16), 640 (3), 693, 696, 696, 891.
Moufflon, 621 (18).
Otter, 534 (81).
Panther, 696.
Turtle, 620 (13).
Wild dog, 601 (17).

B. CLASSIFICATION OF SELECTED OLD KINGDOM TEXTS

I. Texts in K. Sethe, *Urkunden des Alten Reichs* (1933)

Urk. i	*Present location*	*Page*
1–6 [1, A–E]	Ṣaqqâra Tomb LS 6	493–4
6–7 [1, F]	Berlin (West) Mus. 1106	493
10 [8]	Cairo Mus. CG 1566	693
33 [19, A]	Cairo Mus. CG 1415	484 (4)
33 [19, B]	Cairo Mus. CG 1417	483 (2)
33–4 [20]	Ṣaqqâra Tomb C 25	690
34 [21]	Cairo Mus. CG 1691	693
34–5 [22]	Ṣaqqâra Tomb No. 83 [D 6; S 907]	488 (2)
36–7 [24]	Ṣaqqâra Tomb D 52	582
37 [25]	Berlin (East) Mus. 15004	578
38–40 [26, A, B]	Cairo Mus. CG 1482	482–3
40–5 [27]	Cairo Mus. CG 1569, 1674, 1570, 1673, 1702, JE 55937	456
	Aberdeen Mus. 1558a, b, c, 1560	
48–9 [30, A, B]	Ṣaqqâra Tomb D 70 [LS 15]	492 (5)
49–51 [31]	Leyden Mus. F.1904/3/1	593 (1)
51–3 [32, A, B]	Brit. Mus. 682	464
58 [40]	Cairo Mus. CG 1461	468

Urk. i	*Present location*	*Page*
58 [41]	Cairo Mus. CG 1308	462
68–9 [45]	Ṣaqqâra Tomb No. 75 [D 10]	483
73 [50]	Cairo Mus. CG 376	722
75 [1]	Cairo Mus. CG 1732	611
80 [4]	Ṣaqqâra Tomb D 65	606
81 [5, A, B]	Ṣaqqâra Tomb of Ptaḥshepses [II]	460 (1)
82–4 [5, C, D]	Cairo Mus. CG 1565	460 (4)
84–5 [6]	Cairo Mus. CG 1709, 1756	463
87–8 [8, A]	Ṣaqqâra Tomb of Mereruka	526 (10)
88 [8, B]	Ṣaqqâra Tomb of Mereruka	532 (70)
97 [15, C]	Berlin (East) Mus. 7715	423
97 [16]	Cairo Mus.	424
153 [1 (92)]	Cairo Mus. JE 49889	407
173–4 [19 (110), A]	Ṣaqqâra Tomb No. 60 [D 22]	469 (1) (e)
174 [19 (110), B]	Ṣaqqâra Tomb No. 60 [D 22]	469 (1) (f)
175 [20 (111), A, B]	New York, M.M.A. 26.9.1	541
176 [20 (111), C, D]	Ṣaqqâra Tomb of Kaemsenu	541
177 [21 (112), A]	Ṣaqqâra Tomb of Sekhemka	596
177 [21 (112), B]	Philadelphia Mus. E 15729	455–6 (5)
177 [21 (112), C]	Cairo Mus. CG 1565	460 (4)
178 [21 (112), D]	Cairo Mus. CG 1421	468
179–80 [24 (115)]	Ṣaqqâra Tomb LS 16 [S 902]	496
180–6 [25 (116), A–E]	Ṣaqqâra Tomb No. 84 [D 7; S 919]	489 (1), (5), (6), (3) and (4)
188–9 [28–9 (119–20)]	Ṣaqqâra Tomb of Ptaḥḥotp [II]	604 (20)
190–1 [30 (121)]	Ṣaqqâra Tomb No. 75 [D 10]	483
191–2 [31 (122) A, B]	Ṣaqqâra Tomb No. 14 [D 43]	452
192 [31 (122), C]	Brooklyn Mus. 37.25E	452
192–3 [31 (122), D, E]	Brooklyn Mus. 37.27–8E	452
193 [32 (123)]	Ṣaqqâra Tomb of Seshemnūfer	615 (6)
194–6 [33 (124), A–D]	Ṣaqqâra Tomb LS 10	521 (5) and (6)
197 [34 (125)]	Unknown	546
198 [35 (126)]	Unknown	546
198–200 [36–7 (127–8)]	Ṣaqqâra Tomb of Neferseshemrēᶜ Sheshi	512 (6)
200–1 [38 (129)]	Ṣaqqâra Tomb of Uzaḥateti Neferseshemptaḥ	515
201–3 [39 (130), A, B]	Ṣaqqâra Tomb of ᶜAnkhmaᶜḥor	512 (1)
203 [39 (130), C]	Ṣaqqâra Tomb of ᶜAnkhmaᶜḥor	513 (12)
203 [39 (130), D]	Ṣaqqâra Tomb of ᶜAnkhmaᶜḥor	514 (20)
204–5 [41 (132), A]	Ṣaqqâra Tomb of ᶜAnkhmaᶜḥor	515
205 [41 (132), B]	Ṣaqqâra Tomb of Khentka Ikhekhi	511
206–7 [42 (133)]	Cairo Mus. JE 47749	543
209–13 [45 (136)]	Berlin (East) Mus. 17500	876
227 [5 (145), A]	Brit. Mus. 1324	893
227 [5 (145), B]	Manchester Mus. 10780	745
228 [5 (145), E]	Cairo Mus. CG 394	736
228 [5 (145), F]	Cairo Mus. CG 1365	768
235–49 [10 (150)]	Palermo Mus. and Cairo Mus. CG 39734–5, 44859–60	873
249–50 [11 (151)]	Unknown	547
255–6 [14 (154)]	Brussels, Mus. Roy. E.2243	694
260 [18 (158)]	Leipzig Mus. Inv.359	686
262 [19 (159), C]	Ṣaqqâra tomb-group N. IV	677
271–2 [26 (166), A]	Pyramid-enclosure of Iput II	432
272 [26 (166), B]	Pyramid-enclosure of Wezebten	433
272–3 [27 (167), A]	Cairo Mus. JE 49681	432
273–4 [27 (167), B, C]	Pyramid-enclosure of Wezebten	433
307 [38 (178)]	Cairo Mus. JE 56370	431

II. Other Old Kingdom texts

Address, 508 (7)–(9), 519, 520, 570, 609, 610, 623, 625 (1), 626, 626 (3), 630, 646, 763.
Appointment as *ka*-servant, 674.
Biographical text, 508 (10), 569, 605, 626 (3), 629, 646, 646.
Contract with funerary priests, 642 (8).

C. PYRAMIDS

in this volume

[1] 'Pyramids' XXXIII and XXXIV are the North and South Buildings in the Step Pyramid Enclosure, p. 412, XLVIII is the easternmost of the South Mastabas in the Pyramid-complex of Sesostris III, p. 885, LV is the tomb of Siēsi, p. 898. Pyramids XXIX, XLV, L, LII, and LIII have been omitted here.

[2] Numbering of the Ṣaqqâra pyramids.

		Lepsius	*Perring and Vyse*		*Page*
Amenemḥēt III	Dyn. XII	LVIII		Black	887
?	Dyn. XIII				890
?	Dyn. XIII				890
Ameny-Ḳemau	Dyn. XIII				890

D. NUMBERED ṢAQQÂRA TOMBS

in this volume

Approximate location of tombs marked 'Position unknown' is in some cases indicated by headings in the text

(*a*) *Mariette and de Morgan*

No.	*Position on map*	*Page*
1	XLV, B–1	448
2	XLV, B–1	449
3	XLV, B–1	449
4	XLV, C–1	449
5	XLV, C–3	449
6	XLV, B–3	450
7	XLV, B–2	450
8	XLV, B–2	451
9	XLV, B–2	451 *and* Addenda
10	XLV, B–3	451
11	XLV, B–2	451
12	XLV, B–3	451
13	XLV, B–3	451
14	XLV, B–3	452 *and* Addenda
15	XLV, B/C–3	452
16	XLVI, D–2	453
17	identification not certain	
18	XLV, C–3	453
19	XLV, C–1	453
20	XLV, C–1	454
21	XLV, C–1	455
22	XLV, C–1	455
23	XLV, C–1	456
24	XLV, C–2	456
25	XLV, C–2	456
26	XLV, C–2	456
27	XLV, C–2	457
28	XLV, C–2	457
29	XLV, C–2	457
30	XLV, C–2	457
31	XLV, C–2	458
32	XLV, C–2	458
33	XLV, C–2	458
34	XLV, C–2	458
35	XLVI, D–3	458
36	XLVI, D–2	459, *724*
37–8	XLVI, D–2	460
39	XLVI, D–2	461
40	XLVI, D–2	461
41–2	XLVI, D–2	462
43	XLVI, D–2	463
44	XLVI, D–2	463
45	XLVI, D–2	463
46	XLVI, D–2	463
47	XLVI, D–2	463 *and* Addenda
48	XLVI, D–2	464, *465 note 1*
49	XLVI, D–2	464, *505, 583*
50	XLVI, D–2	464
51	XLVI, D–2	465
52	XLVI, D–2	465
53	XLVI, D–2	465
54	XLVI, D–2	465
55	XLVI, D–2	466
56	XLVI, D–2	466
57	XLVI, D–1	467
58	XLVI, D–1	468
59	XLVI, D–1	468
60	XLVI, D–1	468, *507*
61	XLVI, D–1	478
62	XLVI, D–1	478
63	XLVI, D–1	479
64	XLVI, D–1	479
65	XLVI, D–2	480
66	XLVI, D–2	*457 note 1*, 480
67	XLVI, D–2	481
68	XLVI, D–2	481
69	XLVI, D–2	481
70	XLVI, D–2	482
71	XLVI, D–3	482
72	XLVI, E–3	482
73	XLVI, E–3	482 *and* Addenda
74	XLVI, E–3	482
75	XLVI, E–3	483
76	XLVI, E–3	483
77	XLVI, E–3	484
78	XLVI, E–3	485
79	XLVI, E–3	485
80 (probably)	XLVI, E–3	487
81	XLVI, E–3	488
82	XLVI, E–3	488
83	XLVI, E–3	488
84	XLVI, E–3	489
85	XLVI, E–2	489
86	Galleries in the Step Pyramid Enclosure	415
87	tomb not identified	
88	unknown	489

(*b*) *Mariette*

No.	*Position on map or equation*	*Page*
A 1	= No. 18	453
A 2	= No. 5	449
A 3	= S 2405	437
A 4	= No. 86	415
B 1	= No. 71	482
B 2	unknown	490
B 3	unknown	490
B 4	= No. 9	451 *and* Addenda
B 5	= No. 1	448
B 6	= No. 3	449
B 7	unknown	490
B 8	unknown	689
B 9	= No. 88	489
B 10	= No. 2	449
B 11	= No. 4	449
B 12	= No. 12	451
B 13	= No. 11	451
B 14	unknown	690
B 15	XLV, C–1	491
B 16	= No. 15	452
C 1	= No. 48	464, *465 note*
C 2	= No. 8	451
C 3	= No. 25	456
C 4	= No. 68	481
C 5	= No. 40	461
C 6 and 7	= Nos. 41–2	462
C 8	= No. 36	459
C 9	= No. 50	464
C 10	= No. 49	464, *505*, *583*
C 11	= LS 22	579
C 12	unknown	690
C 13	= No. 7	450
C 14	= No. 10	451
C 15	= No. 6	450
C 16	= No. 39	461
C 17	= No. 43	463
C 18	= No. 72	482
C 19	= No. 54	465
C 20	= No. 35	458
C 21	= No. 45	463
C 22	= No. 51	465
C 23	= No. 44	463
C 24	= No. 66	*457 note 1*, 480
C 25	unknown	690
C 26	= LS 20	565
C 27	unknown	690
D 1	= No. 78	485
D 2	= No. 79	485
D 3	= No. 80	487
D 4	= No. 81	488
D 5	= No. 82	488
D 6	= No. 83	488
D 7	= No. 84	489
D 8	= No. 85	489
D 9	= No. 77	484
D 10	= No. 75	483
D 11	= No. 76	483
D 12	= No. 74	482
D 13	= No. 73	482 *and* Addenda
D 14	= No. 70	482
D 15	= No. 69	481
D 16	= No. 67	481
D 17	= No. 65	480
D 18	= No. 64	479
D 19	= No. 63	479
D 20	= No. 62	478
D 21	= No. 61	478
D 22	= No. 60	468, *507*
D 23	= No. 57	467
D 24	= No. 56	466
D 25	= No. 55	466
D 26	= No. 52	465
D 27	= No. 53	465
D 28	= No. 46	463
D 29	= No. 34	458
D 30	= No. 33	458
D 31	= No. 32	458
D 32	= No. 31	458
D 33	= No. 30	457
D 34	= No. 29	457
D 35	= No. 28	457
D 36	= No. 27	457
D 37	= No. 26	456
D 38	= No. 24	456
D 39	= No. 22	455
D 40	= No. 21	455
D 41	= No. 20	454
D 42	= No. 19	453
D 43	= No. 14	452 *and* Addenda
D 44	= No. 13	451
D 45	LVIII, G–4	577
D 46	LVIII, F–4	577
D 47	unknown	580
D 48	LVIII, G–4	577
D 49	LVIII, G–4	578
D 50	unknown	581
D 51	unknown	581
D 52	unknown	582
D 53	unknown	582
D 54	unknown	582, *464 note 1*
D 55	unknown	583
D 56	unknown	584
D 57	LVIII, G–4	579
D 58	unknown	585
D 59	LVIII, F–2	595
D 60	LVIII, F–1	*459*, 593
D 61	LVIII, F–2	608
D 62	LVIII, F–2	596
D 63	LVIII, F–2	598
D 64	LVIII, F–2	598
D 65	LVIII, F–2	606
D 66	Sarcophagus-Shaped Tomb of Shepseskaf	434

No.	Position on map or equation	Page
D 67	unknown	689
D 68	unknown	689
D 69	unknown	689
D 70	XLVI, E–3	491
E 1, 2	= Nos. 37–8	460
E 3	= No. 47	463 *and* Addenda
E 4	= No. 16	453
E 5	= No. 23	456
E 6	= No. 58	468
E 7	= No. 59	468
E 8	LVIII, F–1	595
E 9	LVIII, F–2	596
E 10	unknown	585
E 11	unknown	585
E 12	unknown	586
E 13	unknown	586
E 14	unknown	611
E 15	unknown	611
E 16	unknown	689
E 17	LXII	633
F 1	unknown	586
F 2 (lintel)		753
F 3	unknown	586

No.	Position on map or equation	Page
F 4	= Nos. 41–2	462
H 1	unknown	611
H 2	= LS 17	575
H 3	= Nos. 37–8	460
H 4 (statue)		828
H 5 (false-door)		466
H 6 (lintel)		762 *and* Addenda
H 7 (coffin)		767
H 8 (stela)		667
H 9	unknown	666
H 10 (block)		753
H 11 (false-door)		483
H 12	unknown	492
H 13 (false-door)		586
H 14	= No. 48	464
H 15 (false-door)		608
H 15 (statue)		818
H 16 (coffin)		507
H 17 (coffin)		767

(*c*) *S* (= *Ṣaqqâra*) *series, used by Quibell, Firth, and Egypt Exploration Society*

For another set of Quibell's numbers see Sect. (*g*)

No.	Position on map or equation	Page
S 901	= No. 78	485
S 902	= LS 16	494
S 903	= No. 80	487
S 905	= No. 79	485
S 906	XLVI, E–3	496
S 907	= No. 83	488
S 908	= No. 82	488
S 909	XLVI, E–3	496
S 910	= No. 85	489
S 911	XLVI, E–3	496
S 912	XLVI, E–3	496
S 913	XLVI, E–3	497
S 915	XLVI, E–3	498
S 916	XLVI, E–2	498
S 919	= No. 84	489
S 920	XLVI, D–1	499
S 2146E	unknown	436
S 2171	XLV, B/C–4	436, *436*
S 2171H	XLV, B/C–4	436, *436*
S 2185	XLV, B/C–4	437
S 2302	XLV, B–4	437
S 2305	XLV, B–4	437
S 2322	XLV, B–4	437
S 2331	XLV, B–4	437
S 2347	XLV, B–4	437
S 2400	XLV, A–4	437
S 2401	XLV, A–4	437
S 2405	XLV, B–3	437

No.	Position on map or equation	Page
S 2407	XLV, B–3	439
S 2427	XLV, B–3	439
S 2429	XLV, B–3	440
S 2437	XLV, B–3/4	440
S 2446	XLV, B–4	440
S 2452	XLV, B–3/4	440
S 2466	unknown	440
S 2498	XLV, B–3/4	440
S 2608	unknown	*547, 547*
S 2720	LII	*556, 557*
S 2721	unknown	*556*
S 2727	LII	*557*
S 2730	LII	555
S 2734	LII	*547*
S 2735	LII	556
S 2736	LII	555
S 2740	unknown	*547*
S 2741	unknown	*547*
S 2745	unknown	*547*
S 2748	unknown	*547*
S 2757	LII	549
S 3009	XLV, B–3	440
S 3014	unknown	440
S 3017	XLV, B–3	440
S 3035	XLV, A–3/4	440
S 3036	XLV, A–3	442
S 3036X	XLV, A–3	442
S 3037	unknown	442

No.	*Position on map or equation*	*Page*
S 3038	XLV, A–3	442
S 3038X	= S 3037	442
S 3050	XLV, A/B–3	*505*
S 3073	= No. 5	449
S 3073X	unknown	442
S 3076	= No. 18	453
S 3078	XLV, C–2/3	443
S 3080	XLV, C–2	443
S 3111	XLV, A–3	443
S 3120	XLV, A–4	443
S 3121	XLV, A–4	443
S 3302	unknown	443
S 3357	XLV, B–4	443
S 3471	XLV, B–4	444
S 3477	unknown	444
S 3500	XLV, B/C–4	444
S 3503	XLV, C–4	444
S 3504	XLV, C–4/5	445
S 3505	XLV, C–5	446
S 3506	XLV, C–5	446
S 3507	XLVI, D–5	447
S 3508	XLV, C–2	447
S 3509	XLV, C–2	447
S 3510	XLV, C–2	448
S 3511	XLV, C–2	448
S 3513	XLV, C–2	448, *506*
S 3514	XLV, C–2	448, *506*
S 3516	XLV, C–2	*448 note 1*
S 3518	XLV, B–2/3	448

(*d*) *Lepsius*[1]

No.	*Position on map or equation*	*Page*
LS 4 (Ibis Galleries)		821
LS 5	XLVI, D–2	492
LS 6	XLVI, D–3	493, *506*
LS 7	XLVI, D–3	503, *506*
LS 8	LI, D–4	556
LS 10	LII (Kagemni)	521
LS 12	= S 2735	556
LS 13	LI, E–5	558
LS 14	XLVI, E–4	494
LS 15	= D 70	491
LS 16	XLVI, E–3	494
LS 17	LVIII, F–4	575
LS 18	LI, E–4	565
LS 19	LI, F–5	566
LS 20	LI, E–5	565
LS 22	LVIII, G–4	579
LS 23	LVIII, G–6	588
LS 24	LVIII, G–6	588 *and* Addenda
LS 25	LXII	661 *and* Addenda
LS 26	LXII	667
LS 27	LXI	661
LS 28	LXI	663
LS 29	LXI	664
LS 31	LXI	653
LS 32	unknown	686

(*e*) *Jéquier*

Map LXVII [2]

No.		*Page*
M. II		680
M. III		680
M. IV		680
M. VI		681
M. VII		681
M. VIII	position not marked on map	688
M. IX		682
M. X (west part)		682
M. XI		682
M. XII		682
M. XIII		683
M. XIV		684
M. XV		684
M. XVI		685
M. XVII		685
N. I		676
N. II		677
N. III		677
N. IV		677
N. V		678
N. VI		678
N. VII		679
N. VIII		679
N. IX		679
N. X		679
N. XI		680
O. I	position not marked on map	686
O. II	position not marked on map	686

[1] Tomb LS 1, see *Bibl.* iii², Pt. 1, p. 351. LS 2–3, 9, 11, 21, and 30 have been omitted here.

(*f*) *Firth* (*C. M.*) *and Gunn* (*B.*), Teti Pyramid Cemeteries (*1926*)

Map LII

No.		*Page*	*No.*		*Page*
33		*544*	HMK. 6		540
47		538	HMK. 26		540
81		539	HMK. 30		538
213		*544*	HMK. 37		539
225		540	HMK. 40		543
227		540	HMK. 69		538
240	shaft in mastaba of Kaemsenu	541	HMK. 120		538
			HMK. 125		538
255	shaft in mastaba of Kaemsenu	542	HMK. 140		538
			HMK. 159	position unknown	543

(*g*) *Quibell*

No.	*Position on map*	*Page*
289	LI, E–5	561 *and* Addenda
75	LI, E–6	560
276	LI, E–5/6	562

(*h*) *Loret*

Map LII

No.	*Page*
2	552
4	553
5	553

(*i*) *Various*

Name	*Position on map or equation*	*Page*
'Tomb with Cow'		592
'Tombe du Defterdar'	LS 16	494
'Mastaba du Louvre'		634
'Rue de Tombeaux'		511–16
Mastaba X	XLV, C–5	499

E. VIZIERS

The list includes Viziers quoted in *Top. Bibl.* iii², Part 1

Old Kingdom[1]

	Date	A. Weil, *Die Veziere des Pharaonenreiches*	*Pages*
Menka	Dyn. III(?)	—	404
Neferma'et	Snefru	AR 2	122
Ḥemyunu	Khufu	—	122
Kawa'b	Khufu	—	118, 155, 187, 864
Minkha'ef	Khufu to Khephren	—	195
Khufukha'ef [I]	Khufu to end of Dyn. IV	—	188
Nebemakhet	Khephren to Menkaurē' or a little later	—	198, 199, 229, 230
Nikaurē'	Khephren to end of Dyn. IV	AR 4	232

[1] For Imḥōtep (later tradition), see p. 571. See also 'Ankh-ḥaf, p. 196; Babaf, p. 155; Neferma'et, p. 183; Duaenrē', p. 148.

	Date	A. Weil, *Die Veziere des Pharaonenreiches*	*Pages*
Sekhemkarēʿ	Khephren to early Dyn. V	AR 5	233
Kanūfer	advanced Dyn. IV or later	—	893
ʿAnkhmaʿrēʿ	end of Dyn. IV	—	246
Yunmin	end of Dyn. IV	AR 3	237
Werbauba	Saḥurēʿ	—	327
Washptaḥ (Isi)	Neferirkarēʿ	AR 7	456
name lost	early Dyn. V	—	150
Minnūfer	Neuserrēʿ	AR 9	337, 764
Ptaḥshepses	middle Dyn. V	AR 8	337, 340, 571
Peḥnuika	middle Dyn. V or later	AR 6	482, 491
Ptaḥḥotp	middle Dyn. V or later	AR 12	462
Ptaḥḥotp	middle Dyn. V or later	AR 10	653
Ptaḥḥotp-desher	middle Dyn. V or later	AR 11 and 13	462
Kai	middle Dyn. V or later	AR 19	479
Thenti	middle Dyn. V or later	AR 33	482
Seshemnūfer [III]	Isesi (early)	—	82, 153, 153
Ptaḥḥotp [I]	Isesi	AR 14	596, 599, 608
Raʿshepses	Isesi	—	485, 489, 494, 497
Senezemib (Inti)	Isesi	AR 16	85, 229
Akhtiḥotp	Isesi–Unis	AR 15	597, 599, 605
Ptaḥḥotp [II] (Thefi)	Isesi–Unis	—	599, 600, 606
Senezemib (Meḥi)	Unis	AR 17	84, 85, 86, 87, 92, 129
Sekhemʿankhptaḥ	late Dyn. V or Dyn. VI	—	191
Akhtiḥotp (Ḥemi)	end of Dyn. V or early Dyn. VI	—	627
Tepemʿankh [I]	end of Dyn. V. or Dyn. VI	AR 18	483
Kagemni (Memi, Gemni)	Teti	AR 25	521, 546, 546
Mereruka (Meri)	Teti	AR 26	525, 546, 569
Khentka (Ikhekhi)	Pepy I	—	508
Raʿwēr	probably Pepy I (rather than late Dyn. VI)	—	558
Meryteti (Meri)	Pepy I or later	AR 27	536 (see name-index for other references)
Meḥu	Pepy I or later	—	619
ʿAnkhmaʿḥor (Sesi)	early Dyn. VI	—	512
Neferseshemrēʿ (Sheshi)	early Dyn. VI	AR 24	511
Nūfer (Idu [I])	early Dyn. VI	—	165
Imameryrēʿ (Imapepy)	Pepy II	—	683
Iḥykhent	Pepy II	—	428
Idi	Pepy II	—	428, 678
Niḥebsed-neferkarēʿ	Pepy II	—	683
Khaʿbaukhnum (Biu)	Pepy II	—	684
Khenu	Pepy II	—	427
Shenaʿy	Pepy II	—	678
Teti	Pepy II	—	684
Mereri	late Dyn. VI	—	607
Thethu	probably late Dyn. VI	—	537
Sesi	end of Dyn. VI or 1st Int. Period	AR 28	689
Iynefert	Dyn. VI	—	616
Iḥy	Dyn. VI	—	617, 619
Niʿankhba	Dyn. VI	—	629
Nebkauḥor (Idu)	Dyn. VI	—	627
Neferseshem-seshet (Khenu)	Dyn. VI	AR 23	585

Middle Kingdom

	Date	M. Valloggia in *B.I.F.A.O.* 74 (1974), pp. 124–32	*Pages*
Ameny	Sesostris I	7	832
Sebkemḥēt	probably Sesostris III	11	897
Khnemḥotp	probably Sesostris III	12	896

New Kingdom[1]

		W. Helck, *Zur Verwaltung des Mittleren und Neuen Reichs*, pp. 433–65	
Neferweben	Tuthmosis III	7	865
Ptaḥmosi	Tuthmosis III	8	773, 774
Ptaḥmosi	Amenophis III	14	721, 725
Ḏḥutmosi	Amenophis III	15	712
ʿAperir	probably Amenophis IV	—	562
?	late Dyn. XVIII or Ramesside	—	755
Paser	Sethos I–Ramesses II	24	771, 783, 783, 821, 838, 838
Neferronpet	Ramesses II	27	706
Paraʿḥotp (Raʿḥotp)	Ramesses II	28/29	665
Ḥori	Merneptaḥ–Siptaḥ to Ramesses III	39	731, 851, 861, 871
To	Ramesses III	40	861
Neferronpet	Ramesses IV–VI	41	707, 860
Khaʿemwēset	Ramesses IX	43	859

Late Period

		A. Weil, *Die Veziere des Pharaonenreiches*	
Bekenrenef	Psammetikhos I	SP 19	588
Psammethek-sonb	Dyn. XXIX	SP 27	867
Pedeneit (Pashe(n)tiḥet)	Dyn. XXX	—	591

F. HIGH PRIESTS OF MEMPHIS

The title has been rendered 'Greatest of the Directors of craftsmen', with variants for the Old Kingdom (see Appendix G, titles 135–7). The list includes HPM quoted in *Top. Bibl.* iii², Part 1

Old Kingdom[2]

	Date	D. W[ildung] in *Lexikon der Ägyptologie* (ed. W. Helck and W. Westendorf), ii. 1258–63	*Pages*
Raʿnūfer	early Dyn. V	5	461
Raʿneferefʿankh	Raʿneferef or later	6	698
Ptaḥshepses	Neuserrēʿ	3	327, 464
Ptaḥshepses	probably middle Dyn. V	9	464
Sabu-kem	Dyn. V	10	463
Sethu	probably Dyn. V	11	698
Sabu (Ibebi)	Teti	7	460

[1] The title of Ḥatiay, p. 43, is to be corrected to 'Head of chisellers'.
[2] For No. 14 of *Lexikon der Ägyptologie*, see p. 730.

	Date	D. W[ildung] in *Lexikon der Ägyptologie* (ed. W. Helck and W. Westendorf), ii. 1258–63	*Pages*
Ptaḥshepses [II]	Teti or later	8	460
Sabu (Thety)	Pepy II or later[1]	12	463
Ptaḥshepses [I]	Dyn. VI	—	499
Middle Kingdom and 2nd Int. Period			
Sebkḥotp-ḥenku	Middle Kingdom	—	858
Seḥetepebrēʿ-ʿankh	Middle Kingdom	17	571
Senbuy	2nd Int. Period	—	738
New Kingdom and 3rd Int. Period			
Ptaḥmosi	Tuthmosis III	28	773, 774
Ptaḥmosi	Amenophis III	30	712, 727
Ḏḥutmosi[2]	Amenophis III	31	780, 781, 851
Ptaḥmosi	Amenophis III	32/33	571, 712
Ptaḥemḥēt (Ty)	Tutʿankhamūn or Ay	38	571, 711
Meryptaḥ	probably Ḥaremḥab	37	706
Khaʿemwēset	Ramesses II	50/57	704 (see name-index for other references)
Neferronpet	Ramesses II	55	706
Paḥemneter	probably Ramesses II	34/47	571, 708, 727
Iyiry	Sethos II	59	704, 845, 865
?	Dyn. XIX	—	669
Paḥemneter	probably Dyn. XIX	46	871
Ptaḥmosi	probably Dyn. XIX	—	759
Ḥori	Merneptaḥ-Siptaḥ to Ramesses III	58	851, 871
Ḥori	late Dyn. XIX to early Dyn. XX	58	703, 871
Paḥemneter	late Dyn. XIX to Dyn. XX	60	314, 731
Khaʿemwēset	Ramesses IX	61	859
Ḥori	probably Ramesside	39	873
Bekenamūn	New Kingdom	—	861
Ptaḥmosi	New Kingdom	—	861
Neterkheperrēʿ-mer(y)ptaḥ (Paupau)	Siamūn	64	853
ʿAnkhefensekhmet	Sesonchis I	68	760, 841, 866, 872
Shedsunefertem	Sesonchis I	69	760, 786, 823, 841, 842, 858, 866, 872
?	Sesonchis I	—	873
Sheshonḳ	Osorkon II	73	722, 785, 846, 875
Merenptaḥ	Takelothis II	72	785
Thekerti	probably Sesonchis III	74	786, 847, 873
Pedēsi	Sesonchis III and later	75	786, 786, 847
Ḥarsiēsi	Pemu or later	77	786, 847, 848
ʿAnkhefensekhmet	Sesonchis V	78	848
Late Period			
ʿAḥmosi-men (Irʿaḥeka)	Darius I	80	801, 801, 803
Khnemebrēʿ-siptaḥ (Nekau)	Darius I	82	803
?	probably Late Period	—	592

[1] Rather than Pepy I, since the name appears in the Mortuary Temple of Pepy II (Jéquier, *Le Monument néraire de Pepi II*, ii, pl. 74).
[2] The title not mentioned in *Top. Bibl.*

	Date	D. W[ildung] in *Lexikon der Ägyptologie* (ed. W. Helck and W. Westendorf), ii. 1258–63	*Pages*
Ptolemaic Period			
Esisut (Pedubaste)	Ptolemy II Philadelphus	85/86/87	743, 743, 747
Zeḥo	Ptolemy III Euergetes I	89	748
Ḥaremakhet	probably Ptolemy V Epiphanes	90	718, 749
ʿAnemḥo	probably Ptolemy V Epiphanes	88	718, 747, 748
Pedubaste	Cleopatra VII Philopator	92	743
Pashenptaḥ	Cleopatra VII Philopator	93	743, 744, 744, 744
Pedubaste (Imḥōtep)	Cleopatra VII Philopator	95	744

G. OLD KINGDOM AND FIRST INTERMEDIATE PERIOD TITLES

The list includes several epithets, and also titles quoted in *Top. Bibl.* iii², Part 1

I. Occurrences

See Section II for hieroglyphic forms

1. Abdominal physician, 564.
2. Administrator of the Treasury, 295.
3. Adorer of Ḥarzedef, 192.
4. Adorner of Horus, 451.
5. Assistant of Duau, 239, 258, 404, 426, 768.
6. Assistant leather-worker, 117.
7. Assistant royal scribe, 824.
8. ꜣṯw-official, 100, 103.

   Attendant of the Great House, *see* Keeper of the legs of the Great House.
9. Barber, 350, 769.
10. Belonging to the foremost seat, 157, 190, 236.
11. Boat-builder, 728.
12. Book-keeper of the Great House, 298.
13. Book-keeper of the *mert*(?), 604.
14. Book-keeper of the royal documents, 306.
15. Boundary official, 117, 293, 632.
16. Boundary official of Dep, 125, 265, 281, 344.
17. Boundary official of a frontier-district, 143, 222, 721, 894.
18. Boundary official of a settlement, 68.
19. Boundary official of (the district) 'Star of Horus Foremost of Heaven', 133, 723.
20. Boundary official (ʿḏ) of the northern settlement, 693.
21. Brewer, 48.
22. 'Brother of the endowment', 82, 640.
23. 'Brother of the endowment' of Ptaḥḥotp [II], 606.
24. Butcher of the Great House, 641.
25. Butcher of the slaughterhouse, 465, 502.
26. Butcher of the slaughterhouse of the Great House, 253. *See also Title* 352.
27. Carpenter of the Great Dockyard, 143.
28. Carpenter of Nekhen, 633.
29. Carpenter of the Royal House, 110.
30. Chief of *bat*, 141, 223, 227, 263.
31. Chief of the estate, 538, 567, 569, 671, 673, 675, 677, 677, 679, 680, 681, 681, 681, 681, 682, 682, 682, 683, 683, 683, 684, 684, 685, 892.
32. Chief of the estate 'Mansion of Khufu', 50, 50.
33. Chief of the estate of Meresʿankh, 502.
34. Chief of an estate of the Pyramid of Khephren, 292.
35. Chief of an estate of the Pyramid of Pepy I, 609, 609, 610.
36. Chief of an estate of the Pyramid of Pepy II, 609.
37. Chief of a funerary estate of Snefru in the Letopolite nome, 493.
38. Chief of the Great Estate, 405, 451, 493, 637.
39. Chief Justice and Vizier, *see* Appendix E.
40. Chief of the King, 260.
41. Chief lector-priest, 31, 74, 133, 187, 241, 427, 459, 487, 568, 736.
42. Chief lector-priest of his father, 234, 243.
43. Companion, 120, 155, 403, 403, 683.

129. Great overlord of the Thinite nome, 685, 691.
130. Great *waʿb*-priest, 545, 563.
131. Greatest of the *best*, 257, 258.
132. Greatest of the craftsmen of the King, 211.
133. Greatest of the dentists, 563.
134. Greatest of the Directors of craftsmen, 499, 698, 698.
135. Greatest of the Directors of craftsmen on the day of the festival, 461, 463.
136. Greatest of the Directors of craftsmen in the Two Houses, 460, 464.
137. Greatest of the Directors of craftsmen in the Two Houses on the day of the festival, 460, 463, 464.
138. Greatest of the Five, 678, 684.
139. [*cancelled*]
140. Greatest of leather-craftsmen, 738.
141. Greatest of physicians and dentists, 437.
142. Greatest of the physicians of the Great House, 482.
143. Greatest of the physicians of Lower Egypt, 451.
144. Greatest of the physicians of Upper and Lower Egypt, 634.
145. Greatest of the seers, 394, 403, 509.
146. Greatest of the seers in On, 71.
147. Greatest of the Ten of the Great Court, 253.
148. Greatest of the Ten of the Mansion of Life, 253.
149. Greatest of the Ten of Upper Egypt, 4, 48, 49, 59, 79, 84, 96, 124, 149, 158, 161, 190, 202, 241, 241, 248, 248, 252, 437, 693, 722.

150. Hairdresser of the Great House, 62, 253.
151. He who has command over Selkis, 137.
152. [*cancelled*]
153. *heka*-priest of Meḥyt, 57.
154. Herdsman of Apis, 183, 205, 216.
155. Hersdman of *rekhyt*, 5, 228.
156. Herdsman of Thentet-cattle, 261.
157. Herdsman of the White Bull, 77, 159, 344.
158. Hereditary prince, 155, 183, 187, 203, 203, 205, 228, 230, 239, 241, 274, 403, 427, 548, 645, 681, 683, 849.
159. Honoured by Ḥarzedef, 143.
160. Honoured by Iny (Neuserrēʿ), 345.
160A. Honoured by Kagemni, 546.
161. Honoured by the Lord of Panopolis, 687.
162. Honoured by Merenrēʿ I, 694.
162A. Honoured by Meri, 569.

163. *ỉmy-ḫnt*, 307.
164. Inspector, 246, 758.
165. Inspector of administrators, 61.
166. Inspector of administrators of the granary, 69.
167. Inspector of administrators of the Treasury, 131, 191, 207, 207.
168. [*cancelled*]
169. Inspector of boat(s), 58, 299, 448, 768, 895.
170. Inspector of book-keepers, 216.
171. Inspector of builders, 54, 54, 80, 121, 178, 296.
172. Inspector of carpenters of the Royal House, 114.
173. Inspector of cooling of the Great House, 262.
174. Inspector of corn-measurers of the estates, 115.
175. Inspector of craftsmen, 108, 113, 116, 213, 281.
176. Inspector of craftsmen of the *waʿbt*, 54, 287, 611.
177. Inspector of dancers, 571.
178. Inspector of embalmers, 87, 565.
179. Inspector of an estate of Neferkarēʿ, 738.
180. Inspector of the Great House, 115, 145, 193 (*in error, see title* 44), 548, 570, 760.
181. Inspector of hairdressers of the Great House, 447, 722.
182. Inspector of *ka*-servants, 65, 83, 110, 112, 121, 139, 151, 161, 164, 177, 209, 228, 261, 261, 267, 271, 272, 275, 278, 544, 629, 678, 727, 727.
183. Inspector of King's adorners of the Great House, 582.
184. Inspector of King's hairdressers, 217, 306, 466, 540, 575, 586.
185. [*cancelled*]
186. Inspector of magazines(?), 447.
187. Inspector of manicurists of the Great House, 213, 571 (*as* hairdressers *in error*).
188. Inspector of masters of the largesse, 214.
189. Inspector of metal-workers of the *waʿbt*, 63.
190. Inspector of the most select of those who are in attendance (...), 448, 734.
191. Inspector of Nubians, 247.
192. Inspector of officials (*śrw*), 308, 310, 458, 548.
193. Inspector of oils of King's adorners, 823, 827.
194. Inspector of oils of King's adorners of the Great House, 451.
195. Inspector of physicians, 288, 619, 736.
196. Inspector of physicians of the Great House, 137, 209, 223, 288.
197. Inspector of prophets, 116, 131, 144, 306, 545, 678, 686.
198. Inspector of prophets of Ḥatḥor, 109, 214, 238. *See also Title* 201.
199. Inspector of prophets of Ḥatḥor of the *mert*-temple, 633.
200. Inspector of prophets of Ḥatḥor of the *mert*-temple of Unis, 483.
201. Inspector of prophets of Ḥatḥor in the Sun-temple of Neferirkarēʿ, 582.
202. Inspector of prophets of her (i.e. of Wezebten's) funerary estate, 432.
203. Inspector of prophets of Horus in the chapel (*snwt*), 608.
204. Inspector of prophets of the *ka*-temple of Pepy I, 609.
205. Inspector of prophets of the King's mother, 260.
206. Inspector of prophets of Menkaurēʿ, 261.
207. Inspector of prophets of the *mert*-temple of Pepy I, 689.

279. Judge and Keeper of Nekhen who judges rightly, 246.
280. Judge and Master of the largesse, 405, 451, 692, 769.
281. Judge and Overseer of scribes, 84, 111, 138, 158, 160, 163, 167, 179, 222, 222, 238, 293, 456, 480, 481, 482 (of the book), 490, 583, 606, 606, 637, 699, 736, 898.
282. Judge and Overseer of scribes of the herds, 544 (*perhaps thus*).
283. Judge and Overseer of scribes of the secret judgement of the Great Court, 160.
284. Judge and Real keeper of Nekhen, 769.
285. Judge and Royal scribe, 54.
286. Judge and Scribe, 97, 202, 493, 568, 593, 692, 723.
287. Judge and Scribe of the crews, 135.
288. Judge and Scribe of petitions, 570.
289. Judge in the Six Great Courts, 673.
290. Judge and Strong-of-voice, 52.
291. Judge and Strong-of-voice of the granary, 62.
292. Judge and Supervisor of police, 308, 722.

293. *ka*-servant, *passim*.
294. *ka*-servant of the endowment of Sole companion Raʿwēr, 271.
295. *ka*-servant of the endowment of Werirni, 478.
296. *ka*-servant of the King's mother, 284.
297. *ka*-servant of (Senezemib) Meḥi, 92.
298. *ka*-servant of Ptaḥḥotp [I], 608.
299. Keeper of the diadem, 208, 217, 253, 274, 277, 306.
300. Keeper of the diadem in the place of the King(?), 243.
301. Keeper of the dining-room(?) of the royal repast of the Great House, 739.
302. Keeper of the dockyard, 220.
303. Keeper of the gate, 761.
304. Keeper of the legs (*better*: Attendant) of the Great House, 192.
305. Keeper of the linen (*śšrw*) of the Royal House, 306.
306. Keeper of the magazine, 610.
307. Keeper of the magazine of gold, 178.
308. Keeper of Nekhen, 191.
309. Keeper of oils of the Great House, 133.
310. Keeper of the whole Pe, 216.
311. Keeper of the writing material of the King, 739.
312. *khet*-priest of Ḥa, 339.
313. *khet*-priest of Thentet-cattle, 134.
314. *khet*-priest of Wēr, 134.
315. *khet*-priestess of Horus, 179 note 1.
316. King's adorner, 72, 96, 99, 274, 286, 299, 485, 671, 678, 678, 690, 727, 769, 893.
317. King's adorner and Keeper of gold, 247.
318. King's adorner and Keeper of unguents, 99.
319. King's architect and builder, 542, 542, 543.
320. King's architect and builder in the Two Houses, 85, 87, 89–90.
321. King's daughter, 59, 72, 139, 139, 153, 277, 281, 340, 343, 403, 407, 431 note 1, 432 note 1, 482, 496, 545, 895.
322. King's daughter of his body, 3, 3, 52, 71, 87, 124, 134, 136, 139, 191, 194, 197, 200, 216, 230, 233, 249, 256, 396 note 1, 515, 518, 521, 606, 617, 619, 723, 878.
323. King's eldest daughter, 464.
324. King's eldest daughter of his body, 243, 273, 508, 525, 614.
325. King's eldest son, 3, 230, 679, 683, 684, 684.
326. King's eldest son of his body, 3, 3, 26, 187, 214, 232, 233, 237, 246, 274, 293, 487, 536, 627, 675, 893.
327. King's hairdresser, 265.
328. King's mother, 273, 396 note 1, 577, 676.
329. King's [secretary] of all secret commands of the frontier-posts, 519.
330. King's sole adorner, 271, 282, 301, 492, 496, 511, 539, 544, 545, 563, 564, 568, 568, 568, 610, 610, 674, 674, 674, 676, 676, 677, 681, 681, 686, 686, 687, 688, 688, 741.
331. King's son, 10, 57, 59, 124, 183, 194, 201, 202, 219, 234, 239, 241, 241, 403, 403, 489, 489, 616, 630, 645, 879, 892, 894.
332. King's son of his body, 5, 31, 71, 74, 78, 99, 122, 125, 149, 153, 188, 191, 195, 200, 203, 203, 204, 211, 230, 234, 277, 548, 577, 585, 864, 878, 890, 893.
333. King's *waʿb*-priest, *passim*.
334. King's *waʿb*-priest of the Great House, 70, 259, 449.
335. King's *waʿb*-priest of the *mert* of Userkaf, 581.
336. King's *waʿb*-priest of the Palace (*ḏbꜣt*), 238.
337. King's *waʿb*-priest of the Pyramid of Khufu, 50, 211.
338. King's wife, 194, 233, 249, 256, 273, 396 note 1, 397 note 1, 431 note 1, 432 note 1, 432 note 2, 479, 482, 488, 624, 676.

339. Leader of the land of the Aphroditopolite nome, 143.
340. Leader of the land of the Oryx-nome, 405.
341. Leader of the land of the Thinite nome, 143.
342. Leather-worker, 311.
343. Lector-priest, *passim*.
344. Lector-priest of the *ḏꜣt*-bark of Horus, 519, 630.
345. Lector-priest of the endowment, 736.
346. Lector-priest of his father, 31.
347. Lector-priest of the *mit*-bark of Horus, 519, 630.
348. Lector-priest of Neferirkarēʿ, 161.
349. Lector-priest of Saḥurēʿ, 161.

350. Magician of Selkis of the Great House, 272.
351. Manicurist, 271, 350.
352. Master butcher of the Great House, 614, 639, 644. *See also Title* 26.
353. Master of the Great House, 238.
354. Master of the house of the Great House, 137, 165, 178.

355. Master of the house of tenants of the Great House, 287.
356. Master of the largesse in the Mansion of Life, 135, 235, 254, 281, 307, 478.
357. Master of the largesse in the Mansion of Life of Seshet, 452.
358. Master of the largesse of *rekhyt*, 214, 215.
359. Master of the Palace (*ḏbꜣt*), 68.
360. Master of the royal largesse, 219.
361. Master of wood, 279.
362. Metal-worker of the Great House, 506, 608.
363. Metal-worker in the Two Houses, 452.
364. *mḥnk* of the King, 461, 499, 611, 768.
365. Mistress of the house, 54.
366. *mitrt*, 12, 50, 62, 63, 64, 72, 82, 97, 97, 99, 99, 100, 100, 103, 103, 104, 114, 117, 119, 120, 121, 129, 176, 178, 203, 207, 212, 217, 218, 220, 286, 302, 307, 490, 502, 506, 586, 652, 692, 735, 738, 740, 895.
367. Mother of the King of Upper and Lower Egypt, 179 note 1.
368. Mother of the two Kings of Upper and Lower Egypt, 288 note 1.
369. Mourner (*ḏrt*), 349.

370. Noble of the King, 60, 167, 167, 168, 192, 520, 546, 546, 547, 547, 548, 548, 569, 608, 622, 623, 625, 646, 652, 747, 770.
371. Noble of the King of the Great House, 625.
372. Noblewoman of the King, 539, 681, 683, 688, 688, 723, 774, 898.

373. Official (*śr*) of the Acacia-house, 507.
374. Official (*iry-ḫt*) of the Chamber of unguents of King's adorners, 458.
375. One belonging to the endowment of Niʿankh-khnum and Khnemḥotp, 644.
376. One belonging to the estate 'Mansion of Ḥar-kheper (Raʿzedef)', 142.
377. One belonging to the Great Estate, 121, 121.
378. One who is in the magistracy, 748.
379. One who sets right the judgement, 686.
380. One who sets right the judgement of the Great Court, 248, 306, 308.
381. Overlord of linen (*ḏꜣt*), 678.
382. Overlord of linen (*śśrw*), 106.
383. Overlord of Nekheb, 183, 235, 272, 585, 694, 723.
384. Overseer of all craftsmen, 465.
385. Overseer of all his (Raʿwēr's) properties in and outside the endowment, 269.
386. Overseer of all trees of Memphis, 761.
387. Overseer of all works, 243.
388. Overseer of all works of the King, 48, 89, 137, 146, 149, 155, 161, 163, 212, 234, 242, 344, 452, 481, 485, 489, 500, 502, 586.
389. Overseer (*mḏḥ*) of Anubis foremost of the Sacred Land, 449.
390. Overseer of barbers, 84, 116.
391. Overseer of beef fat, 641, 644.
392. Overseer of bleachers of linen, 735.
393. Overseer of boat-nets, 98.
394. Overseer of the Broad Hall, 241.
395. Overseer of builders, 54, 203.
396. Overseer of butchers of the slaughterhouses of the Great House, 690.
397. Overseer of butlers, 255.
398. Overseer of carpenters, 63.
399. Overseer of carpenters of the *is*-chamber of the Royal House, 72.
400. Overseer of cattle of the Ibis-nome, 7.
401. Overseer of cattle-stalls, 276.
402. Overseer of the chamber of dancers, 895.
403. Overseer of commands (of the King), 262.
404. Overseer of commissions, 57, 77, 94, 159, 165, 308, 563, 596, 898.
405. Overseer of commissions in the whole country, 159.
406. Overseer of commissions of cedar, 158.
407. Overseer of commissions of the Great House, 75, 162, 247.
408. Overseer of commissions of the Pyramid of Isesi, 424.
409. Overseer of commissions of the Pyramid of Neuserrēʿ, 315.
410. Overseer of co mmissions of the Pyramid of Pepy I, 753.
411. Overseer of commissions of the Pyramid of Unis, 748.
412. Overseer of commissions of the Sun-temple of Neuserrēʿ, 315.
413. Overseer of commissions of tenants of the Great House, 109, 153.
414. Overseer of commissions of tenants of the Pyramid of Isesi, 424.
415. Overseer of commissions of tenants of the Pyramid of Pepy I, 546, 630.
416. Overseer of commissions of tenants of the Pyramid of Teti, 520.
417. Overseer of corn-measurers, 62, 120.
418. Overseer of craftsmen, 108, 117, 140, 192, 689, 762, 768.
419. Overseer of craftsmen of the Great House, 138.
420. Overseer of craftsmen of the *waʿbt*, 273, 453.
421. Overseer of the crew of rowers, 114.
422. Overseer of dancers of the King, 282.
423. Overseer of dates, 309.
424. Overseer of dentists, 295 (*as* physicians).
425. Overseer of the department, 116, 176, 260.
426. Overseer of the department of the Great House, 104, 287, 652, 680, 686.
427. Overseer of the department of tenants, 545.
428. Overseer of the department of tenants of the Great House, 53, 56, 80, 109, 126, 134, 148, 152, 160, 164, 269, 284, 286, 518, 547, 570, 614, 646, 698, 892.
429. Overseer of the desert(s), 238, 729.
430. Overseer of directors, 741.
431. Overseer of the dockyard, 99.
432. Overseer of draughts-players of the crews, 100.
433. Overseer of the duck-pond, 450, 478.
434. Overseer of entertainment, 145.
435. Overseer of the expedition, 58, 137, 148, 204, 238, 240, 246, 262, 482, 489, 489, 492, 544, 544, 562, 564, 565, 569, 570, 611, 681, 685, 890.

436. Overseer of faience-workers, 652.
437. Overseer of Farâfra Oasis, 721.
438. Overseer of female dancers, 61.
439. Overseer of female singers, 450.
440. Overseer of female weavers, 120.
441. Overseer of the fields, 450.
442. Overseer of the five of the boat, 214.
443. Overseer of the five . . . of the Great House, 898.
444. Overseer of flutists, 129.
445. Overseer of the four of the boat, 214.
446. Overseer of fringed cloth (*sꜣt*) of the King, 488.
447. Overseer of the gangs, 272.
448. Overseer of the gates in the Two Houses, 222.
449. Overseer of gold of the magazines in the Two Houses, 586.
450. Overseer of gold-workers, 645.
451. Overseer of gold-workers of King's adorners, 456.
452. Overseer of the granary, 262, 491, 610, 691, 696.
453. Overseer of the Great Court, 159, 586, 633.
454. Overseer of the Great Estate, 51, 109, 698.
455. Overseer of the *gś-pr*, 301, 622, 675, 681, 682, 682, 682, 684.
456. Overseer of the *gś-pr* of the Necropolis, 212.
457. Overseer of the *gś-pr* of tomb-makers, 50.
458. Overseer of 'Hair of the Earth', 517, 569.
459. Overseer of hairdressers of the Great House, 453, 637, 698.
460. Overseer of herds, 211.
461. Overseer of the House of Cedar, 165.
462. Overseer of the House of Weapons, 72, 87.
463. Overseer of the House of weaving women, 65, 109.
464. Overseer of the House of weaving women of the Residence, 269 (*translated differently*), 465.
465. Overseer of the House of *weḥaꜥ*-boats, 264.
466. Overseer of the houses of the King's children, 50, 135.
467. Overseer of hunters, 292.
468. Overseer of interpreters, 311, 892.
469. Overseer of the *is*-chamber, 118.
470. Overseer of the *is*-chamber of hairdressing, 727.
471. Overseer of the *is*-chamber of the *waꜥbt*, 116.
472. Overseer of judgement, 506.
473. Overseer of the jury, 723.
474. Overseer of the jury of the Pyramid of Menkaurēꜥ, 294.
475. Overseer of *ka*-servants, 62, 75, 82, 105, 106, 108, 121, 135, 137, 202, 204, 210, 213, 244, 245, 251, 271, 271, 280, 285, 285, 286, 470, 506, 690.
476. Overseer of *ka*-servants of the endowment of Kanenesut, 144.
477. Overseer of *ka*-servants of the endowment (of Rekhetrēꜥ), 250.
478. Overseer of *ka*-servants of the King's mother, 210, 284, 284.
479. Overseer of *ka*-servants of the King's wife (probably Rekhetrēꜥ), 262.
480. Overseer of *ka*-servants of the Pyramid of Raꜥzedef, 7.
481. Overseer of *ka*-servants of Send in the Necropolis, 490.
482. Overseer of the King in all his departments, 96.
483. Overseer of King's adorners, 586.
484. Overseer of King's adorners of the Great House, 691.
485. Overseer of King's ḥarîm, 152 (*translated differently*), 453.
486. Overseer of the King's house, 545.
487. Overseer of the King's *waꜥbt*, 64, 736.
488. Overseer of ladies of the ḥarîm, 450.
489. Overseer of the ladies of the ḥarîm of the King, 282.
490. Overseer of leather-workers, 570, 758.
491. Overseer of the Letopolite nome, 166, 179, 201.
492. Overseer of linen (*śšrw*), 127, 275, 278, 488, 511, 548, 678, 678, 682, 687, 722, 736.
493. Overseer of linen (*śšrw*) of the endowment, 265.
494. Overseer of linen (*śšrw*) of the Pyramid of Khephren, 295.
495. Overseer of linen (*śšrw*) of the Pyramid of Khufu, 295.
496. Overseer of manicurists of the Great House, 242, 453, 455, 641.
497. Overseer of the marsh-lands, 478.
498. Overseer of the Memphite nome, 166, 179, 201.
499. Overseer of metal-workers, 645, 767.
500. Overseer of metal-workers of the Great House, 609, 611.
501. Overseer of miners, 736.
502. Overseer of the *nehet*-sanctuary of the *mert* of Ḥatḥor, 578.
503. Overseer of the new settlements, 55.
504. Overseer of the new settlements of the Pyramid of Isesi, 166, 201.
505. Overseer of the nomes of Lower Egypt, 609.
506. Overseer of the Nubian troops, 439.
507. Overseer of officials (*śrw*), 246, 262, 307, 613, 722.
508. Overseer of oils of the King's adorners, 577.
509. Overseer of oils in the Two Houses, 826.
510. Overseer of the Palace (*ꜥḥ*), 242, 598, 741.
511. Overseer of the Palace (*ḏbꜣt*), 768.
512. Overseer of Per-nu of the Great House, 262.
513. Overseer of the phylai of Upper Egypt, 59, 124, 158, 894, 895.
514. Overseer of physicians, 284. *See also title* 424.
515. Overseer of prophets of Ḥatḥor Mistress of Nidua-snefru, 678.
516. Overseer of prophets of Onuris, 691.
517. Overseer of prophets of the Pyramid of Userkaf, 769.
518. Overseer of the Pyramid of Khephren, 241, 248, 248, 249, 302.
519. Overseer of the Pyramid of Khufu, 58.

520. Overseer of the Pyramid of Menkaurēʿ, 298.
521. Overseer of the Pyramid of Neferirkarēʿ, 468.
522. Overseer of the Pyramid of Neuserrēʿ, 468.
523. Overseer of the 'Pyramid' of Shepseskaf, 213.
524. Overseer of the Pyramid of Snefru, 893.
525. Overseer of the Pyramid-town of Kakai (Neferirkarēʿ), 344.
526. Overseer of the Pyramid-town of Khephren, 257.
527. Overseer of the Pyramid-town of Khufu, 48, 64, 66, 68, 184, 306.
528. Overseer of the Pyramid-town of Menkauḥor, 599.
529. Overseer of the Pyramid-town of Menkaurēʿ, 184.
530. Overseer of the Pyramid-town of Neuserrēʿ, 599.
531. Overseer of the Pyramid-town of Teti, 521.
532. Overseer of the Pyramid-town of Zadkarēʿ (Isesi), 599.
533. Overseer of the Residence (*ẖnw*), 277.
534. Overseer of the Road of Horus, 238.
535. Overseer of the royal commissions of the Pyramid of Pepy I, 90.
536. Overseer of royal fortresses, 729.
537. Overseer of the royal granary/ies, 137, 449.
538. Overseer (*mḏḥ*) of the royal scribes, 84, 437.
539. Overseer of the royal sealed documents of the Great House, 213.
540. Overseer of the royal sealed documents of the land, 213.
541. Overseer of the royal sealed documents of the *meret*, 213.
542. Overseer of the sail(?), 548.
543. Overseer of scribes, 157, 160, 163, 251, 307, 565, 596, 652.
544. Overseer of scribes of the crews, 72, 96, 211, 211, 457, 592, 611, 735.
545. [*cancelled*]
546. Overseer of scribes of the Great Court, 606.
547. Overseer of scribes of the land, 236, 241, 451, 760.
548. Overseer of scribes of the land of the Sebennite nome, 768.
549. Overseer of scribes of the land of [hieroglyph] nome, 443.
550. Overseer of scribes of the land in the Two Houses, 450, 465, 608.
551. Overseer of the scribes of the land in the Two Houses of Upper and Lower Egypt, 451.
552. Overseer of scribes of the *meret*, 185.
553. Overseer of scribes of the Pyramid of Khufu, 64, 284.
554. Overseer of scribes of the royal documents, 146, 163, 456, 501, 686.
555. Overseer of scribes of the royal documents of all works of the King, 484.
556. Overseer of scribes of the royal sealed documents, 241.
557. Overseer of scribes of the sealed documents, 566.
558. Overseer of scribes of the Two Granaries, 823.
559. Overseer of sculptors, 52, 451, 601, 690.
560. Overseer (*mḏḥ*) of sculptors, 403, 404, 437, 437.
561. Overseer (*mḏḥ*) of sculptors in the Two Houses, 499.
562. Overseer of the seal(?), 517.
563. Overseer of singers of the Great House, 129, 468, 468.
564. Overseer of singing in the Great House, 174, 282.
565. Overseer of the six of the boat, 448, 768.
566. Overseer of smelters of gold, 546.
567. Overseer of smelters of gold of King's adorners, 754.
568. Overseer of the southern Pyramid of Snefru, 894.
569. Overseer of the store-room, 68 (*translated differently*), 120, 140, 177, 308, 351, 433, 544, 548, 735, 736, 769.
570. Overseer of the store-room of the King's repast, 214, 280, 295, 447.
571. Overseer of the store-room of the Sun-temple of Userkaf, 303.
572. Overseer of strongholds of the Heliopolitan-East nome, 143.
573. Overseer of the Sun-temple of Neferirkarēʿ, 468.
574. Overseer of the Sun-temple of Neuserrēʿ, 468.
575. Overseer of the Sun-temple of Raʿneferef, 468.
576. Overseer of the Sun-temple of Saḥurēʿ, 468.
577. Overseer of the *ṯꜣw* of the Great Bark, 116.
578. Overseer of the ten, 54, 148, 177, 736.
579. Overseer of the ten of the boat, 96, 104, 214, 448.
580. Overseer of the ten craftsmen, 611.
581. Overseer of the ten craftsmen of the *waʿbt*, 54.
582. Overseer of the ten of the Great Bark, 736.
583. Overseer of the ten of the Great Estate, 112.
584. Overseer of the ten of the Great House, 152.
585. Overseer of tenants, 622, 742.
586. Overseer of tenants of the Great House, 60, 94, 120, 261, 545, 604, 622, 673, 675, 679, 679, 680, 687, 687, 694, 699, 774.
587. Overseer of tenants of the Pyramid of Pepy I, 678.
588. Overseer of tenants of the Pyramid of Teti, 567.
589. Overseer of tomb-makers, 116.
590. Overseer of the Treasury, 54, 64, 96, 98, 259, 466, 478, 494, 501, 736, 739.
591. Overseer of the Treasury of Khufu, 760.
592. Overseer of the Treasury of Raʿzedef, 760.
593. Overseer of the Treasury of the Residence, 455.
594. Overseer of the Treasury of Snefru, 760.
595. Overseer of the treasury of the two boat-crews, 276.

596. Overseer of Ṭura quarries, 586.
597. Overseer of tutors of the King's children of his body, 240.
598. Overseer of the Two Canals of the Great House, 698.
599. Overseer of the Two Cool Chambers of the Great House, 678, 680, 680, 681.
600. Overseer of the Two Granaries, 454, 506, 511, 537, 565, 651.
601. Overseer of the Two Houses of Gold, 257, 258, 452.
602. Overseer of the Two Houses of Weapons, 126.
603. Overseer of the two *is*-chambers of the King's adorners of the Great House, 577.
604. Overseer of the two Pyramids of Snefru, 894.
605. Overseer of the Two Treasuries, 137, 205, 212, 257, 258, 506, 604, 684.
606. Overseer of Upper Egypt, 428, 494, 519, 537, 616, 675, 678.
607. [*cancelled*]
608. Overseer of *waʿb*-priests of Peribsen in the Necropolis, 490.
609. Overseer of the *waʿbt*, 54, 138, 611.
610. [*cancelled*]
611. Overseer of washermen, 97, 116.
612. Overseer of weavers of the Great House, 100.
613. Overseer of works, 91, 205, 451.
614. Overseer of works of the King, 138, 202, 693, 697.
615. Overseer of young men, 465.
616. Overseer of the young men in the endowment of Companion Raʿwēr, 269.

617. Painter, 231, 282.
618. Physician, 282, 601.
619. Physician of the Great House, 228, 258, 540.
620. Policeman, 60.
621. Prophet, 153, 276, 724, 829.
622. Prophet of Anubis, 253.
623. Prophet of Anubis foremost-of-Sepa, 223.
624. Prophet of Bubastis, 453.
625. Prophet of Buto, 274, 638.
626. Prophet of Buto in Pe and Dep, 265.
627. Prophet of Duamutf, 122.
628. Prophet of Duau, 288.
629. Prophet of Ḥatḥor, 149, 212, 464.
630. Prophet of Ḥatḥor foremost of the Pyramid of Userkaf, 578.
631. Prophet of Ḥatḥor Mistress of Dendera, 633.
632. Prophet of Ḥatḥor in the Sun-temple of Neferirkarēʿ, 174, 453, 498, 577, 584, 596, 693, 697, 699, 723.
633. Prophet of Ḥatḥor in the Sun-temple of Userkaf, 723.
634. Prophet of Ḥeka, 223, 451, 634.
635. Prophet of Ḥeḳet, 57, 142, 339, 502, 633, 762.
636. Prophet of Horus *ḳmꜣ-ʿ*, 127, 443, 450.
637. Prophet of Horus *mḏdw* (Khufu), 76, 137, 140, 140, 153, 168, 178.
638. Prophet of Horus of Mesen, 579.
639. Prophet of Horus and Sēth foremost of the divine monument, 736.
640. Prophet of Horus of Shenwet(?), 223, 451.
641. Prophet of Horus *wśr-ib* (Khephren), 244.
642. Prophet of *ḥrwy-nb* (Golden Horus name of Khufu), 140, 178.
643. Prophet of Khephren, 7, 98, 213, 241, 241, 244, 247, 248, 253, 258, 272, 308, 467.
644. Prophet of Khnem-khufu, 97, 271.
645. Prophet of Khnum, 453.
646. Prophet of Khnum in all his places, 634.
647. Prophet of Khnum foremost of Ḥer-wēr in all his places, 482.
648. Prophet of Khufu, 53, 56, 58, 58, 64, 64, 70, 76, 79, 98, 101, 105, 109, 110, 116, 117, 118, 126, 137, 140, 140, 141, 152, 153, 155, 168, 169, 170, 178, 200, 210, 220, 273, 278, 482, 483, 693, 756, 824.
649. Prophet of Khufu foremost-of-the-*akhet*-Pyramid, 50.
650. Prophet of the King's mother, 111, 257.
651. Prophet of Maʿet, 79, 94, 162, 221, 236, 252, 280, 293, 632, 722.
652. Prophet of *mḏd-r-nbty* (*nebty*-name of Khufu), 76, 137, 140, 152, 177.
653. Prophet of Menkaurēʿ, 82, 213, 253, 254, 261, 272, 279, 287, 294, 298, 306, 483.
654. Prophet of Mert of Upper Egypt, 639.
655. Prophet of the *mert*-temple of Menkauḥor, 611.
656. Prophet of Min Lord of Panopolis, 567.
657. Prophet of *nbty-wśr-m* (*nebty*-name of Khephren), 244.
658. Prophet of Nebka, 500.
659. Prophet of Neferirkarēʿ, 169, 174, 453, 463, 596, 760.
660. Prophet of Neith, 405.
661. Prophet of Nekhbet, 274, 577.
662. Prophet of Neuserrēʿ, 106, 106, 169, 174, 245, 453, 596.
663. Prophet of Osiris, 254.
664. Prophet of Ptaḥ, 273, 453, 499, 689, 753, 762, 768.
665. Prophet of the Pyramid of Isesi, 260, 455, 633. *See also title* 676.
666. Prophet of the Pyramid of Khephren, 292.
667. Prophet of the Pyramid of Menkauḥor, 55, 191, 585, 595.
668. Prophet of the Pyramid of Merenrēʿ I, 609.
669. Prophet of the Pyramid of Neferirkarēʿ, 447, 584.
670. Prophet of the Pyramid of Neuserrēʿ, 55, 463, 481, 485, 584, 595, 722.
671. Prophet of the Pyramid of Pepy I, 519.
672. Prophet of the Pyramid of Raʿneferef, 584.
673. Prophet of the Pyramid of Saḥurēʿ, 52.
674. Prophet of the Pyramid of Teti, 520, 559, 608.
675. Prophet of the Pyramid of Unis, 460, 608, 622, 626, 627, 633.
676. Prophet of the Pyramid of Zadkarēʿ (Isesi), 595, 693, 697. *See also title* 665.
677. Prophet of Raʿneferef, 453, 581.

740. Rower of the bark, 295.
741. Royal acquaintance, *passim.*
742. Royal acquaintance of the Great House, 129, 638, 759, 768.
743. Royal chamberlain, 5, 66, 142, 154, 167, 218, 228, 244, 249, 255, 263, 280, 280, 345, 402, 440, 496, 517, 539, 579, 586, 595, 596, 605, 605, 622, 633, 633, 653, 671, 677, 677, 677, 681, 742, 756, 762.
744. Royal chamberlain of the Great House, 66, 155, 165, 239, 521, 547.
745. [*cancelled*]
746. Royal scribe, 76, (97 *to be deleted*), 503.

747. Scribe, 20, 54, 97 (*as* Royal scribe *in error*), 103, 121, 145, 292, 439, 517, 544, 546, 567, 723, 724, 727.
748. Scribe of the archives, 114, 170, 503, 768.
749. Scribe of a boat's side, 694, 742.
750. Scribe of the crews, 275.
751. Scribe of divine books/writing, 133, 141, 282, 403, 563, 736, 824.
752. Scribe of the divine treasure in the Temple of Ptaḥ, 746.
753. Scribe of the documents, 405.
754. Scribe of enrolment of the crew of the boat, 611. *See also Title* 778.
755. Scribe of the expedition, 251, 540, 570.
756. Scribe of the four divisions of craftsmen, 281.
757. Scribe of the granary, 129, 176, 272, 296, 458.
758. Scribe of the Great House, 547.
759. Scribe of the house of the master of the largesse, 730.
760. Scribe of the King's expedition in Wenet, Serer, Tepa, and Ida, 501.
761. Scribe of the new settlements of the Great Estate, 51.
762. Scribe of petitions, 264.
763. Scribe of a phyle, 84, 433, 608, 679, 688.
764. Scribe of a phyle of the endowment of Meḥi (probably Senezemib), 129.
765. Scribe of a phyle of the endowment of Senezemib, 163.
766. Scribe of a phyle of the Pyramid of Khufu, 176.
766A. Scribe of the Pyramid of Merykarēʿ, *see* Addenda.
767. Scribe of the Pyramid-town, 567.
768. Scribe of recruits, 114.
769. Scribe of the royal documents, 48, 74, 133, 158, 162, 211, 306, 307, 457, 675, 684, 687, 736, 742.
770. Scribe of the royal documents of the granary, 124, 691.
771. Scribe of the royal documents of the Great House in the presence, 168.
772. Scribe of the royal documents in the presence, 158, 161, 167, 250, 582, 605, 677, 688, 891.
773. Scribe of the royal linen (*ššrw*), 243.
774. Scribe of sacrificial cattle of the slaughter-house of the god, 763.
775. Scribe of the Treasury, 121, 129, 306.
776. Scribe of the treasury of the estate 'Mansion of Menkaurēʿ', 298.
777. Scribe of the treasury of the Pyramid of Merykarēʿ, 562.
778. Scribe of the troop (*ṯst*), 768. *See Title* 754.
779. Scribe of the Two Granaries, 567.
780. Sculptor, 197, 282, 543.
781. Sculptor of the *waʿbt*, 247.
782. Seal-bearer, 442.
783. Sealer of the best provisions of the King of Lower Egypt, 276.
784. Secretary, 64, 77, 110, 137, 143, 178, 209, 307, 878.
785. Secretary of all commands of the King, 228, 579.
786. Secretary of all foreign countries, 565.
787. Secretary of all secret commands of the King, 223.
788. Secretary of all works, 627.
789. Secretary of commissions of the divine offerings, 251.
790. Secretary of craftsmen, 168.
791. Secretary of the estates of Neith, 723.
792. Secretary of every secret judgement of the Great Court, 94.
793. Secretary of the God's treasure, 567, 732.
794. Secretary of his Lord, 79, 94, 152, 190, 286.
795. Secretary of judgement, 68, 115, 222.
796. Secretary of the jury of the Pyramid of Menkaurēʿ, 294.
797. Secretary of the King in all his places, 895.
798. Secretary of the King in all his secrets, 742.
799. Secretary of the King in the Great House, 145.
800. Secretary of the King's repast of the Great House, 350.
801. Secretary of the King's *waʿbt*, 212.
802. Secretary of Neferirkarēʿ, 638.
803. Secretary of the private hearing in the Six Great Courts, 686.
804. Secretary of the Pyramid of Khephren, 302.
805. Secretary of the Pyramid of Menkaurēʿ, 311.
806. Secretary of the royal ḥarîm, 260.
807. Secretary of the secret judgement of the Great Court, 160, 162.
808. Secretary of the Toilet-house, 115, 133, 135, 141, 234, 235, 253, 254, 281, 306, 343, 485, 497, 634, 687, 722, 723, 723, 730, 732.
809. Seer of Horus and Sēth, 136, 273.
810. *sem*-priest, 78, 125, 270, 318, 480.
811. 'Servants of the estate of Shepy', 893.
812. Servant of the Souls of Nekhen, 404.
813. Servant of the throne, 343.
814. Singer of the Great House, 105, 761.
815. 'Sister of the endowment', 485.
816. *sma*-priest of Anubis, 127, 133.
817. *sma*-priest of Horus, 742.
818. Smelter, 768.
819. Sole companion, *passim.*
820. Sole companion of his father, 5, 293.
821. Steward, 62, 65, 92, 108, 114, 129, 154,

155 (of Kawaʿb, Ḥetepḥeres [II], and Meresʿankh [III]), 175, 176, 212, 215, 244, 245, 257, 261, 270 (of Raʿwēr?), 278, 285, 285, 299, 309, 458, 510, 540, 544, 544, 546, 546, 547, 547, 548, 567, 569, 683, 739, 741, 746, 748.
822. Steward of the Great Estate, 169, 170, 205.
823. Steward of the Greatest of the Directors of craftsmen Raʿneferefʿankh, 698.
824. Steward of Shey, 264.
825. Stonemason of the King, 739.
826. Strong-of-voice of the archives, 114.
827. Strong-of-voice of the granary of the residence, 61 (*translated differently*).
828. Supervisor, 99.
829. Supervisor of craftsmen, 461.
830. Supervisor of the dining hall, 344.
831. Supervisor of directors of the expedition, 98.
832. Supervisor of *ka*-servants, 84, 271, 629.
833. Supervisor of *ka*-servants of Khentkaus [I], 344.
834. Supervisor of magazines(?), 447.
835. Supervisor of officials (*śrw*), 310.
836. Supervisor of the police, 56, 98, 203.
837. Supervisor of prophets of the *mert*-temple of Teti, 520.
838. Supervisor of prophets of the Pyramid of Khephren, 250.
839. Supervisor of prophets of the Pyramid of Menkauḥor, 455, 582.
840. Supervisor of prophets of the Pyramid of Merenrēʿ I, 673.
841. Supervisor of prophets of the Pyramid of Neferirkarēʿ, 466.
842. Supervisor of prophets of the Pyramid of Neuserrēʿ, 689.
843. Supervisor of prophets of the Pyramid of Pepy I, 756.
844. Supervisor of prophets of the Pyramid of Raʿneferef, 455.
845. Supervisor of prophets of the Pyramid of Teti, 460, 460.
846. Supervisor of prophets of the Pyramid of Unis, 460, 615.
847. Supervisor of prophets of the Pyramid of Zadkarēʿ (Isesi), 468, 468, 575.
848. Supervisor of prophets of Rēʿ in the Sun-temple of Menkauḥor, 455, 582.
849. Supervisor of prophets of Rēʿ in the Sun-temple of Neferirkarēʿ, 466.
850. Supervisor of prophets of the Sun-temple of Neuserrēʿ, 689.
851. Supervisor of the store-rooms, 736.
852. Supervisor(?) of tenants, 570.
853. Supervisor of tenants of the Great House, 67, 67.
854. Supervisor of the Treasury, 823.
855. Supervisor of the Two Houses, 738.
856. Supervisor . . . of the Pyramid of Khephren, 307.

857. Teacher of the royal singers, 265.
858. Tenant, 67, 67, 67, 67, 67, 67, 77, 82, 93, 108, 120, 129, 130, 140, 163, 178, 298, 736.
859. Tenant of the Great House, 61, 93, 95, 129, 141, 307, 728, 739.
860. Tenant of the Pyramid of Isesi(?), 672.
861. Tenant of the Pyramid of Menkaurēʿ, 311.
862. Tenant of the Pyramid of Merenrēʿ I, 673.
863. Tenant of the Pyramid of Pepy I, 143, 178, 184, 185, 537, 544, 570, 625.
864. Tenant of the Pyramid of Pepy II, 570.
865. Tenant of the Pyramid of Teti, 496, 512, 515, 519, 519, 545, 568.
866. Tenant of the Pyramid of Unis, 625, 626.
867. Tomb-maker, 282, 295.
868. Treasurer of the God, 516, 739.
869. Treasurer of the God in the *ba-neteru*, *baʿ-neteru*, *neb-rekhyt*, and *dua-tawy* boats, 71.
870. Treasurer of the God in the boat, 246, 277, 306.
870A. Treasurer of the God of the Pyramid of Merykarēʿ, *see* Addenda.
871. Treasurer of the God in the two boats, 240, 492, 565.
872. Treasurer of his father the King of Lower Egypt, 246.
873. Treasurer of the King of Lower Egypt, 183, 203, 216, 234, 401, 564, 569, 569, 570, 676, 684, 684, 685, 878.
874. Treasurer of the royal granary, 295.
875. True prophetess of Ḥatḥor, 307.
876. Tutor of the King's sons, 100, 101.

877. Vizier (*no doubt part of* Chief Justice and Vizier), 678.

878. *waʿb*-priest, 93, 177, 758, 769.
879. *waʿb*-priest of the King's mother, 98, 99.
880. *waʿb*-priest of the King's sons, 50.
881. *waʿb*-priest of Neferirkarēʿ, 593 (*thus?*).
882. *waʿb*-priest of the Pyramid of Isesi, 452.
883. *waʿb*-priest of the Pyramid of Khephren, 483.
884. *waʿb*-priest of the Pyramid of Menkauḥor, 468.
885. *waʿb*-priest of the Pyramid of Menkaurēʿ, 483.
886. *waʿb*-priest of the Pyramid of Neuserrēʿ, 282, 467, 541.
887. *waʿb*-priest of the Pyramid of Saḥurēʿ, 467, 483, 541, 580, 582, 735.
888. *waʿb*-priest of the Pyramid of Snefru, 483.
889. *waʿb*-priest of the Pyramid of Userkaf, 449, 483, 894.
890. *waʿb*-priest of Rēʿ, 68 (*rendered differently*).
891. *waʿb*-priest of Rēʿ in the Sun-temple of Saḥurēʿ, 450.
892. *waʿb*-priest of Rēʿ in the Sun-temple of Userkaf, 580.
893. *waʿb*-priest of Saḥurēʿ, 541.
894. *waʿb*-priest of the two hundred, 613, 679.
895. *waʿb*-priest of the two hundred of the Pyramid of Merenrēʿ I, 674.
896. *waʿb*-priest of the two hundred of the Pyramid of Pepy II, 545, 569, 570, 678.
897. Washerman of the God, 52.
898. Workman of the Necropolis, 295.
899. *wrt ḥtś*, 136.

II. Hieroglyphic forms

Only one form given. Numbers refer to Section I

Summary:

A. Ranks and court
B. Filiation and relationship
C. Officials of treasuries
D. Granaries, farming, and husbandry
E. Endowments and estates
F. Tenants
G. Crafts, trades, and professions
H. Physicians
I. Army, expeditions, and police
K. Boats, barks, and dockyards
L. Barbers, hairdressers, and manicurists
M. Attendants, etc.
N. Entertainment
O. Scribes
P. Judiciary
Q. Various officials
R. Priests and temples
S. Necropolis
T. Pyramids and pyramid-towns
U. Sun-temples
V. Buildings
W. Kings
X. Gods
Y. People
Z. Geographical

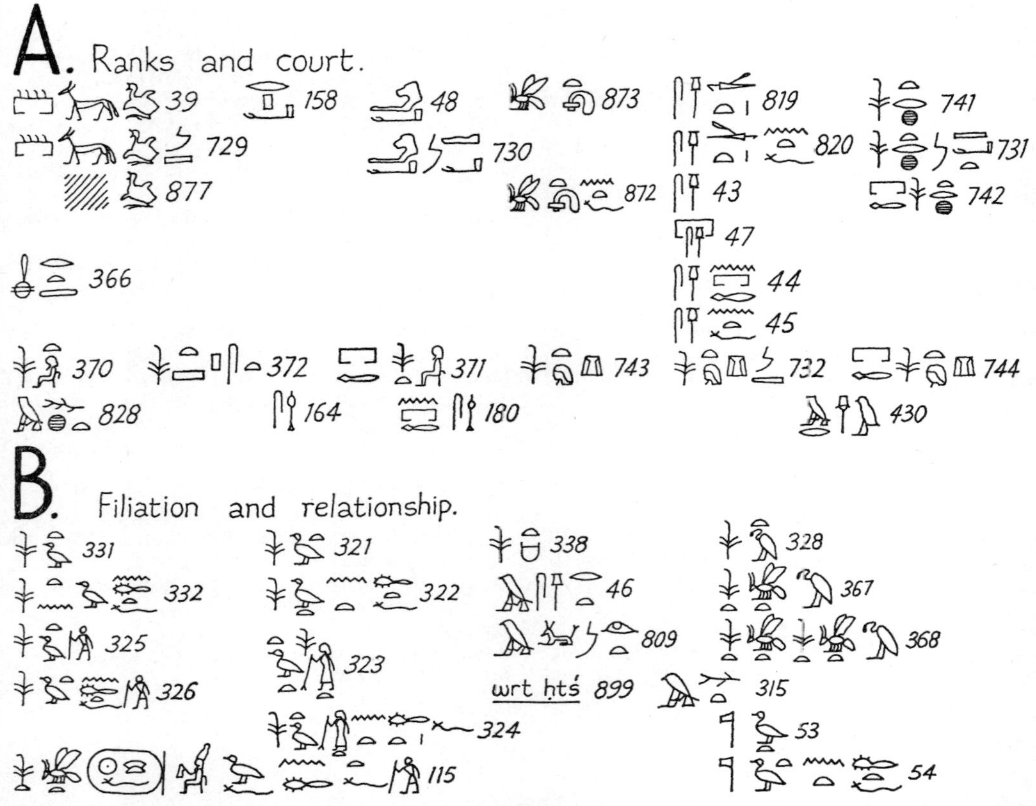

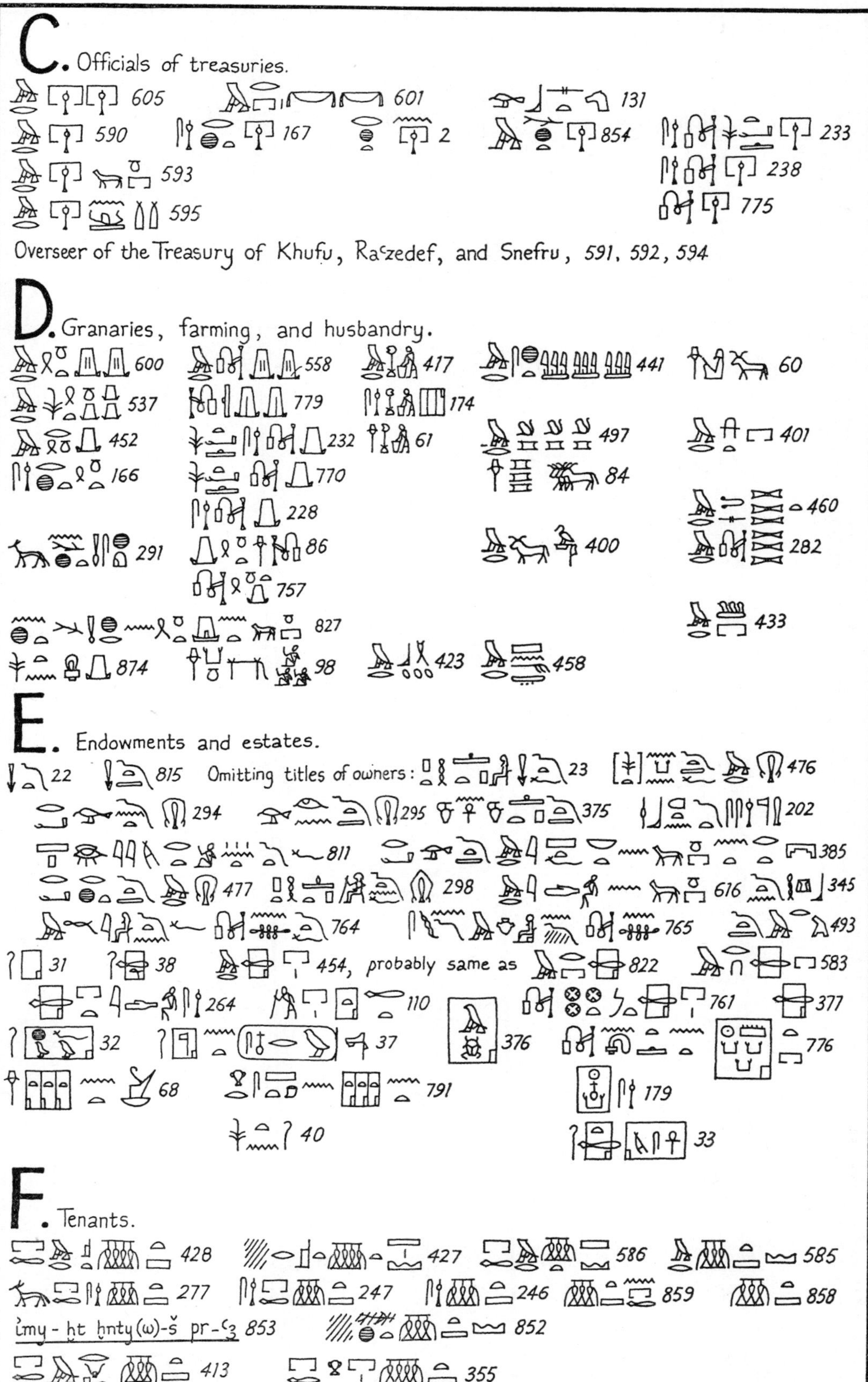
C. Officials of treasuries.
Overseer of the Treasury of Khufu, Raʿzedef, and Snefru, 591, 592, 594
D. Granaries, farming, and husbandry.
E. Endowments and estates.
Omitting titles of owners:
probably same as
F. Tenants.
ỉmy-ḫt ḫnty(w)-š pr-ʿ3 853

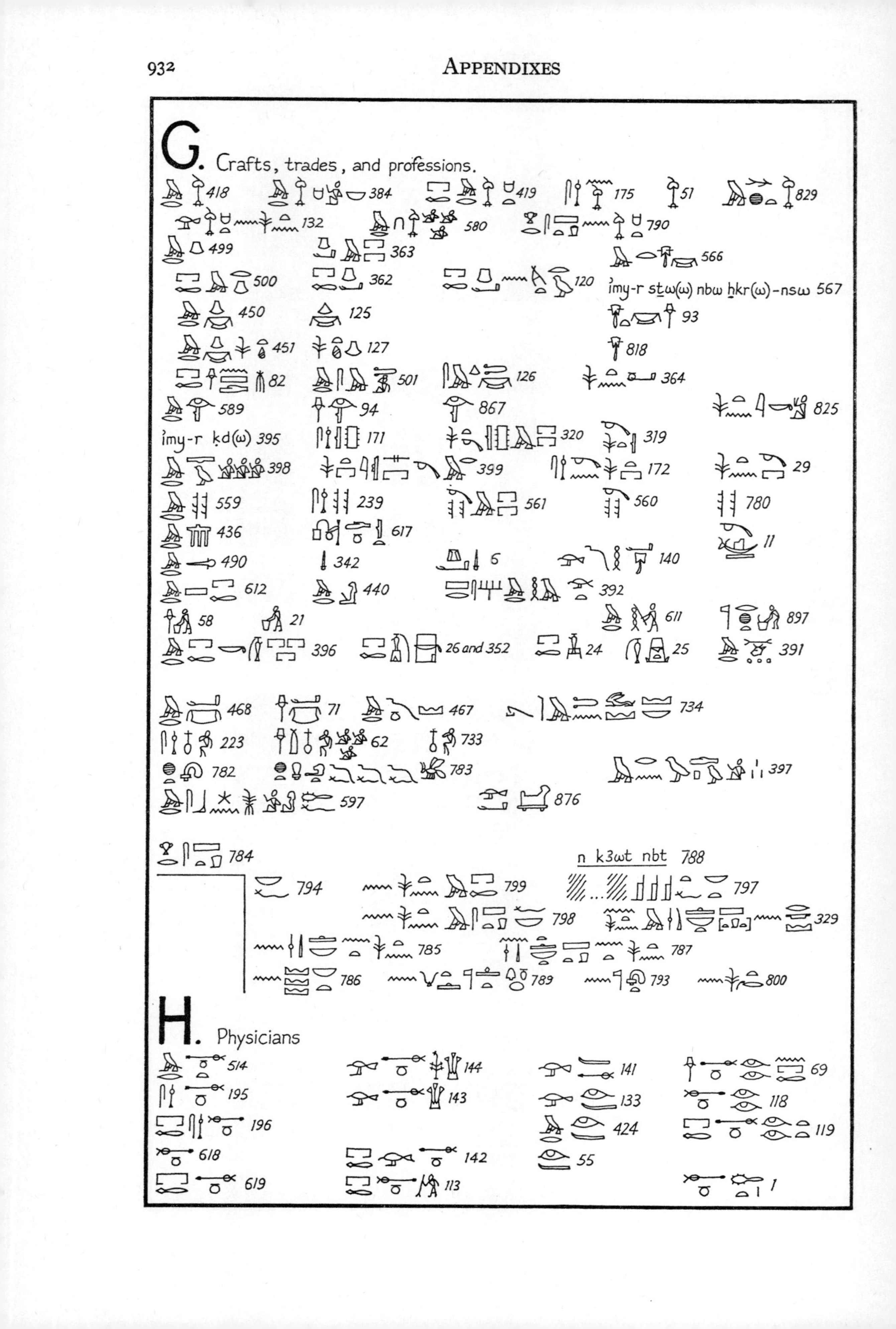

G. Crafts, trades, and professions.

418 384 419 175 51 829
132 580 790
499 363 566
500 362 120 imy-r sṯw(w) nbw ḫkr(w)-nsw 567
450 125 93
451 127 818
82 501 126 364
589 94 867 825
imy-r ḳd(w) 395 171 320 319
398 399 172 29
559 239 561 560 780
436 617 11
490 342 6 140
612 440 392
58 21 611 897
396 26 and 352 24 25 391

468 71 467 734
223 62 733
782 783 397
597 876

784 n k3wt nbt 788
794 799 797
798 329
785 787
786 789 793 800

H. Physicians

514 144 141 69
195 143 133 118
196 424 119
618 142 55
619 113 1

I. Army, expeditions, and police.

435 103 831

755 760

57 506

620 836 292

K. Boats, barks, and dockyards.

169 73 sic? 81 344

445 sic 442 565 579 347

582

393 542 577 749

740 Inspector of rowers of the bark 224 421 754

870 871 869

302 102 273 431 27

465

L. Barbers, hairdressers, and manicurists.

9 390 351 187 496

327 150 70 75

184 181 459

M. Attendants, etc.

316 330 317 318 183 193

194 483 484 508

4 309 509

299 300 190 65

808 Attendant of the Great House 304

N. Entertainment.

814 91 92 241 242

243 244 439

563 564 857

52 177 422 438

124 432

122 123 444 434

O. Scribes.

747 85 226 543 758 746

286 276 281 285

753 769 231 554

772 771

555 556

237 557 539

538 7 311 541

540

762 90 230 288

750 227 544 287

547 550 551

548 549

552 768 763 756

773 235 234 751

774 Inspector of scribes of sacrificial cattle 236 748

12 270 170 275 14 13 826

P. Judiciary.

379 380 289 473 472

795 807 792

803 89 283

Q. Various officials.

613 614 387 388

578 584 447

404 407 405 406

425 426 482

15 271 Judge and Boundary official of the Great House 272

18 20

16 17 19

Overseer of the new settlements 503 534 429

95 598 30

360 280 188 358

835 192 507

Q. Various officials (contd.)

305 382 492
381
74 446
485 806 488 489
834 306 307 186 449
173 599
165 Supervisor of the Two Houses 855 353
868 562
265 615 290
10 96
403 443 147
813 101
8 361 One who is in the magistracy 378

R. Priests and temples.

621 197 130 894
878 333 334 99 76 251
343 Lector-priest of his father 346 41 42 114
134 136 135 137
145 146 138
79 735 56
810 268 269 155 163 314
157 313 156
250 752
266 502

S. Necropolis.

262 609 487 801 781
471 176 420 581
189 898 263
455 457 456
832 293 182 475 481
369 608
116 117 66 67 178

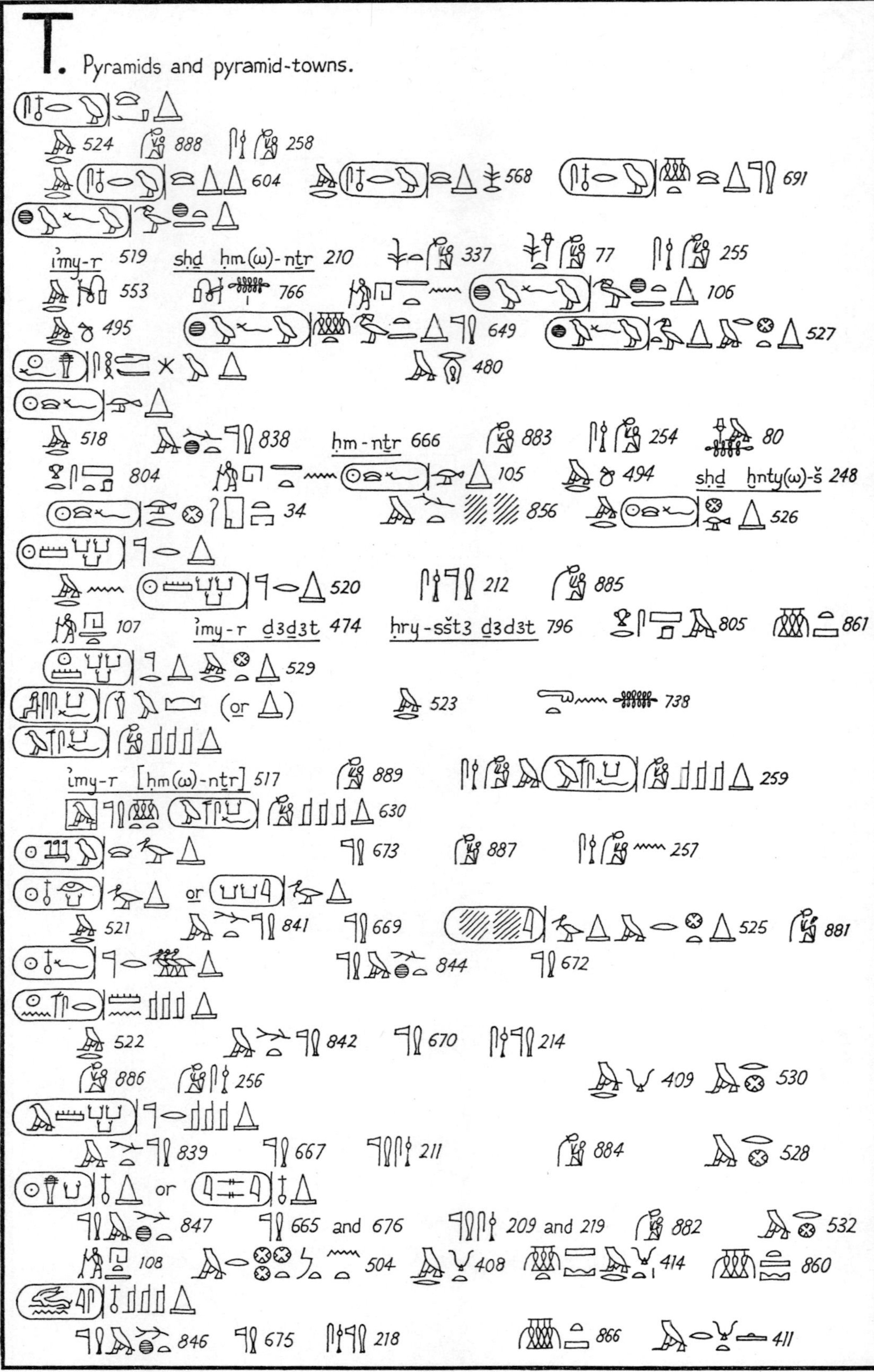
T. Pyramids and pyramid-towns.
524 888 258
604 568 691
imy-r 519 shd hm(ω)-ntr 210 337 77 255
553 766 106
495 649 527
480
518 838 hm-ntr 666 883 254 80
804 105 494 shd hnty(ω)-š 248
34 856 526
520 212 885
107 imy-r d3d3t 474 hry-sšt3 d3d3t 796 805 861
529
(or) 523 738
imy-r [hm(ω)-ntr] 517 889 259
630
673 887 257
or
521 841 669 525 881
844 672
522 842 670 214
886 256 409 530
839 667 211 884 528
or
847 665 and 676 209 and 219 882 532
108 504 408 414 860
846 675 218 866 411

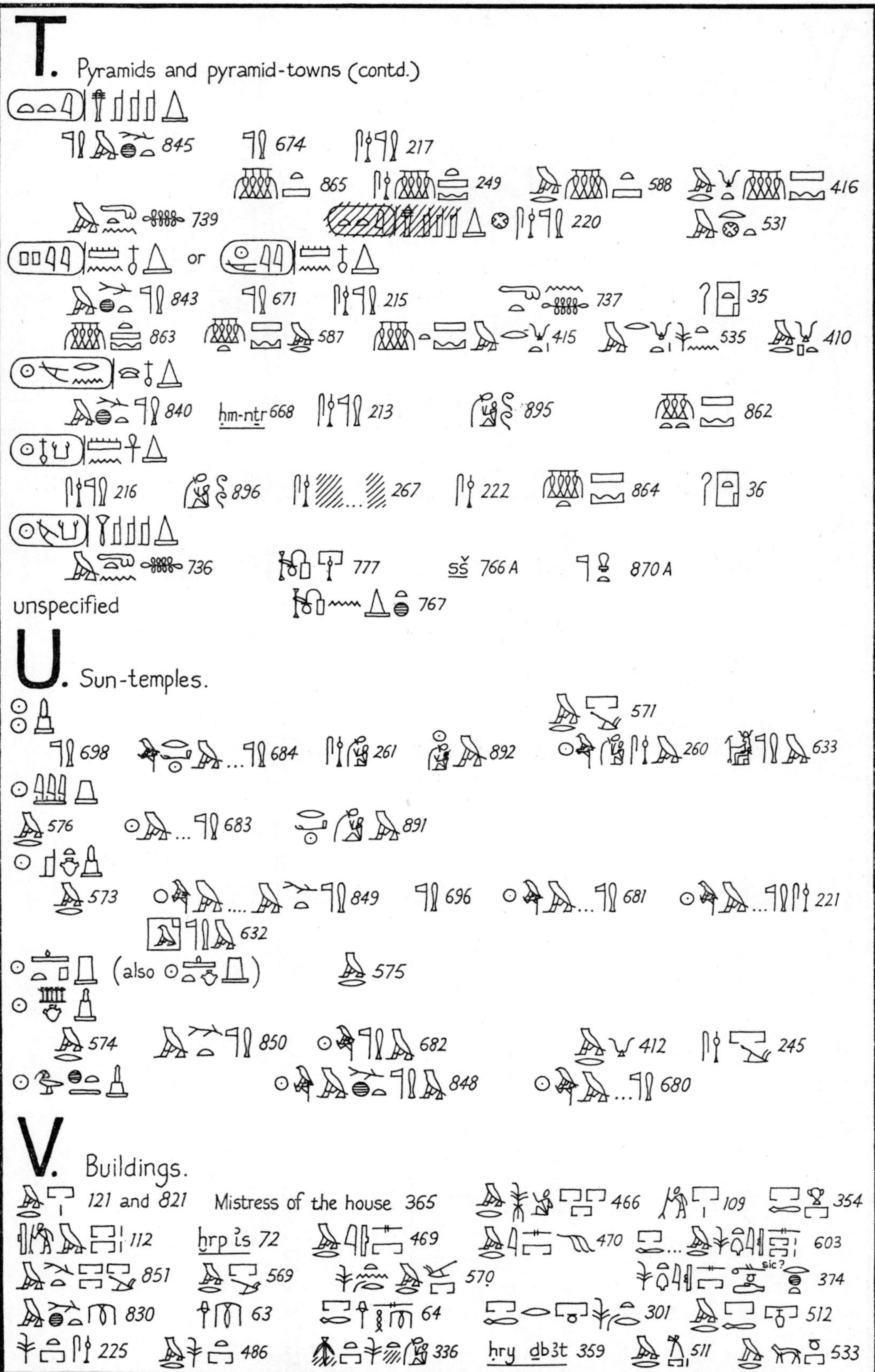
T. Pyramids and pyramid-towns (contd.)
unspecified
U. Sun-temples.
V. Buildings.
121 and 821
Mistress of the house 365
hrp ỉs 72
hry db3t 359

V. Buildings (contd.)

83 510 373
97 356 (preceded by ?) 357 148
59 394 87 104 274
453 546 402
536 462 602 461
463 464 303 448

W. Kings.

(preceded by ?), 658
690 and 727
, also 637, 642, 644, 648, 652, 716
678 and 726
641, 643, 657 695 704 A
721
653 206 253
(i.e. Shepseskaf) 718
701 335
685 349 893
659 348 ḥry-sšt3 802
677
662 160
(preceded by ?), 655
200 705
837 717
207 shd hm(w)-ntr hwt-k3 204
162

X. Gods.

622 623 694 812
816 389 624
516 664 208
625 626 651
702 656
663 654

X. Gods (contd.)

153

660 and 719 720

of

723 722

724 725

661

679 890

699

312

629 and 703 704

198 199

of

True prophetess of Ḥatḥor 875

710 712 711

709

631 and 706 707

708

713

515

154

203 817

640 638 636

639

635

634

645 646

647

692 240

693

151 350

100

687

689

686

728

628 5

627

700

Y. People.

Omitting titles: 297 833 823 824

715 160A 162A 880

3 159 sš pr ḥry-wdb 759 88 229

650 205 879 252 296 478 479

111

Z. Geographical.

606 513 149

28 50 308 278 284 279

383 341 129 128 161

339 688 340

505

498 386 491 310

572 596

437 191

H. APIS-BULLS

in this volume

Apis-bull (numbering of Mariette)		*Date*	*Burial chamber* *Mariette*	*Rhoné*	*Page*
	Dyn. XVIII				
I	I	Amenophis III	A	C1	780
II	V	probably Dyn. XVIII	B	C2	781
III	II	Tutʿankhamūn	C	C3	781
IV and V	III and IV	Ḥaremḥab	D and E	C4 and 5	781
	Dyn. XIX				
VI	I	Sethos I	F	C6	782
VII and IX	II and IV	years 16 and 30 of Ramesses II	G	C8	782
X–XIV	V–IX	Ramesses II	I, J, K	D, D	784
	Dyn. XX				
XVI	II	Ramesses VI			785
XVII	III	Ramesses IX	M	E′	785
	Dyn. XXII				
XXVII	I	year 23 of Osorkon II			785
XXVIII	II	year 14 of Takelothis II			785
XXIX	III	year 28 of Sesonchis III	P	F	786
XXX	IV	year 2 of Pemu			786
XXXI	V	? (Mariette: year 4 of Sesonchis V)	Q	F′	787
XXXII	VI	year 11 of Sesonchis V			787
XXXIII	VII	year 37 of Sesonchis V	R	F″	787
	Dyn. XXIV				
XXXIV = XXXV	I (= I of Dyn. XXV)	year 6 of Bocchoris = year 2 of Sabacon	S	G	789
	Dyn. XXV				
	I (= I of Dyn. XXIV)				
XXXVI	II	year 24 of Taharqa	(T′)	(H*)	791
	Dyn. XXVI				
XXXVII	I	years 20/21 of Psammetikhos I	T	H	791
XXXVIII	II	year 52 of Psammetikhos I	U	I	797
XXXIX	III	year 16 of Necho II	V	J	797
XL	IV	year 12 of Apries	X	K	797
XLI	V	year 23 of Amasis	Y	L	797
	Dyn. XXVII				
XLII		year 6 of Cambyses	Z	M	799
XLIII		year 34 of Darius I	A′	N	800
XLIV		year 4 of Darius I	B′	N′	799
XLV		Darius I	C′	N″	800
	Dyn. XXIX				
unnumbered		year 2 of Nepheritis I			804

Apis-bull (numbering of Mariette)	*Date*	*Burial chamber*		*Page*
		Mariette	*Rhoné*	
contemporary with Dyn. XXXI				
XLVI	year 2 of Khebebesh	D′	O	804
Ptolemaic				
LV	year 17 of Ptolemy VI Philometor		P (2nd on right)	804
LVII	year 52 of Ptolemy VIII Euergetes II			804
unnumbered	unknown		R	804

I. APIS-STELAE IN THE LOUVRE

Only those mentioned in this volume

C No.	*Page*	*IM No.*	*Page*	*IM. No.*	*Page*
316	812	2660	806	2768	793
317	802	2661	809	2775	808
IM. No.	*Page*	2662	794	2782	808
3	813	2663	795	2784	808
6	812	2665	794	2785	809
16	812	2666	796	2787	794
19	805	2672	809	2788	795
36	814	2673	791	2789	795
37	814	2675	791	2795	809
38	807	2676	792	2796	795
42	803	2679	790	2797	796
43	814	2680	789	2799	808
47	814	2681	793	2802	796
64	798	2682	789	2807	809
78	814	2685	793	2809	808
129	814	2686	807	2810	786
132	797	2689	793	2815	795
133	797	2690	788	2819	792
136	815	2692	790	2821	807
137	803	2693	796	2846	788
138	803	2699	794	2847	790
139	814	2702	787	2849	805
176	813	2703	793	2853	794
1244	801	2704	789	2854	795
1805	796	2705	791	2856	792
2619	793	2706	794	2857	803
2620	792	2707	791	2858	795
2621	793	2709	795	2859	796
2623	793	2710	810	2860	810
2624	793	2717	808	2861	795
2631	807	2718	789	2862	810
2634	795	2724	809	2863	790
2637	806	2726	795	2864	810
2640	791	2728	795	2865	805
2642	794	2732	791	2866	794
2645	811	2734	793	2867	792
2650	795	2735	790	3008	806
2651	811	2740	793	3009	792
2653	790	2746	791	3010	809
2656	793	2757	790	3011	797
2658	795	2762	809	3012	789
2659	791	2763	791	3016	806
		2764	794	3017	796

IM. No.	*Page*
3019	807
3020	810
3022	807
3023	793
3024	806
3025	807
3027	793
3028	809
3029	794
3030	809
3031	794
3032	805
3033	806
3034	787
3035	790
3036	790
3037	790
3038	796
3039	793
3040	814
3041	796
3042	796
3043	792
3045	793
3046	793
3047	803
3048	795
3049	787
3050	789
3051	806
3053	794
3054	789
3056	807
3057	794
3058	809
3059	805
3060	807
3061	787
3062	793
3063	794
3064	808
3065	806
3067	793
3068	789
3070	810
3071	796
3072	792
3075	794
3076	792
3077	793
3078	788
3079	788
3080	809
3081	806
3082	792
3083	806
3084	788
3085	788
3087	792
3088	806
3089	792
3090	785
3091	789
3092	789
3093	805
3095	811
3096	811
3097	809
3098	811
3099	815
3100	807
3101	807
3102	809
3103	806
3104	794
3105	794
3106	790
3107	805
3108	795
3109	809
3110	787
3111	811
3112	795
3113	790
3114	799
3116	810
3117	807
3118	790
3123	807
3127	807
3128	806
3129	792
3130	793
3131	799
3132	794
3133	808
3134	794
3135	810
3136	811
3139	810
3141	806
3142	795
3143	788
3144	808
3145	813
3146	807
3148	798
3302	807
3304	796
3305	806
3306	791
3307	795
3308	808
3311	806
3312	810
3316	808
3318	794
3345	812
3424	789
3426	807
3427	787
3428	795
3429	805
3431	814
3432	787
3439	808
3440	807
3441	786
3442	796
3574	794
3577	810
3579	794
3580	790
3582	795
3586	810
3587	809
3588	810
3591	794
3592	789
3595	788
3689	812
3697	786
3717	812
3719	787
3721	789
3727	795
3728	789
3729	813
3732	814
3733	792
3736	786
3745	805
3747	784
3749	786
3756	790
3757	794
3758	813
3760 (probably)	808
3999	801
4000	804
4001	803
4002	798
4003	802
4004	803
4005	814
4006	815
4008	801
4009	798
4010	814
4011	802
4012	813
4013	799
4015	813
4016	800
4017	799
4018	800
4019	798
4020	812
4021	804
4022	815
4025	802
4026	814
4027	803
4029	802
4030	812
4032	802
4033	801
4034	798

IM. No.	*Page*
4037	800
4038	801
4039	800
4040	798
4041	813
4042	810
4043	812
4044	803
4045	800
4046	800
4047	814
4050	802
4051	798
4052	803
4053	798
4054	799
4055	804
4056	802
4057	800
4058	793
4060	802
4061	815
4062	811
4063	800
4065	810
4066	812
4067	811
4068	800
4069	803
4071	813
4072	801
4073	812
4074	798
4075	813
4076	800
4077	802
4079	812
4080	802
4082	813
4083	813
4084	811
4085	813
4086	799
4087	801
4089	811
4091	814
4092	804
4095	803
4097	801
4098	803
4099	802
4100	799
4101	804
4103	804
4104	800
4105	814
4106	812
4107	803
4108	811
4109	801
4110	798
4111	802
4112	812
4113	811
4114	804
4115	813
4116	800
4117	814
4118	800
4119	812
4120	802
4121	802
4122	814
4123	814
4125	801
4126	811
4127	814
4128	799
4129	800
4131	797
4133	799
4134	802
4135	813
4149	802
4150	803
4162	791
4163	815
4167	812
4168	808
4169	803
4170	798
4174	798
4175	798
4187	799
4188	799
4189	811
4190	803
4191	814
4192	798
4193	810
4198	812
4205	786
4207	801
4208	790
4209	814
4210	814
4213	802
4214	801
4215	805
4216	814
4217	811
4218	810
4244	815
4246	804
4963	783
4964	783
5268	783
5269	784
5270	783
5271	783
5305	781
5306	781
5307	781
5341	802
5342	794
5343	811
5427	814
5428	796
5432	806
5936	784
5937	805
5939	790
5941	810
5943	815
5944	795
5945	796
5947	790
5948	790
5949	810
5952	783
5953	784
5954	783
6153	784

N. No.	*Page*
403	792
404	797
405	797
406	797
407	799
408	799
409	804
410	804
411	783
412	784
413	786
414	786
417	791
418	811
419	787
421	790
421	811
421/1	807
421/12	811
421/16	806
421/31	807
421/32	808
421/35	787
421/36	787
421/37	806
421/38 (sic)	790
421/38 (sic)	805
421/39	791
421/44	808
421/46	806
421/48	806
421/50	808
421/51	807
421/52	808
421/57	807
421/59	807
421/63	805
421/64	806
421/65	806
421/74	806
421/77	789
421/94	806
421/97	808
421/107	790

No.	*Page*	*No.*	*Page*	*No.*	*Page*
61	791	133	795	227	794
62	787	136	796	228	810
64	808	137	795	229	809
65	806	138	810	230	794
66	807	139	793	231	796
67	808	142	795	232	792
68	808	143	813	233	796
69	806	144	810	234	793
70	807	148	795	235	813
72	809	149	793	237	795
73	806	150	793	238	793
74	806	154	810	239	797
75	788	155	794	240	797
76	789	156	794	241	793
77	788	158	794	242	809
78 (sic)	789	160	794	245	795
78 (sic)	814	161	793	246	809
79	789	162	793	247	793
80	788	163	796	248	795
81	806	164	795	249	792
82	806	165	794	250	792
83	788	166	792	251	814
84	808	167	796	252	796
85	788	168	794	255	796
86	807	169	794	257	796
87	789	172	808	258	793
88	807	173	808	259	794
89	805	176	793	260	811
90	791	178	795	261	815
91	789	179	795	264	796
92	810	184	795	265	796
93	805	185	794	266	798
94	805	186	794	268	807
95	806	187	809	269	810
96	805	188	791	270	794
98	790	189	811	271	795
99	806	190	792	273	792
100	789	191	793	274	795
102	809	192	797	275	794
103	808	193	797	276	795
104	790	194	794	277	795
105	808	195	807	278	794
106	790	199	796	280	810
107	790	200	808	281	794
108	790	201	790	284	794
110	789	202	793	285	792
111	807	204	814	287	810
112	789	205	808	288	793
113	790	208	792	290	808
114	789	209	811	291	803
115	789	211	795	292	809
116	790	213	791	293	795
117	790	214	809	294	792
118	790	215	809	295	806
119	785	216	793	296	811
120	789	218	794	299	790
121	791	219	802	301	794
123	791	220	796	303	794
124	787	221	792	304	810
126	796	223	809	306	811
127	796	224	795	307	795
128	793	225	794	308	795
129	795	226	810	309	793

INDEXES

1. KINGS

2. PRIVATE NAMES

SECTION I

References to tomb-owners in Roman type.
HPM = High Priest of Memphis.
References to Addenda not included

II. Hieroglyphic forms.
Only one form given. Numbers refer to Section I

1
2
3
5
126
also 6
19
20 See also
See
22
24
25
23
26
18
16
420
426
425
423
424
613
See
625
626

610
462
See also
618
617
See
611
622
623
619
620
621
614
615
616
627
421
427
492
493
(?) 495
494
11 See also
12
13
14
15
422
596

597
598
601
599
600
602
608
607
603
2058
2059
605
604
606
429
430 See also
428 See also
496 See also
498
497
499
502
503 See also

504
505
See
506
507
508
509
510
511
512
513
514
515
527
516
519
520
525

565
560
561
562
563
See
129
550
543
See
557
555
556
553
558
551
552
554
See
559
See
440
439
438
441
See also
442
444
See also
443
449
448
See also

575
See also
577
ʾIzzi 567
568
569
570
579
576
566
578
210
212
211
220
214
213
215
217
571
572
574
573
446
447
450
451
452
See also
445
580
581
589

590 See also
593
591
595
592
See
583 See Addenda below
594
582
584
585
586
See also
588
587
431
432
436
433
See also
435
434
See also
609
2062
624
2061
2056
2060

2054
2057
2055
612
4
63
17
27
137
127
125
124
64
65
66
86
87
88
90
89 See also
91
113
117
119
118
120
106
107
108
109
67
73

Addenda: 135
136

2042 A

2043
2033
2041
2031
2042
2030
1996
2009
2046
2045
2047
1965
1959
1963
1962
Wsr-ḥ3t 1960
1964
1961
2050
2049
2048
2052
1966
1975
1967
1968
1970
Wḏ3-Ḥr-rsnt
Nfr-ỉb-Rʿ-nb-pḥty 1971
1972
1969
1974

1973
1977
1976
2051
140
144
See
1951
1950
147
148
149
153
151
152
154
155
sic 150
142
See also
156
157
141
165
168
See also
167
169
169 A
145 See also

See
See
146
161
See
160
158
759
Bnt-n-dw3-nṯr 166
See
162
143
163
164
1196
1219
1401
1214
1217
1218
1215
(?) 1216
1264
1192
1193
1197

1198
1246
See
1195
1194
1199
1398
1266
1267
1268
1269
1270
1200
1346
1230
1231
1370
1350
1348
(?) 1349
1353
1347
1369
1358
1359
1355
P3-n-Mḥyt 1356
1357
1360
1354
1202

1330
1332
1331
See also (?)
1335
See
1334
1333
1336
(?) … 1338
1272
1404
1394
1395
1212
1213
See
1241
1211
1402
1405
(?) 1457
1458
1455
1454
1456
1273
1372
1373
Ppy-ʿnḫ Zṯw 1374

1375
See also
1376
1377
1378
1379
1380
1381
See also
1382
See
… 1383
See also
1368
1387
1385
1388
1386
1389
1384
1391
1390
1400
1342
1339
1341
1340
See
1392
1396
See

1397
1406
1409
See
1407
1408
1410
See
1412
1411
See also
1413
See
1415
1414
1416
1418
1417
1421
1419
1420
1452
1453
1451
1446
1430
(?) 1422
1427
(?) (?) 1426
1424

1425
1423
1428
1429
1439
1440
1441
1442
1445
1444
1443
1434
1435
1433
1432
1431
See also
1437
1436
1438
1447
1448
1449
1450
See also
236
236 A
See also
200
812

818
819
810
821
822
823
809
820
907
938
915
908
909
910
911
914
See also
913
912
824
825
See
916
917
918
See
922
923
924 (?)
919
920
921

925
949 …
1108
950
952
951
960
961
993
953
963
958
959
See
1135
1150
1132
1142
1143
1141
1139
See also
1140
1144
1145
1133
1134
1138
1136
1137
1147

1146
1148
1149
See
1171
1102
1167
1168
1169
1170
1153
1152
1154
1166
1172
201
216
218
219
234
1174
1115
202
203
204
227
226
228
229
See also

223
1114A
1113
222
225
224
207
209
1173
208
206
221
230
1112
231
232
233
See
205
235
See
1155
See
1156
1159
1160
1163
1164
1162
1161
1165
1157

1053
1044
1047
1052
1011
1061
1175
1057
1010
1092
1091
1094
1095
1096
1097
1103
(?) 1104
1105
1099
1101
1100
1098
1106
1107
1071
1072
1066
1068
1067
1069
1063
1065
1064
1070

1090
1081
954
955
1082
1089
1087
1084
1085
1086
1088
956
1083
957
1111
1116
1114
1109
1110
See
1080
1079
1122
1117
1121
1119
1118
1120
1127
1128
1129
1130
1123

1124
1125
1126
1500
1506
1503
1502
1501
1479 See also
1477
1484
1490
1472 See also
1471
1470
1468
1464
1465
1466
1469
1467
1474
1473
1475
1459
1485
1460
See also
1463
1462

1498
1476
1461
1478
1507
1509
1508
1510
1511
1480
1504
1505
See
1491
1492
1494
1495
1496
See also
1493
1497
1486
1488
1487
1499
1489
1481
1483
1482
307
330
359

411
412
[H]r[w] 287
259
380
382
384
385
381
383
See
308
312
309
310
314
311
317
315
316
313
See
387
See
407
405
401
400
402
403
404
393

392
394
395
390
391
397
398
399
389
406
See
396
See
388
295
292
293
296
294
297
See
See
715
724
722
723
725
720
719
727
707
713
709

708
710
711
712
See also
717
718
714
716
726
800
801
802
803
799
782
also
783
785
784
797
786
788
787
789 See also
798
790 (?)
795
791
794
796
792

793
804
756
730
731
749
750
See also
752
754
755
770
775
778
(?) 733
734
735
732
779
See
740
741
737
736
748
743
744
746
See also
745
738

1534
1543
1535
1536
1537
1539
1540
1538
1541
1542
1746
1533
See also
1749
1748
1547
1546
1548
1549
1583
1578
1735
1736
1737
1579
1581
1580
1577
1576
1607 See also

1608
1597
1609
1610
1598
1600
1599
1612
1613
1614
(?) 1584
1616
1617.
1747
1588
1593
1594
1592
1595
1589
1596
1590
1591
1585
1586
1587
1783
See also ...
1739
1742
1740
1741

1743
1744
1745
1606
1601
1603
1604
1605
1602
1624
1620
1621
1550
1552
1551
1553
1566
1556
1562
1560
1561
1557
1558
1559
1567
1569
(?) 1568
1571
1570
See
1565
1563
1564

See
1626
1625
1627
1628
1629
1555
1572
1573
1575
1574
1636
1647
1637
1642
1648
1649
1644
1639
1640
1544
1545
1650
1651
1688
1669
1670
1668
1673
1672
1671
1675
1682

249
248
251
242
243
244
245
247
250
246
239
252
237
1787
1942
1754
1788
1789
1846
1786
1753
1756
1758
1755
T3-ʿš3-ḫt 1757
1839
1844
1840
1841
1842
1838

1759
1760
1816
1818
1817
1806
1804
1805
1812
1862
1858
T3-nt-ʾImntt 1857
See
1867
1865
1866
1813
1859
See also
1861
1864
1863
1860
1807
1815
1809
1808
1810
1811
1823
1821
1820
1822
1819

1778
1780
1784
1779
1781
1782
1783
1797
1803
1796
1798
1802
1801
1800
or 1799
1833
1834
1824
1825
1832
1830
1826
1831
1828
1827
1829
1793
1791
1794
1790
1792
1795
1776
1777

1835
1836
1837
1761
1763
1762
1770
1772
1773
1768
1769
1765
1764
1766
1767
1771
1774
1775
1944
See also
1843
1785
1814
1940
1941
1886
See
1949
1943
See
1848

2074
or 183
185
188
186
189
190
184
187
2079
2069
2070
2084

2082
2083
2065
2081
2076
2077
2078
See also
2075
2080
2066

2064
See also
2089
2099
2090
2085
?
? 2098
2086
2091
... 2092

...ms 2093
2095
2094
2097
...
2096
See
2088
2087
2100
2101

3. DIVINITIES

4. GEOGRAPHICAL

Names in italics are Ancient Egyptian, names in capitals classical. The article *el-* does not affect the alphabetical order of the place-names. References to toponyms which do not occur in titles are indicated by an asterisk

5. OBJECTS IN MUSEUMS

JE No.	*Page*
59175	888
86764	846
91520	826
Temp. No.	
25.11.60.1–4	890

Cat sarcophagus, CG 5003, p. 851. **Granite chest,** CG 4046, p. 883. **Columns,** JE 35131, p. 420; 41525, p. 704; 56371–5, p. 434; Temp. No. 20.1.25.4, p. 873. **Column-capital,** No. ?, p. 855. **Cups,** JE 48885–6, p. 397; 58346–7, p. 432; No. ?, p. 441. **Cylinder-seals,** JE 45495, p. 875; 72209, p. 598; 72625, p. 542. **Dagger,** CG 52768, p. 552. **Death-mask,** No. ?, p. 395. **Decree,** JE 63398, p. 684. **Dish-fragment,** JE 49857, p. 681. **Disks,** JE 58342–5, p. 432; 70160, p. 441; 70164–5, p. 441. **Doorways,** CG 1552, p. 894; JE 45029, p. 857; Temp. No. 3.2.21.1 (now in Philadelphia), p. 857. **Door-wings,** CG 1568, p. 693; JE 47749, p. 543. **Draughts-board,** CG 68001, p. 559. **Drum (wooden) of doorway,** JE 44175, p. 542. **Dummy mummy of Apis-bull,** JE 91318, p. 825. **Embalming-tables,** CG 1321–2, p. 415. **Faience fragment,** JE 41293, p. 875. **Fan-handles,** JE 86161, p. 652; Temp. No. 6.4.23.12, p. 774. **Foundation deposit,** JE 35174, p. 842. **Head-rests,** CG 1792, p. 774; 1797, p. 699; JE 39155–6, p. 560; 52545, p. 677; 88559–60, p. 540. **Implements, etc.,** No. ?, p. 444. **Jackal-coffins,** CG 29760, p. 777; 29765, p. 777. **Labels,** JE 63346, p. 436; 70114–16, p. 441; JE 86172–5, p. 436; No. ?, p. 436. **Linen,** No. ?, p. 424.

Mace-heads, JE 39163, p. 395; 47225, p. 395; 49372–3, p. 395. **Measuring-vessel,** JE 86754, p. 842. **Mirrors,** CG 44075, p. 875; 44076–80, p. 831; JE 50280, p. 688.

Models, JE 39126, p. 561; 39129–32, p. 561; 39146–7, p. 561; 45319–21, p. 550; 45496, p. 550; 46765, p. 550; 46769–72, p. 550; 47929, p. 539; Temp. No. 4.3.23.1, p. 560; No. ?, p. 561 (two).

Model boats

CG No.	*Page*
4913	774
4915–17	774
4924	835
4930	835
JE No.	
35920–2	650
39127–8	560
39144	560
39145	561 *and* Addenda
45318	550
46766–8	550
56386–97	432
63183–94	541

Number ? P. 673.

Mummy-masks, etc., CG 28107, p. 888; 53779–80, p. 588; JE 52538, p. 682; 89386, p. 698; Temp. No. 11.12.25.18, p. 504; 20.12.25.1, p. 774.

Naos, CG 70035, p. 888. **Necklace-clasp,** CG 53834, p. 525. **Necklace-fragment,** CG 53839, p. 525.

Obelisks, CG 1308, p. 462; 1312, p. 462; 1315, p. 898; 17005, p. 774; 17006, p. 537; 17007–8, p. 548; JE 63404, p. 684.

Offering-stands, CG 1295, p. 689; 1296, p. 774; 1297, p. 689; 1298, p. 491; 1299, p. 479; 1300, p. 698; 1301, p. 491; 1302–3, p. 479.

Ointment-slabs, CG 1337, p. 582; 1338, p. 691; 1339, p. 698; 1340–2, p. 768; JE 47033, p. 515; 50674, p. 677; 59153–4, p. 397.

Palette, CG 69021, p. 557. **Panels,** JE 52021, p. 426; 52343, p. 426; 62950, p. 685. **Pectorals,** CG 52001, p. 883; 52002–3, p. 884. **Pendants,** CG 53247, p. 648; 53249, p. 648. **Pilaster-fragments,** JE 43272–3, p. 662. **Pillars,** CG 1550–1, p. 613; JE 15048 (probably), p. 463; 18928, p. 755; 43270, p. 668; 43271, p. 703; Temp. No. 20.1.25.5, p. 755; number ?, *see* Addenda. **Plaques,** JE 30082, p. 875; 35107, p. 831; 39148, p. 395; 39171, p. 559; 59119, p. 507; 92679, p. 416; Temp. Nos. 27.11.26.3, 4, p. 831. **Pyramidia,** CG 17109 (JE 8371), p. 770; JE 35133 (*also* JE 35745), p. 888; 41665, p. 553; 48841, p. 770; 53045, p. 435; 54855–6, p. 435; Temp. No. 7.11.24.1, p. 770. **Rudder,** CG 4927, p. 885.

Sealings

JE No.	*Page*
35584–8	613
35590–5	613
35598–619	613
44372 (probably)	437
44373	439
44378	437
72205–6	598
91311	448
Temp. No.	
24.12.23.4	437
24.12.23.5	436

Number ? P. 441 (twice).

Shrines, CG 70010, p. 874; JE 91103, p. 824. **Sickle,** JE 70204, p. 441. **Sistra,** CG 69324, p. 863; 69334, p. 875. **Sled,** CG 4928, p. 885. **Sphinx from furniture,** JE 91111, p. 824. **Clay statuettes with execration-texts,** JE 70221, p. 549. **Sticks and clubs,** Temp. Nos. 20.3.31.7–10, p. 561 *and* Addenda. **Stopper,** JE 72204, p. 598.

Vessels (vases, jars, etc.) and lids

CG No.	*Page*
4028–9	889
5019–22	430
18037	820

CONTENTS OF FASCICLE 3

PYRAMID-FIELD OF ṢAQQÂRA
(continued)

LXVIII. Ṣaqqâra.
Sacred Animal Complexes.
Western Group with
the Serapeum.
See pp. 778–820.

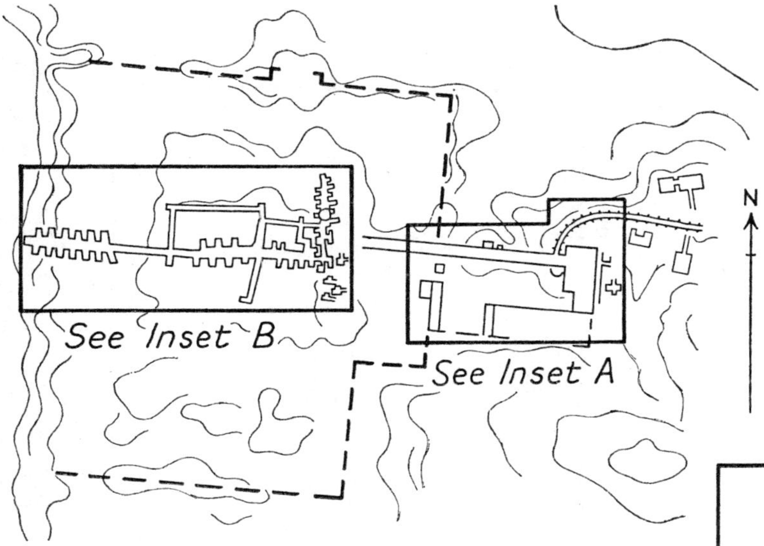

See Inset B
See Inset A
N

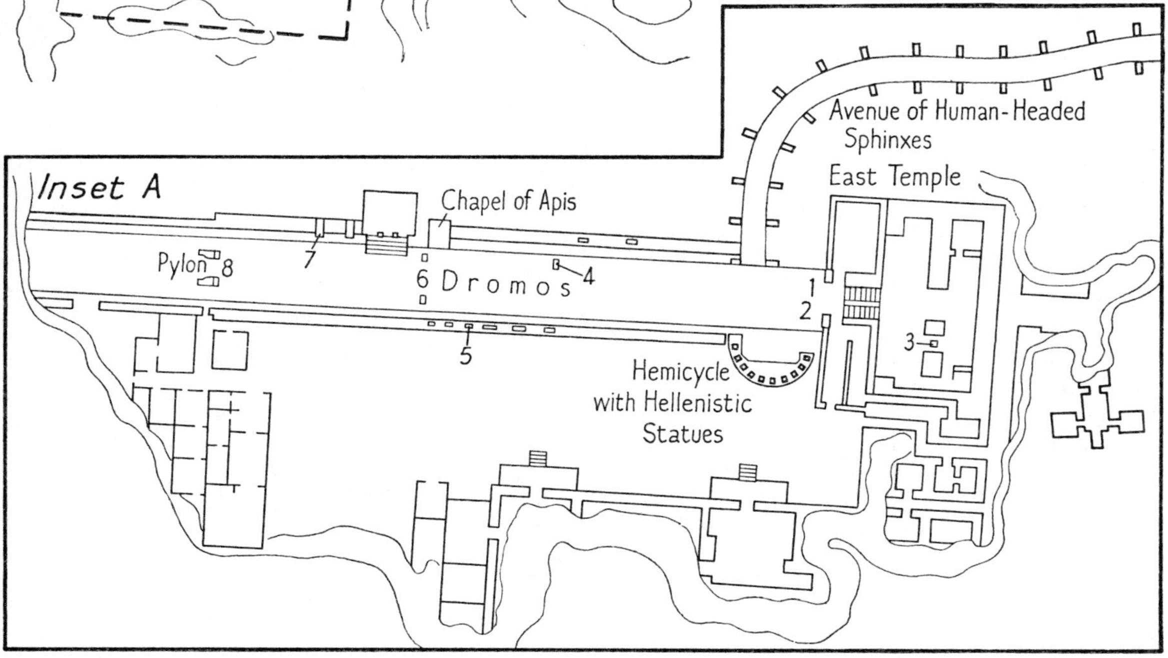

Inset A
Avenue of Human-Headed
Sphinxes
East Temple
Chapel of Apis
Pylon 8
7
6 Dromos 4
1
2
3
5
Hemicycle
with Hellenistic
Statues

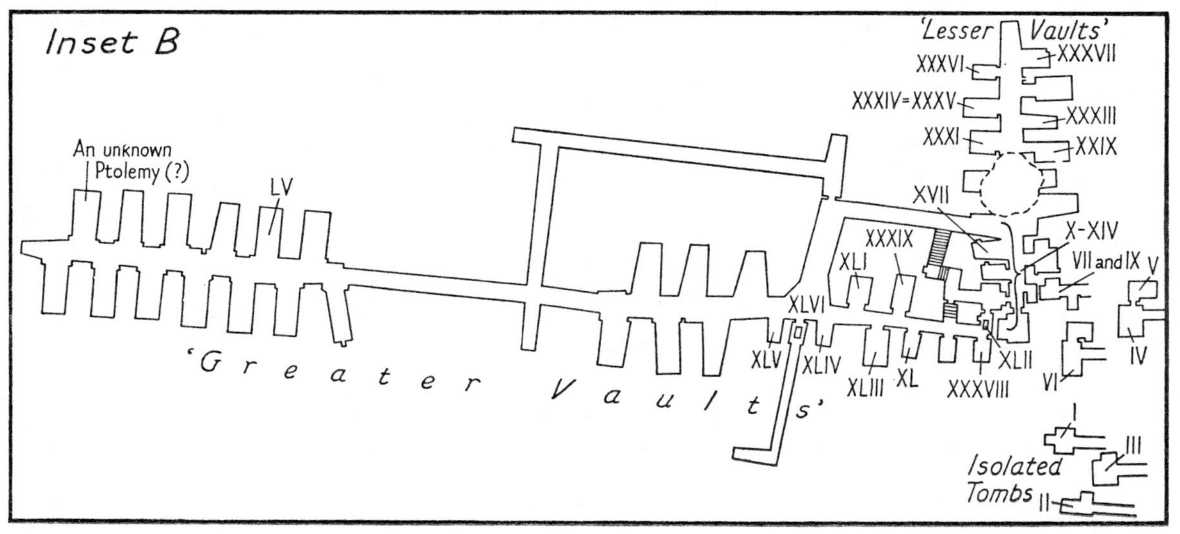

LXIX. Ṣaqqâra.
Sacred Animal Complexes (west section).
See pp. 777–827.

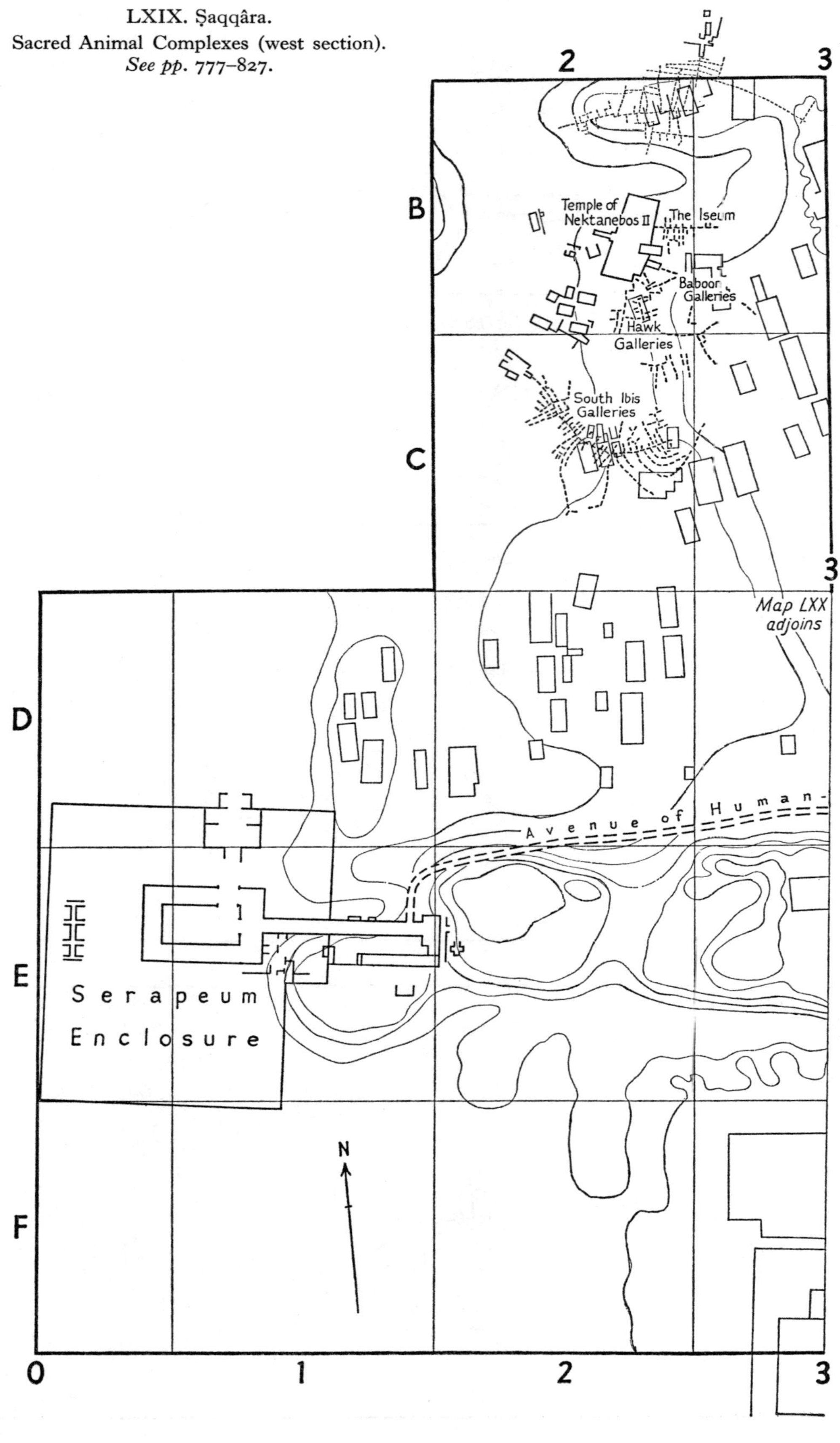

LXX. Ṣaqqâra. Sacred Animal Complexes (east section). *See pp.* 777–827.
Areas D/E–5/6 have been corrected according to the plan published by Smith (H. S.) and Jeffreys in *J.E.A.* 64 (1978), fig. 1 on p. 14.

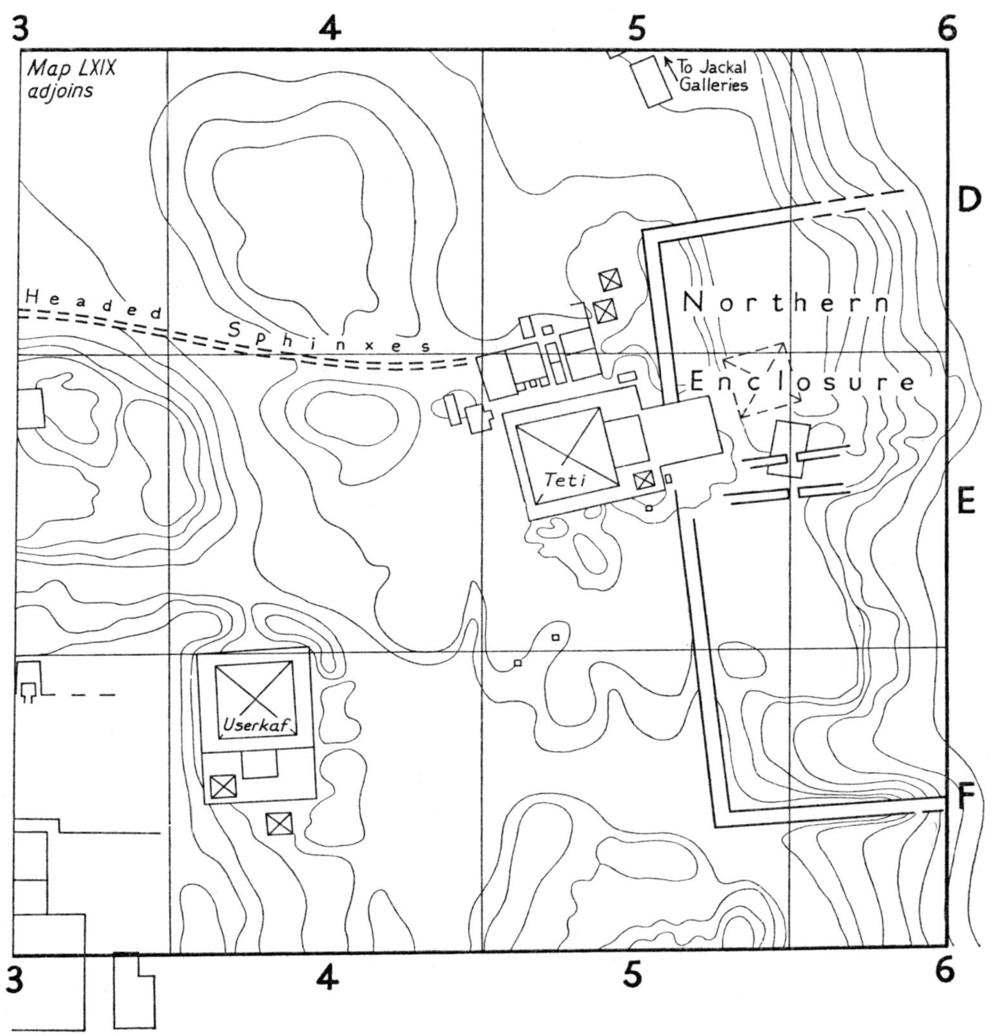

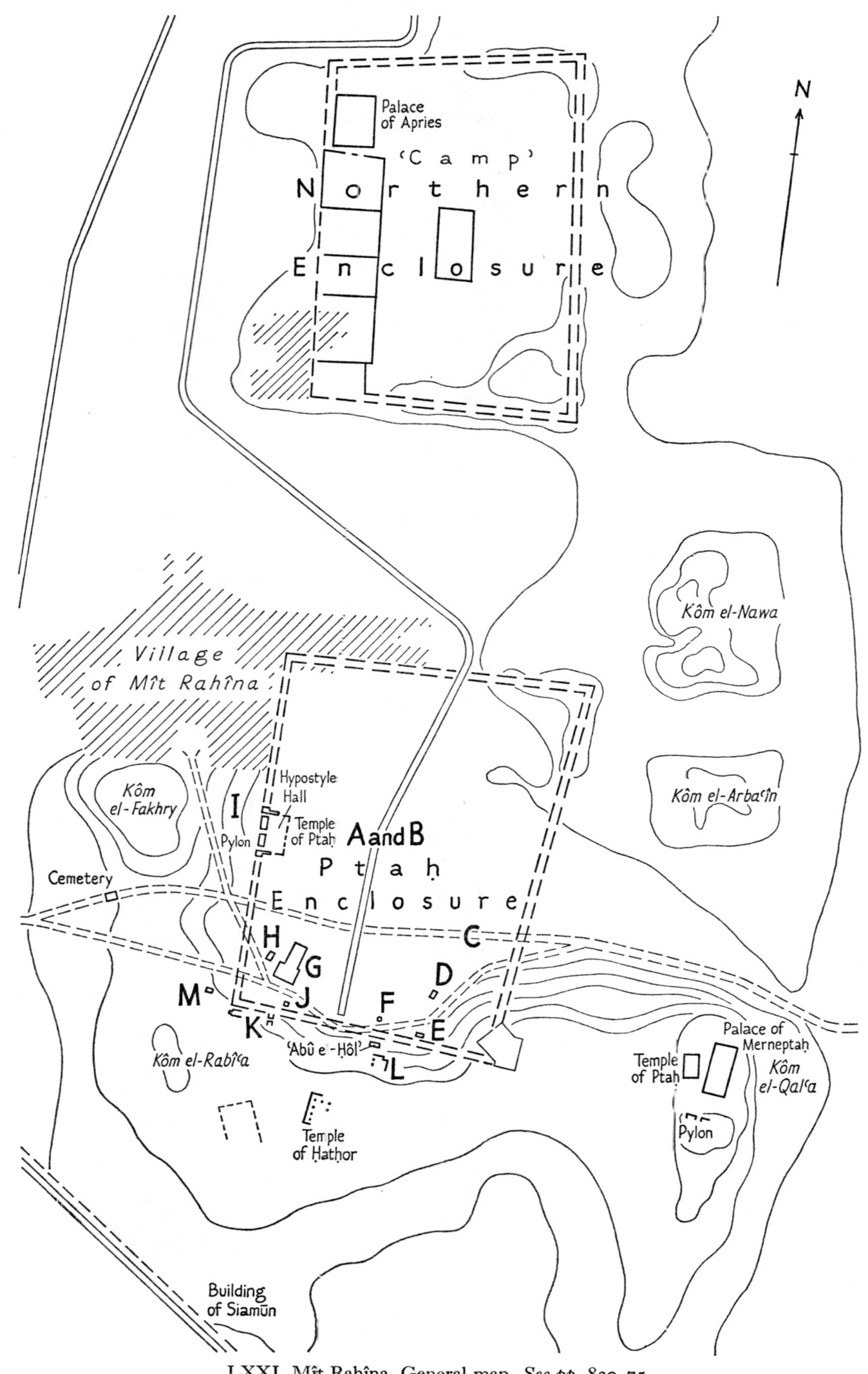

LXXI. Mît Rahîna. General map. *See pp.* 830–75.

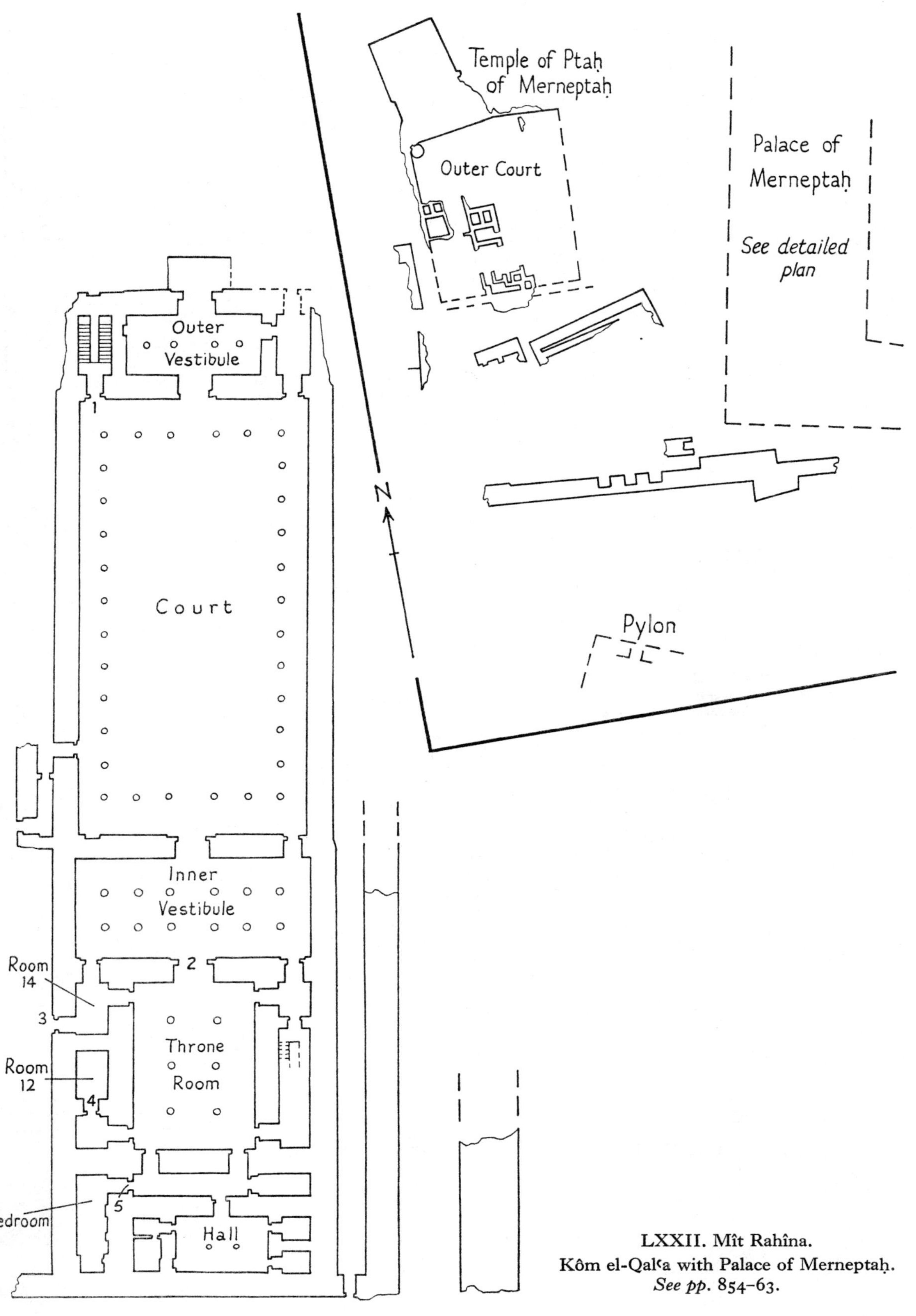

LXXII. Mît Rahîna.
Kôm el-Qalʿa with Palace of Merneptaḥ.
See pp. 854–63.

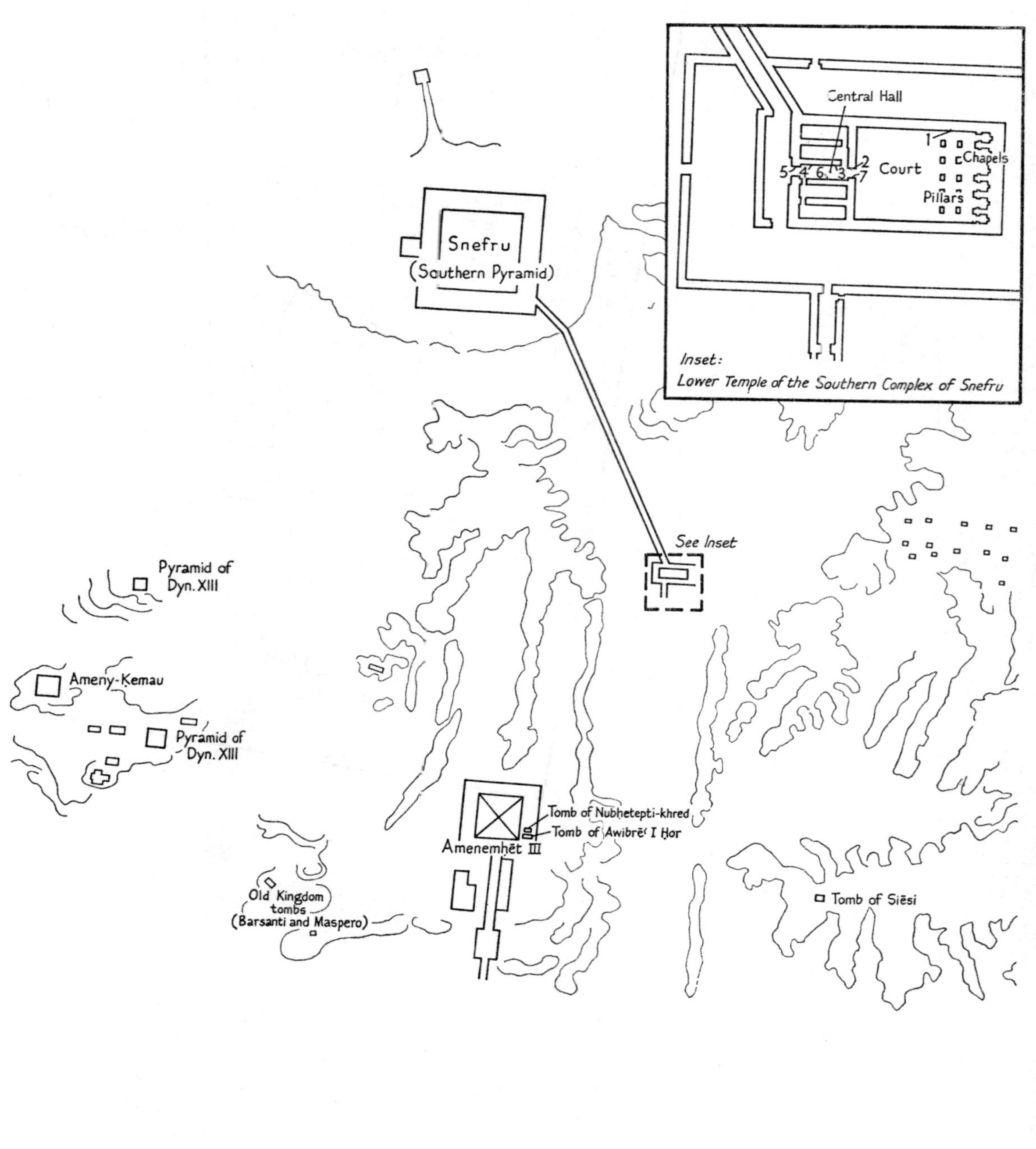

Map LXXIV adjoins

LXXIII. Dahshûr. General map (south section). *See pp.* 876–99.

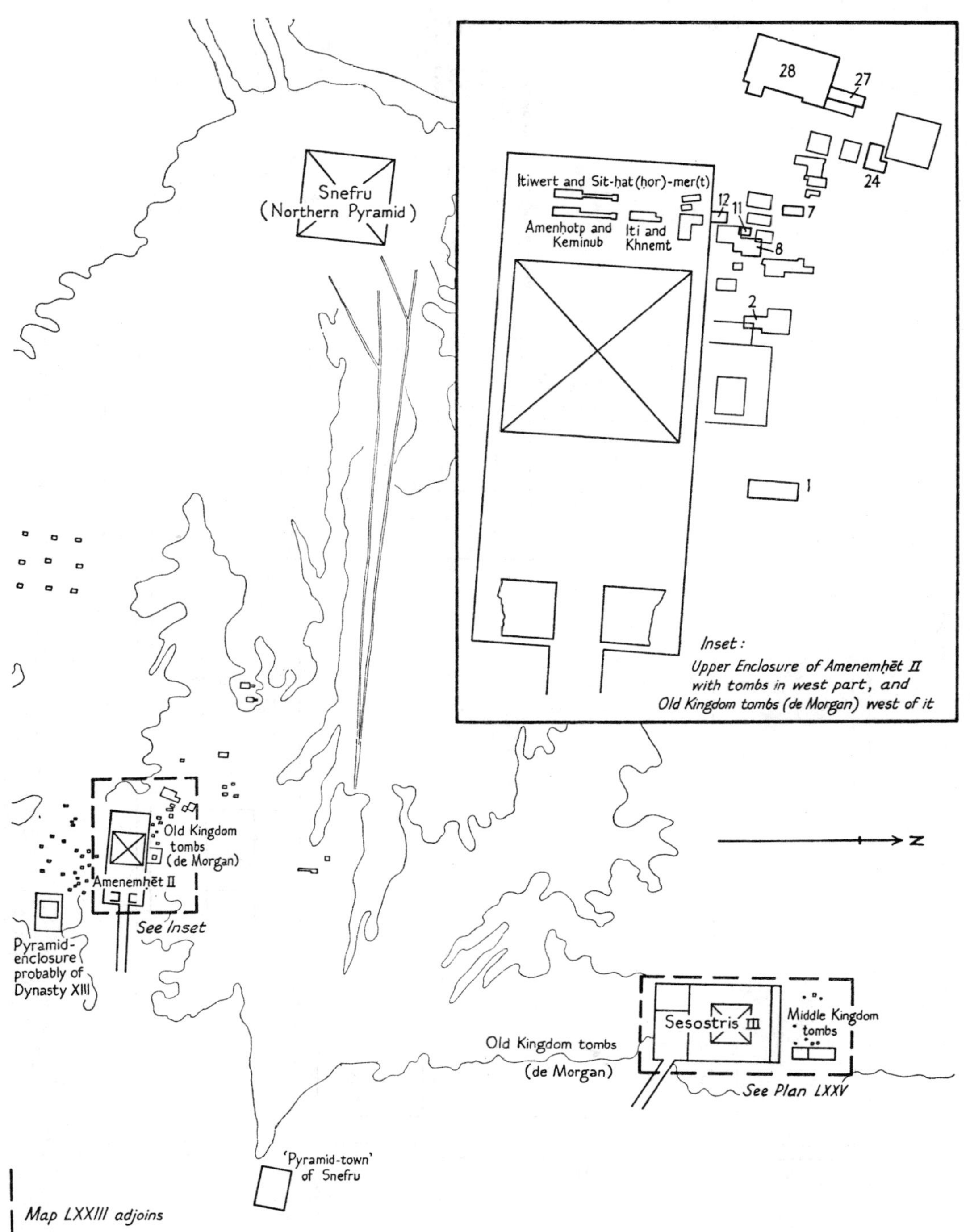

LXXIV. Dahshûr. General map (north section). *See pp.* 876–99.

LXXV. Dahshûr.
Pyramid-complex of Sesostris III and Middle Kingdom tombs north of the enclosure.
See pp. 882–5, 896–8.

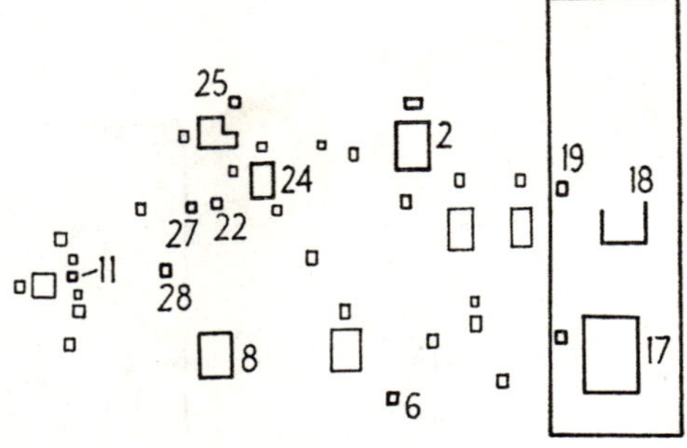

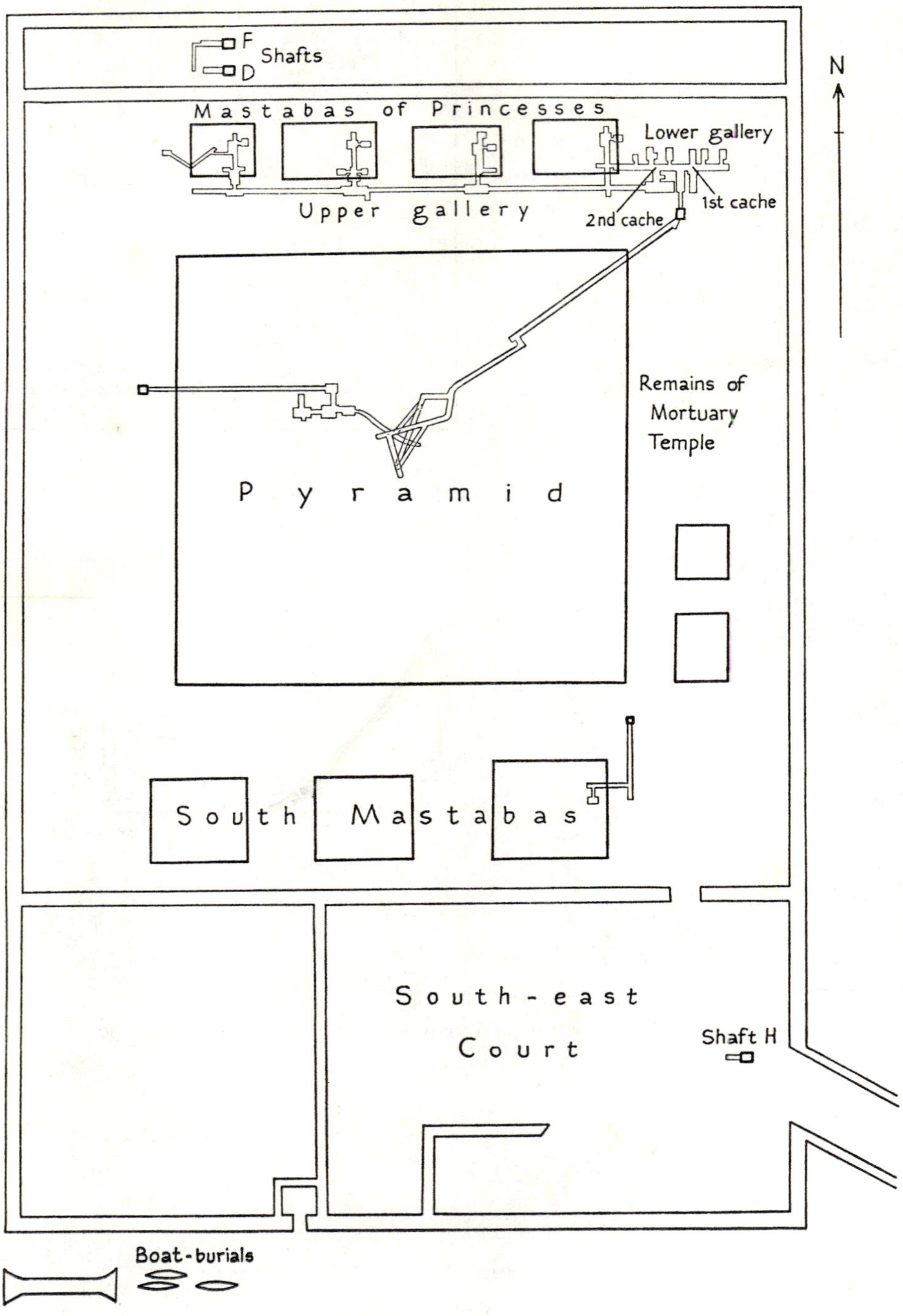

F
Shafts
D
N
Mastabas of Princesses
Lower gallery
1st cache
2nd cache
Upper gallery
Remains of Mortuary Temple
Pyramid
South Mastabas
South-east Court
Shaft H
Boat-burials